This book is published with financial support from the
Chinese Fund for Humanities and Social Sciences (本书获中华社会科学基金资助)

Sixty Years of the Protection and Development of Human Rights in China

Liu Hainian

Translated by Bi Xiaoqing

中国社会科学出版社
CHINA SOCIAL SCIENCES PRESS

Paths International Ltd

Contents

Part I Human Rights in General

Part II Specific Human Rights

Part III Foreign Exchange in the Field of Human Rights

Appendix

Preface

I learnt the term "civil rights" (or "people's rights") far earlier than I learnt the term "human rights". In Chinese language, although the terms "people" and "human", as subjects of rights, have different connotations and denotations, they are closely related to each other. As far as myself is concerned, the understanding of the former had laid a foundation for the understanding of the latter.

My first encounter with the term "civil rights" occurred in 1941, when I began to attend primary school. Each Saturday afternoon, a weekly meeting was held at my primary school at which all the pupils were gathered together to commemorate Dr. Sun Yat-sen, the first President of the Republic of China. On the agenda of such meetings were the singing of the Kuomintang (KMT, namely the Nationalist Party) party song, the collective recitation of "Premier (Sun Yat-sen)'s Last Will and Testament", bowing to a portrait of Dr. Sun Yat-sen, and a speech given by the director of discipline or the principal of the school. The first line in the Kuomintang Party Song went: "The purpose of the Party is to realize the 'Three Principles of the People'" and the Premier's Last Will and Testament included the following admonition: "all comrades must make continued efforts to implement the principles laid out in my writings, such as Nation-building Strategy, Outline of the Constitution of the Republic of China, and The Three Principles of the People... " The Three Principles of the People refer to the Principle of Mínzú (nationalism), the Principle of Mínquán ("democracy", "government by the People" or "civil rights"), and the Principle of Mínshēng ("people's welfare/livelihood," or "government for the People") . Every pupil in the school was required to memorize them. At that time, I was not quite clear what the last two principles meant, but was beginning to feel the importance of the first principle because, at that time, the Japanese invaders had already arrived at my hometown, a remote village in southwestern Henan Province, where they committed all kinds of atrocities such as burning, killing and pillaging. Many innocent lives had been lost. I myself was almost killed in one of the by one of the Japanese air raids. People were living in fear all day long and truly felt that "the Chinese nation was facing it greatest peril" —namely national subjugation and genocide. In the countryside, people were hiding in the green curtain of tall crops and trenches day and night. In August 1945, this nightmare of the Chinese nation ended with the surrender of the Japanese invaders, and Chinese people believed that peace, democracy, and people's livelihood would be finally put on the agenda of the Chinese government. Instead, the Kuomintang Government, supported by the United States, launched a civil war against the communists. As a result, the areas under the rule of Kuomintang were plagued by rampaging soldiers and bandits, skyrocketing inflation, and economic recession and people were living on the edge of starvation. It not was until 1949 that this chaotic situation finally ended with the victory of the People's Revolutionary War and the establishment of the People's Republic of China. Although I was still a child at that time, my personal experience under the Japanese occupation and Kuomintang rule had sew the seek of strong nationalist and patriotic feeling in my heart and laid an ideological foundation for me to participate in revolutionary work in my early years and to engage in legal and human rights research later in my life.

My first encounter with the term "human rights" was in the

world history class in university in late 1950s. At that time, the "left" ideology was already prevalent in the academic circle. Humanism and the theory of human nature were denounced and "human rights" was naturally considered to be hypocrisy and deception. In 1964, I graduated from university and began to work at the Law Institute of Chinese Academy of Social Sciences (CASS). My first task was to collect and sort out materials on the legal system in the communist "revolutionary bases" before 1949. To my great surprise, I discovered some legal documents on the protection of human rights promulgated by the political powers in the Communist-controlled anti-Japanese bases or "liberated areas". Since, at that time, China was still implementing the spirit of the Tenth Plenary Session of the Eighth Central Committee of the Chinese Communist Party, which required people to remind themselves of class struggle "every year, every month and every day", I dared not to dwell on this issue. However, deep in my mind I began to question the appropriateness of simple negation of human rights. With the end of the Cultural Revolution and the convening of the Third Plenary Session of the Eleventh Central Committee of the CPC, people began to reflect on the violations of human rights the past political campaigns, especially during the "Cultural Revolution". In 1979, based on the materials on the legal system of protection of human rights promulgated in the communist revolutionary bases before 1949, Mr. *Chang Zhaoru* and I published in the journal *Studies in Law* an article entitled "Safeguarding People's Rights: a Fine Tradition of Revolutionary System" —we used this title because at that time "human rights" was still considered by the mainstream Chinese mass media "a bourgeois slogan". Even at a time of "emancipation of the mind, reform and opening up", very few Chinese scholars dared to step into the field of human rights, not only because the human rights issue was totally messed up some bourgeois scholars, and double standard on human rights was frequently used by bourgeois politicians to attack China, but also because no in-depth studies had been carried out by Chinese scholars on the Marxist theory of human rights. This silence was finally broken in early 1990s when the then Chinese

President Jiang Zemin pointed out that: "We must carry out studies on human rights, which is an issue China cannot avoid."

After President Jiang Zemin's instruction was given, immediate actions were taken by the Propaganda Department of the Central Committee of the CPC, the CASS, the Party School of the CPC Central Committee and other relevant state organs and institutions. More specifically, the division of work among these organs was as follows: the Ministry of Foreign Affairs was responsible for policy-making, the Information Office of the State Council for dissemination and education, and the CASS for theoretical research. It was probably because human rights protection involves many legal issues that the then President of the CASS, Mr. Hu Sheng, decided to give the concrete task of human rights research to Professor Wang Jiafu and me, the director and deputy-director of CASS Institute of Law at that time. Soon after that, the Theoretical Research Bureau of the Propaganda Department of the Central Committee of the CPC decided to organize the compilation of a large book series entitled "Materials on Human Rights Research", the Information Office of the State Council began to draft white books on "Human Rights Conditions in China", and the CASS Law Institute held a nation-wide seminar on human rights theories, thereby started a more extensive mobilization for human rights research in China. In order to accomplish the task, I had to shift the focus of my research from Chinese legal history to human rights theory.

During the past 20 years, I have studied the Marxist theories on human rights, read relevant human rights literature, carried out investigations in various areas of China and in various countries in Americas, Europe, and South Asia, conducted repeated exchange of views with Chinese and foreign human rights researchers, and participated in dozens of human rights dialogues, seminars, and other human rights-related activities. All these have enabled me to deepen my understanding of human rights issues by studying them from different perspectives.

Human rights was a slogan put forward at the beginning of the Bourgeois Revolution to fight against religious authority and monarchical power and was established as an important constitutional principle after the victory of the Revolution. The Marxists fully recognize the historical progressive role played by bourgeois democracy, freedom and human rights while at the same time point out the incompleteness of such human rights. In fact, after seizing political power, the bourgeoisie not only treacherously abandoned their former allies, but also deprived the suffrage and the right to political participation of women belonging to their own class. Nevertheless, the Marxists still believe that the proletariat should expand their own rights "within democratic republic" through continuous struggle and "raise themselves to the position of ruling class and win the battle of democracy" when conditions are ripe, and ultimately establish an "association, in which the free development of each is the condition for the free development of all" . The day on which this "association" is establish will be the day of complete liberation of the mankind and the full enjoyment of human rights by all human beings. The 1917 October Revolution in Russia and the 1949 victory of the New-Democratic Revolution in China were two examples of the progresses made by mankind towards this great goal.

In 1949, Chinese people won the victory of revolution. They liberated themselves from the exploitation and oppression of imperialism, feudalism and bureaucrat capitalism and established a new China. The Chinese nation washed off the insult and the humiliation inflicted on them by western powers and the Japanese imperialists and upheld national independence and dignity. The emancipation and the independence of the nation is the most important human right. The land reform, the socialist transformation, and socialist industrialization carried out after the establishment of People's Republic of China had increased China's national strength, improved people's living standard and strengthened the protection of human rights. However, beginning from the late 1950s, due to the influence of the "left" ideology, human rights research became a forbidden area. In practice, people's consciousness of human rights protection was very low. As a result, the economic, political, cultural and personal rights of a large number of cadres and ordinary citizens had been infringed upon during numerous political movements, especially during the "Cultural Revolution". The situation began to change after the Third Plenary Session of the 11th CPC Central Committee and people's human rights consciousness was enhanced. In 1991, the central government decided to conduct research on human rights, thereby forcefully promoted human rights protection in China. In 2002, the Constitution of the CPC was revised at the Sixteenth National CPC Congress and a new provision stipulating that "the state respects and safeguards human rights" was included in the revised Party Constitution. In 2004, the same provision was added to the Chinese Constitution, thereby became an important principle on ruling the country and dealing with politics by the Party and the Government. From then on, the existing human rights system has been further improved and the standard of human rights protection raised rapidly. Although, because of a large population and weak economic foundation, China still has many problems in the field of human rights protection, under the leadership of the CPC and on the basis of summarization of many years of experience, now it has charted the course and laid a sound foundation for the development of human rights course in China, which, I can predict with confidence, will have a very bright future.

China is a country with an ancient civilization and a population of 1.3 billion. It is also one of the permanent members of the UN Security Council. In 2010, China's GDP ranked second in the world and this strong momentum of development will continue in the future. Because of China's important international influence, it is not surprising that the social development and construction of human rights protection system in China have become the focus of attention of many countries in the world. As one of the important founding members of the United Nations, China participated in the drafting of the United Nations Charter and the Universal Declaration of Human Rights. The People's Republic of China, after restoring its lawful seat in the UN, has ratified a series of international human rights conventions. It recognizes the universality of human rights and advocates the strengthening of international protection of human rights within the scope of the International Bill of Human Rights while at the same time stresses the particularity of human rights. Different human rights protection systems developed in countries with different historical and cultural backgrounds and at different stages of social and economic development should be respected. Human rights protection is a matter which is essentially within the sovereignty of each state. We oppose the practice of some countries of using their own value or institutional mode as criteria to assess the human rights systems in other countries, especially using double standard to judge countries with ideologies different from their own for the purpose of provoking confrontation in international community. It should be acknowledged that each country has its own human rights problems that need to be solved in the process of social development. Against the background of rapid scientific and technological advancement and economic globalization, the international community is also faced with many human rights problems, such as environmental protection, provision of relief to people faced with severe natural disasters, prohibition and prevention of the production and proliferation of weapons of mass destruction, and the fight against international terrorism. These problems need to be solved through equal dialogue, exchange of views and cooperation. For this reason, the Chinese government proposed in early 1990s to carry out equal dialogues in the field of human rights between different countries and the proposal received extensive responses from the international community. The practice in the past 20 years shows that such dialogues have achieved good results in deepening mutual understandings, eliminating misunderstandings, promoting exchange of experiences, and cooperation between different countries in the field of human rights. We are confident that by adhering to the principle of equal dialogue, China will be able to further promote the development of international protection of human rights and the construction of a harmonious world.

When I was visiting Harvard University in 1991, an American friend asked me how I plan to carry out research on human rights. Maybe because I had devoted many years in studying legal history, a subject which I love dearly, I answered without much thinking that I would study human rights from the historical and cultural perspectives. In the past 20 years, I have always been trying my best to base my study on the human rights reality in China and on the international human rights conventions and relevant codes of conduct, and to study various human rights issues, whether theoretical or practical, and the construction of human rights system in China, as well as China's foreign exchange in the field of human rights, from historical perspective, so as to form scientific opinions on the past, present and future of human rights in China. This book, which introduces the development of the human rights cause in China from different perspectives, is entitled "Sixty Years of Development of Human Rights Protection in China", although it is not a history book. The articles, reports and speeches collected in this book are divided into three parts: the first one is the comprehensive part, which contains comprehensive discussions on theories and the history of human rights, especially the development of human rights protection system in the People's Republic of China, arranged according to their internal logical order; the second part is the part on specific human rights, which contains discussions on specific rights in various areas of human rights, arranged according to the classification of human rights in the two 1966 UN human rights covenants, namely economic, social, cultural, civil and political rights; the third one is the part on foreign exchanges, which contains the reports, lectures and important speeches given by me during various foreign exchange activities, arranged chronological. The book also contains some declassified internal reports on various human rights issues prepared by myself. Although various parts of the book form an organic system, they have been written and published in different periods of time and, therefore, overlaps and repetitions in content are unavoidable. Also, the materials cited in different articles were those available at time of writing of these articles whereas the construction of human rights protection system in China has been progressing with each passing day. It is neither appropriate nor necessary to revise them. Moreover, keeping those materials as they were at the time of publication can enable readers to have a better understanding of the process of development of the human rights cause in China.

The contents of human rights are extensive and complicated and human rights concepts are variegated. A famous professor at UC Berkeley once told me that there are as many human rights concepts in the U. S. as there are human rights scholars in the country. Although such a saying is apparently exaggerated, it nevertheless reflects to some extent the characteristics of the understanding of the human rights issue by American scholars, which is based on free capitalist economy. In China, although the historical and cultural backgrounds and social system are different from those of the U. S., in a time of social transition, rapid economic growth, and diversification of interests, different people also have different understandings of human rights. Although the articles collected in this book were published in different time periods, the basic viewpoints expressed in them have been consistent. Readers are welcome to point out any inappropriateness in the viewpoints or content of this book.

The inscription on the title page of this book was written by Mr. Zhu Muzhi, a famous Marxist theoretician, journalist, as well as excellent calligrapher. His inscription for Xibaipo Revolutionary Memorial Hall— "The Fate of China Was Determined in This Village" —is in itself a precious revolutionary artifact because of its powerful and vigorous calligraphic style and profound message conveyed by it. I first met Mr. Zhu Muzhi in 1980 when I was engaged in the preparatory work for the trial of members of Lin Biao and Jiang Qing Counter-revolutionary Cliques. At that time, Mr. Zhu was the President of Xinhua News Agency and I was a member of the group responsible for the drafting of legal documents for the trial of Lin Biao and Jiang Qing Counter-Revolutionary Cliques. In a press conference on the relevant researches, I accompanied the leaders of the Group to brief him about our drafting work. In 1991, as the Director of the Information Office of the State Council, he presided over the drafting of the white paper on "The Human Rights Situation in China". The CASS Institute of Law provided the materials on the legal framework for the drafting of the white paper and Professor Wang Jiafu and myself participated in part of the drafting work. Since then, we have had frequent contact with each other and I have benefited greatly from his overall design of the white paper, the introduction he personally wrote for the white paper, and the many speeches he later gave on various human rights issues, which, based on the actual situations both in China and abroad, expounded and further developed the Marxist human rights theories. His inscription for this book is a great encouragement and inspiration for me. During the many years of research I have realized deeply that it is not easy to incarcerate people's mind, but it is even more difficult to emancipate people's mind in some areas, such as in the area of human rights. Mr. Zhu has set a good example for us all in emancipating the mind in the field of human rights, especially in developing Marxist human rights theories. My understanding of human rights issues benefited greatly from the teachings of Mr. Zhu Muzhi and other revolutionary predecessors as well as from the ideas of my colleagues in the law circle, especially my colleagues at the CASS Law Institute. In the future, I will continue to try my best to further deepen my understanding of various human rights issues.

The author

Part I

Human Rights in General

The Concept of Human Rights[①]

Currently the following interpretations have been given to the concept of human rights in the Chinese academic circle:

1. "Human rights are the basic rights of the people". This interpretation has been rejected by the majority of scholars for lack of accuracy. Firstly, the interpretation is too narrow by limiting the subjects of human rights to "people", which can be understood as a group concept such as nation or a race, or as a political concept as opposite to enemy. The first understanding is still acceptable, but it could easily lead to the neglect of the individual in practice of human rights protection; the second understanding excludes enemies from the subjects of human rights. Moreover, people as a political concept changes with the change of the nature and objects of revolution in different historical periods. Even at the present stage, with the elimination of classes and expansion of the scope of people, it is still inappropriate to limit the scope of the subjects of human rights to people, thereby excluding enemies and hostile elements who are punished in accordance with law. Secondly it is not appropriate to limit the objects of human rights to "basic rights". The so-called basic rights are usually understood as important rights provided for in the constitution and state laws. They do not include all the legal rights, let along those rights which are not provided for by law but aught to be enjoyed by the people in light of the levels of social, economic scientific and cultural developments. To carry out research on and adopt policies according to the understanding of human rights as the basic rights of the people will neglect certain individuals and rights which should not be neglected and therefore not conducive to the improvement of the socialist human rights system in China and to the international exchanges in the field of human rights and can invite heavy criticisms from other countries

---

① Originally published in CASS News Brief, June 1991

and lead China in the wrong direction.

2. "Human rights are the rights of citizens". This interpretation, which equals human rights with the rights of citizens, is based on the following arguments: human rights are concrete rather than abstract rights; the realization of any right depends on constitutional legal safeguards; and human rights are meaningless without rights of citizens. The majority of Chinese scholars hold that, although the scope of "citizens" is wider than that of "people", this interpretation of the concept of human rights is still inexact. As far as the subjects of human rights are concerned, the limitation of their scope to citizens will exclude stateless persons, refugees and foreigners. As far as the objects of rights are concerned, rights of citizens are only the expression of the human rights concept in domestic law which still do not include all the rights that aught to be enjoyed by human beings; besides, as mentioned above, "rights of citizens" is a domestic law concept whereas "human rights" is a concept of both domestic and international law. If human rights are equaled with rights of citizens, it will be difficult to explain the universality of human rights or for the representatives of Chinese government to logically participate in international protection of human rights.

3. "Human rights are the rights enjoyed or ought to be enjoyed by all human beings by virtue of their natural and social attributes and restricted by the level of social, economic and cultural development." I believe that this interpretation of human rights is more scientific than the previous ones. It has three levels of meanings: firstly, the subjects of human rights are human beings. They include all human beings, including people or citizens, stateless persons, refugees and foreigners. Here, human beings mainly refer to individuals, but also include groups of people. At the domestic level, the subjects of collective human rights refer to women, children, the elderly, the disabled, religious groups; at the international level, the mainly refer to specific ethnic or racial groups. Collective human rights are the extension of individual human rights; secondly, the objects of human rights are the rights that ought to be enjoyed by human beings in light of the level of social, economic and cultural development including not only the rights actually enjoyed by human beings (actual rights), but also rights prescribed by law (legal rights) and rights that ought to be enjoyed by people according to moral principles (due rights). Due rights embody the common aspiration of mankind and are the motive force of the continuous improvement of legal

rights and actual rights.

Thirdly, this interpretation can more scientifically reveal the origins of human rights. It shows that human rights originate from the natural attributes of human beings, for example, the right to life. Meanwhile, they are also the products of the development of the sum total of all social relations, such as political, economic, social and cultural rights. The two natures are unified.

This concept of human rights distinguishes itself from that of "natural rights" put forward by western bourgeois scholars and at the same time avoids the one-sidedness of the popular doctrines that claim human rights are the products of the commodity economy or the products of law. In recognizing the social attributes of human beings, this concept also recognizes the class attribute of human rights. In capitalist society, it embodies the privileges of rich people who consist of only a small proportion of society. Only in socialist society have the subjects of rights expanded to all human beings. This concept also reveals the relationship between human rights and social, economic and cultural developments, without which human rights are only empty talks. This concept accords with Marxism and tallies with historical development and social reality.

This interpretation also recognizes the particularity and universality of human rights. The particularity of human rights is determined by such factors as the national, historical and cultural traditions, geological environment, and social, economic and political systems of each country and manifested itself in different human rights institutions and national characteristics. In a country in which there are classes and class antagonism, human rights have apparent class nature. This is because classes in a dominant political and economic position will always try to seek their own special interests by legal means. The universality of human rights is based on the common interests of mankind and refers to the ideal and demand that human rights be enjoyed by all human beings. Its concrete manifestations include the various rights listed in the United Nations Charter and the Universal Declaration of Human Rights; international human rights treaties; joint actions taken by the international community in accordance with universally recognized principles of international law for the denunciation or punishment of acts of colonialism, enslavement, racial discrimination, aggression and other violations of human rights. The particularity and universality of human rights are interrelated. When making human rights policies, we should pay attention to both of them. Overemphasizing or neglecting either one of them may result in mistakes and negative consequences in practice.

Of course, recognizing the universality of human rights does not mean to ignore the different interpretations of the same international conventions, even the same provision in the same convention, made by different countries based on their own national interests in international intercourses. We should guard against the attempts by western countries to use human rights as excuse to impose their own values on or to change the economic and political systems of other countries.

Research on Human Rights Must Be Based on Correct Concepts[1]

Human Rights are important and lofty ideas and the realization of full enjoyment of human rights is an arduous and complicated task. It is exactly for this reason that the research on human rights must be based on correct concepts.

I

Human rights are important because they concern the enjoyment of the basic rights by every individual and every group of people in the world; the realization of human rights is an arduous and complicated task because, in real world, rights claims can differ in thousands of ways due to the differences in historical background and social status between different individuals, between individuals and groups of people and between different groups of people. It is very difficult to coordinate the relationships between various economic, political, cultural and social rights at different stages and levels of social development, to satisfy and balance the rights and interests of different groups of people, and to correctly deal with and resolve the conflicts of rights so as to prevent them from intensifying into fierce struggles that can affect the development and stability of and cause serious damage to society.

II

The complexity of human rights research also lies in the fact that the

---

① This was originally a speech given by the author at the "Second National Meeting for the Exchange of Work Experience by Human Rights Organs in China", organized by China Society for Human Rights Studies and held in Nankai University in April 2010.

concept of human rights, like the concept of the state, has been totally messed up by bourgeois politicians and their intellectual mercenaries. Originally, bourgeois enlightenment thinkers put forward the concept of human rights to oppose religious authority and monarchical power advocated and practiced by the feudal class and therefore was a huge progress in history. During the Bourgeois Revolution, the bourgeoisie had also recognized the universality of human rights. However, once they seized the political power, they began to use law to restrict and deprive the rights of the working class, cruelly exploit and enslave people of colonial and semi-colonial countries, even engage in slave trade. Not only so, but, for a long period of time, they had even deprived "in accordance with law" the rights of women who belonged to their own class. At the end of the Second World War, the international community adopted the Charter of the United Nations, thc Universal Declaration of Human Rights, the two international human rights covenants and many other human rights conventions. However, in the process of implementing international human rights conventions, some western countries ignore their own history of racial, ethnic and gender discriminations and oppression of the working people, refuse to reflect on the disastrous consequences of their long-term colonialist aggressions on Asian, African and Latin American countries, take their own national interests as the starting point and their own level of development and their own values as standards, and use the protection of human rights as excuse to apply double standard, try their best to smear, bully, and suppress countries with ideologies different from their own, even use their inherited economic and military powers to launch aggressive wars against their former colonies or semi-colonies. In this process, they manipulate domestic and international public opinions to disguise themselves as human rights defenders, impose their own values on other people, and turn international human rights organs into wrestling rings for bashing countries with ideologies different from their own. For a long period of time after the establishment of the People's Republic of China, Chinese scholars had neglected the study of Marxist theory of human rights, resulting in major reversals in the understanding of the human rights concept. Beginning from late 1950s, as a result of the policy of "taking class struggle as the central task", human rights became a forbidden zone into which no Chinese scholar dared to set foot. Even during a period after adoption by the CPC (CPC) of the policy of emancipation of the mind, reform and opening up at its Third Plenary Session of the Eleventh Central

Committee in 1978, the research on human rights theory in China was still in a state of lingering hesitation. Some mainstream media even asserted that " 'Human rights' is a slogan of the bourgeoisie." It seemed that human rights had become a privilege of the bourgeoisie. As a result, China had adopted an "ostrich policy" in the faced of the bourgeois propaganda. Now, after many years of efforts, the principle of "The state respects and safeguards human rights" has finally been enshrined in the Constitution of the CPC and established as a constitutional principle. Nevertheless, it is still necessary for us to further emancipate the mind, deepen the understanding of human rights, and remove ideological and institutional obstacles to the realization of human rights in certain areas.

III

The complexity of the task of realization of human rights determines that it is bound to meet with various obstacles and demands that human rights researchers to have appropriate ideas and objectives. The objectives of carrying out human rights research are not merely to complete a project, write several research reports or articles, public a book, or offer a new course in college. Of course, all these could be short-term objectives of the research work of a human rights researcher or teacher. However, if they are taken as the ultimate objectives of human rights research, the research will be subjected to various limitations and lose its objectivity. The ultimate objective of human rights research is to enable everyone to enjoy human rights. More specifically, in our own country, the objectives of human rights research are to improve the human rights protection system, to carry out international exchange and cooperation in the field of human rights, and to promote the construction of a world of harmony, so as to enable Chinese people and people around the world to fully enjoy human rights.

To achieve these objectives, human rights research must be guided by Marxism. Classical Marxist writers have made profound criticism of bourgeois human rights, but they have never negated human rights themselves. On the contrary, Marx and Engels fully recognized in all their works the emancipation of men through the replacement of one form of society by another since the primitive society. From these social transformations they discovered the laws of development of human society and established the theory of scientific socialism. They fully recognized the historical progressiveness of capitalism, and the significance of capitalist constitutions and laws to the protection of human rights. Carl Marx had once said that: "A man's duty is to demand human rights and citizen's rights not only for himself, but also for all individuals who have fulfilled their obligations."①

Marx called the American Declaration of Independence "the first declaration of human rights" in human history and Engels said that the U. S. Constitution "recognized human rights for the first time" in human history. They pointed out that "Bourgeois society is positively represented by the bourgeoisie. The bourgeoisie, therefore, begins its rule. The rights of man cease to exist merely in theory."② Meanwhile, they also pointed out the historical limitations of capitalism and the hypocrisy of the capitalist "freedom", "equality" and "democracy", and revealed the essence of bourgeois human rights. Engels pointed out that bourgeois equality of rights merely "replaced all former individual and hereditary privileges with the privilege of money. Thus the principle of election is, by property qualifications for the right of electing and being elected, retained for their own class. Equality is set aside again by restraining it to a mere 'equality before the law', which means equality in spite of the inequality of rich and poor."③ Under such a system, "The right of man to liberty ceases to be a right as soon as it comes into conflict with political life."④ It was for this reason that Lenin pointed out sharply that capitalist freedom, equality and democracy "is bound to remain restricted, truncated, false and hypocritical, a paradise for the rich and a snare and deception for the exploited, for the poor."⑤ The reason why classical Marxist writers revealed the essence of capitalist freedom, equality and democracy was to demonstrate that human rights are concrete rather than abstract and are closely related to specific social system. To make human rights genuine

---

① *Complete Works of Karl Marx and Frederick Engels* (The Second Chinese Edition), vol. 16, Beijing: People's Publishing House, 1998, p. 16.

② *Complete Works of Karl Marx and Frederick Engels* (The First Chinese Edition), vol. 2, Beijing: People's Publishing House, 1957, p. 16.

③ Ibid, p. 648.

④ *Complete Works of Karl Marx and Frederick Engels* (The First Chinese Edition), vol. 1, Beijing: People's Publishing House, 1957, p. 440.

⑤ *Complete Works of Vladimir Lenin* (Chinese Edition), vol. 35, Beijing: People's Publishing House, 1985, p. 244.

rights enjoyed by everyone, we must reform the social basis on which they depend. Thus, they closely connected the fight for human rights to the proletarian revolution and pointed that: "the first step in the revolution by the working class is to raise the proletariat to the position of ruling class to win the battle of democracy." After that, it must construct socialism through proletarian dictatorship. By then, "in place of the old bourgeois society, with its classes and class antagonisms, we shall have an association in which the free development of each is the condition for the free development of all."① To emancipate all mankind and realize the free development of each individual—this is the ultimate objective of the Marxist theory of human rights. Today, although over or nearly one century has passed since the above-mentioned expositions on human rights by classical Marxist writers were published, during which period the bourgeoisie has made various repairs to the capitalist system, the basic principles of Marxism still have strong vitality. In the practice of socialist revolution and construction, the Chinese communists have developed the Marxist human rights theory by combining the basic principles of Marxism with the Chinese experience and, during the long period of democratic revolution, had taken the fight for national independence, freedom, and people's welfare—namely human rights—as their banner. Today, they have enshrined the principle that "the state respects and safeguards human rights" in the Chinese Constitution and established it as an important principle of ruling the country and, in light of the human rights need of the Chinese people and the current level of development of human rights cause in China, identified the right to existence and the right to development as the most important human rights. The new achievements made by China in the construction of human rights system further proved the correctness of the Marxist human rights theory.

IV

Historical experience shows that, in order to further improve the human rights protection system under the new situations, China must observe and study human rights from the perspective of Marxist historical materialism and dialectical materialism and, while fully recognizing the great

① *Complete Works of Karl Marx and Frederick Engels* (The Second Chinese Edition), vol. 1, Beijing: People's Publishing House, 1998, p. 273.

achievements already made, face up to the existing problems in the field of human rights protection. China has made great achievements in safeguarding human rights in the 60 years since the establishment of the People's Republic of China, especially in the 30 years since the Third Plenary Session of the Eleventh Central Committee of the CPC. After the success of the people's revolution, China had achieved genuine national independence and people's liberation, as Mao Zedong had said "The Chinese people have stood up from now on." These are the most important and most basic human rights. Then, however, in an effort to fight against imperialist invasion and blockage, Chinese leaders became too eager for success in the construction of socialism and launched "the Great Leap Forward". They also over-emphasized class struggle, resulting in great harms to the broad masses of ordinary people and cadres. At the Third Plenary Session of it Eleventh Central Committee in 1978, the Party took decisive measures to clear up what was confused and put things to rights. It adopted a series of basic policies, including emancipating the mind, reforming and opening up, strengthening the socialist democracy and legal system, taking economic construction as the central task, establishing a socialist market economy, constructing a socialist legal system with Chinese characteristics, building a socialist well-off society in a all-round way, adopting people-orient Scientific Outlook on Development, and building a socialist harmonious society. During the past 30 years, China has made remarkable achievements in the construction of socialism and protection of human rights. Only by recognizing the huge achievements China has already made, can we keep the right direction in the face of complicated situation and accurately identify the problems to be solved in the field of human rights. For example, although China has realized the steady growth of the national economic, there are imbalances in development between different regions of country; although China is gradually improving its social security system, the system will not be able to cover all urban and rural residents in a short period of time; although state-owned and private enterprises are developing vigorously, the systems relating to corporate social responsibility still need to be further improved and implemented; although a primary socialist legal system has already been established in China, the system still far from perfect: because of the influence of the bureaucratic ideology in law enforcement and judicial practice, the effect of law enforcement has been greatly reduced by hidden rules; although judicial organs and personnel have been strengthened, the exercise of adjudicative and procuratorial powers by people's courts and people's procuratorates is often subjected to the influence of power and money; for many years, the Party and the state has been strengthening the fight against corruption in Party and government organs, state-owned enterprises and public institutions, but so far this effort has not achieve satisfactory results, and this seriously affects the credibility of the Party and the government. Moreover, there is also the problem of the protection of the rights and interests of disadvantaged groups, such as women, children, the elderly and the disabled. Human rights researchers should pay proper attention and contribute their efforts to the solution of all the above problems.

V

Another important objective of research on human rights is to carry out international exchange and cooperation in the field of human rights. In the past, we often talked about "struggle" in the field of international human rights. Later, we also talked about "exchange". In a letter to China Society for Human Rights Studies, President Hu Jingtao mentioned "exchange and cooperation". The change in the wording itself reflects the deepening of the understanding of human rights. However, the fact that "struggle" is no longer mentioned does not mean there is no more struggle in the field of international human rights. In today's world, with the rapid development of science and technology (the development will even faster in the future), the distances between individuals and between states have been greatly shortened. The interdependency and indivisibility of human rights become more and more apparent in the international protection of human rights. Problems such as the climate change, environmental protection, natural disaster, international terrorism, piracy, wars between states and various problems resulting from wars, and economic crises triggered by financial crises, etc, will all endanger the human rights in different countries and they cannot be solved by any one country or even several countries. China is a world power and a permanent member of the UN Security Council. With the development of China's economy and the increase in its national strength, western powers demand China to undertake more international responsibilities and developing countries hope China will play a greater role in international affairs. Under this situation, China has put forward the proposal of building a harmonious world of lasting peace and common prosperity. This is a new thinking about international relationship and human rights protection. To promote the exchange and cooperation in the field of human rights and the construction of a harmonious world, we should carry out careful research on the rules of conduct in the field of international human rights, especially the Universal Declaration of Human Rights and the two 1966 international human rights covenants, which form an important part of the International Bill of Human Rights, and over 20 other international human rights conventions already ratified by China, and make efforts to further improve some of these conventions. We also need to carry out research on the relevant human rights organs of the UN and their operation mechanisms and establish close contact with them. In the intercourse with UN human rights organs, other international human rights organizations and human rights organizations in other countries, China should adhere to principles while at the same time be flexible, so as to uphold national dignity while at the same time show the manner of a great civilized socialist country. The key to international exchange and cooperation is the correct understanding of and scientific attitude towards the human rights safeguarding system in China. Just as mentioned before, we should acknowledge both achievements and existing problems in our own countries; adhere to our own successful experiences while at the same time draw on the useful experience of other countries. We do not advocate politicization and ideologicalization of international human rights dialogue. However, we should be aware that some countries, out of their our interests and their ambition to dominate the world, claim to take human rights as the cornerstone of their foreign policy and that some western people have over the years developed the bad habit of looking down on people in non-western countries as inferiors. Therefore, we must be prepared to fight back with good reason, to our advantage and with restraint. Experience shows that to do so can not only uphold national dignity, but also win the respect of our adversaries.

VI

In order to achieve the above-mentioned two objectives, we must draw on the fruits of the progress of human civilization, which can be divided into domestic and foreign, historical and contemporary. The Chinese nation, which makes up one fifth of the total world population and have a five-thousand-year-old history of civilization, have created brilliant historical culture and possess strong ideological and institutional cohesive power. The traditional Chinese culture contains many elements of human rights. They include ideas about "human", such as "humanism", "human sympathy", "humanitarianism", "human relations", and the principle of "valuing people above everything else in the universe"; ideas about "harmony", such as "harmony", "peace", and "seeking harmony in diversity"; and the ideas about "stability", such as "peace and stability", "giving peace to the people", and "peace is a blessing", as well as ideas about "respecting the old and cherishing the young", "helping the poor and assisting the needy", "being strict to oneself and more tolerant to others", "peaceful coexistence of different ethnic and religious groups", etc. People all around the world have the same human nature: they all pursue human dignity and happiness. And in the process of pursuing these ideals, each nation and each country has accumulated rich experiences. Just as western thinkers have put forward the ideas of freedom, equality, democracy, and human rights, China has advanced the ideas of people-oriented scientific outlook on development and the construction of a harmonious socialist country. The western countries have enjoyed rapid development in modern history and China should learn from their successful experience. However, practice has shown that a precondition for drawing on the achievements of the progress of human civilization, especially in the field of human rights, is to further emancipate the mind. With respect to traditional culture, we should neither bow in worship to outdated ideas, nor adopt a nihilistic attitude, but should discard its dregs and take its essence; likewise, with respect to western culture, we should neither worship it blindly, nor negate it totally, but to identify and draw on its useful elements. Just as comrade Deng Xiaoping had pointed out, China has a long history of feudal rule and little tradition of democracy and the rule of law. Feudal law stressed people's obligations while ignoring their rights. After the establishment of the People's Republic of China, no systematic publicity and education on the protection of rights have been carried out and, as a result, the rights consciousness among cadres and the people has been weak. In real life, carrying out research on and disseminating knowledge of human rights, especially advancing ideas considered by some as new, will often met with obstacles, even misunderstandings. Even if so, we should not lose our heart. We should be confident that, as long as we have the right footing and the support of the Party leaders and the great masses of people, we will be able to make greater contribution to the human rights cause in China through our research work.

The Formation and Development of the Human Rights Concept in China (an Outline)[①]

The world is about to enter into the 21st century. With the rapid scientific and technological advancement and social and economic development, the levels of human civilization and human rights protection have also been raised. In order to implement the spirit of the Universal Declaration of Human Rights, and the provisions of the International Covenant on Economic, Social and Cultural Rights and the International Covenant on Civil and Political Rights and promote the domestic and international protection of human rights, it is necessary to strengthen the research on the human rights concepts and institutions in different cultural contexts (namely the particularity of human rights) while recognizing the universality of human rights.

For many years, I have been conducting research on the human rights concept in China from the perspective of historical and cultural perspective in the hope of communicating with scholars who study human rights concepts in other cultural context, and, while basing my research on the actual situations in China, draw on the essence of the human rights concepts formed in different cultural contexts, so as to contribute to the construction of Chinese and international human rights protection systems. To discuss this subject in little more detail, I will have to write a very long article, even a very thick book. But here I will only share with you my thoughts on the following main points:

First, China is a united multi-ethic nation with vast territory, huge population and a 5000—year-old history of civilization. Since the era of

---

① Originally a keynote speech given by the author at the "Sino-U. S. Seminar on Human Rights and Administration of Justice", held in Washington in December 1998.

legends, the ancestors of Chinese nation, out of the natural instinct of sustaining their own life and maintaining their own existence, began to fight against all forces of nature, including flood. From the flood control by Dayu recorded in the earliest Chinese historical records to the flood fighting in the Yangtze River Basin and Songhuajiang River Basin in 1998, in almost every dynasty or period in history in China, a large amount of manpower and material resources have been use to fight against flood. Flood fighting and other big projects often requires the human and material resources of not only one region or ethnic group, but many different regions or even the whole country. Such projects cannot succeed without collective efforts or centralized and unified leadership. In history, this is not only the main factor in the formation of the spirit of solidarity, cooperation and self-sacrifice of the Chinese nation, but also the main objective cause for the long history of the system of absolute monarch in China.

Second, for a long period of time in history, China had been a feudal monarchy based on agricultural natural economy. However, the Chinese people have never ceased the struggle for their rights, although the concept of "human rights" was introduced to China from the West only during the period when the feudal system was on the verge of collapse. As early as in the end of the Qin Dynasty, Chen Sheng and Wu Guang, the two peasant leaders, had raised the question "Do those gentry have blue blood certainly?" so as to awaken the people's rights consciousness and call on them to fight for their own rights. Thereafter, every peasant uprising or peasant war has been a struggle by peasants for their due rights. In order to prevent society from falling apart as a result of intense class struggle, the Confucian ideas were developed on the basis of agricultural natural economy and the clan system formed through blood relationship and, through evolution, became the orthodox ideology that upheld social stability and guided the establishment and operation of the state political system.

Third, Confucianism is a huge ideological system. It has the following three aspects that are relevant to human rights: first, the idea of minben (taking people as root or basis). Confucius advocated universal love and said that: "A benevolent person always cares for others." And Mencius said that: "The people are the most important element in a nation; the spirits of the land and grain are the next; the sovereign is the lightest." Li Shimin, the Emperor of the Tang Dynasty further explained this idea:

"The monarch is like a ship while the people are like water: the water can carry a ship, it can also upset it." In another words, rulers could stay in power only if they took people as the root and love the people. Second, the doctrine of the mean. The so-called "mean" refers to harmony, namely, "the man of perfect virtue, wishing to be established himself, seeks also to establish others; wishing to be enlarged himself, he seeks also to enlarge others" and "don't do to others what you don't want others to do to you". In managing state affairs, the doctrine of the mean requires the ruler "to know the two extremes way of governing, but govern the people according to the way of mean;" To be fair and upright, and "to be sparing in the use of punishments and fines, and make the taxes and levies light". Third, the system of ethics and morals, which is a hierarchical order established according to Confucius ideas. They advocate "Five Cardinal Relations", a moral order based on the relationships between the ruler and subjects, between parents and offspring, between husband and wife, among siblings, and between friends, namely beneficent emperors and faithful ministers, fatherly father, obedient children, kind elder brothers, brotherly younger brothers, loyal husband, docile wife, modest elders, compliant youngers. This system embodies both the feudal hierarchical relationship, and bilateral obligations. It required those in high positions, including emperors, to exercise self-control and self-discipline. This ethical system takes "Cultivate individual moral character, run the family in unison, manage the nation in order, and peace will prevail throughout the universe" as its motto, so as to create a harmonious society with domestic peace and good governance. Confucianism has its hypocritical aspects and emphasizes hierarchical obligations. However, from the historical perspective, this ideology and the institutions established under its influence has upheld the unity of China and increased the cohesion of the Chinese nation, and promoted the development of the ancient civilization. Although no concept of human rights had been put forward in ancient China, the idea of taking people as root, the doctrine of the mean and the ethics of traditional Chinese culture provide fertile soil that allowed the concept of human rights to take root and develop in China.

Fourth, another important element affecting the formation and development of human rights concept in China is religion. Religion is a form of social culture that takes human faith as its core. Essentially belonging to the sphere of ideology, it is the product of social development at certain historical stage. China is a country of many religions, including Taoism, Buddhism, Islam, Catholicism and Christianity, patriarchal traditional religion, and witchcraft religion. Among these religions, only Daoism and patriarchy religions, and witchcraft religions are native to China. All the others are introduced from foreign countries. Daoism originated during the Han Dynasty; Buddhism was introduced to China from India during the Han Dynasty; Islam was introduced into China from Arabian countries during the Tang Dynasty; Catholicism and Christianity was introduced into China three times in Tang Dynasty, Yuan Dynasty and Ming Dynasty, but all the three attempts made these two religions to establish themselves in China had failed for lack of the effort to integrate themselves into Chinese culture. They began to take roots in China only after the Opium War in 1840. Although there are many different religions in China, those different religions have inevitably been influenced by Chinese culture that takes "unity in diversity" as one of its main values. The traditional Chinese culture, with Confucianism as its main body, contains many doctrines that are consistent with the main teachings of various religions, For example, it is hard to tell whether such principles as "Don't do to others what you don't want others to do to you", "Harmony is what matters", "Content is happiness", "Tolerance brings security", "Good has its reward and evil has its recompense. The payback is just a matter of time", and "Enjoying reading and conducting oneself in a sincere and honest way in society", etc. are Confucian doctrines or religious teachings. Under the influence of traditional Chinese culture, a relationship of harmonious coexistence and mutual respect has been development between followers of different religions and between religious believers and non believers. The rulers in Chinese history have basically adopted a policy of equality and tolerance towards various religions. Throughout several thousand years of Chinese history, there had never been a nationwide religious war, a state religion with monopoly position or a theocratic central dynasty like those in the western history. Such a harmonious and tolerant environment had inevitably exerted a strong influence on the formation and development of human rights concept in China.

Fifth, against the above mentioned cultural background, modern western ideas of democracy, freedom and human rights was introduced into China in the process of economic and cultural interactions and armed aggressions thereby injecting new elements into the ancient Chinese culture. Such ideas had led to many revolutions and reforms in modern Chinese history, such as the Taiping Heavenly Kingdom Movement, the Hundred Days Reform, and the Revolution of 1911, and inspired many reformers and revolutionaries, such as Hong Xiuquan, Kang Youwei, Liang Qichao and Sun Yat-sen, to devote their whole lives to the human rights cause in China. Unfortunately, western colonialists under the pretext of such wonderful words as democracy, freedom and human rights, used their superior military forces against China and forced it to cede territory and pay indemnities under a series of unequal treaties and to slaughter and humiliate the Chinese people. As an inevitable result of such aggressions by "teachers" against "students", the Chinese people had equaled the slogan of "democracy and human rights" of western powers with the slogan of "East Asia co-prosperity" used by the Japanese militarists to savagely slaughter Chinese people. It therefore is understandable that many Chinese people today, based on their historical experience, still have strong suspicion over the behavior of western countries of taking human rights as political instrument and treat China with double standard.

Sixth, to fight for genuine human rights, the founders of the Communist Party of China (CPC) had at the very beginning of the Party written the slogan of human rights on their banner and carried out unyielding struggle against western imperialists and their agents in China and against Japanese militarists. As early as in the 1930s and 1940s, the CPC had adopted laws on the protection of human rights in the "Soviet areas" and anti-Japanese bases under its control. During the 1940s, the CPC had adopted over a dozen regulations on the protection of human rights in the anti-Japanese bases and "liberated areas" under its control. In 1949, the CPC won the nationwide victory in revolution and liberated the Chinese people, the Chinese nation stood up in the world, and various fundamental human rights were recognized by the Constitution. However, since the beginning of the 1950s, especially during the "Cultural Revolution", under the influence of "the left line", constitutional and legal principles were trampled upon. After the end of the "Cultural Revolution", the 1982 Constitution restored various fundamental human rights. During the 20 years that had followed, China had made remarkable achievements in human rights protection. On the basis of these achievements, the Chinese government signed the International Covenant on Economic, Social and Cultural Rights and the International Covenant on Civil and Political Rights in 1997 and 1998, respectively, which will further promote the construction of human rights system in China as well as the cause of international protection of human rights.

Seventh, as a result of China's cultural background and level of social development, the human rights concept and human rights protection in China have the following characteristics: first, China believes that the right to existence is the primary human right. For this reason, China needs to, on the one hand, maintain ecological balance and mobilize social forces to fight against natural disasters and, on the other hand, resist foreign aggression and uphold national independence. Second, China attaches great importance to the right to development. As a result of long period of feudal rule and imperialist aggression, China is still a developing country today, with very unbalanced economic and cultural development in different parts of the country, tens of millions people living in poverty, and over 100 million illiterates and semi-illiterates. Therefore, it must develop its economy and cultural undertakings. Third, China attaches great importance to internal harmony and stability. In order to survive and develop, China must strengthen the unity and solidarity between various ethnic groups, carry forward the fine tradition of the Chinese nation, and establish harmonious social relationships and a stable social order. Fourth, China has achieved great progress in the legalization and institutionalization of human rights protection. Various fundamental rights have not only been confirmed by the Constitution, but provided for in such basic laws as the General Principles of Civil Law, the Civil Procedure Law, the Criminal Law, the Criminal Procedure Law, the State Compensation Law as well as in some important policy documents and are beginning to be conscientiously implemented. Fifth, in response to the demands of the development of the market economy and the construction of democratic politics, China, while attaching importance to collectively human rights, is paying increasing attention to the protection of individual human rights. Six, historically, China has always advocated the peaceful coexistence with all the countries and people around the world, active participated in international protection of human rights. However, it opposes the use of human rights as pretext for interfering in the internal affairs of other countries, especially the interference by big powers of internal affairs of countries which today remain underdeveloped as a result of their aggression and oppression.

Eighthly, when we look back at China's human rights history in the

20th century, we can feel both the pain and humiliation of being trampled upon by imperialists and the joy of wining great victory through unyielding struggle. Today, Chinese people cherish very much their hard-won rights, and follow closely the cause of international protection of human rights. Looking into the future, we can see that, with the development of the socialist market economy and the implementation of the strategy of ruling the country in accordance with law and constructing a socialist state under the rule of law, the freedoms of Chinese people, whether in the economic or political fields, will continue to expand and the human rights protection will also expand from the economic, political social and cultural fields to the fields of the protection of the ecological environment and natural resources. China will draw on more useful experiences from other countries and make greater contribution to the international protection of human rights. However, in any case, China will not copy the institutional model of western countries or over-emphasizes individual freedom like some countries do. The Chinese human rights protection system will be an organic combination the individual and the collective, rights and obligations, freedom and order, and the state and society so as to create a new harmonious situation in a new historical condition. History will determine whether the human rights concept and system with Chinese and oriental characteristics have more vitality than the western ones, or whether people from different parts of the world will form new human rights concept by learning from each other.

The Struggle for Human Rights by the Communist Party of China (1921—1949)[①]

The objective of the Communist Party of China (CPC) has always been to struggle for the realization of socialism and communist as well as for the full enjoyment of human rights by Chinese people. Therefore, it can be said that the history of the CPC is a history of struggle for the human rights of people all ethnic groups in China. For many years, however, this fact has been distorted by the enemies of the CPC, who used the mass media under their control to create misunderstandings among our friends about the human rights record of the CPC. For some more complicated reasons, there are confusions about this issue even among our own ranks for a long period of time. In view of this situation, carrying out a review of the literatures on the historical facts of the struggle by the CPC for human rights is beneficial to clearing up misunderstandings and confusions both for our friends and for ourselves.

I

The so-called human rights are the rights enjoyed or ought to be enjoyed by every human being. In other words, they are rights of human beings. Here "human beings" refers to all individuals, including men, women, the elderly, minors, healthy persons, the disabled, citizens, foreigners, stateless persons, prisoners of war, and criminals. And the rights here refer to all the rights that ought to be enjoyed by human beings, including civil and political rights, economic, social and cultural rights, as well as the right to environment. Although the concept of human rights

---

① This article was originally published in *Oriental Law*, No. 3, 2011.

was introduced into China in modern history, Chinese people's rights consciousness is as old as the Chinese civilization. The countless slave uprisings, peasant wars, and resistance against foreign aggressions occurred on Chinese territory have shown that the struggle by Chinese people for human rights has never ceased in the 5, 000 years of Chinese history and, with the rise of their rights consciousness, the Chinese people become increasingly determined in their struggle for human rights.

China was invaded by many imperialist powers after losing the Opium War in 1840. A large part of Chinese territory was ceded to or divided up as sphere of influence by foreign powers. Imperialist powers also forcibly occupied many Chinese harbors and ports and large areas of neighborhoods in major Chinese cities as their concessions. They not only established security forces, but also stationed troops in China. Some imperialists acted in a tyrannous manner on Chinese territory: they wantonly humiliated the Chinese people, trampled upon their human rights; they even designated some parks in China as forbidden zones for Chinese people and put up the sign "No Dogs and Chinese Allowed" at the entrance of these parks; and under the protection of extra territoriality, they could commit all kinds of crimes without being punished. Because of the above fact, the struggle by Chinese people for human rights was a struggle not only against domestic rulers, but also against foreign invaders. And this was also why Dr. Sun Yat-zen took the "Three Principles of the People", namely the principles of nationalism, democracy, and the people's livelihood, as the banner of his democratic revolution in early 20th century to arouse the Chinese people (and succeeded to a certain extent in doing so) . The 1911 Revolution led by Dr. Sun Yat-zen brought to an end to the autocratic monarchical system that had lasted for over 2, 000 years and overthrew the last emperor of China. From then on, the concept of democratic republic has been deeply rooted in the mind of Chinese people. However, because of the congenital weakness of the Chinese national bourgeoisie, the revolution was not based on solid ground. As a result, it had failed to establish a bourgeois republic envisaged by it. The fruit of revolution was soon usurped by northern warlords backed by imperialist powers and headed by Yuan Shih-kai. From Yuan Shih-kai on, a series of warlords had entrenched themselves in Beijing and controlled the central government. Although they ultimately failed to abolish the "republic", they continued to act in the same way as that of the feudal rulers in the Qing Dynasty. In this "republic", Chinese people continued to be oppressed by feudal warlords and imperialists. Under this circumstance, Yuan Shih-kai signed "The Twenty-One Demands" in exchange for support by Japanese imperialists. Later, the Beiyang Government attended the Paris Peace Conference and intended to agree on the transfer of Germany's privileges in Shandong Peninsula to Japan. This had greatly angered Chinese intellectuals and workers. On May 4, 1919, students took to the streets and chanted such slogans as "Down with imperialists", "Down with warlords", "Severely punish traitors to the country", "Fight for civil rights" and "Fight for freedom". Staunchly supported by the working class, the patriotic actions of the students and other intellectuals developed into a great patriotic movement—the May 4th Movement. Later Mao Zedong pointed out: "The outstanding historical significance of the May 4th Movement is to be seen in a feature which was absent from the Revolution of 1911, namely, its thorough and uncompromising opposition to imperialism as well as to feudalism."① It was against this historical background that the advanced elements in the May 4th Movement—the communists—established the CPC in 1921. As soon as it stepped onto historical stage, the CPC began to shout loudly: "Arise! All those who don't want to be slaves! Arise, the wretched people of the world! ... The earth shall rise on new foundations, and we will be the masters of the world." From the above song that embodies the purpose of the working class party we can see that the CPC from its very beginning has linked the struggle for human rights and freedoms with the struggle for the overthrow of the old rule and for making people the masters of their own country—namely the struggle for political power. Just as the white paper "Human Rights in China", promulgated by the Information Office of the State Council in November 1991, points out: "Under long years of oppression by the 'three big mountains' -imperialism, feudalism and bureaucrat-capitalism-people in old China did not have any human rights to speak of. Suffering bitterly from this, the Chinese people fought for more than a century, defying death and personal sacrifices and advancing wave upon wave, in an arduous struggle to overthrow the 'three big mountains' and gain their human rights."②

---

① *Selected Works of Mao Zedong*, vol. II, Beijing: People's Publishing House, 1991, p. 699.

② Information Office of the State Council of the People's Republic of China, *Human Rights Conditions in China*, Beijing: The Central Literature Press, 1991, p. 1.

II

Historical facts show that the 1911 Revolution led by Dr. Sun Yat-sen, the May Fourth Movement, and the New Democratic Revolution led by the CPC all took the fight for the rights of Chinese people as their starting point and ultimate goal. The person who first introduced the concept of human rights into China was Mr. Chen Duxiu, one of the founders of the CPC. As early as before the establishment of the CPC, Chen Duxiu pointed out that human rights and science are indispensable to national prosperity, just like two wheels to a carriage. "In order to deliver themselves from ignorance and catch up with western nations, the Chinese people must attach equal importance to science and human rights."① After its establishment, the CPC led a major strike by Jinghan (Peking-Hankou) Railway workers in 1923, during which it put forward the slogan of "Fight for freedom and human rights; march forward and never retreat". In August of the same year, Mr. Chen Duxiu, then the Secretary-General of the CPC, stated in his report to the Third National Congress of the CPC that: "With respect to the campaign for human rights, we have already established alliances for human rights in Beijing, Guangzhou, Shanghai, Shandong and Jiangxi in accordance with a resolution adopted at the Second National Congress of the Party. In Beijing, most members of the alliance are students while in Shandong and Guangzhou, the majority of the members of the alliance are workers."② I have not been able to find the original text of the resolution on the campaign for human rights adopted at the Second National Congress of the CPC, but the above report on the work carried out by the CPC since its second national congress shows that the CPC did adopted such a resolution, established corresponding organizations, and carried out a campaign for human rights.

The existing historical documents show that the human rights mentioned in almost all of the CPC's political programs and in all the slogans put forward by the CPC in the workers' and peasants' movements in its early years and during the First Revolutionary Civil War were specific rights. The only exception was the slogan of "fight for freedom and human rights" put

① Chen Duxiu, "A Letter to Youth", in *La Jeunesse*, vol. 1 No. 1, September 15, 1915.

② Declaration of the Second National Congress of the CPC, July 1922.

forward during 1923 strike by Jing-Han Railway workers. The reason for this maybe was that the mention of specific rights could enable the broad masses of Chinese people to better understand the relationship between the CPC's political campaigns and their own personal interests.

For example, the Declaration of the Second National Congress of the CPC stated that the goals of the current struggle were: "to overthrow the oppressive rule of imperialists and achieve complete independence of the Chinese nation"; "to ensure that workers and peasants, regardless of their sex, have unlimited right to vote in the election of the parliaments at all levels, including municipal councils, and that they enjoy absolute freedoms of express, of the press, of assembly, of association, and of strike". The Declaration also demanded the adoption of a series of laws on safeguarding the rights of workers, peasants and women, on reforming the educational system and implementing the system of compulsory education, and on limiting the rate of farm rent. With respect to improving the treatment of workers, the CPC's demands included: "(1) to abolish the system of bonded labor; (2) to implement the system of eight-hour working day; (3) to establish workers' hospital and other health facilities in factors; (4) to establish an insurance system for factories; (5) to protect female and minor workers; (6) to protect unemployed workers"; "to abolish all laws restricting the rights and freedoms of women, to ensure women enjoy equal political, economic, social and educational rights with men"; and "to reform the educational system and implement the system of compulsory education".[①] The human rights advocated by the CPC in other programmatic documents and workers' movements were basically the same as those mentioned above, only they revealed more profoundly the existing human rights problems and put forward more specific and targeted rights demands in light of specific situations of different time periods and locations. For example, the Declaration on General Strike in Kailuan Coal Mines, published in October 1922, pointed out that: "The Kailuan Coal Mine Bureau treated its workers worse than mules. When there is mining accident, the foreign bosses of the mines asked only how many mules have died. They don't care how many miners have died. This is because mules cost them 200—300

---

① See "Declaration of the Second National Congress of the CPC (July 1922)", in *Selected Documents of the Central Committee of CPC*, Beijing: the Central Party School Press, 1982.

yuan a head whereas for miners died in an accident they need only to pay 100 yuan compensation "per head" ."[①] Soon afterwards, the Combined Secretary of China Labor Organizations, led by the CPC, pointed out in the Appeal to All Workers in China for Supporting the Strikes by the Miners of Kailuan Mines and the Cotton Spinners in Japanese-Run Textile Factories that: "Shanghai Japanese Textile Factory, run by Japanese capitalists, is the biggest blood sucker for Chinese workers. Workers in this factory went on a strike in the end of May because their wages were too low to maintain a basic livelihood. But the strike failed because the Japanese capitalists bribed Shanghai police who then closed down the trade union to which all the workers entrust their fate for no reason at all... now the workers of the factory are at the end of their tether. They have no choice but to go on a second strike. The Chinese Constitution clearly provides that "People have the freedom of assembly" . But they have deprived us of this natural right. If this can be tolerated, what cannot?"[②]

Historical documents show that, compared with international campaigns for human rights, those led by the CPC had the following characteristics: firstly, they were clearly goal-oriented. The CPC had learnt from historical experience and practice that the invasion by imperialist powers and the rule by feudal warlords were like two big mountains that weighed heavily on the back of Chinese people. Without overthrowing these two big mountains, the Chinese nation would never become independent and the Chinese people would never be liberated or have any human rights to talk about. Therefore, in order to protect their human rights, the Chinese people must overthrow imperialists and feudal warlords. Secondly, the scope of the subjects of rights was more extensive. For a long period of time, the subjects of human rights in western countries had been mainly the male members of the bourgeoisie. The protection of many of the rights of the working class and women was placed on the agenda of western countries only during the 1960s and 1970s, whereas the CPC had paid attention to the protection of the human rights of workers and peasants, who made up the majority of the Chinese population, at a relatively early

① See "Declaration of General Strike by Workers of the Five Mines in Kailuan", in *Ta Kung Pao*, October 28, 1922.

② "Appeal by the Combined Secretariat of Chinese Labor Organizations to all the Workers in China for supporting the Strikes by the Miners of Kairuan Coal Mines and the Cotton Spinners of Shanghai Rihua Textile Factory", in *Beijing Morning Post*, November 10, 1922.

stage and its campaigns for women's rights was decades earlier than those in some developed western countries. Thirdly, the objects of rights are more extensive. At the every early stage, the CPC had campaigned not only for civil and political rights, but also for economic, social, cultural and educational rights. Fourth, it is especially noteworthy that the CPC had not only put forward the slogan of human rights, but also participated in workers' and peasants' organizations and led the actual struggles for human rights. Many CPC members had laid down their precious lives in such struggles.

Through these struggles, the CPC realized that, in order to defeat the imperialist invasion and overthrow the oppressive rule of feudal warlords, it must establish a broad alliance with various social forces and cooperate with the Nationalist Party led by Dr. Sun Yat-sen. For this purpose, the CPC adopted at its Third National Congress the Resolution on National Movement and KMT, in which it was decided to establish an alliance with the KMT and jointly launch a campaign of national revolution. Thereafter, many members of the CPC jointed the KMT and some of them become part of the KMT leadership. At the first National Congress of KMT, held in Guangzhou in January 1924, Dr. Sun Yat-sen, with the help of the CPC, developed his "Three Principles of the People" into "New Three Principles of the People". As was pointed out by the Declaration of the First National Congress of KMT, the main content of the "New Three Principles of the People" were: (1) The principle of nationalism. In terms of external relations, nationalism means "to emancipate the Chinese nation so that it can become a free and independent nation in the world." For this purpose, the Chinese people must resist foreign aggression. The Declaration pointed out that: "To any class, nationalism means nothing more than freedom from the aggression by imperialists. Without national independence, Chinese national enterprises will be economically oppressed by foreign powers and never have any chance to develop; as for Chinese workers, they will be drained dry by warlords and domestic and foreign capitalists who are dependent on imperialism. Therefore, to most Chinese people, the fight for national liberation is nothing more than the fight against imperialism." In terms of internal relations, nationalism means "the equality of all ethnic groups and opposition to the oppression of one ethnic group by another ethnic group." (2) The Principle of democracy. According to this principle, the right to vote and to stand for election, the right to recall, the right of initiative, and the right to referendum "should be enjoyed by all citizens, rather than the privilege of a few." Especially they should not "become the tools of oppression against the common people." In order to truly realize democratic rights and freedoms, it is necessary to provide for civil rights in the constitution and to safeguard them by the constitution and laws. (3) The third principle is the principle of people's livelihood. The main content of this principle includes equalization of land ownership and regulation of capital. China was an agricultural country, "the main cause of the economic inequality in China is the concentration of the ownership of land in a small number of people." "Of all classes in Chinese society, peasants suffer the greatest hardship... Therefore, for those peasants who have lost their land and become tenants, the state should provide them land to cultivate and undertake water conservancy projects for them. It shall establish such relief organs as peasants' banks to provide relief to peasants who are in urgent need of money to prevent them from becoming lifelong debtors, so that they can lead a happy life." "To regulate the capital means that the state should take over the management of Chinese and foreign enterprises that are of monopolistic nature or industries that are too large in scale to be managed by private enterprises, such as banks, railroad, and airlines, so that the people's livelihood will not be controlled by private capital." "The state shall provide unemployed workers with relief and adopt labor laws to raise their living standard. Moreover, the state should also make efforts to implement other social welfare systems aimed at safeguarding people's livelihood, such as the pension system, the child-raising system, the system of social assistance to disabled people, and the system of compulsory education."

The "New Three Principles of the People" comprehensively explained Dr. Sun's proposition of realizing human rights in China through national revolution, which was basically the same as the political program of the CPC during the period of Democratic Revolution. After the First National Congress of the KMT, it became the common program of the KMT-CPC cooperation. Under the guidance of this common program, the revolutionary forces in China had made brilliant achievements in the fight for human rights.

III

Under the banner of "Three Principles of the People", the Great

Revolution led by CPC and the KMT had dealt a heavy blow to the reactionary rules of imperialists and feudal warlords. However, Chiang Kai-shek and Wang Jingwei, who for a long period of time had disguised themselves as left-wing members of the KMT and ultimately seized the military and political power of the KMT, launched a counterrevolutionary coup in Shanghai and Wuhan in April and July 1927, respectively, in which a large number of CPC members and other revolutionaries had been massacred. The coup marked the failure of the Great Revolution and a big setback in the struggle for human rights in China. Faced with such grim situation, members of the CPC were not intimidated by Chiang Kai-shek's "white terror" . They buried their fallen comrades, wiped the blood off their own wounds, and went on fighting with dauntless spirit.

Because of the change of situation, the CPC's struggle for human rights during the Period of the Second Civil War that began in 1927 showed the following new characteristics:

1. As the representative of the working class and oppressed people, the CPC continued to lead the Chinese people in the struggle against reactionaries headed by Chiang Kai-shek

In view of the fact that Chiang Kai-shek had completely betrayed the revolution and used military force to massacre communists and ordinary people, the CPC decided to organize armed uprisings, establish its own armed forces, and fight armed enemies with revolutionary armed forces. In accordance with a decision of the Central Committee of the CPC, the communists organized a series of uprisings, including: the Nanchang Uprising in Jiangxi Province on August 1, 1927; the Autumn Harvest Uprising in Hunan Province in September 1927; the uprisings in Gaiyang and Huang'an of Hubei Province, in Haifeng and Qiongya of Canton Province, in Ji'an and Wan'an of Jiangxi Province, as well as in various places in Henan Province, Hebei Province, and Shanxi Province in the Autumn of 1927; the Guangzhou Uprising in December 1927; the uprisings in Yiyang and Hengfeng of Jiangxi Province, in Yizhang of Hunan Province, and in Honghu and Sangzhi of Hubei Province in January 1928, the uprisings in Jianping of Fujian Province in February 1928; the uprisings in Weinan, Huaxian and Tongguan of Shaanxi Province in the Spring of 1928; and the uprising in Pingjiang of Hunan Province in July 1928. Although the above-mentioned uprisings occurred in different locations with different participants, they all had the same objective, namely to overthrow the rule of new warlords headed by Chiang Kai-shek and backed by Imperialists, to resist the oppression by feudal landlord class and comprador class, and to fight for people's rights.

The followings were the conditions of negotiation raised by the CPC Canton Party Committee to Zhang Fakui, a local warlord, in its Declaration of Uprising: "(1) to immediate release all political prisoners; (2) to immediate return to trade unions their union clubs occupied by the Reorganization Committee, which was a running dog of the warlords; (3) to completely restore and protect all the rights of workers who had participated in the Canton-Hong Kong Strike; (4) to completely restore the freedoms of speech, of publication, of assembly, of demonstration, of strike and other freedoms of the working class; (5) to arrest and punish all criminals who terrorize members of the working class; and (6) to immediately arm the workers in Canton Province and put them under the command of Canton Workers' Congress. ①The Basic Program of the Canton Uprising included the followings: "with respect to the working class: ordinances shall be promulgated to implement the eight-hour day system, and similar systems shall be implemented for workers in handicraft industry and in small enterprises; the rights of the workers who participated in the Canton-Hong Kong Strike shall be restored and expanded; the state shall provide subsidies to the unemployed workers in light of their original wages and raise the wages of all employed workers." "With respect to peasants: ordinances shall be promulgated to declare that all land belongs to the state and be handed over to peasants for cultivation." With respect to common working people and petty bourgeoisie urban citizens: orders shall be issued to confiscate the housings and properties of bourgeoisie and distribute them among the poor people, to abolish all taxes for the poor, to cancel all debts, especially debts that are due in the end of the year, for the poor, and to abolish all housing taxes for the poor—all housings in the city shall be owned publicly; all the pawns in all the pawn shops shall be confiscated and those belonging to the poor shall be returned to their original owners." With respect to soldiers, the state-owned land shall be assigned to soldiers and unemployed people for cultivation; soldiers' committees shall be set up in all armed forces; and revolutionary army of workers and peasants

① "Declaration of Uprising by the CPC Canton Party Committee (November 28, 1927)", in *Bolshevik*, vol. 1, no. 9.

shall be established."[1]

The documents adopted by the CPC during the Canton Uprising and the Guangzhou Uprising were, to some extent, representative of the documents adopted by the CPC at that time. Their objectives were to overthrow the rule of warlords headed by Chiang Kai-shek, to uphold the rights of workers, the poor people and the petty bourgeoisie in urban areas, and to overthrow local tyrants, evil gentry and feudal landlord class which formed the basis of Chiang Kai-shek's rule. Some people might say that this kind of political program was too radical. Actually it was not. Dr. Sun Yat-sen, when explaining his Three Principles of the People, stated that: "Civil rights can only be enjoyed by the citizens of the Republic. They should not be granted to those who are against the Republic to be used by them to sabotage the Republic. More specifically, all individuals and groups who are truly against imperialism should be able to enjoy all the freedoms and rights whereas no one, whether individual or group, who betrays his own country and pledges loyalty to imperials and warlords may enjoy such rights and freedoms."[2] After the 1927 Counterrevolutionary Coup, the new warlords headed by Chiang Kai-shek had already become willing pawns of imperialists in their aggression against China. When they began to massacre the Chinese people, the CPC had no choice but to pay them back in their coin. Any act of mercy towards them would be a crime against the people. It was exactly by summarizing international and Chinese historical experiences, especially the revolutionary experience in China, that the CPC had succeeded in organizing and leading a series of armed uprisings against Chiang Kai-shek's rule, establishing its own armed forces, fighting violent enemies through violent revolution, and eventually winning human rights for Chinese people.

It should be pointed out that during the 1920s and 1930s, there had emerged a group of intellectuals called the "human rights school" in China. Represented by Mr. Hu Shi and Mr. Luo Rongji, these intellectuals put forward or expounded on a series human rights theories which had had some positive impacts in China. However, in the violent struggle between revolutionaries and counterrevolutionaries, this group of intellectuals began to waver in their political stance and soon break up. Nevertheless,

---

① See Basic Program of the Uprising of Canton Workers, October 11, 1922.

② See Declaration of the First National Congress of the KMT, January 23, 1923.

their historical role in the struggle for human rights in China should be fully recognized.

2. As the creator and leader of the "red bases", the CPC adopted a serious of laws on the protection of human rights during the early 1930s

In order to win the battle against powerful enemies, the revolutionary armed forces must avoid key cities, which were the strongholds of enemies, and transfer its main forces to and establish revolutionary bases in rural areas, especially remote and border regions, where the enemies' rule were relatively weak. By 1930, the CPC had established over a dozen rural revolutionary bases of varying seize throughout the country, mainly in the remote mountainous regions in the provinces of Hunan, Hubei, Jiangxi, Fujian, Canton, Guangxi, Henan, Anhui, Jiangsu, Zhejiang and Sichuan. "In these economically and culturally backward regions, the transportation was poor and the dominant economy was small-scale peasant economy with outdated cultivation methods and low productivity. Most of the people there were illiterate. Feudal clan organizations and superstitious practices were prevalent. [1]Men in these regions were usually subjected to the oppression by three systems of authority, namely political authority, clan authority, and religious authority. As for women, in addition to being oppressed by these three systems of authority, they were also dominated by men (the authority of the husband). As was pointed out by comrade Mao Zedong, "These four authorities-political, clan, religious and masculine-are the embodiment of the whole feudal-patriarchal system and ideology, and are the four thick ropes binding the Chinese people, particularly the peasants."[2] The political authority of the landlords established on the basis of the feudal land ownership system was the backbone of all the other systems of authority. Bound by the four thick ropes and oppressed by the political authority of the landlords, Chinese peasants, like Chinese workers in cities, had no human right to talk about. In order to fight for human rights and to mobilize peasants to participate in the revolution, the CPC carried out land reform and adopted

---

① Party History Research Center of the CPC Central Committee, *The History of the Communist Party of China*, Beijing: People's Publishing House, 1991, p. 259.

② *Selected Works of Mao Zedong*, vol. I, Beijing: People's Publishing House, 1991, p. 33.

a series of relevant laws and regulations in the revolutionary bases, including the land struggle and the promulgation of the Land Law in Jinggangshan area, Jiangxi Province; the formulation of the Land Law in Xingguo County, Jiangxi Province, which was presided over by Mao Zedong; the adoption of the Land Resolution in western Fujian Province; the adoption of Political Program on Land Issues in northwest Hubei Province; and the adoption of the Interim Regulations on Land Law in Zuojiang area of Guangxi Province. Although these land laws and policies varied in their concrete contents, they were consistent in general spirit and basic principle, namely to rely on poor peasants who made up the majority of the rural population, establish alliance with middle peasants, restrict rich peasants, eliminate the feudal landlord class, abolish the system of ownership of land by feudal landlord and establish the system of ownership of land by peasants, so as to truly realize the ideal of "land to the tiller". The land reform carried out by the CPC in revolutionary bases had led to huge changes in rural areas: the poor peasants who had long been under the oppression of feudal landlords finally gained political emancipation and became the master of the rural areas; middle peasants also "have had their say along with poor peasants".[①] The land reform had greatly raised the peasants' enthusiasm for production and the raise of productivity had in turn led to rapid improvement of peasants' livelihood. Political empowerment, economic development and the improvement of livelihood had motivated more peasants to joint the revolutionary ranks and to fight for the rights of the Chinese people.

Apart from the land issue, another urgent human rights issue in rural China was the protection of the rights of women who suffered the most severe oppression in Chinese society. Therefore, great importance was attached by the CPC to the adoption of laws on the protection of women's rights in revolutionary bases. The laws, regulations and policies adopted by the CPC during this period included: the Marriage Law adopted by the first Workers', Peasants', and Soldiers' Congress of Western Fujian Province in March 1930; the Marriage Regulations adopted by the Soviet Area in Hunan-Jiangxi-Jiangsu Border Region and the Resolution on the Issue of Marriage" promulgated by the Second Workers', Peasants', and Soldiers' Congress of Hubei-Henan-Anhui Border Region later in the

① Mao Zedong, "Investigation in Xingguo County, Jiangxi Province", in *Collection of Rural Investigation Reports by Mao Zedong*, September 12, 1930.

same year; the Regulations of the Soviet Republic of China on Marriage and the Marriage Law of the Soviet Republic of China, adopted by the Central Soviet Area in December 1931 and April 1934, respectively, with the support of Mao Zedong; the Decision on the Adoption of the Marriage Law, adopted by the Soviet Government of Western Fujian Area in March 1930, which pointed out that: "In the past several thousand years, under the influence of the old moral codes, China has implemented a very shameful mercenary marriage system. Under this system, men treated women as their appendants and family property. In order to economically exploit women's labor so as to uphold family economy, men always tried to lower women's political and social status by restricting them with such old moral codes as "the three obediences and the four virtues", "parents deciding the marriages of their children", and "ignorance being the virtue for women".① In November 1931, the Central Executive Committee of the Soviet Republic of China adopted at its first meeting a Resolution on the Adoption of the Marriage Regulations, which pointed out that: "Under the feudal rule, the marriage between men and women are barbaric and inhumane. The oppression and the pain suffered by women are far worse than those suffered by men."② In order to change this situation, the above-mentioned marriage laws and regulations all embodied the following principles: first, freedom of marriage, which requires the abolition of all arranged, forced or mercenary marriages and the prohibition of the practice of child-bride. Marriage must be based on the consent of both the men and women and no party may use compulsion on the other party and no third party may interfere in marriage. Second, the implementation of the monogamy system and prohibition of polygamy. Third, the minimum ages for marriage are 20 for men and 18 for women. Marriage shall be prohibited if the man and the woman are lineal relatives by blood or collateral relatives by blood up to the fifth (or third in some of these laws) degree of kinship or for those suffering from venereal diseases or leprosy. Fourth, freedom of divorce. Divorce shall be granted if either the husband or the wife insists on divorce. Fifth, marriage and

① "Bulletin No. 7 of the Soviet Government of Western Fujian Province (April 1930)", in Han Yanlong and Chang Zhaoru (eds.), *Selected Legal Documents Adopted in Revolutionary Areas during the Period of New Democratic Revolution in China*, vol. 4, Beijing: China Social Sciences Publishing House, 1981, p. 796.

② Ibid., p. 788.

divorce must be registered at the county government. Sixth, after divorce, the husband and the wife shall dispose of their own pre-marital properties or debts; marital properties shall be divided equally between the husband and the wife; if there are children in the family, marital properties shall be divided equally among all the members of the family. The debts incurred by the family after marriage shall be paid by the husband after divorce. Seventh, the wife shall have the custody of the children born or conceived before divorce; if the wife refuses to take custody of the children, then the husband shall take over the custody. If the wife takes the custody of a child, the husband must pay two thirds of the living expense of the child till he or she reaches the age of 16. Eighth, children born out of wedlock shall be protected by law and it is prohibited to abuse or abandon such children. The above principles, while recognizing the freedom of marriage, provided special protection to women and children. This was because "women had just been liberated from feudal oppression. They have not yet recovered from the various harms caused by the oppression (such as foot-binding), or gained complete economic independence. Therefore, laws and policies should put more emphasis on the protection of women, and require men to take on more duties and obligations resulting from divorce. Children are the masters of new society, but the care of children was often neglected in by the old custom. Therefore, the laws must contain special provisions on the protection of children."① The marriage laws and regulations adopted by the CPC during the period of the Second Revolutionary Civil War were progressive and led to a revolution in the protection of women's rights. Not only so, they had also laid a legal foundation for the protection of women's rights in China during the later stages of revolution, even after the establishment of the People's Republic of China.

The main legal provisions on human rights protection in the "red bases" during the period of the Second Revolutionary Civil War were contained in several constitutional documents promulgated by the CPC in the Soviet areas. They included the Outline Constitution of the Soviet Republic of China, promulgated by the government of the Central Soviet Area in 1931 and 1934; the Ten Main Political Programs of the Soviet Republic of

① " Resolution on the Trial Implementation of the Marriage Regulations, Adopted at the First Meeting of the Central Executive Committee of the Soviet Republic of China", in Han Yanlong and Chang Zhaoru (eds.), *supra* note 14, p. 788.

China, the Declaration of Guangzhou Soviet, the Revolutionary Political Programs of the Revolutionary Committee of Hunan-Hubei-Jiangxi Border Region, and the Interim Political Program of Jiangxi Soviet, adopted in 1933. The main content of these constitutional documents included:

Firstly, the Chinese Soviet was a state of democratic dictatorship by workers and peasants. "All workers, peasants, soldiers of the red army, and all other working people and their family members, regardless of their gender, race, ... religion, shall be equal before the Soviet law... all the above-mentioned Soviet citizens who have reached the age of 16 have the right to vote and stand for election in the Soviet, to choose their representative, to participate in the Soviets at various levels to discuss and decide all local political affairs of the state."①

Secondly, "the political power of Chinese Soviet takes the safeguarding workers' and peasants' freedoms of expression, of the press, of assembly, and of association as its objective. It opposes the democracy of the landlords and the bourgeoisie, and advocate the democracy of workers and peasants; it strives to abolish the economic and political rights of the landlords and the bourgeoisie, and remove all obstacles set up by reactionary society to the enjoyed of freedoms by workers and peasants."②

Thirdly, "the political power of Chinese Soviet takes the safeguarding of the religious freedom of workers and peasants as its objective, and absolutely adheres to the principle of separation of political power from religion."

Fourthly, "The political power of Chinese Soviet recognizes the right to self-determination of ethnic minorities in China... currently it will try its best to help these weak ethnic groups to free themselves from the oppressive rules of imperialists, the KMT, warlords, aristocrats, lamas, and chieftains and achieve complete autonomy. It will help them to develop their own cultures and languages."

Fifth, "The political power of the Chinese Soviet takes the complete improvement of the livelihood of the working class as its objective. To this end, it adopts labor law, implements the eight-hour working day system, provides for the standard of minimum wage, establishes social insurance

① "Outline Constitution of the Soviet Republic of China (adopted at the Second National Congress of the Soviet Republic of China)", in ibid., pp. 13—14.

② Ibid., p. 15.

system and state unemployment allowance system, and declares that workers have the right to supervise over production."

Sixth, "The political power of the Chinese Soviet takes the elimination of feudal exploitation and improvement of peasants' livelihood as its objective. To this end, it promulgates the land law, deprives the landlord class of all its land and distributes it to farmhands, poor peasants and middle peasants, and takes the realization of the nationalization of land as its ultimate objective."

Seventh, "The political power of the Chinese Soviet takes the complete realization of women's liberation as its objective. To this end, it recognizes the freedom of marriage, implements various measures for the protection of women, so as to gradually lay the material foundation for women to truly free themselves from the bondage of housework, and to participate in the economic, political and cultural life of society."

Eighth, "The political power of the Chinese Soviet takes the safeguarding of the right to education of workers and peasants as its objective. To this end, it implements a complete free universal education system to the extent allowed by the conditions of revolutionary war. This system shall be implemented first among the young people. It shall safeguard all the rights of young working people, actively encourage them to participate in political, cultural and revolutionary activities, so as to cultivate new social forces."①

A review of the legal provisions on the protection of human rights promulgated by the CPC during the Second Revolutionary Civil War gives one the impression that some of these provisions were too radical and did not offer sufficient protection to national bourgeoisie and rich peasants. This is true. However, in order to make a more objective assessment of these provisions, we should analyze them in their historical context. In 1927, when Chiang Kai-shek betrayed the revolution, he was supported not only by big bourgeoisie, but also by the upper stratum of the national bourgeoisie. Landlords and rich peasants also tried their best to oppose revolution and were Chiang's social basis in rural areas. Under such circumstances, it was impossible for the CPC to give the same rights protection to landlords and rich peasants as that given to the broad masses of peasants and it is understandable that CPC leaders at that time, filled

① "Outline Constitution of the Soviet Republic of China (adopted at the Second National Congress of the Soviet Republic of China)", in ibid., pp. 13—16.

with hatred against the enemies who massacred their comrades and sometimes misguided wrong ideologies, had made certain mistakes in human rights policies and laws. Of course, we can also look at this issue from another perspective: although human rights are universal, different countries and areas are faced with different situations and have different priorities, and their human rights laws and policies must reflect such differences. Therefore, it is not appropriate to expect the policies and laws adopted by the CPC at that time to be perfect or make indiscreet remarks or criticisms against them. Although there were defects in these laws and policies, the basic purpose of the CPC was to serve the people and tens of thousands of communists and revolutionary soldiers had sacrificed their lives in the struggle for the realization of human rights in China, thereby winning the heartfelt support of the great masses of Chinese people. In just a few years, a new situation of political and economic development and human rights protection had emerged in the revolutionary bases. Later, Chiang Kai-shek personally commanded massive forces to carry out repeated campaigns of "encirclement and suppression" against the revolutionary bases. Faced with the strong enemy, the red army was forced to evacuate from their bases and begin the Long March. After they left, the people in the revolutionary bases were deprived of their newly-gained rights and once again plunged into the abyss of misery.

IV

At the time when the Chinese warlords were busy fighting each other in a scramble for power and wealth and Chiang Kai-shek busy suppressing with massive forces red armies in various revolutionary bases, the Japanese invaders, who had long since entrenched themselves in Northeast China, began to carry out their plan to annex the entire Chinese territory. The situation in China at that time was exactly the same as that described in the Appeal to All Fellow Countrymen to Resist Japanese Invasion and Save the Chinese Nation, issued by the Central Committee of the CPC on August 1, 1935 (The August First Declaration): In less than four years since the Mukden Incident of 1931, the Japanese had occupied and annexed over half of the Chinese territory, marching from Manchuria to Rehe, from Rehe to the Great Wall Fortress, from the Great Wall Fortress to "Luandong De-militarized Zone", and from the Demilitarized Zone to Hebei, Shanxi and other northern provinces. Now they have already occupied half of the Chinese territory and are actually carrying out the vicious plan of conquering the entire China laid out in the Tanaka Memorandum. Before long, the Yangtze River Basin, the Pearl River Basin and other regions in China will be under the occupation of the Japanese invaders, our five-thousand-year-old homeland will become a conquered land, and four hundred million Chinese people will become slaves of a foreign power. When province after province of China were occupied by the Japanese, thousands after thousands of the Chinese people become slaves, village after village and city after city being bathed in blood, millions after millions of countrymen driven from their homes, and one internal affair after another being interfered with, can China still be regarded as an independent country? Can Chinese people still regarded as an independent nation? In view of the above situation, the Appeal pointed out that: "The Chinese state and the Chinese nation are now at their crucial moment of life and death. They will survive only if we rise up to resist the Japanese invasion. Therefore, fighting against Japanese invasion has become a sacred duty of every fellow Chinese." The Appeal finally called upon all Chinese compatriots to "Fight for our homeland! Fight for the survival of the Chinese nation! Fight for national independence! Fight for territorial integrity! And fight for human rights and freedom!"

The Appeal was issued by the CPC during the Long March when the Red Army was constantly pursued and intercepted by enemies. When the Red Army, after breaking through one barrier after another, finally reached northern Shaanxi Province, the CPC issued two declarations with contents identical to that of the August First Declaration. The first one, Declaration on the Annexation of Northern China by Japan and on the Betrayal of Northern China and Entire China by Chiang Kai-shek, was issued on November 13, 1935 in the name of the Central Committee of the CPC. The second one, Declaration on Resisting Japanese Invasion and Saving the Chinese Nation, was issued on November 28, 1935 in the name of Mao Zedong and Zhu De. Apparently, the main human rights issue faced by China around the year 1935 had become the independence and survival of the Chinese nation, endangered by Japanese invasion. During this period of time, the emphasis of the struggle for human rights led by the CPC was to unit the Chinese people to resist Japanese invasion and uphold national independence. Therefore, the CPC's struggle for human rights during the period between 1935 and August 1945 had been carried out mainly in the following three fronts:

1. Leading Chinese people in the fight for democracy, freedom and the right to resist against Japanese invasion

After betraying the revolution, Chiang Kai-shek adopted a domestic policy of dictatorship and suppression of dissenters and a foreign policy of "stabilizing the country first and resisting foreign aggression afterwards", which actually was a capitulation policy. In the Declaration of the Great Alliance of Freedom Movement in China in 1930, Yu Dafu and Lu Xun described the situation in China at that time as the following: "under the rule of the current government, people have no freedom to talk about. Books and newspapers are banned, so there is no freedom of thought; the press is censored, so people cannot freely express their opinion; colleges and universities are closed down, so people are not able to freely receive education; all mass organizations which are not designated by the government are disbanded, so there is no freedom of association. All political movements and strikes or acts of resistance against rent taken by poor working people for the purpose of improving their livelihood are absolutely prohibited and the organizers of such activities are even arrested. Chance remarks can lead to public execution; there is no security of person or life whatsoever. The Chinese people, being deprived of their freedoms, are living in extreme misery."① Under the KMT rule, no publication was allowed to advocate the resistance against Japanese invasion and all anti-Japanese statements and actions were regarded as the crime of "communist propaganda". The CPC had carried out various forms of struggle against the KMT's suppression of Chinese people's resistance against Japanese invasion. In October 1935, students in ten middle schools and universities in Beiping and Tianjin, under the influence and leadership of the CPC, establish a student council, which issued the "Declaration on Resisting Japanese Invasion, Saving the Chinese Nation, and Fighting for Freedom" in November of the same year. On December 6, the student council of 15 universities and middle schools in Beiping published an Open Telegram from the Students of Various Universities and Schools in Beiping, which denounced the appeasement and capitulation policy adopted the KMT government towards

① Yu Dafu, Lu Xun et al., "Declaration of the Great Alliance of Freedom Movement in China" in *Sprouts*, vol. 1, no. 3, March 1930.

Japanese invaders since the Mukden Incident, and eloquently explained that there was only one way out for China, that is to mobilize the people in the whole country to resist Japanese invasion. On December 9th, thousands of students broke the numerous blockages set up by KMT military police to demonstrate in the street of Beiping and petitioned the KMT government to cease all acts of civil war, stop arbitrary arrests, ensure local territorial security, and safeguard the freedoms of expression, of assembly, of association, and of the press. This was the famous "December 9th Movement", which shocked China and the world and mobilized the entire nation to rise up against Japanese aggression.

In 1936, under the influence of the CPC, the literary and art circles in Shanghai, represented by such famous writers as Lu Xun, Ba Jin and Mao Dun, published the "Declaration of Literary and Art Circles on the Resistance against Japanese Aggression and Protection of the Freedom of Express", which pointed out that: "The Japanese invasion is intensifying with each passing day and the subjugation of the Chinese nation is imminent: the four provinces in northeast China have long fallen into enemy hands, the five provisions in north China as well as Fujian province are now also in imminent danger." The Declaration demanded that all anti-Japanese forces be united and earnestly pointed out that: "the freedom of expression and the freedom of literary and artistic activity are the key not only to cultural development, but also to the survival of the nation. Today, to freely express the demand to save the nation is not only a right, but also a bounden duty of Chinese citizens. Unless it is prohibited for citizens to love their own country, it is a matter of course that they should enjoy the freedom to express their patriotic opinions. Therefore, we demand that the government immediately grant the people their freedom of expression and abolish all laws and regulations that obstruct the exercise by people of their freedom of expression, such as those on the censorship of newspapers and banning and seizure of publications."[①] The Declaration expressed common wishes of Chinese intellectuals and forcefully promoted the anti-Japanese struggle in KMT controlled areas.

Apart from mobilizing students and other intellectuals to join the anti-Japanese campaign, the CPC had also made much efforts in wining the support of democratic personages, social activists and high-ranking

---

① See Declaration of Literary and Art Circles on the Resistance of Japanese Aggression and the Protection of the Freedom of Express (1936).

officials of various KMT factors, such as Soong Ching-ling, Cai Yuanpei, Zhang Xueliang, Shao Zongnan, Shao Zili, Li Jishen, Li Zongren, Bai Chongxi, Jiang Guangnai, Cai Tingkai, Chen Guofu, Chen Lifu, Hu Zongnan, Chen Cheng, and Chiang Kai-shek himself. From the second half of 1936 to the first half of 1937, the CPC had been sending them letters or using other channels to explain to them the importance of stopping the civil war, implementing democracy, and establishing a united front to fight against the Japanese aggression. In October 1939, Mao Zedong, Zhu De and other Red Army leaders sent a letter to Chiang Kai-shek and other leaders of the National Revolutionary Army in which they pointed out that: "Now the Chinese nation is facing its greatest peril. 'When a bird's nest is overturned, no egg can remain intact.' When a nation is in such a critical condition, there is no longer any room for internal strife."① On December 1, 1936, Mao Zedong and Zhu De pointed out in a letter to Chiang Kai-shek that: "Recently the situation in Suiyuan is deteriorating. Because of the civil war, the number of soldiers available for defending the Chinese territory against Japanese is very small. The Great Wall Campaign and the Battle of January 18th in Shanghai were two examples... If we could only stop the civil war today, we will be able to pull our troops out of the internecine battlefields and sent them to the frontlines of anti-Japanese war tomorrow, thereby increasing the defense capability in Shuiyuan by ten times... In this way, we can avenge our nation for the humiliation it had suffered at the hand of the Japanese invaders, defend our homeland, and recover our lost territory... It is for this reason that we are now personally writing to you to once again earnestly requesting you to make a prompt decision to grant our request to save our country. Let us turn hostility into friendship, to joint our efforts in the fight against the Japanese because this is not only beneficial to both of us, but also the only way for the Chinese nation to get itself out of the current crisis."② As for what kind of joint government should be established through the KMT-CPC cooperation, the Central Committee of the CPC had made it very clear in a previous letter to the Central Committee of the

① "A Letter from Leaders of the Red Army to Commander-in-Chief Chiang Kai-shek and Other Leaders of the Northwest Army of the National Revolution Army (October 26, 1936)", in *Reference Materials on the History of the CPC*, vol. 7, p. 435.

② "A Letter from Mao Zedong, Zhu De and Others to Chiang Kai-shek (December 1, 1936)", ibid., p. 438.

KMT: "Chinese people demand for a democratic republic government that works in the interests of the people. The political program of such a government must: firstly, to resist foreign aggression; secondly, to safeguard people's democratic rights; and thirdly, to alleviate, even to eliminate, people's sufferings in their daily life."①

The CPC's call for the stop of civil war and the establishment of an anti-Japanese alliance had not only won the support of workers, peasants, students, intellectuals and community leaders, but also caused strong reaction in the military and political circles of the KMT. On December 12, 1936, Zhang Xueliang and Yang Hucheng, the two generals of the KMT army stationed in Xi'an, driven beyond their limits of forbearance by Chiang Kai-shek's anti-communist policy, detained Chiang who came to the city to urgent them to send their troops to the frontline of the civil war against the CPC, and in December 13 sent circular telegrams to the relevant parties throughout the country in which they put forward the following Eight-point Proposal: "first, to restructure the Nanjing Government and to form an anti-Japanese united front composed of all parties and factions; second, to stop all acts of civil war; third, to immediately release patriotic leaders arrested in Shanghai; fourth, to release all political prisoners; fifth, to lift the ban on patriot movement; sixth, to safeguard the freedom of assembly, the freedom of association and all other political rights; seventh, to truly implement the will of Dr. Sun Yat-sen; and eighth, to immediately convene a national salvation conference."② On December 15, Mao Zedong, Zhu De, Zhou Enlai and other Red Army leaders sent a telegram to the KMT and the national government expressing their support to the Eight-Point Proposal put forward by Zhang Xueliang and Yang Hucheng. The telegram pointed out that: "The Eight-Point Proposal expressed the common wish of the Chinese people"; and that "the KMT and the national government should accept the Proposal, stop the civil war they are launching right now, remove Chiang Kai-shek from his office and hand him over to the Chinese people for trial; establish a government of united front consisting representatives of all parties, factions, all circles of society and all armed forces, abandon the concentration of power and the bureaucracy so indulged in by Chiang Kai-

① "A Letter from CPC to KMT (August 25, 1936)", ibid., p. 438.

② "Circular Telegram by Zhang Xueliang and Yang Hucheng (December 13, 1936)", ibid., p. 446.

shek, carry out political reform, lift the ban on the freedom of expression and on patriotic publications, release patriotic political prisoners, pull all troops out of battlefields of civil war and send them to Shanxi and Suiyuan to fight against Japanese invaders, so as to save the Chinese nation from foreign subjugation."① After successfully mediating a peaceful solution to the Xi'an Incident, the Central Committee of the CPC raised a five-point demand to the Third Plenary Session of the Central Committee of the KMT: "first, to stop all acts of civil war so as to concentrate national strength on resisting foreign aggression; second, to safeguard the freedoms expression, of assembly, and of association, and release all political prisoners; third, to convene a national congress participated by representatives of all political parties, sections, social circles, and armed forces so as to draw on collective wisdom and absorb all useful ideas to save the nation; fourth, to complete as soon as possible all preparation for the war of resistance against Japanese aggression; and fifth, to improve people's livelihood."② Through its strenuous efforts, the CPC finally established an anti-Japanese united front, realized the second KMT-CPC cooperation, and removed the obstacles to the anti-Japanese national salvation movement.

2. Leading Chinese people in resisting Japanese aggression and upholding national independence

The Japanese had long since made a strategic plan to conquer China and dominate entire Asia. "According to this plan, eight divisions would be deployed in North China to take Beiping, Tianjin and other major cities and carry out military campaigns in five provinces of North China; five divisions would be deployed in Central China: one attacks Shanghai; one force-lands from Hangzhou Bay, and the other two take coordinated action to attack Nanjing; and one division would be deployed in South China to take Guangzhou and the surrounding area. From the beginning, the Japanese navy would take control of the Chinese coasts and the Yangtze River Basin and assist the ground forces to capture strategic areas. The Japan's military campaigns in China were carried out basically according to

① "Telegram from Red Army Leaders to the KMT and the National Government Concern the Xi' an Incident" (December 15, 1936), ibid., p. 439.

② "Telegram from the Central Committee of the CPC to the Third Plenary Session of the Central Committee of the KMT (February 10, 1937)" ibid., p. 449.

this plan, only the strength of the military force used in these campaigns far exceeded that in the original plan."① In the process of execution of this plan, the Japanese invaders pursued the policy of "burn all, kill all, and loot all", savagely slaughtered Chinese people—most of them were civilians—and beastly raped Chinese women—many of them were old women or girl children and many died as a result of the rape. The Japanese invaders carried out thousands of massacres in urban and rural areas in China. According to incomplete statistics, a total of 21 million Chinese people had been killed or wounded and another 10 million tortured to death during Japan's all-out war of aggression against China that began in 1937. During the six weeks beginning from December 13, 1937, the Japanese invaders carried out systematic massacres in the city of Nanjing in which over 300, 000 civilians were killed;② between July 1937 and July 1945, the Japanese invaders carried out 498 massacres—in each of them no less than 10 civilians were slaughtered—in Hebei Province alone; between May and June 1942, 50, 000 Japanese soldiers were sent to eastern Hebei Province to carry out the "May First Mopping-up Campaigns", in which over 50, 000 civilians were killed;③ among the 78 counties and cities in Hunan Province, 44 were occupied, eleven invaded and harassed, and nine bombed by the Japanese troops during the eight-year Anti-Japanese War, resulting in 2, 622, 383 casualties;④ the Japanese invaders had left numerous mass graves in many parts of China during the war. Faced with the atrocious slaughter by the Japanese invaders and national subjugation and genocide, the CPC, while organizing the united front and calling Chinese people to resist Japanese invasion, also carried out coordinated military campaigns alongside friendly forces in frontline battlefields against the Japanese troops. It led the independent guerrilla warfare against the Japanese carried out by the Eighth Route Army and the

① War History Office, Defense Research Institute of Japan Defense Agency (ed.), *History of Japanese Military Campaigns in China During the Second World War* (*Part I*), Tokyo: Asagumo Shinbunsha Inc., 1975, pp. 102—103.

② See Information Office of the State Council Of the People's Republic of China, *Human Rights in China*, December 1991.

③ Cheng Bofeng and Zhuang Jianping (eds.), *Bloody Evidences: Documentary Records of the Atrocities Committed by Japanese Invaders in China*, Chengdu: Chengdu Publishing House, 1955, p. 2.

④ Ibid., p. 329.

New Fourth Army in North, Central and East China and the military campaign against the Japanese carried out by Northeast Anti-Japanese United Army in Northeast China. The CPC led armies eliminated over 1, 000 Japanese soldiers in the Battle of Pingxinguan Pass and over 2, 000 enemies in the ambushes in Pingding County and Xiyang County of Shanxi Province; destroyed or seriously damaged over 20 enemy planes in the surprise attack on Mingyangbao Airport in Dai County, Shanxi Province; and, in coordination with the KMT armies, engaged in pitched battles with Japanese troops in Xikou Town of Shanxi Province, which lasted for 20 days and dealt a serious blow to the arrogant Japanese invaders. The above campaigns effective contained the main forces of Japanese invaders and upset their plan to annex China. Between August and December 1940, the Eighth Route Army launched the "Hundred Regiments Offensive" against Japanese invaders in North China area. A total of 105 regiments participated in the offensive, "killing and wounding 30, 000 Japanese soldiers and soldiers of collaborationist Chinese armies and capturing 281 Japanese soldiers and 1, 400 soldiers of collaborationist Chinese armies",[①] thereby dealing an even heavier blow to the Japanese army, and cutting it vanguards off from it rear. In the meantime, the strategy of protracted war, put forward by Mao Zedong and implemented by the CPC, had enhanced the confidence of Chinese soldiers and civilians in the ultimate victory of the war against Japanese invasion. Despite the policy of passive resistance adopted by the KMT and the continuous obstructions and frictions created by the capitulationist factions in the KMT, the war of resistance against Japanese aggression by Chinese people, including the majority of officers and soldiers in the KMT army, like an unstoppable deluge, finally engulfed and overwhelmed the Japanese invaders and a small band of collaborationist Chinese who surrendered themselves to the Japanese imperialists. In August 1945, the Chinese people finally won the great victory of war of resistance against Japanese invasion.

3. Adopting a series of laws on the protection of human rights in various anti-Japanese bases

Anti-Japanese bases were the bases established by the CPC to support the

---

① Cheng Bofeng and Zhuang Jianping (eds.), *Bloody Evidences: Documentary Records of the Atrocities Committed by Japanese Invaders in China*, Chengdu: Chengdu Publishing House, 1955, p. 543.

war of resistance against Japanese invasion. During the entire anti-Japanese war period, these bases, while under tremendous military, economic and political pressure and blockage, had undertaken the difficult task of providing human and material resources for the war effort. In order to unit broader range of social forces in the fight against Japanese aggressors, and to uphold the independence, freedoms and human rights of the Chinese people, the CPC needed to further strengthen the construction of the legal system of protection of human rights in light of the new situation.

The legal provisions on the protection of human rights adopted by CPC can be found in the administrative programs adopted by the governments of anti-Japanese bases in the Shaanxi-Gansu-Ningxia Border Region, the Shanxi-Chahar-Hebei Border Region, the Shanxi-Hebei-Shandong-Henan Border Region, Northwestern Shanxi Province and Shandong Province between 1939 and 1942. These administrative programs contain extensive provisions on the protection of human rights. For example, the Administrative Program of the Government of the Shaanxi-Gansu-Ningxia Border Region during the Anti-Japanese War Period, promulgated in April 1939 contained the following provisions: (1) "to consolidate and expand the anti-Japanese national united front, to unit all people and political parties in the Border Region, and mobilize all human, material, financial and intellectual resources to defend the border region, the northwest China, and the whole of China and to recover the lost land"; (2) "to actively carry out the work of eliminating traitors, to increase people's alertness, to completely eliminate traitors, enemy spies, and bandits, so as to strengthen the base areas"; (3) "to realize the equality of political and economic rights for Mongolian, Hui and Han nationalities and to form an anti-Japanese alliance of Mongolian, Hui and Han nationalities in accordance with the principle of equality of nationalities"; (4) "to respect the beliefs, religions, cultures, customs, and habits of the Mongolian and Hui nationalities, and help them to develop their own cultures"; (5) "to develop democracy, to adopt a direct, universal, equal and anonymous election system, to improve the political institutions of centralized democracy, and to enhance people's ability of self-government"; (6) "to safeguard people's freedoms of expression, of the press, of association, of belief, of residence, of movement and of communication, to encourage the development of anti-Japanese organizations and armed forces among the people, and to raise their enthusiasm for resisting Japanese invasion"; (7) "to implement the policy of gender equality and improve the political, economic and social status of women, implement the voluntary marriage system, and prohibit the systems of mercenary marriage and child bride"; (8) "to establish a judicial system that is convenient for the people, and safeguard people's right to report on crimes committed by any government officials"; (9) "to develop universal education, eliminate illiteracy, enhance national consciousness and raise the political and cultural levels of the adult people in the Border Region"; (10) "to confirm people's right to private property, and protect the interests of the people in the Border Region gained from the land reform"; (11) "to reclaim waste land, undertake water conservancy projects, improve farming, increase agricultural production, and organize ploughing in spring and harvest in autumn"; (12) "to develop handicraft industry and other industries, encourage investment by businessmen, and raise industrial production"; (13) "to establish eight-hour working day system, improve labor conditions, protect workers' interests, enhance workers' enthusiasm for work and increase productivity"; (14) "to protect children and prohibit maltreatment of children"; and (15) "to provide assistance to the elderly, the weak, orphans, and widows, to provide relief to victims of natural disasters so as to prevent them from becoming destitute and homeless".① In May 1941, in order to expand the basis of the anti-Japanese political power and establish a broader anti-Japanese united front, the Politburo of the Central Committee of the CPC promulgated the Administrative Program of the Government of Shaanxi-Gansu-Ningxia Border Region, which declared that a "three-thirds system" would be implemented in the construction of political power in the Border Region, namely only one third of the offices in the government of the Border Region would be held by the CPC members and the other two thirds would be held by non-CPC members. Moreover, the Program also strengthened the provisions on the protection of human rights. For example, it provided in Article 6 that: "The government shall safeguard the personal right, political right, property right and the freedoms of expression, of press, of association, of belief, of residence, and of movement of all anti-Japanese people (including landlords, capitalists, peasants and workers). No one may be arrested, interrogated or punished by any state organ, armed force, or organization, except by judicial or public security organs in the performance of functions; people have the right to report on or make

① Han Yanlong and Chang Zhaoru (eds.), *supra* note 14, pp. 31—33.

charge against any unlawful act by public officials." Article 7 of the Program provided that: "The government shall improve the judicial system, resolutely abolish corporal punishment, and lay stress on evidence rather than confession. With regard to those who had collaborated with Japanese invaders, except for those who refuse to repent, a policy of lenience shall be adopted to help them to change by education and persuasion, to allow them put their past behind them and start a new life, and it is prohibited to kill or humiliate them, or to force them to surrender themselves or write a statement of repentance. The same policy shall be adopted for anyone who tried to sabotage the government of the Border Region, such as traitors and anti-communists." Article 16 provided that: "Vagrants shall be given land to cultivate and the opportunity to get job and education; measures shall be adopted to change the bad habit among civil servants and common people of discriminating against vagrants and to help vagrants to change their way of life through education and persuasion." Article 20 provided that: "A policy of leniency shall be adopted for all prisoners of war and no question of their past shall be asked. Those who are willing to join the resistance forces shall be accepted and given preferential treatments; it is prohibited to kill or humiliate them, or to force them to surrender themselves or write a statement of repentance. The same policy shall be adopted for those who, after their release, joined the enemy force and being captured again. Those who had attacked the Eighth Route Army, the New Fourth Army and any other anti-Japanese forces shall be dealt with in a similar way."①

Shaanxi-Gansu-Ningxia Border Region was the seat of the Central Committee of the CPC, the Administrative Program of this Region had a demonstrative effect. The administrative programs of all other revolutionary bases contained roughly the same content.

In order to truly safeguard human rights, the various revolutionary bases, after promulgating their administrative programs, adopted regulations on the protection of human rights in accordance with the basic spirit of these administrative programs. Examples of such regulations include: the Regulations of Shaanxi-Gansu-Ningxia Border Region on the Protection of Human Rights and Property Rights, Regulations of Shandong Province on the Protection of Human Rights, Interim Regulations of Hebei-Shandong-Henan Border Region on the Protection of People's

① Han Yanlong and Chang Zhaoru (eds.), *supra* note 14, pp. 34—37.

Rights, Regulations of Northwest Shanxi Province on the Protection of Human Rights, and the Rules for the Implementation of Regulations of Bohai District on the Protection of Human Rights. These instruments contained specific provisions on the political, economic, cultural and personal rights of the people in these bases. With respect to political rights, the Regulations of Shandong Province on the Protection of Human Rights provided in Article 2 that: "All citizens of the Republic of China, regardless of their gender, race, religion, profession and class, are equal in legal and political rights"; in Article 3 that "All citizens of the Republic of China, with the exception of traitors and those deprived of their citizens' rights, have the right to election, the right to recall, the right of initiative, and the right of referendum. The above-mentioned exception does not include political prisoners arrested before the start of the anti-Japanese war"; in Article 4 that: "to the extent of not jeopardizing the war of resistance against Japanese invasion, people shall have the following freedoms: (1) the freedom of person and the freedom of organizing anti-Japanese armed groups; (2) the freedom of movement and the freedom of residence; (3) the freedoms of expression, of writing, of the press, of assembly, of association, and of communication; (4) the freedom of belief, of religion and of political activity."① With respect to the right to property, the Regulations of Shaanxi-Gansu-Ningxia Border Region on the Protection of Human Rights and the Right to Property provided in Article 3 that: "The government protects the right to private property and the right to usufruct of private property (including land, house, creditor's right and all other property) of all anti-Japanese people"; in Article 4 that: "in areas where the land allocation system had already been implemented, the right to private ownership of land of peasants who have already been allocated land shall be protected; in areas where the land allocation system had not yet been implemented, the landlords' ownership of land and the debtors' right shall be protected."② With regard to personal rights, the Regulations of Northwest Shanxi Province on Human Rights provided in Article 3 that: "People shall enjoy the right to person. No one may be arrested, detained, interrogated or punished unless in accordance with law"; in Article 4 that: "People shall have the freedom of action. No one maybe searched or

① Han Yanlong and Chang Zhaoru (eds.), *supra* note 14, p. 90.

② Ibid., p. 92.

stopped unless in accordance with law"; in Article 5 that: "People shall have the freedom of residence. Their residence may not be broken into, searched or sealed up unless in accordance with law"; in Article 9 that: "no armed force or mass organization has the right to arrest, detain, interrogate or punish any individual. In case the armed force needs to arrest an individual in relation to a military secret, it must do so through the local government or the relevant government organ"; and in Article 10 that: "District or village offices of the government have no power to arrest any person without the order from the county government; when arresting a person, the government (including public security bureaus) at various levels must produce a formal arrest warrant or a similar document."① Moreover, each of the above-mentioned human rights instruments strictly prohibited the practice of extorting confessions by torture and required that a criminal suspect be brought before a judge for trial in accordance with legal procedures within 24 hours under normal circumstance and no more than 48 hours under special circumstance after arrest. Both the Regulations of Shandong Province on the Protection of Human Rights, and the Rules for the Implementation of Regulations of Bohai District on the Protection of Human Rights provided for criminal punishments for public officials who infringe upon people's freedoms or rights, extort confessions by torture or by other illegal means, and for the right of victims of such violations to request compensation for the damages they have suffered as a result of the violations.

The laws on the protection of human rights adopted by anti-Japanese bases were comprehensive and operable. Some people, based on western legislative standard, hold that the human rights protection laws in revolutionary bases failed to give a strict definition and theoretical generalization to the human rights concept and therefore doubt whether a human rights protection system really existed at that time or, if such a system did exist at that time, whether it could be regarded as a genuine human rights protection system. Such doubt is unjustified. Although defining human rights in a human rights law is important, definition of human rights should not be taken as the only standard for judging human rights laws. The protection of human rights is concrete. Faced with the grim situation at that time, when the revolutionary bases were under frequent attacks by both the Japanese invaders and KMT armies, the human rights

① Han Yanlong and Chang Zhaoru (eds.), *supra* note 14, pp. 98 and 99.

protection in these bases depended on concrete codes of conduct, which must use concise and clear language to inform soldiers and civilians what rights they were entitled to, what rules they must abide by, what acts were prohibited, and what kind of violation of human rights were crimes punishable under the law. These regulations, together with other laws, constituted the revolutionary legal system in the revolutionary bases, which effectively united the people and consolidated the people's democratic political power of these bases, and turned these remote culturally and economically backward border regions into politically, economically and culturally developed model regions, and strongholds of the Eighth Route Army, the New Fourth Army and other anti-Japanese armed forces. Historical facts have already proved that the human rights protection laws in these bases were comprehensive and concrete and were truly implemented under the leadership of the CPC and that the human rights in these bases were genuinely protected.

V

The victory of the war of resistance against Japanese aggression removed one of the major obstacles to the independence and emancipation of the Chinese nation. The Chinese people, who had suffered from many years of war, longed for a peaceful environment in which they could recover from the trauma of the war. The CPC, representing the will of the people, advocated that all patriotic and democratic forces in China should unit and seize the rare historical opportunity to build China into an independent, democratic, and prosperous new country, and to help Chinese people to get rid of oppression and poverty and to enjoy a free and happy new life. However, the situation did not develop according to the good will of the people. Chiang Kai-shek, who had adopted a policy of compromise towards Japanese imperialists, who had been ever on the retreat before the Japanese forces during the eight-year war of resistance, and who holed up all his main forces in a small corner of southwest China during the final years of the war, came out of his hiding place posing himself as a "hero of resistance against Japanese invasion" after the surrender of Japan and tried to seize the fruit of victory. Since his main military force was too far away from the frontline, Chiang and his backstage boss—the American imperialists—adopted two unusual steps: first, the U. S. government "tried to use Japanese armies to hold back the communists" .[1] It ordered the Japanese invaders, whose hands were stained with the blood of Chinese people, to continue to maintain the so-called order in the occupied areas and forbade them from surrendering to the people's armed forces led by the CPC, thereby actually allowing them to continue oppressing the Chinese people. Second, Chiang Kai-shek used the collaborationist Chinese armies as garrisons "to be responsible for effective defense" against the recovery of occupied Chinese territories by people's armies, took the opportunity to incorporate half a million collaborationist Chinese troops into the KMT armies as "underground armies" or "vanguards", and ordered them to attack liberated areas. The Military Committee of the KMT even went as far as appointing Zhou Fohai, the President of the Executive Yuan of Nanjing puppet government, as the General Director of the Campaign Headquarters of Shanghai Municipality. Meanwhile, the U. S. Government, in the name of repatriating Japanese POWs and helping the KMT government to take over occupied areas, transported KMT armies by air and sea from Southwest and Northwest China to North China, East China, Central China and Northeast China, and order the U. S. marines to enter and be stationed in coastal port cities and large inland cities to help KMT armies to grab strategic areas.

What happened at that time was exactly what China had repeated experienced during the 100 years since 1840: the foreign invaders could realize their invasion of China only with the help of their agents in China whereas the reactionaries in China could put to good use of their despotic power only by relying on their foreign backstage bosses. After the end of the World War II, the U. S. government, in order to "contain the Soviet influence" and "establish the dominant position of the U. S. in the world", tried to gain control over China and, for some historical and practical reasons, it had chosen Chiang Kai-shek and his KMT government as the piece on its chessboard. As the U. S. Secretary of State Dean Acheson later admitted, the method adopted by the U. S. at that time was to enhance the strength of KMT government and "to help it establish

---

[1] Harry S. Truman, *Memoirs by Harry S. Truman*, Chinese Edition, vol. 2, Beijing: SDX Joint Publishing Company, 1974, p. 72.

its power in as broad areas as possible. "[①] Thus, Chiang Kai-shek and his reactionary KMT government, acting in collusion with the U. S. government, became the biggest obstacle to the achievement of national dependence and full enjoyment of human rights by Chinese people after the World War II. Faced with complicated new situation and seemingly formidable enemy, the CPC, as always, stood together with the Chinese people, and carried out persistent struggle against KMT reactionaries and their backstage boss—the U. S. imperialists.

1. Defeating KMT reactionaries through the people's war of liberation, thereby realizing national independence and emancipation

After winning the victory of the war of resistance against Japanese invasion, the Chinese people were eager to re-build their own country in peace and to realize genuine national independence, freedom and prosperity. On August 25, 1945, the Central Committee of the CPC pointed out in the Declaration on the Current Situation of China that: "The main tasks of the Chinese nation today are to strengthen national unity, ensure domestic peace, realize democracy, improve people's livelihood, so as to realize the unification of the country and establish an independent, free and prosperous new China based on peace, democracy, and solidarity." To achieve this goal, Mao Zedong, "with tremendous courage"[②] and in complete disregard of his own safety, personally went to Chongqing to negotiate with Chiang Kai-shek. On October 10, 1945, after more than one and a half months of hard negotiation, a Summary of Conversations Between Representatives of the KMT and the CPC (namely the so-called "Double Tenth Agreement") was signed. According to the Agreement, the KMT accepted the basic policy of peaceful state building, promised to "take peace, democracy, solidarity, and unity as the basis, make concerted efforts to avoid civil war, and build an independent, free, and prosperous new China" . The Double Tenth Agreement also required the KMT government to convene a political consultative conference participated by representatives of all political parties and non-party personages in the country to discuss plans

---

① A Letter from U. S. Secretary of State Acheson to U. S. President Truman (July 30, 1949), in Party History Research Center of the CPC Central Committee, *supra*note 11, p. 665.

② Party History Research Center of the CPC Central Committee, *supra* note 11, p. 675.

for state building, end the "Political Tutelage" as soon as possible, realize political democratization, recognize people's democratic rights and freedoms and the lawfulness and the equality all political parties, abolish secret services, release political prisoners, and hold general election.

This Agreement, if implemented earnestly, could have avoided civil war, realized the plan of peaceful state building, and safeguarded people's democratic rights and freedoms. However, the negotiation with the CPC and the signing of the Double Tenth Agreement was only a stalling tactics adopted by Chiang Kai-shek to achieve the ultimately objective of eliminating the CPC and the revolutionary forces led by it. On September 29, 1945, while still in the process of negotiating with the CPC, Chiang Kai-shek sent a secret telegram to commanders-in-chief of various theaters of operations, which stated that: "The purpose of the current negotiation with the treacherous Communist Party is to find out its demands and purposes and to reduce international pressure on us. You should take this opportunity to rapidly take over the major cities in occupied areas. Once the National army has gained control over strategic areas and lines of communication and completed the acceptance of the surrender of the Japanese armies, we will conduct concrete negotiation with the treacherous Communist Party on the basis of our military advantages. Should the CPC refuse to submit itself to the unified political and military rule of the government, we will eliminate them as bandits."① Meanwhile, He Yingqin, the Commander-in-Chief of the KMT army, also sent secret orders to various theaters of operations to print and distribute the Manual on the Suppression of Bandits, compiled by Chiang Kai-shek during the "encirclement and suppression" of the red armies in 1933, and required the commanders of the KMT armies to "supervise and encourage those under your command to make arduous effort to complete as soon as possible the task of suppressing bandits".② According to the secret order and deployment of Chiang Kai-shek, the KMT armies launched attacks on liberated areas. The people armies led by CPC were forced to fight back, wiping out near 110, 000 KMT troops in areas of Shangdang, Suiyuan, Handan, Xuzhou and Jinan. On October 1, 1946, the KMT reactionaries were forced to sign a "Truce Agreement" with the CPC.

① Party History Research Center of the CPC Central Committee, *supra* note 11, pp. 678—679.

② Ibid., p. 679.

It turned out that the "Truce Agreement" was just another stalling tactic employed by Chiang Kai-shek after the "Double Tenth Agreement". He needed time to deploy troops and strategic materials with the help of the American imperialists. As for the U. S., it realized that the KMT at that time "has absolutely no ability to suppress the CPC by military force" and that Chiang Kai-shek's launching of a civil war without sufficient preparation "might result in the control of the entire China by the CPC",[①] thereby putting the U. S. in an disadvantaged position in the struggle with the Soviet Union for sphere of influence. Both the U. S. government and Chiang Kai-shek took their own interest as the starting point of their actions and totally ignored Chinese people's aspiration for peace. Soon afterwards, blinded by the lust for gain, they believed that they were ready for the war and consequently started war machine. In the second half of 1946, they started a full-scale civil war by launching large-scale attacks on liberated areas. The CPC armies, supported by the Chinese people, rose in defense of themselves and, after fierce battles, quickly turned the tides in their favor. In a little more than three years, they defeated the KMT reactionaries who had been so arrogant and overbearing only a short while ago and drove them out of the Chinese Mainland.

2. The United Front and Democratic Movement led by the CPC: the second front of the struggle for human rights

While launching armed attacks on the liberated areas, the KMT reactionaries also suppressed the democratic movement undertaken by democratic parties and patriotic teachers and students in areas under its control. On January 31, 1946, in order to safeguard human rights in a state of emergency, the Political Consultative Conference participated by various political parties decided to establish a Committee on the Protection of People's Rights. In a speech at the preparatory meeting of the Committee, the CPC representative, Mr. Dong Biwu, called on all Chinese people to unit and take joint actions to protect their own human rights.[②] In the next day, the KMT reactionaries sent special agents to a

① *General George C. Marshall's Mission to China, 1945—1947*, Beijing: Zhonghua Book Company, 1981, p. 210.

② *Chronology of Dong Biwu*, Beijing: Central Literature Publishing House, 2007, p. 244.

meeting celebrating the successful convening of the Political Consultative Conference and beat up 60 participants of the meeting, including Guo Moruo, a representative to the Chinese People's Political Consultative Conference, Mr. Li Gongpu, the Chairman of the Conference, Activists Shi Fuliang and Zhang Naiqi, as well as many news reporters. Thereafter, the KMT had created a series of incidents in which many revolutionaries were beaten up or murdered and their homes or offices smashed or looted. However, the more severe the regime's repression, the more people resisted. The KMT's retrograde act of stubbornly launching the civil war by relying on its American master had sparked widespread protests both in China and abroad. Various political parties, mass organizations, and overseas Chinese organizations sent circular telegrams or published declarations to call for the implementation of democracy, for the stop of the civil war and for the U. S. government to cease interfering in China's internal affairs.

The democratic movement began in the city of Kunming, where a large number of universities and colleges were located at that time. In the evening of January 25, 1945, over 6, 000 students held an assembly in Southwest Associated University, in which anti-civil war speeches were given by such famous professors as Mr. Qian Duansheng, Mr. Fei Xiaotong, Mr. Pan Dakui and Mr. Wu Qiyuan. The KMT troops surrounded the gathering and fired shots to scare its participants. On December 26, over 30, 000 students in more than 30 universities, colleges and high schools declared a general strike and published a declaration, demanding an immediate stop to the civil war, the withdrawal of U. S. troops from China, the establishment of a democratic confederate government, and genuine protection of people's rights and freedoms. The students also established a General Strike Committee to lead the struggle against KMT reactionaries. Under the leadership of CPC Yunan Provincial Committee, members of the CPC and of the Youth Democrat Union played a key role in the strike. On December 29 and 30, the students of the city held a demonstration. On December 1, the KMT government sent a large number of special agents and soldiers to Southwest Associated University and Yunnan University to beat up and throw grenades at students, resulting in the death of four students, two of them were members of the CPC. The incident, later became known as "December 1 Massacre", shocked the whole country. On December 23, 1943, eleven members of the Shanghai Association against Civil War and for the Promotion of Democracy, including Mr. Ma Xulun, Mr. Yan Baohang, Mr. Hu Juewen and Ms. Lei Jieqiong, went to Nanjing to submit a petition to the KMT Government. They were beaten up by KMT reactionaries as soon as they arrived at the Xiaguan Railway Station of Nanjing City and many of them were wounded. On July 11 and 15, 1946, special agents of the KMT in Kunming murdered two members of the Central Committee of China Democratic League—Mr. Li Gongpu and Mr. Wen Yiduo—who were against the dictatorship of Chiang Kai-shek and actively advocated peace and democracy. On December 24 of the same year, a female student of Peking University, Ms. Shen Chong, was raped by an American soldier. The incident further enraged the Chinese people. The unprincipled protection by the KMT controlled media of the American soldier added more fuel to the fire. The protest spread from Peking University to Yanjing University and Tsinghua University, and from Beijing to other large and medium-sized cities, including Tianjin, Shanghai, Nanjing, Kunming, Wuhan, Kaifeng, Chongqing, Guangzhou, Hangzhou, Fuzhou, Guilin, and Taipei, developing into a large-scale anti-American patriotic movement that had lasted for several months. ①

The KMT reactionaries, while brutally repressing the intellectual circle, also intensified the plunder and exploitation of Chinese people. As a result of war, peasants' land laid waste and agricultural production dropped; and as a result of the dumping of American commodities in China, Chinese national industries were on the brink of bankruptcy. In order to carry on with the civil war, the KMT government increased the land tax rate and intensified press-ganging of soldiers and civilian workers. The decrease in the industrial and agricultural production had resulted in the shortage of goods, the raise in commodity prices, and devaluation of currency. The deepening of economic crisis led to the general and drastic decrease in educational expenditure. Teachers in universities, colleges, and primary and secondary schools were on the brink of starvation and the masses of people found it hard to live on. Under such circumstances, workers and peasants quickly joined the intellectuals in the democratic movement. Between the second half of 1946 and 1947, "rice riot" had

① Party History Research Center of the CPC Central Committee, *supra* note 11, p. 690; *Draft of Modern Chinese History*, Harbin: Heilongjiang People's Publishing House, 1981, pp. 333, 335 and 336.

broke out in over 40 cities and towns in the provinces of Jiangsu, Zhejiang, Anhui, Sichuan, Hubei, Hunan, Henan, Shandong, Shaanxi, Suiyuan, Jiangxi and Canton. Peasants rose up to resist rent, tax, and press-ganging. In May 1947, a democratic movement against civil war, hunger, and persecution broke out. The democratic movements in KMT areas, although peaceful, had shaken the foundation of the reactionary rule of the KMT. As Mao Zedong pointed out that now a second front has emerged, that is, the sharp struggle between the great and righteous student movement and the reactionary Chiang Kai-shek government. The slogan of the student movement is "Food, Peace, Freedom" or "Against Hunger, Against Civil War, Against Persecution". ①

3. Buildingcontinuously expanding liberated areas into strongholds of people's war of liberation and model regions of human rights protection

As the Chinese say goes, "A just cause enjoys abundant support while an unjust cause finds little support." Chiang Kai-shek's retrograde act of relying on the support of the U. S. government to launch civil war met with strong opposition by people throughout the country. With the material and personnel support from the U. S., the KMT's large-scale attack on liberated areas reached its climax when the troops led by Hu Zongnan captured Yanan on March 19, 1947. From then on, the People's Liberation Army had turned the table on the KMT armies, went from victory to victory, and continuously expanded the liberated areas. To support the people's war of liberation, and to enable people in liberated areas to further enjoy their rights, a series of reform had been carried out under the leadership of the CPC. Firstly, on the basis of summarization of past rural land policy, the Outline Land Law of China, adopted in September 1947 and promulgated in October of the same year, abolished the exploitative feudal and semi-feudal land system, and implemented a "land-to-the-tiller" system. The land reform in the vast liberated areas enabled over 100 millions peasants, or one fourth of the total peasant population in the whole country, to become land owners. An American author pointed out that "The New Draft Agrarian Law was destined to play

① *Selected Works of Mao Zedong*, vol. IV, Beijing: People's Publishing House, 1991, p. 1223.

as important a role in China's Civil War of 1946—1950 as the Emancipation Proclamation played in the American Civil War of 1861—1865."[①] Actually the land reform in China was of much larger scale and more profound than the emancipation of the black slaves in the U. S. because it enabled the poor peasants who had been enslaved in the past to become the owner of their land and master of their own country. Secondly, while carrying out land reform in old liberated areas, the CPC implemented the policy of reducing rent and lowering the interest rate in newly liberated rural areas and the policy of protecting national industry and commerce in newly liberated cities. On the basis of the human rights protection law which had already existed in the revolutionary bases, the CPC adopted a series of new regulations, including the Administrative Program of the Autonomous Government of Inner Mongolia, the Announcement of the Government of Special Municipality of Harbin on the Prohibition of Unlawful Detention, Arrest, and Interrogation and Other Violations of Human Rights, the Order of the Administrative Office of Henan-Anhui-Jiangsu Border Region Instructing Governments at Various Levels to Truly Protect Human Rights and Strictly Prohibit Arbitrary Arrest, Corporal Punishment and Extorting a Confession by Torture, and the Revised Regulations of Bohai District on the Protection of Human Rights—all of them contained further stipulations on the protection of human rights. Thirdly, the work of building democratic government was carried out in various liberated areas after the completion of the land reform. The main purposes and tasks of such work was to support the People's Liberation Army in eliminating KMT forces in these areas and in establishing a stable social order; to establish political power at various level on the basis of democracy, to develop production, to invigorate the economy, to safeguard people's political, economic and cultural rights, to give full support to the troops in the front line, to defeat the KMT reactionaries and liberate the whole of China. The North China People's Government was the first government established in main liberated areas. The experience accumulated, the laws adopted and the various institutions established by this government laid a foundation for the establishment of a central government of the new China.

---

① William Hilton, *Fanshen: A Documentary of Revolution in a Chinese Village*, Chinese translation, quoted in Party History Research Center of the CPC Central Committee, *supra* note 11, p. 758.

Under the combined impact of the offensives by the People's Liberation Army, led by the CPC and supported by the people of revolutionary bases and liberated areas, and the magnificent upsurges of democratic movement in KMT areas, the once ferocious and arrogant KMT reactionaries were finally defeated. On October 1, 1949, the People's Republic of China was established, opening a new chapter in the development of the human rights cause in China.

Although human rights are beautiful and lofty ideas, the struggle for human rights is an arduous task, and the struggle for human rights for hundreds of millions of Chinese people who had suffered from oppression, exploitation and humiliation at the hands of imperialists and colonialists for over a century was an even more arduous task. Just as mentioned above, the CPC had undertaken this historical task with Marxism as its guidance from the day of its birth in 1921 and, after 28 years of efforts, finally achieved great victory in 1949. From the perspective of human rights protection, the history of the CPC can be summarized as the followings:

Firstly, the CPC had put an end to the invasion of China by imperialists and colonialists and achieved national independence. Beginning from 1840, as a result of invasions by imperialists, China had been reduced to a semi-colonial and semi-feudal society. At the gunpoint, the Chinese government was forced to sign a series of unequal treaties under which large pieces of Chinese land were ceded to or divided up as sphere of influence among various imperialist powers, many Chinese cities were forced to be open as trading ports, large areas in some Chinese cities were designated as foreign concessions, and Chinese people had become "second-class citizens" in their own country and suffered oppression and humiliation. From the date of its establishment, the CPC had taken the resistance of the imperialist aggression and oppression as its task, and fought bloody battles first against British, U. S., French, German and Japanese colonialists, then against Japanese militarists, and finally against American imperialists and its agents in China and ultimately driven all of them from Chinese Mainland, thereby realizing national independence. To Chinese people who had suffered the oppression by imperialists and colonialists, the realization of national independence was the most important human right.

Secondly, the CPC had led the Chinese people in overthrowing imperialism, feudalism, bureaucrat capitalism and achieving genuine emancipation. Before 1840, China was a feudal monarchy dominated by the landlord class. After the invasion by imperialists, the feudal class, imperialists and bureaucratic capitalists acted in collusion with each other to exploit and oppress the Chinese people. Together they became "the three big mountains" weighing on the backs of the Chinese people. Long period of plunder and years of war had turned the once fertile land of China into a desolated wasteland. The peasants had no land to till or home to return to. They had never been able to get enough food and clothing. Many of them were forced to leave their native homes and die in foreign land. Workers were oppressed by domestic and foreign capitalists and feudal bosses, some even became indentured laborers and the tools used by big capitalists to obtain exorbitant profit, and there was no place where they could get redress for injustice. With the victory of people's revolution in 1949, the Chinese people had finally overthrown the "three mountains", liberated themselves from economic exploitation, and achieved political emancipation.

Thirdly, national independence and emancipation of the people had laid a sound foundation for the development of the new China and for the full enjoyment of human rights by Chinese people. In the 60 years since the establishment of the People's Republic of China, the CPC have defeated aggressions and harassments by imperialists, and crushed their plot to strangle the newly-born People's Republic while it was still in the crib. Under extremely difficult conditions, in which China was blockaded, contained, and encircled by western countries led by the U. S. and Japan, China has succeeded in implementing democratic reform and socialist revolution and construction. Especially during the thirty years since the "reform and opening up", the socialist market economy has developed rapidly, Chinese people have enjoyed unprecedented level of protection of their human rights, and the Chinese nation has enjoyed high prestige in the international community.

The entire modern history had shown that no oppressor class would easily return to the people the rights they have grabbed from them. As a result, the struggle for human rights is not like drawing or embroidery, and could never succeed by sitting down on a table and prattling about general principles. When imperialists, feudalists and bureaucratic capitalists use violence against the Chinese people, the only way for Chinese people to save themselves was to use revolutionary violence against counterrevolutionary violence. In such life-and-death struggles, the older generation of revolutionaries, chanting the slogan "for a new China", charged weave up weave towards enemy positions with fearless heroism and sacrificed their lives without hesitation. We should never forget that the monument of victory of revolution was cast with the lives and blood of countless revolutionary martyrs and men and women with lofty ideals. Today, good-hearted people might feel sad when seeing such historical images of revolution, even think that such revolutions were too cruel, and they can hardly link the bloody life-and-death struggle with the protection of human rights. Actually, the realization of human rights in any country has been achieved through long and bitter struggle and the adoption of harsh measures against enemies who stubbornly resist revolution. The French Declaration of the Rights of Man and of the Citizen, adopted during the French Revolution, was the result of the long struggle by the French people and of the 1789 Uprising by the revolutionaries in Paris. In order to implement the content of the Declaration, the French people had to fight continuous battles against royalists who tried to restore the feudal rule. Struggle was not over even after the French people guillotined Louis the XVI, who tried to suppress the revolution by colluding with foreign powers. The American people fought two wars with British colonialists in order to gain independence. And after gaining independence, again fought a four-year war against southern slave-owners in order to emancipate the black slaves and to realize the human rights enshrined in the Declaration of Independence and the U. S. Constitution.

The struggle for independence, emancipation and human rights by Chinese people was carried out in conditions even harsher, more complicated and more difficult than those in which the French and American revolutions were carried out. China is a country with a huge population, vast territory, and very unbalanced development in different regions. And Chinese people were faced with the oppression by many imperialist powers and their Chinese agents who were armed to the teeth. When enemies came towards the Chinese people with butcher's knife, the Chinese people would have helplessly waited for their death like lamb to the slaughter were it not for the CPC, which led them in a resolute struggle against the enemies. Today, when recalling this period of history, we cannot but feel proud and fortunate that Chinese people had such a brilliant leader as the CPC at that time. Of course, today China still has many problems to be solved and many tasks to be accomplished with respect to the protection of human rights. However, looking back in history, we should be confident that, as long as we are under the leadership of the CPC and continue on the path opened up by older generations of revolutionaries, we will be able to bring socialism with Chinese characteristics and human rights protection cause in China to a new level.

Sixty Years of Development of Human Rights and the Rule of Law in China①

After long period of struggle since the establishment of the People's Republic of China in 1949, especially since the Third Plenary Session of the Eleventh Central Committee of the Communist Party of China, China has made remarkable achievements in improving its legal system of human rights protection and developing the human rights cause. Today, at a new beginning, the Chinese people are creating better economic, political, cultural and social conditions for the fuller enjoyment of human rights in accordance with the constitutional principle of "the state respects and safeguards human rights", the blueprint put forward by the CPC at its Seventeenth National Congress and the National Human Rights Action Plan of China (2009—2010).

I. Chinese People's Long Struggle for Human Rights

Historical records show that, ever since the beginning of civilization, Chinese people have started the struggle for human rights out of the human instinct for survival. However, conscious struggle for human rights in modern sense was developed gradually under the influence of the concept of "natural rights" put forward by western bourgeois enlightenment thinkers and in the struggle against western imperialists, colonialists and their agents in China. The industrialization process, which started in the 17th century, greatly stimulated the desire of capitalists for external expansion. By relying on their powerful gunboats, they began to seek row material bases and commodity markets in Asia, Africa and Latin

---

① Originally published in *Academic Forum of Nandu* (No. 1 2009). The original title was "The Establishment and Development of Legal System of Human Rights Protection in China".

America. The expansion reached the peak in the beginning of the 19th Century, when the Qing Dynasty in China was on the decline and lagging farther and farther behind western countries in development because it was unable to reform itself to adapt to new situation. The British Empire, known at that time as "an empire on which the sun never sets", had long been coveting China for its rich raw material base and potential huge market. It first tried to use opium as weapon to destroy the physical and mental health of Chinese people. When met with resistance, it used military force to launch war of aggression against China. After the 1840 Opium War, the U. K., the U. S., France, Portugal, Germany, Russia, Japan and other imperialist powers had launched many wars of aggression, either unitarily or jointly, against China and forced the Qing Government to sign a series of unequal treaties. As a result, the Chinese government lost its sovereignty, the Chinese nation was faced with great peril, the Chinese people humiliated and their homeland trampled upon and became a semi-colony of western powers. Cruel reality had taught the Chinese people about the aggressive intension of western countries under the guise of protecting human rights and enabled them to see clearly the true nature of the human rights advocated by western countries. In order to realize national independence and truly enjoy human rights, countless Chinese patriots, including both the ordinary people and government officials, had carried out arduous struggle against imperialists and their agents in China.

1. Struggle for Human Rights by Patriots and Reformists after the Opium War

Beginning from the Opium War, Chinese people have been engaged in a long resistance against imperialist invasions and struggle for freedom and human rights. During this process, a large number of national heroes whose stories were capable of evoking praises and tears have emerged. They included Lin Zexu, Deng Tingzhen and Guan Tianpei, who resolutely advocated the prohibition of opium and resistance against British invasion during the Opium War; patriotic old general Feng Zicai and Liu Mingchuan, the first governor of Taiwan, during the Sino-French War; generals Ding Ruchang, Deng Shichang and Lin Shuisheng, who sacrificed their lives during the First Sino-Japanese War of 1894—1895. Some of them laid down one's life for one's country, some others were demoted and banished to remote provinces under false charges, but all of them faced danger fearlessly and stood firm for the cause of justice. For example, Lin Zexu, while being exiled to Xinjiang, wrote that: "I would rather die for the benefit of my country than shirking my duty to pursue personal interests" . Meanwhile, the broad masses of Chinese had also played an important role in resisting foreign invasion and upholding national independence. In May 1841, tens of thousands of local people in Sanyuanli of Guangzhou City organized themselves to resist the British invasion troops who committed rape, pillage and other atrocities in the area, thereby setting a precedent of large-scale spontaneous armed resistance by the broad masses of Chinese people against foreign invasions. In 1895, the people of Taiwan, upon learning that Taiwan and the surrounding islands was ceded to Japan, protested by going on strike and closing up all shops and issued an official call to arms, stating that: "We would rather die defending Taiwan than surrendering it to Japan submissively." Together with the Black Flag Army led by General Liu Yongfu, they fought bloody battles with two modernized divisions of Japanese army and one Japanese navy fleet, causing them 32, 000 casualties. ①

During the invasion by the Eight-Power Allied Forces in 1900, members of the Boxer Movement and some troops of the Qing Government engaged in fierce battles with the invading troops and dealt heavy blows to the British and Russian armies in Beijing, Tianjin and Northeast China.

Despite the joint resistance by troops and civilians against foreign invaders in the frontline, the corrupt and weak Qing Government humiliated the country and forfeited its sovereignty again and again by ceding land and paying compensations to foreign powers. At this critical moment when China was faced with national subjugation and genocide, bourgeois reformists such as Kang Youwei, Liang Qichao, Yan Fu, and Tan Sitong, based themselves on the principle of "natural rights", wrote books and set up theories, submitted reports to the emperors to advocate reforms and restriction of monarchical power by civil rights. Kang Youwei wrote that: "Today, 400 million Chinese people, without distinction of noble and simple, are faced with great peril like birds in a cage, fish in a cauldron, inmates in a prison or lamb to the slaughter. This is a situation

① *Outline of Modern Chinese History*, Beijing: Higher Education Press, 2007, p. 32.

unheard of in 4, 000 years of Chinese history. "① Liang Qichao wrote that: "China really woke up from a 4, 000—year long dream only after it was defeated in the Sino-Japanese War of 1894—1895 and was forced to cede Taiwan and pay an indemnity of over 200 million taels of silver to Japan. "② He also wrote that: "Human rights are nature rights, namely autonomous rights equally enjoyed by every human beings. "③ They disseminated the ideas of human rights and equality and opposed imperialist invasion and the system of feudal autocratic monarchy. Based on the theory of evolution, Yan Fu rejected the "divine rights of the monarch" by pointing out that a monarch is set up by the people. People select upright and wise people as their monarch to be responsible for safeguarding their property and life so that they can concentrate on farming, weaving, and other social productive activities. "④ Tan Sitong also pointed out that: "The monarch is like the cart the people are like the horse. You cannot put the monarch before the people, just as you cannot put the cart before the horse... the monarch is someone who works for the people and ministers are those who help him in serving the people. "⑤ According to common sense, if a monarch or ministers refuse to serve people, people are justified to depose and replace the monarchy with democracy. "Among various types of political system, only democracy is compatible with universal truth. "⑥ The reformists, with their lofty ideals and advanced theories, played the role of enlightenment at that time. The reform they pushed Emperor Guangxu to implement was actually far less radical than that they had advocated in their writings, it nevertheless greatly enraged the conservative forces. When Kang Youwei, Liang Qichao

---

① Kang Youwei, *Collection of Political Comments of Kang Youwei*, Part I, Beijing: Zhonghua Book Company, 1981, p. 237.

② See Liang Qichao, "The Hundred Days Reform", in *Collected Works of Yinbingshi*, Beijing: Zhonghua Book Company, 1951.

③ Zhang Dan and Wang Renzhi (eds.), *SelectedEditorials in the Decade Before the 1911 Revolution*, Part I, vol. 1, Beijing: SDX Joint Publishing Company, 1960, p. 30.

④ Yan Fu, *Collected Works of Yan Fu*, vol. 1, Beijing: Zhonghua Book Company, 1986, p. 34.

⑤ Tan Sitong, *Complete Works of Tan Sitong*, Part II, Beijing: Zhonghua Book Company, 1981, p. 339.

⑥ See Tan Sitong, "Jean Jacques Rousseau's Theory of Social Contract", in *Xinmin Congbao*, No. 12, June 15, 1902.

and others were enthusiastically persuading Emperor Guangxu to implement the reform, Empress Cixi was busy sharpening her knives. In the end, Tan Sitong and other five "Gentlemen of Hundred Day Reform" were executed, while other leading reformists either fled to other countries or lost their moral and turned into royalists. Although the Hundred Day Reform had failed, the ideas put forward in the writings of the reformists continued to spread in intellectual circles and had exerted influence on the broad masses of people.

2. Struggle by Bourgeois Revolutionaries for Human Rights Before and After the1911 Revolution

The failure of the Hundred Day Reform and the execution of Tan Sitong and other reformists enabled bourgeois revolutionaries headed by Dr. Sun Yat-sen to see clearly the true nature of the feudal monarchy upheld by the ruling circle headed by Empress Cixi, and strengthened their resolve to overthrow the Qing Government and struggle for human rights through "national revolution". In his article "The Real Solution to China's Problem", Sun Yat-sen enumerated the various crimes of violation of human rights committed by the Qing Regime: "They treated us as a conquered race and deny us equal rights."[①] He stated that "people's sovereignty is a universally accepted political principle"[②] and that "the state belongs to all the people, rather than to one person or one family."[③] Zou Rong, in his article "The Revolutionary Army", called on Chinese people to "kill the monarch who oppress us, so as to restore our natural rights." And he pointed out that: "Why must we carry out revolution? It is because the evil regime has deprived us of our natural rights. In order to restore our natural rights, we must overthrow this evil regime."[④] In 1905, Sun Yat-sen summarized the program of Tongmenghui (Chinese Revolutionary League) as the Three Principles of the People, namely nationalism, democracy and people's livelihood. Nationalism included the

① Sun Yat-sen, *Complete Works of Sun Yat-sen*, vol. 1, Beijing: Zhonghua Book Company, 1981, p. 252.

② Sun Yat-sen, *Complete Works of Sun Yat-sen*, vol. 3, Beijing: Zhonghua Book Company, 1984, p. 319.

③ Sun Yat-sen, *Complete Works of Sun Yat-sen*, vol. 5, Beijing: Zhonghua Book Company, 1985, pp. 628—629.

④ Supra note 4, p. 665.

goal of "expelling the Manchu and reviving Zhonghua", namely to overthrow the Qing Government and establish a state of national independence; democracy meant to overthrow feudal autocratic monarchy and establish a republic; people's livelihood meant to distribute land equally among the people and carry out social reform. He hoped to "achieve victories of political revolution and social reform in a one-time effort". In October 1911, revolutionaries launched an uprising in the City of Wuchang under the banner of the Three Principles of People and overthrew the system of feudal autocratic monarchy that had ruled China for over 2,000 years. On January 1, 1912, Sun Yat-sen was elected the provisional president of the Republic of China and promulgated Presidential Decree, which declared that: "All citizens are entitled to human rights and are equal before the law". [①] In March of the same year, Provisional Constitution of the Republic of China was promulgated, which confirmed the bourgeois republic system and various democratic rights and freedoms, including political and economic rights, of citizens. The 1911 Revolution ended the feudal monarchy and established a bourgeois republic, dealt a heavy blow to imperialism and feudalism, and promoted the awakening of Asian people. Lenin pointed out that: "The revolutionary struggle of the Chinese people has a world-wide importance because it is bringing emancipation to Asia and undermining the rule of the European bourgeoisie." [②]

The 1911 Revolution, by overthrowing the feudal monarchy, advocating people's sovereignty and upholding human rights, had become a milestone in modern Chinese history. However, for various reasons, including the failure to mobilize the common people, the revolution ultimately failed under the threat of feudal warlords supported by imperialists and the fruit of revolution was seized by the Northern Warlords headed by Yuan Shih-kai. Later, Yuan Shih-kai assassinated Song Jiaoren, the leader of KMT which had won the victory in the election of the National Assemble, disbanded the KMT, tore up the Provisional Constitution, and appointed himself a president who could stay in office permanently and recommend his own successor. In 1915, Yuan Shih-kai believed that he had

---

① See Association of Chinese Historians (ed.), *The 1911 Revolution*, Shanghai: Shanghai People's Publishing House, 2000.

② V. I. Lenin, *Complete Works of Lenin*, Chinese Edition, vol. 21, Beijing: People's Publishing House, 1990, p. 163.

made all necessary preparations and decided to openly revive the monarchy and make himself emperor. To achieve this goal, he became politically dependent on foreign imperialist powers, economically upheld the interests of imperialists, feudal landlords, and comprador bourgeoisie, culturally implement the policy of "worshiping Confucianism and restoring the ancient ways". He issued decrees to restore ceremonies of worshiping Confucius, to study of Confucian classics in primary and secondary schools, and to advocate "the three cardinal guides and the five constant virtues". Faced with such perverse acts and reactionary policies, Sun Yat-sen realized that: "A constitution on paper alone will never be enough to protect civil rights from violation by warlords... A constitution can be truly implemented only after overthrow on imperialism and warlords."① It was based on this understanding that Sun Yat-sen and the revolutionaries led by him had fought even more resolutely against feudal warlords.

Meanwhile, a large number of advanced intellectuals, including Li Dazhao, Chen Duxiu, Lu Xun, Cai Yuanpei and Hu Shi, had launched the New Cultural Movement, which played the role of enlightenment in the ideological field at that time, and put forward the slogans of "Eradicating Superstitions" and "Down with the Confucianism". Li Dazhao held that Confucianism was the "soul of despotism" and "protective talisman of autocratic monarchs throughout the Chinese history". Therefore, "all monarchs throughout Chinese history had always worshiped Confucius as their patron saint."② Chen Duxiu pointed out that the patriarchal clan system and clan ethics advocated by Confucianism "undermine the independence and dignity of individuals, suffocate their freedom of thought, deprive them of the right to be equal before the law (for example, people of different social status receive different criminal punishments for committing the same crime), and make them dependent on others and destroy their productivity."③ To break this pattern, all the main proponents of the New Cultural Movement opposed autocratic monarchy and advocated the emancipation of human beings and human

---

① Sun Yat-sen, *Selected Works of Sun Yat-sen*, People's Publishing House, 1956, p. 522.

② Li Dazhao, *Collected Works of Li Dazhao*, Part I, People's Publishing House, 1984, p. 264.

③ Chen Duxiu, *Selected Works of Chen Duxiu*, vol. 1, People's Publishing House, 1984, p. 167.

nature. Chen Duxiu wrote that: "political emancipation can be achieved only through the abolition of monarchical power, religious emancipation can be achieved only through the negation of ecclesiastical power, economic emancipation can be achieved only through the equal distribution of wealth, and women can be emancipated from male authority only through political participation."① He also wrote that "in order to be fully emancipated, women must get rid of the bondage of marriage, and be restored their free and autonomous personality."② Hu Shi maintained that: "the greatest evil in a society is to destroy the personality of an individual and prevent him from freely developing himself."③ In order to realize individual freedom, Chinese people must resolutely oppose despotism and attach importance to democracy, constitutionalism and the rule of law. Li Dazhao pointed out: "The constitution is the embodiment of the spirit of modern citizens, their certificate of freedom and the creed of all citizens of the Republic of China."④ Chen Duxiu held that human rights can be safeguarded only through the adoption and implementation of a constitution: "The so-called human rights are the individual rights and freedoms that are enshrined in the constitution and can not be deprived even by state laws."⑤ The New Cultural Movement was initially unfolded in the intellectual circle, but quickly spread throughout the country and played a positive role in the enlightenment of the Chinese people.

It was during the period of New Cultural Movement that Marxism was brought toChina by the socialist revolution in Russia in October 1917. Marxism reveals the laws of the development of human society, denounces the hypocrisy of the capitalist system and the bourgeois human rights concept, and expounds the doctrines of class struggle, of revolutions by the proletariat and other oppressed people, and of proletarian dictatorship. Marx and Engels pointed out in the Communist Manifesto that: "The history of all hitherto existing societies is the history of class struggles." "The oppressor and the oppressed, stood in constant opposition

① Chen Duxiu, *Selected Works of Chen Duxiu*, vol. 1, People's Publishing House, 1984, p. 130.

② Ibid.

③ Hu Shi, *Selected Works of Hu Shi*, China Writers Publishing House, 1991, p. 74.

④ Li Dazhao, *Collected Works of Li Dazhao*, Part I, People's Publishing House, 1984, pp. 157 and 168.

⑤ *Supra* note 16, p. 166.

to one another, carried on an uninterrupted, now hidden, now open fight, a fight that each time ended either in a revolutionary reconstitution of society at large, or in the common ruin of the contending classes." In order to realize "a revolutionary reconstitution of society at large", they pointed out that the proletariat must, by means of a revolution, make itself the ruling class, and, as such, sweep away the conditions for the existence of class antagonisms and of classes generally, and thereby abolish its own supremacy as a class. "This struggle, however, has now reached a stage where the exploited and oppressed class (the proletariat) can no longer emancipate itself from the class which exploits and oppresses it (the bourgeoisie), without at the same time forever freeing the whole of society from exploitation, oppression, and class struggles."①

Lenin further developed Marxism in light of the actual situation in Russia. He pointed out that: "The period of the awakening of the East in the contemporary revolution is being succeeded by a period in which all the Eastern peoples will participate in deciding the destiny of the whole world, so as not to be simply objects of the enrichment of others."② The victory of the October Revolution proved that economically backward nations could also achieve self-emancipation under the guidance of socialist ideology.

The ideological enlightenment by the New Cultural Movement and the dissemination of Marxism in China after the October Revolution in Russia had deepened the understanding of the Chinese intellectuals and Chinese people of the decadent nature of feudalism and the aggressive nature of imperialism and colonialism. At the end of the World War I in 1918, China, as a victorious nation, not only failed to get any compensation from defeated nations, but its reasonable demands, such as abolishment of foreign spheres of influence in China, withdrawal of foreign troops from Chinese territory and annulment of the "Twenty-one Demands" imposed by Japan on China, were rejected at the Paris Peace Conference. What was more, the Conference also decided to transfer German concession in Shandong Province to Japan. Such "gangster logic" had greatly enraged the Chinese people. On May 4, 1919, college students in Beijing took to

① Friedrich Engels, "Preface to the 1883 German Edition of the Communist Manifesto", in Karl Marx and Friedrich Engels, *Selected Works of Marx and Engels*, Chinese Edition, vol. 1, Beijing: People's Publishing House, 1995, p. 232.

② V. I. Lenin, *Complete Works of Lenin*, Chinese Edition, vol. 37, Beijing: People's Publishing House, 1986, p. 322.

the street in protest. When the protest was suppressed by the Beiyang Government, the workers and merchants in Shanghai went on strike in support of the students. The movement rapidly spread to over 100 cities in 20 provinces. This was the so-called May 4th Movement. It was the first genuine and thorough anti-imperialism and ant-feudalism movement in modern Chinese history and also the beginning of a new stage of revolution and struggle for human rights by Chinese people.

3. The Struggle for Human Rights by the CPC and Patriotic Democratic Personages

Guided by Marxism, influenced by the October Revolution in Russia, and baptized by the May 4th Movement, some leaders of the New Cultural Movement established communist groups in Beijing, Shanghai, Wuhan, Guangzhou, Hunan and Hubei while participating in workers' and students' movements which were raging like storms at that time. In July 1921, they convened the first national congress of communists in Shanghai and established the Communist Party of China (CPC). The CPC took it as its own duty to help Chinese people of various nationalities to fundamentally change their fate of being oppressed and exploited and uphold their rights. To this end, it carried out unyielding and arduous struggle against imperialists and feudal warlords in a more organized and guided way. From its birth in 1921 to the establishment of the People's Republic in 1949, the CPC had experienced the First Revolutionary Civil War, the Second Revolutionary Civil War, the War of Resistance against Japanese Invasion and the War of People's Revolution, during which it had twice cooperated with the KMT. The struggle at this historical stage can be divided into three battle fronts.

Mobilizing and Organizing Chinese People to Fight for National Independence and Human Rights

The CPC pointed out at its second national congress that "the Chinese people, in the struggle for their own rights, must fight against capitalist imperialism and the feudal forces of warlords and bureaucrats."① In

① Declaration of the Second National Congress of the CPC, in *Selected Documents of the Central Committee of the CPC*, Beijing: the Party School of the Central Committee of the CPC Press, 1989, p. 64.

accordance with the spirit of this congress, the CPC established "alliances for human rights" in Beijing, Guangzhou, Shanghai, Shandong and Jiangxi, and organized the Strike by Anyuan Railroad and Mine workers in September 1922, the strike by workers in four flower factories in British Concession in Hankou city in November 1922, the strike by the workers of Kailuan Coal Mine in October 1922, and the strike by Beijing-Hankou Railway workers in February 1923. During the Beijing-Hankou Railroad Strike, faced with bloody suppression by warlord Wu Peifu, the CPC put forward the resounding slogan of "Fight for freedom and human rights". Although the strike was brutally suppressed, it trained and built up the workers' class in China. From that time on, the workers' movements rose one after another like raging fires. As these movements grew in scale, the CPC's rights consciousness rose continuously and the slogans it put forward became more and more specific. Since many of the demands raised by the CPC concerns the survival of the nation and the interests of the people, it had won the continuous sympathy and support from students and broad masses of people. For examples, supported by urban residents and students, the May Thirtieth Movement and the Guangzhou-Hong Kong Strike in 1925 had greatly increased the CPC's influence and dealt a heavy blow to the forces of imperialism and feudal warlords in Shanghai, Guangzhou and Hong Kong.

However, the CPC had also learnt from these struggles that, in China, a semi-colonial and semi-feudal country in which the farmers made up 90% of the population, a revolution could not succeed without the full participation by farmers. "Under such circumstance, 'land to the tiller' became an urgent demand of poor farmers."① "The farmers' problem became a central issue of the national revolution. Whether the revolution can progress and succeed depends on whether the peasants' movement can progress and succeed."② In order to mobilize peasants to participate in revolution, Peng Pai and other CPC leaders had, through arduous work, established peasants' associations and carried out a large-scale peasants' movement in Haifeng County, Guangdong Province. Mao Zedong and others established National Institute of Peasant Movement and personally

① Li Dazhao, *Selected Works of Li Dazhao*, Beijing: People's Publishing House, 1959, p. 532.

② See *Resolution on the Position of Peasants' Movement in National Revolution*, adopted at the Second Peasants' Congress of Guangdong Province in May 1926.

went to Hunan Province to carry out investigation, and lead and organize peasants in the struggle against local tyrants and evil gentry. In areas where peasant movement was carried out in the provinces of Hunan, Hubei and Guangdong, poor peasants not only realized their economic rights, but also improved their political status and gained spiritual emancipation. The vigorous peasant movement during the period of Great Revolution forcefully supported the war against feudal warlords and its continuous development later also laid a sound foundation for the armed struggle and the building of revolutionary basis by the CPC. In September 18, 1931, Japanese imperialists launched an all-out war of aggression against China: "Province after province of China were occupied by the Japanese, thousands after thousands of the Chinese people become slaves, village after village and city after city are bathed in blood, millions after millions of countrymen driven from their homes, and one internal affair after another are interfered with."① Chinese nation was at it crucial moment of life and death. In order to same the motherland, the Central Committee of the CPC issued on August 1, 1935 the Appeal to All Fellow Countrymen to Resist Japanese Invasion and Save the Chinese Nation (The August First Declaration), calling on all Chinese people to unite and "Fight for our homeland! Fight for the survival of the Chinese nation! Fight for national independence! Fight for territorial integrity! And fight for human rights and freedom!" Afterwards, the CPC led the December 9th Movement, and launched a nation-wide campaign for stopping the civil war and resisting the Japanese aggression. After the victory of the Anti-Japanese War, Chiang Kai-shek started a full-scale civil war by relying on the support of the U. S. imperialists. Supported by the people in liberated areas and the workers' and students' movements in KMT-controlled areas, the CPC ultimately won the revolutionary war.

It should be pointed out that while the CPC was leading and organizing Chinese people in the struggle for human rights and faced with the betray of revolution, the massacre of communists and suppression of workers' and peasants' movements by Chiang Kai-shek and the all-round invasion of China by Japanese imperialists, a large number of patriots, including Song Qingling, Cai Yuanpei, Lu Xun, Yang Xingfo, Hu Shi, Luo

① "The Appeal to All Fellow Countrymen to Resist Japanese Invasion and Save the Chinese Nation", in *Reference Materials on the History of Revolution in China*, vol. , Beijing: Remin University of China Press, 1956, pp. 140—141.

Rongji, Pan Guangdan, and Xu Zhimo, also carried out struggle for human rights in Beijing, Shanghai and other major citizens. Most of these people had studied abroad and accepted education in the U. S. , Europe or Japan. Some of them had accepted Marxism, and were sympathetic to the revolutionary struggle led by the CPC, while some other, although did not understand, even were against Marxism and the struggled led by the CPC, but hated the corrupt KMT government and the dictatorship by Chiang Kai-shek, and resolutely opposed the brutal aggression by Japanese imperialists. For this reason, Hu Shi, Luo Rongji and others called for the protection of human rights and establishment of legal safeguards for human rights. They pointed out that: "In short, human rights are rights of human beings. They are the sine qua non of human beings. Human rights differ from civil rights in that the former are the due rights of human beings whereas the latter are legal rights, namely rights provided for by the Constitution and laws. "① Hu Shi pointed out that: "Today, in order to truly safeguard human rights and establish a rule-of-law basis for the safeguarding of human rights, China must adopt as soon as possible the Constitution of the Republic of China, or at least, a temporary constitution for the period of political tutelage. " And he called on the government to "adopt as soon as possible a temporary constitution, so as to establish a rule-of-law basis for the protection of human rights. "②

Although these persons tried to take a so-called third road between the KMT's dictatorship and CPC's revolutionary struggle, which was impossible to realize in China at that time, they did play an enlightenment role in the dissemination of human rights theories. Soon afterwards, Song Qingling and others who had been struggling by various means against Chiang Kai-shek's military dictatorship, established the China League for Civil Rights in Shanghai in December 1932 with branches in Shanghai and Beijing: Lu Xun and eight others were in charge of Shanghai Branch and Hu Shi and eight others were in charge of the Beijing Branch. The League took "raising people's civil rights consciousness and safeguarding civil rights" as its objective. It had the following tasks: "1. Struggle for the release of political prisoners and oppose the practice of imprisonment, torture and execution of political prisoners currently prevalent in China. The main target group of the League in this respect is a large number of anonymous prisoners. 2. Ensuring

① Luo Rongji, "On Human Rights", in *New Moon*, vol. 2, No. 5.

② Hu Shi, "Human Rights and Temporary Constitution", in *New Moon*, vol. 2, No. 5.

the right to defense and other legal assistance to political prisoners, investigating the conditions in prisons and exposing the violations of civil rights; 3. Striving for the freedom of the press, the freedom of speech, the freedom of assembly, the freedom of association and other civil rights. Because the initiators and participants of the human rights activities during this period of time, including the members of the China League for Civil Rights, had high status and prestige in China, especially in the academic circle, their activities had a major impact on society and became an important part of the human rights cause in China. Their struggle was frustrated during the period of "white terror" when Yang Xingfo was assassinated and Luo Rongji and other members of the League were imprisoned. However, when the Japanese intensified the invasion of China and the Chinese nation was in peril, they soon became active again. Some of these personages later joined the united front led by the CPC during the period of People's War of Liberation and played an important role in the democratic movement in KMT-controlled areas and contributed to the liberation of Chinese people.

Upholding National Independence, Freedom and Human Rights through Armed Struggle

The feudal rulers and old and new warlords in China were very weak in the face of the savage aggression and oppression by imperialists and colonialists, but took their gloves off when suppressing the struggle for national independence and freedom by the Chinese people. The suppression became even more brutal when their interests were combined with those of imperialists and they themselves became the agents of imperialists. Just as Lenin pointed out that: "The reactionary classes themselves are usually the first to resort to violence, to civil war; they are the first to 'place the bayonet on the agenda'"[①] and that: "Great revolutions, even when they commence peacefully, as was the case with the great French Revolution, end in furious wars which are instigated by the counter-revolutionary bourgeoisie."[②] The Chinese people were forced to take up arms to fight

① V. I. Lenin, *Complete Works of Lenin*, Chinese Edition, vol. 39, Beijing: People's Publishing House, 1990, p. 116—117.

② V. I. Lenin, *Complete Works of Lenin*, Chinese Edition, vol. 29, Beijing: People's Publishing House, 1990, p. 326.

against armed counterrevolutionaries and imperialists through armed revolution. In 1927, just as the Northern Expeditionary Army entered into the Yangtze River Basin and victory was in sight, Chiang Kai-shek staged the "April 12 Coup", in which he adopted a policy of "rather killing one thousand by mistake than letting one escape" towards the communists and carried out massacres of revolutionaries, thereby beginning a period of "white terror" . In response, CPC-led armies launched an armed uprising in the city of Nanchang in August 1927 and, after several twists and turns, jointed force with peasant armed forces that had launched the Autumn Harvest Uprising and formed the Red Army in Jinggangshan, Jiangxi Province. Since this army and other CPC-led revolutionary armed forces were people's army, they were able to grow continuously despite the harsh conditions of survival and the encirclement, pursuit, obstruction and interception by KMT armies led by Chiang Kai-shek, and created under very difficult conditions revolutionary bases in Jianggangshan region of Jiangxi Province, Hubei-Henan-Anhui Border Region, and Northern Shaanxi Province, and effectively upheld the rights of people in these bases.

In 1931, Japan launched the September 18th Incident. It first occupied the three northeast provinces and then invaded Northern China in an attempt to turn entire China into its colony. The Marco Polo Bridge Incident in July 7, 1937 marked the beginning of the Anti-Japanese War. In September of the same year, the second KMT-CPC cooperation was formally established. In order to save the Chinese nation from subjugation, the CPC agreed to re-designate the Red Army under its leadership as the Eighth Army and the New Fourth Army and established Anti-Japanese Democratic Coalition in Northeast China, together with people of the whole country, including members of the KMT armies and local armed forces, rose up to resist the Japanese aggression. As the song March of the Volunteers went: "Arise! All those who don't want to be slaves! Let our flesh and blood forge our new Great Wall! ... As the Chinese nation has arrived at its most perilous time, our million hearts beating as one. Brave the enemy's fire, March on! On!" This song showed vividly the fearless spirit of the Chinese people and the righteousness of the war of resistance against Japanese aggression. The Anti-Japanese War lasted longer and was of much bigger scale than the War of Independence in North America and the 1789 French Revolution. Since Japan formed an Axis with Nazi Germany and Fascist Italy and invaded many countries in Southeast Asian and South Asia, the resistance by Chinese armies against Japanese invasions in China and abroad became a part of the Second World War. Therefore, the victory of the Anti-Japanese War not only effectively upheld the independence and freedom of Chinese people of all nationalities, returned Taiwan to China, but also provided strong support to other countries invaded by Japan, Germany, and Italy, thereby contributing to the cause of international human rights protection.

After eight years of arduous war of resistance, Chinese people earnestly expected peace, democracy, and reconstruction of the country. For this purpose, Mao Zedong personally went to Chongqing to negotiate with Chiang Kai-shek. However, Chiang Kai-shek, relying on his million-strong army equipped with American weapons, launched full-scale civil war even before the inks on the October 10th Agreement signed between the KMT and CPC and the ceasefire order became dry, in the hope of "eliminating the people's army in a quick battle". Because the civil war was against the will of the people, the KMT troops were steadily losing ground in the battlefields despite the personnel and materials support from the U. S. Meanwhile, large-scale student movements and popular "No Hunger, No Civil War, No Persecution" Movement broke out in KMT-controlled areas. Being attacked both from behind and in front, the once overbearing KMT troops were driven out of the Mainland only after three years of War of Liberation. The remnants of the KMT troops led by Chiang Kai-shek fled to Taiwan.

Promoting the Construction of the Legal System for the Protection of Human Rights in Revolutionary Bases

Human rights have both universality and particularity and can take the forms of due rights, legal rights and actual rights. Human rights in political programs for revolution and construction are often put forward from the point of view of the universality and due rights. However, consideration must also be taken of the particularity of human rights under the concrete conditions of a particular period and region in order to transform these rights into actual rights. Due rights must be transformed into legal rights and be safeguarded by a legal system before they can be actually enjoyed by individuals. It was for this reason that the CPC attached great importance to the construction of the legal system for the protection of human rights in the revolutionary bases, despite that fact that, because of the war, most of these bases were in a very unstable condition. For example, under the conditional of continued military "encirclement and suppression" and economic blockade against the Central Soviet Base Area by KMT reactionaries, the First National Congress of Chinese Soviet Republic adopted in November 1931 the Outline Constitution of the Chinese Soviet Republic, which was revised at the Second National Congress of Chinese Soviet Republic in January 1934. The main content of the Constitution included: the Soviet political power belongs to workers, peasants, Red Army soldiers and all poor laboring people; all workers, peasants, Red Army soldiers, all poor laboring people and their family members, regardless of gender, race, or religious belief, are equal before the law; all citizens who have reached the age of 16 shall have the right to vote, the right to stand for election, and the right to directly send representatives to Soviets at various levels to discuss and decide all national or local political affairs; the Soviet political power takes the complete improvement of the lives of workers and peasants as its objective, adopts labor law, implements eight-hour workday system in urban areas, provides for minimum wages, establishes social security system, promulgates land law in rural areas, confiscates the lands of the landlord class and distributes them to poor and middle peasants; declares the complete independence of the Chinese nation, refuses to recognize all political and economic privileges of imperialists in China and all unequal treaties concluded between counterrevolutionary governments and imperialists, strives to liberate China from the oppression by imperialism; ensures that workers, peasants and other poor working people enjoy the freedom of speech, freedom of the press, freedom of assembly, freedom of association, and freedom of religion; ensures the liberation of women, recognizes the freedom of marriage, enables women to gradually acquire the material basis necessary for liberating themselves from the bondage of housework, so that they can participate in the economic, political, and cultural life of society; implements complete compulsory education so as to ensure that workers, peasants and other laboring people enjoy the right to education; and ensures to all foreigners residing in Soviet areas all the political rights provided for by law.

After the breakout of the Anti-Japanese War, the CPC, in order to unit all Chinese people in the resistance against Japanese aggression, established the Anti-Japanese National United Front, and promulgated a series of laws and regulations on the protection of human rights in anti-Japanese base areas behind the enemy lines. The more important ones among them included the Administrative Program of the Government of the Shaanxi-Gansu-Ningxia Border Region, the Regulations of Shaanxi-Gansu-Ningxia Border Region on the Protection of Human Rights and Property Rights, the Regulations of Shandong Province on the Protection of Human Rights, the Interim Regulations of Hebei-Shandong-Henan Border Region on the Protection of People's Rights, the Regulations of Northwest Shanxi Province on the Protection of Human Rights, the Revised Regulations of Bohai District on the Protection of Human Rights, and the Rules for the Implementation of the Regulations of Bohai District on the Protection of Human Rights. All these laws and regulations contained specific provisions on the protection of people's right to life, personal rights, property right and political rights, freedom of action, freedom of movement, freedom of residence, freedom of speech, freedom of the press, freedom of assembly, freedom of association, freedom of communication, freedom of belief, freedom of religion, and freedom of political activity. They especially stressed the legal protection of personal rights. For example, "No armed force, state organ, organization or armed organization of the masses may infringe upon the lawful personal rights, property rights or other rights of the people, unless in accordance with law."[①] "No organ, armed force, or organization, except for a judicial or public security organ in the performance of its functions, may arrest, interrogate or impose punishment on anyone." "When arresting a person, it is prohibited to insult or beat him, to extort a confession from him by torture, or to force him to confess. A trial should be based on evidence, rather than confession."[②] "A criminal suspect must be brought within 24 hours of arrest to a trial organ, which then must hold a hearing within 24 hours." "Uphold receipt a civil or criminal case, a trial organ must make a judgment within 15 days if the circumstance of the case is not complicated, or 30 days if the circumstance of the case is complicated."[③]

The above human rights laws and regulations adopted by the CPC in

① "The Rules for the Implementation of Regulations of Bohai District on the Protection of Human Rights", in Dong Yunhu & Liu Wuping, *World Documents of Human Rights*, Chengdu: Sichuan People's Publishing House, 1990, p. 770.

② "Regulations of Shaanxi-Gansu-Ningxia Border Region on the Protection of Human Rights and Property Rights", in ibid., p. 764.

③ "Regulations of Northwest Shanxi Province on the Protection of Human Rights", in ibid., p. 769.

revolutionary bases may seem incomprehensive from the contemporary perspective. For example, the subjects of human rights in these laws and regulations were workers, peasants, Red Army soldiers and all poor laboring people, and were expanded to include landlords and capitalists only during the Anti-Japanese War. However, considering these laws and regulations were adopted during the war time when the CPC was engaged in complicated life-or-death struggles against enemies, we can not but be deeply impressed by the great importance it had attached to the protection of human rights. Especially the judicial protection of personal rights in these laws and regulations were later embodied in the laws and regulations adopted by the CPC during the People's War of Liberation, such as the Announcement of the Government of Special Municipality of Harbin on the Prohibition of Unlawful Detention, Arrest, and Interrogation and Other Violations of Human Rights, the Order of the Administrative Office of Henan-Anhui-Jiangsu Border Region Instructing Governments at Various Levels to Truly Protect Human Rights and Strictly Prohibit Arbitrary Arrest, Corporal Punishment and Extorting a Confession by Torture. The construction of a legal system for the protection of human rights was one of the important reasons why the CPC was able to enjoy enthusiastic support from the masses of people and continuously expand its bases despite blockades, sieges, and sabotages by Japanese invaders and KMT reactionaries. The construction of these bases had laid an important foundation for victory of the New Democratic Revolution.

After the Opium War, China became a semi-colonial and semi-feudal society and Chinese people were under the triple oppression of imperialism, feudalism and bureaucratic capitalism. National independence was not only an inherent content, but also a precondition for the realization, of human rights. The victory of the People's Revolution in 1949 marked the end of the rule of imperialism, feudalism and bureaucratic capitalism in China. The Chinese people have stood up from then on. In the above-described historical process, various mass organizations and revolutionary parties in China, despite their differences in political opinions, had united in the struggle for national independence and countless excellent sons and daughters of the Chinese nation had laid down their lives for this cause. Just as the inscription on the Monument to the People's Heroes reads: "Eternal glory to the heroes of the people who from 1840 on laid down their lives in the many struggles against domestic and foreign enemies and for national independence and the freedom and well-being of the people!" All men and women with high ideals who had struggled for human rights in China will go down in history and always be remembered as heroes of the Chinese nation.

II. Historical Development of Human Rights Cause in the People's Republic of China

The founding of the PRC washed off the humiliation suffered by Chinese people in the past century and opened a new chapter in the development of human rights cause in China. Before the founding of the PRC, the national political power was controlled by feudal warlords and KMT reactionaries while the CPC led the Chinese people in various forms of struggle for human rights. After the founding of the PRC, although the CPC has continued to lead Chinese people in the struggle for human rights, it has been doing so mainly by exercising state power to create conditions for the realization of human rights. When reviewing the revolutionary in China, Mao Zedong once said that the CPC had explored for many years the law of new democratic revolution and was able to understand and master it only after paying heavy prices. He hoped that it would not take that long time for the CPC to understand and master the law of socialist revolution and construction. However, things did not turn out the way Mao wanted it. China has also made many mistakes and taken many wrong paths in socialist revolution and construction as well as in the construction of human rights protection system. The CPC and the Chinese people have summarized their experiences and learnt their lessons from these mistakes.

1. Great Achievements Made by China in the Construction of Human Rights Protection System in the 1950s

In the 1950s, the Chinese government had done a large amount of work and made remarkable achievements in human rights construction. In the field of legislation, the government adopted in September 1949 the Common Program of the Chinese People's Political Consultative Conference, which declared the end of the rule of imperialism, feudalism and bureaucratic capitalism in China. The People's Republic of China is a new democratic or a people's democratic state. It implements the system of people's democratic dictatorship based on the leadership of the working class, the alliance of workers and peasants, and unity of all democratic classes and all nationalities in China, and strives for the independence, democracy, peace, unity, prosperity and increase of national strength of China. The Common Program, which served as a temporary constitution at that time, provided for the nature and operational principles of government organs as well as military, economic, cultural, educational, ethnic and foreign policies of the state and affirmed the political, economic, cultural and social rights of the people. In accordance with the Common Program, China promulgated the Marriage Law in April 1950, the Land Reform Law in May 1950, and the Election Law in March 1953. The purpose of these laws was to meet the most urgent needs of protection of people's rights at that time. The 1950 Marriage Law abolished arranged marriage, forced marriage and other feudal marriage systems based on the idea that men are superior to women; established new democratic marriage system based on gender equality and freedom of marriage and the formation of new families based on democracy, harmony, and mutual love. It provided that a monogamous marriage system shall be implemented; marriage must be based upon the complete willingness of both man and woman; both the man and the woman desiring to contract a marriage must have reached the legal age for marriage and they shall register in person with the marriage registration office. Husband and wife are equal in rights and obligations during marriage; the rights of the child are protected by law; a natural child shall have the equal rights of a legitimate child; the freedom of marriage includes both the freedom of marriage and the freedom of divorce. Under the old marriage system, women were under the dual oppression by their fathers and their husbands, enjoyed no freedom of marriage and had low status in family after marriage. The implementation of the Marriage Law liberated both women and men from the bandage of the old marriage system. The Land Reform Law was aimed at "abolishing the exploitative feudal system of ownership of land by landlord class and implementing the system of ownership of land by peasants, so as to liberate productive force, develop agriculture and blaze a trail for the industrialization of country."① To realize this objective, the CPC adopted the policy of "relying on poor peasants and farmhands, uniting middle-peasants, neutralizing the rich peasants, and eliminating exploitative feudal system in a step-by-step and discriminative way, and developing agricultural production." The implementation of the Land Reform Law freed

① See the Land Reform Law of the People's Republic of China.

over 300 million peasants from the bondage of feudal land ownership system and enabled them to acquire land and other means of production. With the exception of a few ethnic minority areas, the CPC had realized in the whole country the ideal of "land to the tiller" put forward by Sun Yat-sen several decades ago, thereby greatly raising the enthusiasm for production and living standard of the broad masses of peasants.

While implementing the marriage law in the whole country and carrying out land reform in rural areas, the CPC started to make arrangements for unemployed workers and former employees of KMT government, thereby beginning a democratic reform movement aimed at liberating the workers from the exploitation and oppression by feudal bosses. The democratic reform in urban areas greatly enhanced the Chinese people's enthusiasm for revolution and production. With their support, the Chinese government defeated the U. S. troops in the Korean War, foiled the bombings of coastal cities by Chiang Kai-shek's forces supported by the U. S. and over 100 invasions of Chinese territorial seas by U. S. warships, eliminated over one million political bandits and a large number of KMT spies and agents, thereby effectively upholding social order and the safety of life and property of the people. In 1952, the national economy was restored to the highest level in history. In 1953, the state began a large-scale economic construction. In 1954, the Constitution of the People's Republic of China was adopted after broad discussion by the people of whole country.

The 1954 Constitution was a "socialist constitution" adopted after thorough discussion by representatives of the people. Based on the Common Program, it provided for the following fundamental rights of citizens: the right of citizens who have reached the age of eighteen to vote and stand for election regardless of their ethnicity, race, sex, occupation, social origin, religious relief, education, property status, or length of residence; the freedoms of speech, of the press, of assembly, of association, of procession and demonstration; the freedom of religious belief; freedom of the persons of citizens is inviolable. No citizens may be arrested except by decision of a people's court or with the approval of a people's procuratorate; the homes of citizens of the People's Republic of China are inviolable, and the privacy of correspondence is protected by law; citizens of the People's Republic of China enjoy freedom of residence and freedom to change their residence; citizens of the People's Republic of China have the right to work. To guarantee enjoyment of this right, the state, by planned development of the national economy, gradually creates more employment and better working conditions and wages; working people have the right to rest and leisure. To guarantee enjoyment of this right, the state prescribes working hours and holidays for workers and office employees; working people have the right to material assistance in old age and in case of illness or disability. To guarantee enjoyment of this right, the state provides social insurance, social assistance and public health services and gradually expands these facilities; citizens have the right to education. To guarantee enjoyment of this right, the state establishes and gradually extends the various types of schools and other cultural and educational institutions; citizens have the freedom to engage in scientific research, literary and artistic creation and other cultural pursuits. The state encourages and assists creative work in science, education, literature, art and other cultural pursuits; women enjoy equal rights with men in all spheres of political, economic, cultural, social and domestic life. The state protects marriage, the family, and the mother and child; citizens have the right to bring complaints against any person working in organs of state for transgression of law or neglect of duty by making a written or verbal statement to any organ of state at any level. People suffering loss by reason of infringement by persons working in organs of state of their rights as citizens have the right to compensation. The 1954 Constitution fully recognized the fundamental rights of citizens, provided a beautiful blueprint of national development, and greatly enhanced the enthusiasm of the Chinese people to participate in socialist revolution and construction. China completed the collectivization of agriculture and the transformation of handicraft industry and individual industrial and commercial enterprises in 1955 and basically completed the socialist transformation of capitalist industry and commerce in 1956, thereby promoting the development of agriculture, industry and the entire national economy. In 1957, the first five-year plan was completed ahead of schedule, with the gross output value of industry and agriculture reaching 124.1 billion yuan, 67.8% higher than that of 1952 in comparable price. Of which, the gross output value of industry was 70.4 billion yuan, 128.6% higher than the pervious year and the gross output value of agriculture was 53.7 billion yuan, 24.8% higher than the pervious year.[①] A very good situation of prosperous market, stable commodity

① See Research Office of the Central Committee of the CPC, "Chronicle of Events of the People's Republic of China", in *Wen Hui Bao*, October 3, 2009.

prices, and marked improvement people's living standard had emerged throughout the country.

However, despite the full recognition of rights of citizens by the Constitution and the rapid development of the agriculture, industry and the national economy, some problems had emerged in the construction of the legal system during this period of time. As Comrade Dong Biwu pointed out in his speech at the Eighth National Congress of the CPC in 1956: "Since the founding of the People's Republic, the Party has done countless pieces of work and made unprecedented achievements in safeguarding the long-term and immediate interests of the people. However, we often find violations of laws and disciplines and infringements of people's democratic rights in the work of many departments of local and central governments. Some government officials even consider themselves above the law."①

The political movements launched by the CPC in the early years of the People's Republic of China, such as the "Suppression of Counterrevolutionaries", the "Three-Anti Movement" and the "Five-Anti Movement", had no doubt made great achievements. However, because these movements were launched before the adoption of the relevant legal norms, they were carried out in accordance with very general policies, rather than concrete laws in the beginning. As a result, excesses and over-expansion were inevitable. The cases of "Pan Hannian and Yang Fan Counterrevolutionary Group" and "Hu Feng Counterrevolutionary Group" in the 1955 movement of "Purge of Internal Counterrevolutionaries" were two obvious examples. Those implicated in these two cases were good comrades who had made great contribution to revolution or faithfully followed the CPC for many years, but were wrongfully accused as counterrevolutionaries. Although they were later rehabilitated by the CPC, the cases had left deep wounds in the history of the People's Republic of China.

2. The Progresses Made and Serious Problems Emerged in the Construction of Human Rights Protection System in Late 1950s

In 1956, Chine continued to carry out large-scale socialist construction. During the 10 years from 1956 to 1966, although China was

① Dong Biwu, "Further Strengthening People's Democratic Legal System and Safeguarding the Cause of Socialist Construction", in Dong Biwu, *Selected Works of Dong Biwu*, Beijing: People's Publishing House, 1985, p. 414.

faced with serious problems in the development of the national economy because the "Great Leap Forward Movement" and the "People's Commune Movement", the situation began to change for the better since 1960, when the CPC Central Committee adopted the policy of "adjustment, reinforcement, enrichment and improvement". As the CPC Central Committee later pointed out: "In the ten years preceding the "Cultural Revolution" we achieved big successes despite serious setbacks. By 1966, the value of fixed industrial assets, calculated on the basis of their original price, was four times greater than in 1956. The output of such major industrial products as cotton yarn, coal, electricity, crude oil, steel and mechanical equipment all recorded impressive increases... The distribution of industries over the country became better balanced. Capital construction in agriculture and technical transformation began on a massive scale and yielded better and better results. Both the number of tractors for farming and the quantity of chemical fertilizers applied increased over seven times and rural consumption of electricity 71 times. The number of graduates from institutions of higher education was 4.9 times that of the previous seven years. Educational work was improved markedly through consolidation. Scientific research and technological work, too, produced notable results."① These developments had created better conditions for the enjoyment by Chinese people of various economic, political, and cultural rights. The Chinese government announced at the Third National People's Congress in 1965 that the economy as a whole would soon enter a new stage of development and that it would make energetic efforts to build China step by step into a socialist power with modern agriculture, industry, national defence and science and technology. However, this magnificent target was not fulfilled owing to the "Cultural Revolution".

The "Cultural Revolution", which lasted from May 1966 to October 1976, was responsible for "the most severe setback and the heaviest losses suffered by the Party, the state and the people since the founding of the People's Republic". It was through the joint struggles waged by the entire

① "Resolution on Certain Questions in the History of the CPC since the Founding of the People's Republic of China", in Department of Educational Administration of Party School of CPC Central Committee (ed.), *Selection of Important Documents of CPC and the Government Since the Third Plenary Session of the Eleventh Central Committee*, Beijing: Party School of CPC Central Committee Press, 2008, pp. 95—56.

Party and the masses of workers, peasants, PLA officers and men, intellectuals, educated youth and cadres that the havoc wrought by the "Cultural Revolution" was somewhat mitigated. During this decade, "Some progress was made in our economy despite tremendous losses. Grain output increased relatively steadily. Significant achievements were scored in industry, communications and capital construction and in science and technology. New railways were built and the Changjiang River Bridge at Nanjing was completed: a number of large enterprises using advanced technology went into operation; hydrogen bomb tests were successfully undertaken and man-made satellites successfully launched and retrieved; and new hybrid strains of long-grained rice were developed and popularized."①

During this period of time, many of the established constitutional principles were abandoned and a series of problems, even extremely serious problems emerged in the protection of human rights.

——In 1957, with the serious escalation of the "Anti-rightist Movement", hundreds of thousands of intellectuals, patriots and Party cadres, especially those in the literary and art circles and political-legal circles (including young students) were labeled "bourgeois rightists". Although these people were treated as "contradictions among the people", they had been persecuted ruthlessly and their human dignity trampled upon from the very beginning under the slogan of "denounce with severity". Later, most of them had been transferred out of their original work posts or sent to labor camps. In a time when class struggle was taken as the paramount task, they were listed together with "landlords, rich peasants, counterrevolutionaries, and bad elements" as the so-called "black five". They were discriminated against even after their "rightist" label was removed.

——In 1958, the main decision-makers of the CPC, ignoring the objective law of economics and exaggerating the role of subjective will, indiscreetly launched the "Great Leap Forward Movement" and "People's Commune Movement". During the "Great Leap Forward Movement", all people were asked to engage in steelmaking. Metal objects were removed

---

① "Resolution on Certain Questions in the History of the CPC since the Founding of the People's Republic of China", in Department of Educational Administration of Party School of CPC Central Committee (ed.), *Selection of Important Documents of CPC and the Government Since the Third Plenary Session of the Eleventh Central Committee*, Beijing: Party School of CPC Central Committee Press, 2008, p. 105.

from public facilities and personal properties such as pots and pans were requisitioned as raw materials and forests cut down to be used as fuel. During the "People's Commune Movement", arbitrary and impractical decisions, exaggeration of production figures, and practice of equalitarianism in the name of communism had disrupted the order of production, dampened farmers'enthusiasm for produce. These, in addition to natural disaster, had led to decline of agricultural production by large margin. On top of that, the Soviet Government at that time acted in bad faith by tearing up contract with China and pressing China for payment of debts. All these had caused serious difficulties in China's national economy during the period between 1959 and 1961. Many people in the provinces of Hebei, Shandong, Anhui, Henan, Shaanxi, and Sichuan were suffering from malnutrition. In some places there was an increase in the rate of abnormal mortality.

——In 1959, Mao Zedong launched a criticism against Peng Dehuai and labeled him and other senior Party officials who adhered to their correct views an "anti-Party Clique". Later, Mao launched a nation-wide "struggle against right deviations" in which many people who dared to report the actual situation at that time and criticize the "Great Leap Forward Movement" and "People's Commune Movement" were denounced as having right deviations. The "struggle against right deviations" further undermined socialist democracy and legal system, and worsened the already grave situation of economic, political and social life.

——Between 1963 and 1965, a socialist education movement was carried out in some rural and urban areas in which the implementation of the "left" policies by some grassroots cadres and problems in their style of work or life were regarded as class struggle or manifestations of class struggle within the Party and the public were mobilized to "rectify" them. As a result, many grassroots cadres came under attack. Some of them were later struggled against as "capitalist roaders in power in the Party", causing great harms to these cadres.

——In 1965, under the slogan of fight against revisionism and bourgeois ideology, a mass denunciation movement was launched in literary and art circles. As a result, for a period of time, not only human rights were regarded as heresy, but even humanitarianism and theory of human nature became forbidden zones into which no one in the academic circle dared to enter.

——In 1966, the Chinese leaders launched the "Cultural Revolution", which was the culmination of the radical "Left line" gradually developed since late 1950s. In the name of solving the problems caused by the dark side of the Party and the state, the initiators of this "Revolution" called for the downfall of "capitalist roaders in power in the Party" and "reactionary academic authorities". As a result, many government officials, renewed scholars, writers, artists and teachers were persecuted and humiliated by being paraded through streets wearing a dunce cap. Students and workers throughout the country had suspended classes or production to "carry out revolution". They attacked Party and state organs and tried to take over state power, and resorted to violence against each other, thereby seriously disrupting social order and production. The human dignity, personal safety, property, even the life of a large number of people, from ordinary citizens to government officials at various levels, even the president of state, had been violated. "History has shown that the 'Cultural Revolution', initiated by a leader laboring under a misapprehension and capitalized on by counter-revolutionary cliques, led to domestic turmoil and brought catastrophe to the Party, the state and the whole people."①

3. Reflections on Problems in the Construction of Human Rights Protection System in China during the Period from the Founding of the New China to the End of the "Cultural Revolution"

With the establishment of the People's Republic of China, Chinese people gained freedom and emancipation and became masters of their own country. This is an important human right. During the twenty year between the establishment of the People's Republic of China and the end of the "Cultural Revolution", with the economic, political, and cultural development, the general level of people's material and cultural life had been continuously raising and, correspondingly, their economic, political, cultural and social rights had been basically safeguarded. However, just as mentioned before, there had been violations of different rights of different groups of people during different periods of time. Some of these violations were large in scale and grave in nature. It is very painful to

① "Resolution on Certain Questions in the History of the CPC since the Founding of the People's Republic of China", in Department of Educational Administration of Party School of CPC Central Committee (ed.), *Selection of Important Documents of CPC and the Government Since the Third Plenary Session of the Eleventh Central Committee*, Beijing: Party School of CPC Central Committee Press, 2008, p. 102.

recall this part of history, but that was what really happened and it happened because of the following reasons:

Firstly, one of the important external causes for the escalation of class struggle and violations of human rights was that was that during this period of time China had been in a state of constant localized wars or preparation for war. During the early years of the People's Republic of China, the war was still going on in some regions of China, including Guangdong, Guangxi, Hainan and some remote boarder regions, which had not been totally liberated. Therefore, the Common Program of the Chinese People's Political Consultative Conference declared in Article 2: "The Central People's Government of the People's Republic of China must undertake to wage the people's war of liberation to the very end, to liberate all the territory of China, and to achieve the unification of China." At that time, there were about one million armed bandits entrenched in the mountain areas in the provinces of Hunan, Hubei, Sichuan, Yunnan, and Guangxi. Supported by the U. S., KMT reactionaries who had fled to Taiwan had been continuously bombing the coastal areas of the Mainland and harassing the inland areas. When the Korean War broke out in 1950, the U. S. invaded Korea and bombed Northeastern China. In response, the Chinese government sent a volunteer army to Korea to help Korean people resist U. S. aggression as well as to defend Chinese territory. The U. S. also sent troops to Taiwan, ordered the Seventh Fleet to cruise the Taiwan Straight and carry out constant provocation in Chinese coastal areas, and instigate other western countries to impose economic blockade against China in the hope of straggling the young republic in its infancy. Faced with fierce resistance by Chinese and Korean people, the U. S. troops suffered heavy losses and a U. S. general admitted that they had been involved in the wrong war, at the wrong place, at the wrong time, and with the wrong enemy". The U. S. was forced to sign an armistice agreement in 1953, but this did not change its aggressive nature. Soon afterwards, it was involved in another large-scale war, this time in Vietnam. Since China and were closely related to and shared the same fate with Vietnam, it generously offered itself as the rear area of Vietnam and provided Vietnamese people with huge manpower and materials in support of their war against U. S. aggression, until the withdrawal of the U. S. troops in the 1970s. Before the end of the Vietnam War, the relationship between China and the Soviet Union began to worsen as a result of the ideological difference between the Chinese and Russian communist parties. The Soviet Union deployed over one million troops at Chinese-Soviet boarder and stationed troops in the People's Republic of Mongolia, which had posed serious treat to China and started a military conflict in Zhenbao Island and in Heilongjiang Province and other boarder areas between the two countries. Although larger-scale armed conflict was avoided later, the tension between the two countries continued until the 1980s. China had a long history of being subjected to foreign aggression and treasured its hard-won national independence. The acts of war and threats of war by the U. S. and other countries forced China to always keep itself on high alert and vigilance. This mentality of vigilance, while was conducive to uniting the Chinese people and mobilizing them for the protection and construction of their motherland, could easily lead many Chinese leaders who grew up in war conditions to observe and make decisions on issues of national development with a strong class struggle mentality and military methods. As a result, "they continue to regard issues unrelated to class struggle as manifestations of class struggle and when confronted with actual class struggle under the new conditions, habitually fell back on the familiar methods and experiences of the large-scale, turbulent mass struggle of the past, which should no longer have been mechanically followed. As a result, we substantially broadened the scope of class struggle."① During the "Cultural Revolution", they even adopted the policies of "taking class struggle as the key link" and "implementing total dictatorship", which caused great harms to a large number of innocent ordinary citizens and cadres and made the provisions on human rights in the Constitution and laws dead letters.

Secondly, the negative influence of feudal autocracy and patriarchal system in traditional culture was a main ideological root cause of the serious problems in the construction of human rights system during that period of time. From the unification of China by the First Emperor of Qin in 221 BC to the overthrow of the Qing Dynasty in 1911, the system of feudal autocratic monarchy had been implemented in China for 2, 000 years. Under such a system, the feudal emperor was the supreme ruler in

① "Resolution on Certain Questions in the History of the CPC since the Founding of the People's Republic of China", in Department of Educational Administration of Party School of CPC Central Committee (ed.), *Selection of Important Documents of CPC and the Government Since the Third Plenary Session of the Eleventh Central Committee*, Party School of CPC Central Committee Press, 2008, p. 106.

the country: "Under the wide heaven, all is the king's land. Within the sea-boundaries of the land, all are the king's servants. "① Under the influence this ideology, government officials at various levels were only representatives and servants of the emperor, and feudal patriarchs, as the basis of feudal autocratic system, had also been given corresponding powers by law. After the overthrow of the Qing Dynasty, the Northern warlords and Chiang Kai-shek became new emperors, only they changed the name of the "emperor" to the "president" . In the "public" under their rule, despotic dictatorship was practiced and there was no democracy to talk about. Against this historical background, it was very difficult for the People's Republic China, established in 1949, to be free from the influence of the old tradition. As Deng Xiaoping pointed out: "From old China we inherited a strong tradition of feudal autocracy and a weak tradition of democratic legality. "② Feudal autocratic tradition and patriarchy system had manifested themselves prominently in the operation of institutions and the ideology and work style of cadres: "Over-concentration of power means inappropriate and indiscriminate concentration of all power in Party committees in the name of strengthening centralized Party leadership. Moreover, the power of the Party committees themselves is often in the hands of a few secretaries, especially the first secretaries, who direct and decide everything. Thus 'centralized Party leadership' often turns into leadership by individuals. "③ Because the over-concentration of and lack of supervision over and restriction on the power of leading cadres, "many places and units have their patriarchal personages with unlimited power. Everyone else has to be absolutely obedient and even personally attached to them. "④ Apparently, under such a circumstance, in the political life, "the relationship between a superior and a subordinate had become the one repeatedly criticized by Comrade Mao Zedong, the relationship between cat and mouse, like the relations in the old society between monarch and subject, or father and son, or the leader of a faction and his followers. "⑤ It was exact because

---

① See *Book of Poetry*: Bei shan.

② Deng Xiaoping, *Selected Works of Deng Xiaoping*, vol. 2, People's Publishing House, 1995, p. 332.

③ Ibid. , pp. 328—329.

④ Ibid. , 331.

⑤ Ibid.

of the above-mentioned factors that democratic life of the Party and the state had been seriously damaged, the ability of Party and state leaders to make correct decision on some major issues impaired, and no effective resistance had been met when they made wrong decisions such as the launching of the "Cultural Revolution" which lasted for ten years and resulted in unprecedented catastrophes, including the persecution to death of many excellent Party cadres, including some founding fathers of the PRC, even the state president.

Thirdly, the failure to fully understand the Marxist theory of human rights was the ideological cause for the problems in human rights construction in China. Confucius had said that: "If the name is not right then speech will not be in order, and if speech is not in order then nothing will be accomplished."① This assertion had always had a profound influence in China, especially among the intellectuals. Although, during the May 4th Movement, Chinese intellectuals put forward the slogan of "Down with Confucianism" and no longer took Confucius' teachings as truth, the philosophies behind some of his statements still have great vitality even today. After the Seventh National Congress of the CPC, Mao Zedong Thought, together with Marxism and Leninism, became a basic guiding theory for the CPC and the state in China. Although Mao Zedong himself opposed "book worship", many people tended to seek support for their own statements and actions in the works of classic Marxist writers. The basic human rights views and theory in the masterworks of Marx, Engels and Lenin are often expressed through the criticism of bourgeois human rights concepts and revelation of the nature of capitalist human rights system. For examples, "the so-called rights of man are 'simply the rights of a member of civil society', that is, of egoistic man, of man separated from other men and from the community";② "the primary human right in capitalism is the right to equally exploit the labor force";③ "human rights in themselves are privileges";④ and that "bourgeois property was proclaimed as one of the essential rights of man".⑤As a result, some

① See *The Analects*: Zilu.

② See *The Analects*: Zilu, p. 648.

③ *Complete Works of Marx and Engels* (Chinese Edition), vol. 23, People's Publishing House, 1972, p. 324.

④ Ibid, p. 229.

⑤ Ibid., p. 720.

people mistook these statements about the hierocracy and narrowness of bourgeois human rights for general comments on human rights. Actually, Marxism has always recognized the historical progressiveness of bourgeois human rights. Marx enthusiastically praised the United States Declaration of Independence as the first declaration of human rights in the world history. ①Engels praised the U. S. Constitution as " the first one to recognizing human rights" . ②Marx pointed out that when the bourgeoisie began it own rule, "human rights was no longer a mere theory"③ . Lenin also pointed out that: " Compared to feudalism, capitalism was an historical advance along the road of ' liberty", "equality', 'democracy' and 'civilization'" . ④Not only so, in their theories, the construction of socialism and the realization of communism have always closely linked with the realization of human rights and the free and comprehensive development of human beings. Marx and Engels pointed out that: "In place of the old bourgeois society, with its classes and class antagonisms, we shall have an association, in which the free development of each is the condition for the free development of all. "⑤ They also pointed out that: "Communism is the necessary form and the dynamic principle of the immediate future, but communism as such is not the goal of human development, the form of human society"⑥ and that "Communism is the doctrine of the conditions of the liberation of the proletariat. "⑦ Here I quote the expositions of classical Marxist writers only to show that ignoring their comprehensive expositions on human rights will lead not only to

---

① *Complete Works of Marx and Engels* (The First Chinese Edition), vol. 1, People's Publishing House, 1957, p. 20.

② *Complete Works of Marx and Engels* (Chinese Edition), vol. 3, People's Publishing House, 1995, p. 447

③ *Complete Works of Marx and Engels* (Chinese Edition), vol. 2, People's Publishing House, 1995, p. 157.

④ *Complete Works of Lenin*, Chinese edition, People's Publishing House, 1986, p. 109.

⑤ *Complete Works of Marx and Engels* (The First Chinese Edition), vol. 1, People's Publishing House, 1957, p. 294.

⑥ Franz Mehring, *Karl Marx: The Story of His Life*, Chinese edition, SDX Joint Publishing, 1954, p. 592.

⑦ *Complete Works of Marx and Engels* (The First Chinese Edition), vol. 1, People's Publishing House, 1957, p. 230.

misunderstandings, but also to many dangers in practice. Beginning from mid-1950s, human rights had been abandoned in Chinese theoretical circle and political life as a bourgeois slogan and no concrete standard on the protection of human rights had been adopted when formulating plans for the development of the national economy or carrying out a series of movements with inspiring and ambitious goals. At that time, even the consideration of material interests in practice, let alone demand for the protection of individual rights, were denounced as bourgeois ideas. The research on human rights theory had become a forbidden zone no one dared to enter.

Fourthly, the lack of legal safeguard was the institutional cause for the problems in human rights construction. As mentioned before, the 1954 Constitution contained a special chapter on the "fundamental rights and duties of citizens", the content of which had been widely praised around the world. Soon afterwards, however, the principles and provisions contained in this chapter were abandoned, mainly because no corresponding laws had been adopted to ensure the implementation of these principles and provisions. The provisions in the constitution are usually general principles that lack operability in administrative law enforcement and administration of justice. In order to ensure their implementation, corresponding laws must be adopted to concretize these general principles and provisions so that they can be enforced by administrative and judicial organs. However, China had failed to adopt any administrative, civil, economic, or criminal law long after the adoption of the 1954 Constitution. Many problems also existed in the implementation of laws. As early as in September 1956, Mr. Dong Biwu pointed out at the Eighth National Congress of the CPC that: "Now it is both necessary and possible for China to gradually improve its legal system. The phenomenon of incomplete legal system, if left unresolved for a long period of time, will become a serious problem." He then listed various phenomena of ignoring the legal system in practice: "some Party members and state functionaries ignore or refuse to abide by state laws and regulations, and no sufficient attention has been paid to this problem by the Party committees at various levels." In some localities, there was no separation of the Party work from the government work, "the Party committee often directly issue orders on behalf of state organs"; "some local governments do not strictly follow legal procedures in handling criminal suspects"; "some judicial personnel arrest suspects without following legally-prescribed procedures, restrict the right of defense and the right of appeal of criminal defendants. Some staff members of detention facilities and prisons maltreat detainees and prisoners in violation of Party policies, state laws and revolutionary humanitarian principle. "[1] However, Dong Biwu's visionary opinions and far-sighted suggestions were ignored by the main leaders of the Central Committee of the CPC. In 1957, the Ant-rightist Movement was launched in violation of the Constitution, resulting in large-scale subversion of the rule of law. In 1958, Mao Zedong even claimed that the editorials of the People's Daily were laws. During the "Cultural Revolution", even the orders issued by the Red Guards were regarded as laws and followed with reverence and awe by many units and people. As a result, the whole country was in a state of complete lawlessness. Some people did whatever they like to do; in some place, beating, smashing, looting, unlawful searching citizens' home and confiscating private property, and illegal detention became prevailing practice. There was no protection of citizens' property right, personal right or the right to life and the whole society descended into chaos.

Fifthly, the failure to carry out comprehensive thanksgiving education and the imbalance between thanksgiving education and the consciousness of subject of rights were the educational causes of the problems in human rights construction in China at that time.

"Human rights are inherent rights". This means that human rights are moral rights or due rights. Long-term struggles are needed in order to turn them into rights actually enjoyed by the people, namely actual rights. The rights and happy life we are enjoying today were secured by revolutionary martyrs with their blood, youth and life. As a Chinese saying goes: "A person should repay as much as he can for even a little bit of favor he has received." We should never forget the great sacrifice and contribution they had made to national independence, freedom, and human rights. This thanksgiving can increase the national cohesion and our sense of national pride. It is proper for us to be grateful, pay respect to, even worship such great revolutionary leaders as Sun Yet-sen and Mao Zedong. But such respect and warship should not be developed into superstition and weaken the subject consciousness and rights conscious of individuals, groups and the people. Otherwise we can easily lose judgment in some questions, even

---

[1] See Dong Biwu, *Collected Legal Writings of Dong Biwu*, Law Press China, 2001, pp. 346—348.

the ability to distinguish right from wrong. As The Internationale, the clarion call for the proletariat, goes:

"Arise you prisoners of starvation
Arise you toilers of the earth
For reason thunders new creation
'Tis a better world in birth.
. . .
We are but naught we shall be all.
. . .
No saviour from on high delivers
No faith have we in prince or peer
Our own right hand the chains must shiver
Chains of hatred, greed and fear."

The song expresses in simple words the Marxist conception of history: the people are the creators of history and their own liberators. The Chinese Constitution provides that "All powers of the state belong to the people." Despite the above theory and constitutional provision, the long-term failure to carry out thanksgiving education and to strike a balance between thanksgiving education and education on the consciousness of subjects of rights had led to moral disorder and lack of respect for human dignity. Moreover, because of the lack of the knowledge of relevant laws and policies, the victims of human rights violations did not know how to uphold their rights while the violators took such violations for granted. Some victims of serious violations of human rights were moved to tears of gratitude even before the policy of rectification had been fully implemented and the violation against them stopped. And there was no sound supervision and accountability system to make the violators of human rights reflect on their own behavior or exercise self-discipline. The violations of human rights were considered justified under the circumstances at the time of their occurrence and that they were later rectified only because of the change of circumstances. Such a mentality made it very difficult to avoid the repetition of violations of human rights.

despite the many mistakes, even serious mistakes like the Cultural Revolution", made by the Party and the government, it is undeniable that historical progresses had been made in the development of human rights cause in China during the period between the founding of the PRC and the "Cultural Revolution" . As mentioned above, the implementation of the Marriage Law in 1950 liberated men and women from the bondage of the feudal system of arranged marriage, which had lasted for thousands of years. The implementation of the Land Reform Law enabled more than 300 million peasants in newly liberated areas, in addition to over 100 million peasants in old liberated areas, to have their own land, thus truly realizing the goal of "land to the tillers" in a big agricultural country. The land reform greatly raised the peasants' enthusiasm for production. Apart from the "Three Years of Natural Disaster", China had been able to maintain a continued growth of grain and oil production. While carrying land reform in rural areas, the CPC and the government carried out democratic reform in urban areas that liberated the workers from the oppression and exploitation by feudal bosses and law-breaking capitalists and turned them into the masters of their factories. Decisive measures had been taken to ban brothels and prostitution and the use and traffic in drugs throughout the country; effectively controlled schistosome, malaria, TB and other infectious diseases; and greatly improved the health and life expectancy of the people. China began a large-scale industrialization in 1953, and completed the first five-year plan for the development of national economy in 1956, which greatly raised the enthusiasm of the Chinese for socialist construction. Later, although the industrial production and national economy suffered great losses as a result of the mistakes made by the Chinese government in its work and the treacherous acts of the Soviet government, China was able to keep the momentum of development. Compared with 1956, there was a substantial increase in industrial fixed asset in 1966. Even during the ten-year "Cultural Revolution", China maintained the momentum of growth in agricultural production, and made many important achievements in industry, transportation, capital construction, science and technology. For example, the successful testing of hydrogen bomb and the successful launching an recovery of man-made satellite were made against the background of continuous harassment by imperialists and hostile forces and economic sanctions and blockade by western countries led by the U. S. The Chinese people under the leadership of the CPC had overcome numerous difficulties in defending national security and upholding national dignity. One can tell the differences only through comparison and only those who had suffered humiliation and oppression in the old society can truly appreciate the freedom and emancipation in the new society. Many foreign friends have made fair comments on this fact. For example, a scholar from a developing country who visited China in early 1990s once said that his country would not be able to reach the level of social, economic, political and cultural development achieved by China since 1949, especially the level of social equality, in another 50 years. Such comments were objective and fair.

III. New Chapter in the Development of Human Rights System since the Third Plenary Session of the Eleventh Central Committee of the CPC

In October 1976, the Gang of Four was overthrown; in July 1977 Deng Xiaoping was formally reinstated; and in December 1978, the Third Plenary Session of the Eleventh Central Committee was held, in which the CPC established the ideological line of liberating the mind and seeking truth from fact and the policy of opening up and reform, "began to correct conscientiously and comprehensively the 'Left' errors of the 'Cultural Revolution' and earlier", [①] and decided to improve socialist democracy and legal system and to shift the focus of work on socialist modernization, thereby creating a new situation in economic, political, cultural and development and the development of human rights cause.

1. Ideological Emancipation in the Field of Human Rights

Human Rights Research Went on a Tortuous Road of Development after the Third Plenary Session of the Eleventh Central Committee of the CPC

After the Third Plenary Session of the Eleventh Central Committee of the CPC, many people began to reflect from the human rights perspective on the many incidents of beating, smashing, looting, unlawful search and confiscation of private property, unlawful detention, persecution to death, even arbitrary execution, occurred during the "Cultural Revolution". The Central Committee of the CPC took decisive police and legal measures to rectify a large number of unjust, false and erroneous cases and rehabilitated the reputation of the victims in these cases and their relatives. Meanwhile, the state strengthened the legislative work, adopted the Criminal Law, the Criminal Procedure Law and a number of other laws

① *Spura* note 38, p. 108.

urgently needed at that time, and restored the judicial organs "smashed during the "Cultural Revolution" . In the economic field, reform was carried out first in rural areas then in urban areas so as to satisfy the basic needs of the people. By early 1990s, the people's political, economic, and cultural rights had been greatly improved. However, because of long period of mental slavery, the theoretical circle was still afraid to directly discuss the issue of human rights. Apart from the article "On Human Rights and Citizens' Rights", written by Mr. Xu Bing and published in Guangming Daily,[①] most articles on human rights at that time discussed the issue from the perspectives of "people's rights" or the rights of a certain category of people, for examples, "Strengthening Construction of the Legal System and Safeguarding People's Rights"[②], "Safeguarding People's Rights: a Fine Tradition of Revolutionary Legal System"[③], "Legal Protection of Literal and Art Workers[④], On the Legal Status of Criminals"[⑤], and "Legal Status of Criminals Revisited" . In spite of these articles, because of some guiding articles published by the official journals of the CPC Central Committee and other mainstream media, such as "Human Rights: a Bourgeois Slogan", there had been many setbacks in the human rights research that had just started in China.

Emancipation of Mind and Theoretical Research in the Field of Human Rights Entered into a New Stage in 1991

In January 1991, the then Chinese President Jiang Zemin wrote the following instruction on a latter from some American and European scientists to Mr. Zhou Guangzhao: "The issue of human rights cannot be avoided by China and therefore needs to be carefully studied and publicized." This instruction was made against the following background: as far as domestic situation was concerned, with the deepening of reform and rapid economic development in rural and urban areas, interest became pluralized. The popularization and education of law, which took the

① Xu Bing, "On Human Rights and Citizens' Rights", in *Guangming Daily*, June 19, 1979.

② See *Hebei Daily*, November 14, 1978.

③ See *Studies in Law*, *(1979) 1.*

④ See *Guangming Daily*, March 3, 1979.

⑤ See People's Daily, November 27, 1979.

popularization of the Constitution as its main content, had greatly raised people's consciousness of democracy, the legal system and rights. With regard to the problems in the protection of rights, Jiang Zemin once said: "We should correctly explain democracy, freedom, and human rights to our cadres, the masses and especially young students from the basic Marxist point of view and in a language they understand."① As far as international situation was concerned, with the collapse of communism in Eastern Europe and the dissolution of the Soviet Union in late 1980s and early 1990s, China, which adhered to the socialist road, became the primary punching bag of western countries led by the U. S. in the field of human rights. They performed an anti-China chorus in different media in an effort to demonize China. As a result, many people, including 42 scientists in Europe and the U. S., were confused about the human rights situation in China. They wrote a joint letter to Mr. Zhou Guangzhao, the then President of the Chinese Academy of Sciences, in which they criticized the human rights situation in China and claimed that they would call on scientists around the world to cut contact with China if China would not improve its human rights conditions. When Jiang Zemin read this letter, he quickly made the above-mentioned instruction and passed it on to the members of the Politburo, to Mr. Li Ruihuan, who was in charge of ideological work at that time, and to Mr. Zhu Muzhi, the then director of Central External Propaganda Group. Meanwhile, he also instructed Mr. Hu Sheng, the then President of the Chinese Academy of Social Sciences, to organize research on human rights theory.

President Jiang Zemin's instruction opened the gate of the forbidden zone of theoretical research on human rights and liberated the theoretical circle from assertion that "human rights" is a bourgeois slogan. In the spring of 1991, a series of seminars on human rights were organized by the Propaganda Department of the CPC Central Committee, the Chinese Academy of Social Sciences (CASS), and the Central Party School, thereby ending over ten years of setback and entering a new phase of emancipation of mind in the field of human rights research in China. At this stage, the research carried out by the CASS and the Central Party School, publication of the large book series "Materials of Human Rights Research", especially the issuance of the white book "Human Rights in

① See a speech given by Jiang Zemin at the National Conference of Heads of Propaganda Departments held in July 2, 1989.

China" by the Information Office of the State Council, had had major impact both in China and abroad.

First, the research on human rights theory carried out by CASS and the Central Party School. After receiving from the CPC Central Committee the task of carrying out human rights research, Professor Hu Shen, the then President of CASS, gave the task to CASS Law Institute. He pointed out that human rights research should be guided by Marxism and serve the purposes of improving the human rights protection system in China and promoting China's international struggle and exchange in the field of human rights. Based on Deng Xiaoping's theory of "boldly absorbing and drawing on all the achievements of civilization attained by mankind", he required that human rights research should be combined with study of scientific achievements attained in the progress of human civilization. To fulfill this task, the CASS Law Institute, on the basis of a series of internal colloquia, organized a large national seminar on human rights theory in Beijing in June 1991. The seminar was participated by not only scholars in the fields of law and philosophy, but also government officials, including diplomats. Before that, Professors Dong Yunhu and Liu Wuping at the Central Party School had already carried out solid work of data collection and research and put forward their own opinions on human rights issues in the chapter "Human Rights Overview" of the book World Documents of Human Rights compiled by them. During the two-day seminar on human rights organized by CASS Law Institute, the participants carried out heated discussions on such issues as "the concept of human rights", "the historical development of human rights" and "the significance of human rights research". Bases on the discussions at the seminar, the CASS Law Institute submitted three reports, "On the Concept of Human Rights", "Holding High the Banner of Socialist Human Rights", and "Making a Clear Distinction Between Human Rights and Violations of Human Rights", to the CPC Central Committee in June 1991. These reports explain the differences between the concepts of "human rights", "people's rights" and "citizens' rights": "human rights are the rights enjoyed or ought to be enjoyed by all human beings by virtue of their natural and social attributes as human beings". The subjects of human rights are human beings, including the people, citizens, stateless persons, refugees, and other foreigners—namely all human beings. Here human beings mainly refer to individuals, but also include collectives. Collective human rights are the extension of individual human rights. The objects of human rights are the rights ought to be enjoyed by human beings, namely due rights. Due rights embody the common aspiration and pursuit of mankind at a certain stage of social, economic, and cultural development and are the driving force and precursors of the continued improvement of legal rights and actual rights. They scientifically reveal the origin of human rights, namely human rights both derive from the natural attributes of human beings and are the products comprehensive development of social relations. Human rights have the dual attributes of universality and particularity. The former reflects the ideals and demands based on the common interests of all human beings while the latter is determined by the cultural tradition, geographical environment, social, economic, and political systems and level of development of each country or nation. Different countries have different human rights systems and national characteristics. Within a country, under the condition of existence of class and class struggle, human rights have obvious class attribute. This is because the classes in politically and economically dominant position always try to use legal means to seek their own special interests. Universality and particularity are in a relationship of interaction and inter-infiltration with each other. When adopting human rights policies, China should pay attention to both particularity and universality of human rights. Over-emphasizing or ignoring either one of them will result in errors and harmful effects in practice. The reports point out that the full protection of human rights is an inherent demand of socialist system and in line with the communist goal of the complete liberation of all mankind. The Chinese Constitution is in itself a bill of rights that comprehensively provides for citizens' economic, political, cultural and social rights. In the past, influenced by the "Left" ideology, we were reluctant to talk about human rights and considered them "bourgeois slogan". This was not conducive to the development of the human rights cause and international exchange and struggle in the field of human rights. In the future, China should hold high the banner of human rights and, to do so, it must establish its own system of human rights theory guided by Marxism and based on the actual situation in China. In this process, we should be aware the trick of western countries of using human rights as excuse to interfere in the internal affairs of other countries and resolutely fight back against some foreign governments and officials who interfere in China's domestic affairs and attempt to demonize China.

In order to promote solid theoretical research and provide more accurate information to the CPC Central Committee for its decision-making in the field of human rights, the CASS decided to carry out a two-year investigation beginning from 1991 on the research on human rights theories and construction of human rights institutions in various countries in North America, Western and Central Europe, and South Asia. The investigation was led by Professor Wang Jiafu and Professor Liu Hainian and investigation tours were made to the above-mentioned four regions. The participants of these tours were: in North America: Liu Hainian, Lin Di, Xin Chunying and Li Lin; in Western Europe: Wang Jiafu, Han Yanlong, Xu Bing and Li Mingde; in South Asia: Liu Hainian, Li Buyun, Liu Nanlai, Huang Lie, and Huang Qianghua, and in Central Europe: Wang Jiafu, Han Yanlong, Wang Keju and Liu Baiju.

These investigation tours, known as "ice-breaking tours" at that time, had immediately drawn the attention of international news media. Some said that this was a sign of reform and opening up in the field of human rights in China, while others saw this only as a preparation made by the CPC for confrontation with western countries in the field of human rights. Some foreign news agencies stationed in China even proposed to follow the team during the investigation tours and report on its activities on a continuous basis. During these investigation tours, the CASS delegations held fruitful discussions and exchange of opinions with human rights scholars, human rights activists, NGOs, members of parliament, and government officials in the host countries. Upon returning to China, they submitted to the Chinese government a series of investigation reports, which accurately reflect the human rights institutions and the human rights ideas of scholars and government officials in the countries visited and therefore were attached great importance to by the Chinese leaders and the relevant government departments. The reform and opening up in China was propelled from top down and the construction of human rights system was no exception. These investigation reports and nation-wide research on human rights theory provided valuable information and reference for the decision-making by the Chinese government in the field of human rights.

Second, the book series "Human Rights Research Materials" compiled under the auspice of the Theoretical Bureau of the Propaganda Department of the CPC Central Committee. At a colloquium on implementing the instructions of CPC leaders to strengthen the research on human rights issues, organized by the Propaganda Department of the CPC Central Committee, many participants complained about the lack of materials on human rights. In order to promote the research on human rights, the Theoretical Bureau of the Propaganda Department of the CPC Central Committee decided to organize relevant units to compile the book series "Human Rights Research Materials". The series consists of six books: (1) "Selected Materials on Human Rights Studies", compiled by the Central Party Committee. Considering that the book "World Documents of Human Rights", edited by Dong Yunhu and Liu Wuping, had already contained a comprehensive collection of international instruments on human rights, it was decided that this book includes only the constitutional provisions on human rights protection in a selected countries, so as to avoid too much repetition; (2) "Marxist Theory on Human Rights", compiled by the Central Compilation & Translation Bureau; (3) "Human Rights Construction in China", compiled by the CASS Law Institute. This book is a detailed introduction to the human rights condition in China and is divided into two parts: legislation on human rights protection and practice of human rights protection; (4) "Developing Countries and Human Rights", compiled by the CASS Law Institute. This book mainly introduces the human rights ideas and institutions of developing countries, the participation by developing countries in international human rights conventions and the contents of regional human rights conventions of Asia, Africa and Latin America; (5) "Human Rights Theories in Western Countries", compiled by Peking University. This two-volume book introduces in a chronological order the human rights ideas of representative scholars and politicians in western countries. (6) "Socialist Parties and Democratic Socialist Human Rights Views", which introduces the human rights views of Socialist International, the Soviet Union and East European countries. This four-million-character book series (it has seven million characters if the book World Documents of Human Rights edited by Dong Yunhu and Liu Wuping is considered a part of the series) was compiled according to the principles of "objectiveness, comprehensiveness, detailedness, and accuracy so as to comprehensively and truthfully reflect the main theories, views and literature in the field of human rights. Just as Professor Jin Huiming, the then Director of the Theoretical Bureau of the Propaganda Department of the CPC Central Committee, pointed out in the Preface of the book series: "There is no denying that, for a long period of time, we had not paid enough attention to the research on human rights issues and lacked the knowledge of human rights. Some comrades indiscriminately rejected human rights as bourgeois ideology while others blindly accepted and are consciously or unconsciously influenced by western human rights ideas. All these are incorrect attitudes towards the human rights issue. "① Under such a circumstance, the publication of this book series was no doubt of great importance because "it is the first comprehensive and systematic compilation of materials on human rights research in China and has great reference value to the research on human rights theory, to the construction of human rights system and to the struggle in the field of foreign relations. "② Of course, the compilation and publication of this book series has another layer of significance: it was organized by Theoretical Bureau of the Propaganda Department of the CPC Central Committee, the Party organ responsible for ideological work. In this process it mobilized many colleges and universities, research institutes, and relevant departments of the State Council, thereby greatly promoting the human rights research in China.

Third, the first white paper published by the Chinese government: "Human Rights in China" . Soon after the instruction on research of human rights issues was given by Chinese leaders, the Information Office of the State Council Decided to publish a white paper on the human rights situation in China. As Mr. Zhu Muzhi pointed out at a press conference after the launching of the white paper, the reason for the publication of the white paper was that: "during a half century and more since the establishment of the People's Republic of China, the Chinese people have made great achievements in all fields, including in the field of human rights. This was a remarkable achievement made by the Chinese people... the human rights situation of the Chinese people today is immeasurably better than that before the founding of the People's Republic of China. However, because of the lack of publicity in this respect, even many Chinese people, especially young people, let alone people in foreign countries, know very little about this achievement... the publication of this white paper will help the Chinese people and the international community to get a comprehensive, systematic, and accurate

---

① See Jin Huiming, "Preface", *Materials on Human Rights Research*, Sichuan People's Publishing House, 1994.

② Ibid.

knowledge of the human rights enjoyed by Chinese people."①

The drafting of the white paper was directly led by Mr. Zhu Muzhi, who was assisted by Mr. Zeng Jianhui and Mr. Zhou Jue. The drafting work carried out by a writing group headed by Mr. Li Yuanchao, the then Chief of the First Bureau of Information Office of the State Council. Other members of the writing group included Qian Xiaoqian, Tian Dan, Dong Yunhu, Liu Fengzhi, Xu Jianyi and Zou Encheng.

The guiding ideology of the drafting work was: to be guided by Marxist human rights view and based on the actual condition in China; to adhere to the principle of seeking truth from fact, to present achievements and progresses as well as problems and shortcomings, and to adopt the method of historical comparison and to set out facts and reason things out. During the drafting process, the Information Office of the State Council invited various ministries and commissions under the State Council and the CASS Law Institute to provide materials and data on human rights construction in China and held many colloquia participated by the responsible persons of dozens of departments under the central government to exchange opinions on the viewpoints, framework and writing style of the white book, so as to draw on collective wisdom and absorb all useful ideas. After repeated deliberation and revision, the white paper is based on logical and sufficient presentation of arguments and has great powers of persuasion.

Apart from the preface, the white paper consists of ten parts: "the Right to Subsistence-the Foremost Human Right the Chinese People Long Fight for"; "the Chinese People Have Gained Extensive Political Rights"; "Citizens Enjoy Economic, Cultural and Social Rights"; "Guarantee of Human Rights in China's Judicial Work"; "Guarantee of the Right to Work"; "Citizens Enjoy Freedom of Religious Belief"; "Guarantee of the Rights of Minority Nationalities"; "Family Planning and Protection of Human Rights"; "Guarantee of the Rights of Disabled Persons"; and "Active Participation in International Human Rights Activities". It points out that all human rights are interrelated and indivisible. However, it is necessary and justifiable for each country to have different priorities in the realization of human rights in different period of time in light of its history, culture and level of development. The white paper makes it clear at the very beginning of its Preface that: "It has been a long-cherished ideal of mankind to

① Zhu Muzhi, *On Human Rights*, China Intercontinental Press, 1998, pp. 20—21.

enjoy human rights in the full sense of the term. Since this great term-human rights-was coined centuries ago, people of all nations have achieved great results in their unremitting struggle for human rights" and that: "Under long years of oppression by the" three big mountains imperialism, feudalism and bureaucrat-capitalism—people in old China did not have any human rights to speak of. Suffering bitterly from this, the Chinese people fought for more than a century, defying death and personal sacrifices and advancing wave upon wave, in an arduous struggle to overthrow the "three big mountains" and gain their human rights. Please note that the "Preface" states that "human rights" is "a great term" and "a long-cherished ideal of mankind" and that the Chinese people always take human rights as their objective of struggle and have carried out arduous struggle to achieve this objective. This statement fully confirms human rights and the universality as well as particularity of human rights. The white paper especially emphasizes the right of subsistence and the right to development because Chinese people have learnt from their own experience that the right to subsistence is the precondition for the enjoyment of all other rights. Without the right to subsistence, the Chinese people would be suffering from the aggression, oppression and pillage of imperialists and have no human rights to talk about. After overthrowing imperialism, feudalism and bureaucratic capitalism, China must guarantee the basic livelihood of its people so as to safeguard their right to subsistence. To this end, it must attach importance to the right to development. That is why China always claims that "development is of overriding importance". Of course, development means not only economic development, but also political, cultural and social development. China has been able to continuously improve the level of human rights protection exactly because it has gasped this main contradiction in socialist construction.

By summarizing history, presenting the present, looking forward to the future, and laying out facts and reasoning things out, the white paper is very compelling and causes major responses both in China and abroad. Deng Xiaoping called it "a magnificent paper, a great paper" . This white paper shows that the CPC's understanding of human rights had reached a new level and it has become new milestone in the construction of human rights system in China.

2. The Gradual Improvement of the Legal System of Human Rights Protection

Basically speaking, the objective of socialist construction is to enable people to fully enjoy human rights and this objective was embodied in the Common Program adopted in the early days of the PRC, the 1954 Constitution, and the outlines of the first few five-year plans. However, because of the above-mentioned reasons, China had gone through a tortuous road in realizing this objective. At the Third Plenary Session of its Eleventh Central Committee, the CPC established the policy of liberating the mind and seeking truth from fact, thereby correcting the course of development. The nation-wide human rights research carried out under the leadership of the CPC Central Committee deepened Chinese people's understanding of human rights, enhanced their consciousness of human rights construction, and further improved the legal system of human rights protection.

Constitutional Guarantees of Human Rights

Major progresses have been made in the constitutional guarantees of human rights since the Third Plenary Session of the Eleventh Central Committee of CPC:

Firstly, in accordance with the will of the people, the 1982 Constitution highlights the protection of the fundamental rights. In August 1980, Deng Xiaoping pointed out in his speech "On the Reform of the System of Party and State Leadership" that: "The Central Committee will submit proposals for revising the Constitution of the People's Republic of China to the Third Session of the Fifth National People's Congress. Our Constitution should be made more complete and precise so as to really ensure the people's right to manage the state organs at all levels as well as the various enterprises and institutions, to guarantee to our people the full enjoyment of their rights as citizens."① The 1982 Constitution inherits the advantages of the 1954 Constitution, contains detailed comprehensive and extensive provisions on citizens' rights, and puts "The Fundamental Rights and Duties of Citizens" in a more prominent position by moving it from Chapter Three to Chapter Two.

Secondly, since the promulgation of the 1982 Constitution, the

---

① *Spura* note 43, p. 339.

National People's Congress, in light of the deepening of the reform and actual needs of socialist construction, adopted in 1988, 1993, 1999 and 2004 four amendments to the Constitution, which contain a total of 31 articles and touch upon such issues as the re-assessment of basic national situation and the basic tasks and objectives of the state, the transition from planed economy to socialist market economy, the constitutional status of non-public sectors of economy, the protection of citizens' private property, the establishment of the strategy of "ruling the country by law and constructing a socialist country under the rule of law", etc. On the basis of existing provisions, these new provisions have strengthened the constitutional protection of citizens' economic, political, cultural, and social rights.

Thirdly, the establishment of the constitutional principle of "the state respects and safeguards human rights." As far as their origins are concerned, human rights are moral rights. The realization of rights is naturally subjected to the constraints of social, economic and cultural conditions. Once conditions permit, the government has the obligation to turn moral rights into legal rights and make further efforts to turn them into the rights actual enjoyed by the people. The constitutional provision of "the state respects and safeguards human rights" embodies the essence of the socialist system with Chinese characteristics, as well as the value-orientation of the Chinese Constitution. The establishment of the principle of "the supremacy of the Constitution and the law" will further impel legislative organs to regulate various relations in accordance with the will of the people and improve the socialist legal system in China; it will inspire and encourage government organs and state personnel to respect the people, to treat all people on an equal basis, to raise their human rights consciousness and quality of service and to truly become people's servants in performing their duties.

Legal Protection of Political Rights

Political rights are the rights of citizens to participate in the administration of state affairs. The Chinese Constitution provides that: "All power in the People's Republic of China belongs to the people. The National People's Congress and the local people's congresses at various levels are the organs through which the people exercise state power." Chinese people's political rights mainly embody in the election of and supervision over duties to the people's congresses and the exercise by elected deputies to people's congresses of rights on behalf of the people. The Chinese Constitution and laws provide for citizens' right to vote: deputies to the people's congresses at the county and the township level shall be elected directly by voters; deputies to the National People's Congress and people's congresses of provinces, autonomous regions, and municipalities directly under the central government shall be elected by the people's congresses at the next lower level. Deputies to the people's congresses at various levels, vice chairmen of the standing committees of people's congresses at various levels, and deputy heads of people's governments at various levels shall be determined by competitive election. Chairmen of the standing committees of people's congresses at various levels, the heads of people's governments, presidents of people's courts and presidents of people's procuratorates at various levels shall also be determined by competitive election. If only one candidate is nominated, a non-competitive election may be conducted. The system of competitive election further improved the election system, and is conducive to enabling more qualified candidates to be elected deputies to people's congresses or state personnel and to exercise state power.

In order to strengthen the supervision over state organs and state personnel, Citizens have the right to criticize and make suggestions regarding any state organ or functionary. Citizens have the right to make to relevant state organs complaints or charges against, or exposures of, any state organ or functionary for violation of the law or dereliction of duty. State organs concerned must deal with complaints, charges or exposures made by citizens in a responsible manner after ascertaining the facts. No one may suppress such complaints, charges and exposures or retaliate against the citizens making them. The implementation of the above provisions has raised the quality and capacity of political participation and consultation, as well as the efficiency of state legislative, administrative and judicial organs.

Legal Protection of Personal Rights and Other Related Rights

Personal rights, including the right of the person, the right to health, the right to personal freedom and the right to personal dignity, are the precondition for the enjoyment of other fundamental human rights. Great importance has been attached to the protection of personal rights by the

Chinese Constitution and laws. The Constitution clearly provides that: "Freedom of the person of citizens is inviolable. No citizen may be arrested except with the approval or by decision of a people's procuratorate or by decision of a people's court, and arrests must be made by a public security organ. Unlawful detention or deprivation or restriction of citizens freedom of the person by other means is prohibited, and unlawful search of the person of citizens is prohibited" and that: "The personal dignity of citizens of the People's Republic of China is inviolable. Insult, libel, false accusation or false incrimination directed against citizens by any means is prohibited." In accordance with the above constitutional provisions, the National People's Congress adopted the Criminal Law and Criminal Procedure Law in September1979. These two laws have strengthened the protection of human rights. Their tasks are to correctly use criminal punishment to fight against all criminal acts, to ensure that innocent people are not incriminated, to uphold the political power of the people's democratic dictatorship and the socialist legal system, and to protect the right of the person, the right to private property, democratic rights, and all other rights of citizens. The Criminal Procedure Law specifically prohibits extorting a confession by torture, and contains strict stipulations on detention, arrest, search, taking of evidence and other coercive measures affecting personal freedom and safety. "Whoever intimidates, insults, beats, or retaliates against a witness or his or her close relatives shall be subject to criminal liability in accordance with law if it constitutes a crime; or shall be subject to punishment in public security administration in accordance with law if it is not criminally punishable."① In order to adapt to the actual situation and in light of the judicial practice in China and useful foreign experiences, China revised the Criminal Procedure Law and the Criminal Law in 1996 and 1997, respectively. The two most important revisions are: first, the recognition of the principle of *nulla poena sine lege* in the General Provisions of the Criminal Law: "Any act deemed by explicit stipulations of law as a crime is to be convicted and given punishment by law and any act that no explicit stipulation of law deems a crime is not to be convicted or given punishment"; and second, the recognition of the principle of presumption of innocence in the General Principles of the Criminal Procedure Law: "No person shall be found guilty without being judged so by a people's court in accordance with law."

① Article 49 of the Criminal Procedure Law.

In order to ensure judicial fairness, both the Constitution and the Criminal Procedure Law stipulate that people's courts shall exercise judicial powers independently in accordance with law, and people's procuratorates shall exercise procuratorial powers independently in accordance with law, without interference by any government authority, social organization, or individual. In the continuous process of practice, China has gradually established the system of open trial, the system of people's assessors, the system of criminal defense, the system of legal supervision, the system of review of death sentences, the system of agent ad litem, and the system of legal aid. Administration of justice is the last line of defense for human rights as well as an indicator of the progress of democratization. The improvement of the above-mentioned laws and systems provides better safeguards for human rights in China.

Legal Safeguards for Economic, Social and Cultural Rights

Attaching importance to the safeguarding of people's economic, social and cultural rights is an essential requirement of socialism as well as an important characteristic of the Chinese Constitution. With respect to economic rights, the Constitution provides that: "The basis of the socialist economic system is socialist public ownership of the means of production, namely, ownership by the whole people and collective ownership by the working people"; that "At the primary stage of socialism, the State upholds the basic economic system in which the public ownership is dominant and diverse forms of ownership develop side by side and keeps to the distribution system in which distribution according to work is dominant and diverse modes of distribution coexist"; and that "The individual economy of urban and rural working people, operating within the limits prescribed by law, is a complement to the socialist public economy." The Constitution also provides that: "Socialist public property is inviolable." and that "The lawful private property of citizens may not be encroached upon. The state protects by law the right of citizens to own private property and the right to inherit private property." In accordance wit the Constitution, the state adopted a series of laws, including the General Principles of Civil Law, the Property Law, the Land Administration Law, the Urban Real Estate Administration Law, the Forest Law, the Grassland Law, the Mineral Resource Law, the Coal Industry Law, the Energy Conservation Law, the Patent Law, the

Copyright Law, the Trade Mark Law and the Contract Law, so as to safeguard the property right and intellectual property right, which are the foundation of socialist market economy. It has also adopted the Company Law, the Partnership Enterprise Law, the Law on Individual Proprietorship Enterprises, the Law on Farmers'Professional Cooperatives, the Anti-Monopoly Law and the Anti-Unfair Competition Law, so as to safeguard the legal status of market subjects, to ensure their equal participation in market competition and the healthy operation of socialist market economy. With respect to social and cultural rights, the Constitution provides that the state, through the development of social production force, properly apportions accumulation and consumption, concerns itself with the interests of the collective and the individual as well as of the state and, on the basis of expanded production, gradually improves the material and cultural life of the people; that the state establishes and improves the social security system fitting in with the level of economic development; that "the state undertakes the development of socialist education and works to raise the scientific and cultural level of the whole nation"; and that "the state promotes the development of the natural and social sciences, disseminates knowledge of science and technology, and commends and rewards achievements in scientific research as well as technological innovations and inventions." In accordance with the Constitution, the state adopted the Labor Law, the Labor Contract Law, the Employment Promotion Law, the Production safety Law, the Law on the Safety of Mines, the Trade Union Law, the Labor Dispute Mediation and Arbitration Law, the Law on the Prevention and Control of Occupational Diseases, the Provisions on Unemployment Insurance of Staff and Workers in State-owned Enterprises, the Regulations on Unemployment Insurance, the Regulation on Work-Related Injury Insurance, the Regulations on Guaranteeing Minimum Subsistence for City Residents and the Decision of the State Council on Establishing Urban Employees'Basic Medical Insurance System, so as to safeguard employment, production safety, and the basic livelihood of retired and unemployed workers and urban residents. China has also adopted the Production Quality Law, the Food Quality Law, the Agricultural Product Quality Safety Law, the Pharmaceutical Administration Law, the Law on the Protection of Consumer Rights and Interests, the Environmental Protection Law, the Law on the Prevention and Control of Atmospheric Pollution, the Water Conservation Law, the Law on the Prevention and

Control of Water Pollution, the Law on the Protection of Marine Environment, and the Law on Prevention of Desertification and Transformation of Deserts, so as to safeguard people's living environment and their right to health; and the state has adopted the Education Law, the Law on Higher Education, the Law on Occupational Education, the Law on Private Education, the National Defense Education Law, the Teachers' Law, the Law on the Popularization of Education in Science, and Sports Law, so as to popularize nine-year compulsory education, develop secondary education, occupational education and higher education, and raise citizens' cultural quality and scientific knowledge.

Legal Safeguards for the Rights of Ethnic Minorities

China is unified multi-ethnic country with a total of 56 ethnic groups. The Han people make up 92% while the other 55 ethnic groups make up 8% of the total population of the country. The Chinese government has always attached great importance to ethnic equality and solidarity. Mao Zedong once pointed out that: "The unification of the country, the unity of the people, and the unity of various ethnic groups in the country are the basic guarantees for the victory of our cause."① On the basis of the 1954 Constitution, the 1982 Constitution contains more detailed provisions on the affairs and rights of ethnic minorities. It stipulates in the General Principles that "All nationalities in the People's Republic of China are equal. The state protects the lawful rights and interests of the minority nationalities and upholds and develops a relationship of equality, unity and mutual assistance among all of China's nationalities. Discrimination against and oppression of any nationality are prohibited; any act which undermines the unity of the nationalities or instigates division is prohibited." and that "Regional autonomy is practiced in areas where people of minority nationalities live in concentrated communities; in these areas, organs of self-government are established to exercise the power of autonomy. All national autonomous areas are integral parts of the People's Republic of China. All nationalities have the freedom to use and develop their own spoken and written languages and to preserve or reform their own folkways and customs."

① Mao Zedong, *Selected Works of Mao Zedong*, vol. 5, People's Publishing House, 1977, p. 363.

Apart from the " Preamble " and " General Principles ", the 1982 Constitution contains a special section on "the Organs of Self-government of National Autonomous Areas" in Chapter Three ("State Organs") . Among the 138 articles in the Constitution, 28 concern ethnic minorities. In accordance with the Constitution, China adopted the Law on Regional National Autonomy in 1984, which indicated that system of regional national autonomy had been brought into the orbit of law. According to the Constitution and the Law on Regional National Autonomy, organs of self-government of national autonomous areas share common characteristics with ordinary local state organs while at the same time have their unique characteristics. For examples, among the chairman and vice-chairmen of the standing committee of the people's congress of a national autonomous area shall be one or more citizens of the nationality exercising regional autonomy in the area. The chairman of an autonomous region, the prefect of an autonomous prefecture or the head of an autonomous county shall be a citizen of the nationality exercising regional autonomy in the area concerned. The people's governments of national autonomous areas shall apply the system of giving overall responsibility to the chairman of an autonomous region. Other posts in the people's government of an autonomous region, an autonomous prefecture or an autonomous county shall rationally be assumed by people of the nationality exercising regional autonomy and of other minority nationalities in the area concerned. Organs of self-government enjoy greater power than other local state organs in making local regulations and separate regulations and in economic management. Ethnic minorities have always given preferential treatment in the right to participation in the highest state organs and local state organs at various levels. The percentage of ethnic minorities among the deputies to each National People's Congress has been much higher than the percentage of ethnic minorities in the total population. The state and economically developed areas have been continuously increasing their support to ethnic minority areas to promote the economic, cultural and social development in these areas. Because of such support, the increase in GDP and per capita income in ethnic minority areas has been higher than other areas for many consecutive years. With the implementation of the strategy of developing western areas, there will be more rapid development in economic, political, cultural and social rights in ethnic minority areas.

Legal Safeguards for the Rights of Women, Children and Disabled Persons

China has always attached great importance to the safeguarding of the rights of women, children and disabled persons, who are disadvantaged groups of society. Women make up one half of the total population in the country and are an important force in the construction of socialism. Children are the future of the country and their healthy development is the wish of the whole society. The Constitution clearly stipulates that: "Women in the People's Republic of China enjoy equal rights with men in all spheres of life, including political, economic, cultural, social and family life" that "Marriage, the family and mother and child are protected by the state" and that: "Violation of the freedom of marriage is prohibited. Maltreatment of old people, women and children is prohibited." In accordance with the Constitution, the state has promulgated the Marriage Law, the Inheritance Law, the Election Law, the General Principles of the Civil Law, and Civil Procedure Law, which contain specific provisions on the protection of the rights of women and children. In order to strengthen the protection of rights of women and children, the state promulgated in early 1990s the Law on the Protection of Minors, the Law on the Protection of Women's Rights and Interests, and the Law on Maternal and Infant Health Care. According to the Constitution and the relevant laws, women enjoy political rights, cultural rights, labor rights, property rights, personal rights, marriage rights and family rights on an equal basis with men. The Law on the Protection of Minors stipulates that "The State shall protect the rights of the person and property as well as other lawful rights and interests of minors from violation." And it provides for various principles on the protection of minors and the responsibilities of families, schools, society and judicial organs in this respect. In order to implement the above legal provisions, the State Council promulgated the Program for the Development of Chinese Women and the Program for the Development of Children's Rights in China. The implementation of these laws and programs has given full play to the role of women in socialist economic construction and in the administration of state and social affairs, promoted the realization of the equal status of women in social and family life, and effectively safeguarded children's right to life, right to health, right to education, their special rights in judicial process.

Because of its huge population, China has a large number of people with disabilities. Currently there are over 83 million disabled people in China, making up about 6.34% of the total population in the country. The protection of the rights of disable people is of great importance to social stability and sustainable economic development. The Constitution provides that: "Citizens of the People's Republic of China have the right to material assistance from the state and society when they are old, ill or disabled. The state and society ensure the livelihood of disabled members of the armed forces and help make arrangements for the work, livelihood and education of the blind, deaf-mutes and other handicapped citizens." In accordance with the Constitution, the state adopted the Law on the Protection of Disabled Persons in 1990 and revised the law in 2008 so as to adapt to new developments of situation. Many other laws, such as Election Law, the General Principles of the Civil Law, the Civil Procedure Law, the Marriage Law, the Inheritance Law, the Military Service Law, and the Law on Compulsory Education, also contain special provisions on the protection of the rights and interests of disabled persons. Moreover, the State Council and the relevant government departments have also adopted a series of administrative rules and regulations on the protection of disabled persons, such as the Five-year Development Plan for Disabled Persons, Several Opinions on the Development of Education for Disabled Persons, the Regulations on the Employment of Disabled Persons, the National Plan for the Implementation of Three Kinds of Rehabilitation Work, the Notice on the Exemption of Taxation for Disabled Persons Who Start Their Own Individual Business, and the Notice on the Taxation of Social Welfare Units. The organs of power of various provinces, autonomous regions and municipalities directly under the Central Government have also adopted local regulations on the protection of rights and interests of disabled persons. The law specifically prohibits discrimination against, insult, maltreatment, and abandoning of and infringement upon the rights of disabled persons. Whoever infringes upon the right of person or other lawful rights of disabled persons by taking advantage of their disabilities and constitutes a crime shall be given a heavier punishment in accordance with the relevant provisions of the Criminal Law. the implementation of the above-mentioned laws have effectively safeguarded the right to vote and the right to stand for election, the property right and other civil rights and interests, the equal rights in family life, the right to education, and the right to preferential treatment in employment of disabled persons. The state has established China Disabled Persons Federation with local branches in all provinces, municipalities, and counties except for Taiwan. These organizations are playing an important role in safeguarding the rights of disabled persons.

The most important characteristic of human rights protection system in China is genuineness. During the thirty years since the reform and opening up, China, by developing the socialist market economy and deepening reform on the political system, has already established a basic human rights safeguarding system and laid a more solid foundation for the protection of human rights. Now the protection of various human rights in China has reached an unprecedented level in history. With respect to political rights and freedom, Chinese people enjoy the right to vote and the right to stand for election in accordance with law. The turnout in the election of each people's congress has been over 90%. People administrate state and social, economic, and cultural affairs through various channels and forms; they enjoy the freedoms of expression, of the press, of association, of procession and of demonstration, and of religious belief; and they supervise over state organs and state personnel by means of communication, meeting, mess media, and the Internet. With respect to economic rights, with the rapid development of the socialist market economy, China became the third biggest economy in the world in 2008, with GDP exceeding 30 trillion yuan. The disposable income of urban residents had increased from 1, 378 yuan in 1990 to 15, 781 yuan in 2008; the per capita net income of rural residents had increased from 686 yuan in 1990 to 4, 761 yuan in 2008; and the saving deposits of urban residents increased from 703. 4 billion yuan at the end of 1990 to 21. 7885 trillion yuan at the end of 2008. The housing of urban residents has not only increased in terms of floor space, but also become an important part of their private property. With respect to employment and social rights, an average of more than 10 million new jobs were created each year in urban areas in the whole country and over 10 million laborers were transferred from rural to urban areas during the past five years. The registered unemployment rate in urban areas has been kept under 5%. The problem of reemployment of laid-off workers and employment of incoming labor force has been basically solved.

In recent years, the pension of enterprise retirees has been continuously raised and urban pension system continuously improved. In 2008, over 200 million people were covered by pension system and over 400 million people covered by basic medical insurance system. In rural areas, an overall minimum living guarantee system was established and the New Rural Co-operative Medical System has been continuously improved, covering 814 million people or 91.5% of the rural population. With respect to cultural rights, all school-age children in rural areas have been exempted from tuition and miscellaneous fees and provided free textbooks and resident students from poverty-stricken families were provided subsistence allowance. Beginning from the second half of 2008, all school-age children in urban areas have also been exempted from tuition and miscellaneous fees. While implementing the nine-year compulsory education system, the state is also energetically developing secondary and higher vocational education and regular higher education. In 2008, there were over 30 million students in institutions of secondary and higher vocational education, and 21.495 million undergraduate and graduate students in regular institutions of higher education. The development of education has promoted economic, cultural, scientific and technological development and created condition for the comprehensive and free development of human beings.

3. Adoption of National Human Rights Action Plans

We can see from the development of the legal system of human rights protection since the Third Plenary Session of the CPC Eleventh Central Committee that every progress made in this field is the result of emancipation of mind and renewal of ideas under the leadership of the CPC. Safeguarding of human rights is the objective of long-term struggle by the CPC and the Chinese government as well as the foundation of the ruling of the country by the CPC. As mentioned above, China has already made great achievements in the construction of human rights legal system. Nevertheless, many improvements still need to be made in this field in light of the inherent requirement of the socialist system with Chinese characteristics and the level of social, economic, and cultural development in the country. In April 2009, in order to further improve the legal system of human rights protection and promote the development of human rights cause in China and in response to the UN's proposal to adopt national human rights action plans, the Chinese government promulgated the National Human Rights Action Plan of China (2009—2010) in accordance with the basic principle of "respecting and safeguarding human rights" in Chinese Constitution and the basic spirit of the Universal

Declaration of Human Rights and the two international human rights covenants.

The Action Plan bases itself on the actual situation in China, adheres to the principle of interdependence and indivisibility of all human rights, pushes in a comprehensive way the coordinated development of economic, cultural, civil and political rights in accordance with state laws, and promotes the harmonious development of mankind and the environment. Apart from the Introduction, this important document is divided into the following five parts: I. Guarantee of Economic, Social and Cultural Rights, including Right to work; Right to basic living conditions; Right to social security; Right to health; Right to education; Cultural rights; Environmental rights; Safeguarding farmers' rights and interests; and Guarantee of human rights in the reconstruction of areas hit by the devastating earthquake in Wenchuan, Sichuan Province; II. Guarantee of Civil and Political Rights, including: Rights of the person; Rights of detainees; The right to a fair trial; Freedom of religious belief; The right to be informed; The right to participate; The right to be heard; and The right to oversee; III. Guarantee of the Rights and Interests of Ethnic Minorities, Women, Children, Elderly People and the Disabled, including The rights of ethnic minorities; Women's rights; Children's rights; Senior citizens' rights; The rights of the disabled; IV. Education in Human Rights; and V. Performing International Human Rights Duties, and Conducting Exchanges and Cooperation in the Field of International Human Rights. This Action Plan has the following characteristics:

Firstly, generally speaking, it is the concretization of constitutional and legal provisions on the safeguarding of human rights. It clearly sets out the concrete objectives to be achieved in the relevant fields within the two-year period covered by the Plan. Using concrete figures in the part on economic, social and cultural rights and putting forward specific requirements in the part on civil and political rights, it has high operability and is easy to assess and supervise.

Secondly, the method of writing and the content of the Part I and Part II of the Action Plan, namely the part on the protection of economic, social and cultural rights and the part on the protection of civil and political rights, dovetail with the International Covenant of Economic, Social and Cultural Rights (ICESCR) and the International Covenant on Civil and Political Rights (ICCPR). China has ratified the ICESCR and signed the

ICCPR. These two parts cover a wide range of fields. Apart from listing safeguards for various rights, the part on economic, social and cultural rights also contains two special sections on the protection of farmers' rights and interests and on the guarantee of human rights in the reconstruction of areas hit by the devastating earthquake in Wenchuan, Sichuan Province. This is because the issue of farmers' rights and interests affects a large number of people and the issue of guarantee of human rights in the reconstruction after Wenchuan Earthquake was a very prominent issue, both need to be attached special importance to. In the part on civil and political rights, emphasis is laid on the prohibition of illegal, wrongful or prolonged detention, and extorting a confession by torture, the right to defense and the right to fair trial, so as to realize fairness and justice in the whole society. Moreover, religious freedom, the right to know, the right to participation, and the right to oversee are inherent parts of socialist democracy and human rights, as well as important guarantees of social stability.

Thirdly, ethnic minorities, women, children, the elderly and the disabled are known as "vulnerable groups", namely groups whose rights are often infringed upon or ignored. The protection of the rights of these groups is an important part of international human rights conventions. The rights of these groups are characterized by comprehensiveness. Namely they involve economic, social and cultural rights as well as civil and political rights. Attention should be paid both to the guarantee of their basic livelihood and to their education and employment, as well as to their democratic rights and judicial protection of their rights. Internationally, the protection of the rights of these vulnerable groups is regarded as an indicator of the level of human rights protection in a country.

Fourth, human rights education is a bright spot in the Human Rights Action Plan. This is the first time since the principle of "the state respects and safeguards human rights" was enshrined in the Constitution that the state actively relies on the present systems of compulsory education, secondary education, higher education and vocational education, training organizations in state agencies, as well as the media, including radio, television, news-papers, magazines and the Internet to carry out education in human rights in various forms in a planned way, and to popularize and spread knowledge of the law and human rights. In the previous parts of this article, I have discussed many causes of the problems in the construction of human rights protection system in China in the first 30 years of the PRC. Today, although the human rights situation is much better, many of the causes of human rights violation have not been totally eliminated. The basic solution to these problems is education, namely to raise through education people's consciousness of democracy, the rule of law, freedom, equality and justice and their consciousness as subjects of rights, and to encourage them to uphold individual and collective rights and to supervise public power. From the short-term and local point of view, the rise of rights consciousness may lead to increase of rights demands and consequently more social conflicts, but from the long term and overall point of view, it is conducive to resolving, mitigating and reducing conflicts and to maintaining political and social stability, as long as the human rights education is focused on priorities and the CPC cadres and state personnel can play an exemplary role and live what they teaches.

Fifth, the implementation of international human rights obligations and exchange and cooperation in the field of international human rights. This part of the Action Plan shows China's basic attitude towards the Universal Declaration of Human Rights and other international human rights conventions ratified by China, namely the human rights commitment made by China to international community. Strengthening international exchange and cooperation in the field of human rights is conducive to China's integration into international community as well as to increasing China's soft power.

The Action Plan is based on strong mass support and social need. After realizing moderate prosperity and enabling people to have adequate food and clothing, the CPC and the Chinese government, in response to people's demand, put forward in a timely manner the policy of adhering to the scientific outlook on development, namely people-oriented, comprehensive, coordinated and sustainable development, and constructing a harmonious socialist well-off society in an all-round way, thus placing safeguarding people's livelihood and rights high on its agenda. The National Human Rights Action Plan is the embodiment of this policy. Once adopted, it has received positive response from state organs, institutions of higher education, research institutes and NGOs. The key to the implementation of the Action Plan is action. It clearly provides that: "Governments and government departments at all levels shall make the action plan part of their responsibilities, and proactively implement it in line with the principle of "each performing its own functions and sharing out the work and responsibilities." All enterprises, public institutions, social and non-governmental organizations, press and media agencies, and the general public shall give vigorous publicity to this action plan, and expedite its implementation." Meanwhile, the government has also established a "joint meeting mechanism for the implementation of the National Human Rights Action Plan", participated by the relevant functional departments of the State Council and legislative and judicial organs, to be responsible for the implementation, supervision, and assessment work, thereby providing organizational safeguard for the implementation of the Action Plan. There is every reason to believe that, with the implementation and fulfillment of the first National Human Rights Action Plan and adoption and implementation of new action plans, the level of human rights protection in China will reach a new level.

4. Active Participation in International Exchange and Cooperation in the Field of Human Rights Protection

Protection of human rights is essentially an internal affair of each sovereign state. However, since many human rights violations, including those committed by theocratic rulers of Western Europe in the Middle Ages, by colonialists and imperialists in the process of aggression against weak and small nations in modern history, and by German Nazis and Japanese militarists during the World War II, have been committed against people in other countries, human rights issue has become an international issue. The UN Charter, adopted in San Francisco in June 1945, declares at its very beginning that: "We the peoples of the United Nations determined to save succeeding generations from the scourge of war, which twice in our lifetime has brought untold sorrow to mankind, and to reaffirm faith in fundamental human rights, in the dignity and worth of the human person, in the equal rights of men and women and of nations large and small, and to establish conditions under which justice and respect for the obligations arising from treaties and other sources of international law can be maintained, and to promote social progress and better standards of life in larger freedom, and for these ends, to practice tolerance and live together in peace with one another as good neighbours, and to unite our strength to maintain international peace and security..."① To strengthen the international protection of human rights, the UN General Assembly adopted the Universal Declaration of Human Rights in December 1948,

① See Charter of the United Nations, in *supra* note 32, pp. 928—929.

which further points out that: "Whereas disregard and contempt for human rights have resulted in barbarous acts which have outraged the conscience of mankind, ... Whereas the peoples of the United Nations have in the Charter reaffirmed their faith in fundamental human rights, in the dignity and worth of the human person and in the equal rights of men and women and have determined to promote social progress and better standards of life in larger freedom, Whereas Member States have pledged themselves to achieve, in cooperation with the United Nations, the promotion of universal respect for and observance of human rights and fundamental freedoms, Whereas a common understanding of these rights and freedoms is of the greatest importance for the full realization of this pledge."① China is among the first signatories of the UN Charter and one of the permanent members of the UN Security Council, and Chinese representatives participated in the drafting of the Universal Declaration of Human Rights. In May 1955, before China's lawful seat in the UN was restored, Chinese Primer Zhou Enlai pointed at an enlarged meeting of the Standing Committee of the National People's Congress that: "The ten principles provided for in Bandung Declaration include the principle of respecting fundamental human rights and respecting the purposes and principles of the United Nations Charter... they are always advocated by Chinese people and abided by the Chinese government." After the restoration of China's legitimate seat in the UN and the UN Security Council in 1971, the Chinese government has actively participated in various activities of international protection of human rights and widely praised for doing so.

Sending Representatives to Participate in Various Human Rights Meetings and in the Drafting and Adoption of Human Rights Instruments Organized by the UN and Its Subsidiary Organs

After the restoration of its legitimate seat in the UN, China has sent delegation to every meeting of the UN General Assembly and the Economic and Social Council participated in the deliberation of various issues, including human rights issues. Chinese delegation attended the annual session of UN Human Rights Commission as observer in 1979, 1980 and

① See Universal Declaration of Human Rights, in Institute of Law, Chinese Academy of Social Sciences (ed.), *International Instruments of Human Rights and International Institutions of Human Rights*, Beijing: Social Sciences Documentation Publishing House, 1993, p. 3.

1981. Since its was elected to the UN Human Rights Commission in 1981, China had been re-elected to the Commission each year until 2006, when the Commission was replaced by newly-established UN Human Rights Council, to which China was also elected as a member. Chinese delegation has participated in the drafting and adoption of many UN human rights instruments, including the Convention on the Rights of the Child, the International Convention on the Protection of the Rights of All Migrant Workers and Members of Their Families, Convention against Torture and Other Cruel, Inhuman or Degrading Treatment or Punishment, Declaration on the Right and Responsibility of Individuals, Groups and Organs of Society to Promote and Protect Universally Recognized Human Rights and Fundamental Freedoms, Declaration on the Rights of Persons Belonging to National or Ethnic, Religious and Linguistic Minorities, and it has played a crucial role in the drafting of the UN Declaration on the Right to Development. China has always maintained that human rights are both individual and collective rights and that the right to development should be given priority to in developing countries. China has made great contribution to the enrichment and development of the concept of human rights. While actively participating in international protection of human rights, the Chinese government has ratified 25 international human rights conventions, including such core human rights conventions as the ICESCR, International Convention on the Elimination of All Forms of Racial Discrimination, Convention on the Elimination of All Forms of Discrimination against Women, Convention against Torture and Other Cruel, Inhuman or Degrading Treatment or Punishment, Convention on the Rights of the Child, and Convention Relating to the Status of Refugees. The Chinese government strictly implements its obligations under various human rights conventions, submits in a timely manner reports on the implementation of these conventions, and takes active measures to improve human rights protection laws and systems in accordance with these conventions.

Opposing Double Standard and Advocating Equal Dialogue instead of Confrontation in the Field of Human Rights

By using their dominant position in international affairs since the modern time, Western countries represented by the U. S. have always take their own national interests as the starting point of treatment of human rights issues. This is prominently reflected in the "double standard" they have always pursued on human rights issues. The so-called "double standard" means to adopt one standard for themselves, their allies, and those considered by them as potential allies, and another standard for those considered by them as enemies or potential adversaries. Actually, all countries in today's world have some unresolved human rights problems. However, the U. S. and other western countries, by relying on their "advantages" formed on the basis of ill-gotten wealth their ancestors grabbed from peoples in Asia, Africa and Latin America, make indiscreet criticisms against China and some other developing countries from high moral ground, introduce ideology into the field of human rights, and try to impose their own values and institutional modes on others. For this purpose, they have long treated UN Human Rights Commission as an arena for political struggle. Every year, the State Department of the U. S. publishes the so-called "country reports on human rights", making accusations against other countries and interfering their internal affairs, and acting like an international human rights police, totally ignoring the large-scale violations of human rights committed by themselves either overtly or covertly in the Persian Gulf region, in the Middle East and in many other countries. To uphold its national dignity, China has carried out struggle against such acts with good reason, to its own advantage and with restraint. Taking the overall situation of international protection of human rights as its starting point, China has also proposed to carry out equal dialogue and exchange between states and between states and intergovernmental organizations, such as EU, in the field of human rights. This proposal has received positive response from major countries in the world. Beginning from the 1990s, China has carried out dozens of bilateral and multilateral dialogues and exchanges with many countries in Americas, Europe, Oceania and other continents. It has been generally recognized that these dialogues and exchanges have to a certain extent increased mutual understanding between China and western countries.

Upholding International Justice, Participating in Humanitarian Assistance and Promoting the Construction of a Harmonious Society

Based on the fine cultural tradition of the Chinese nation and the essential characteristics of socialism, China has always upheld international justice. As early as in the 1950s, China, together with India, Burma and other third world countries, had advocated the "Five Principles of Peaceful Coexistence", namely the principles of mutual respect for each other's territorial integrity and sovereignty, mutual non-aggression, mutual non-interference in each other's internal affairs, equality and cooperation for mutual benefit, and peaceful co-existence, which have been recognized by most developing countries in the world. China has abided by these principles in its foreign relationship and made unremitting efforts in uphold national independence, fighting against hegemonism, and stopping large-scale violation of human rights, thereby wining the trust and support of many third world countries. After the restoration of its legitimate seat in the UN, China, as a permanent member of the UN Security Council, has upheld international justice in dealing many difficult international issues, such as the issues of Cambodia, Palestine and occupied Arab territories, thereby bringing solution to these problems or promoting their development towards a reasonable solution. In order to solve humanitarian crises in some countries and regions, China, at the request of the UN, has sent over 2, 000 peacekeepers to 18 countries, including Haiti, Cambodia, and Darfur, ranking first among permanent members of the UN Security Council in the contribution of soldiers to UN peacekeeping missions and winning worldwide acclaim for the performance of Chinese soldiers in these peacekeeping missions. In order to construct a "social and international order" in which the rights and freedoms set forth in the Universal Declaration of Human Rights can be fully realized, China calls for the establishment of a new international order and promotes the construction of a harmonious world of lasting peace and common prosperity. In the so-called harmonious world, states should promote democracy, harmony, collaboration and win-win solutions in international relations: politically, all countries should respect each other and conduct consultations on an equal footing in a common endeavor to promote democracy in international relations; economically, they should cooperate with each other, draw on each other's strengths and work together to advance economic globalization in the direction of balanced development, shared benefits and win-win progress; culturally, they should learn from each other in the spirit of seeking common ground while shelving differences, respect the diversity of the world, and make joint efforts to advance human civilization; in the area of security, they should trust each other, strengthen cooperation, settle international disputes by peaceful means, rather than by war, and work together to safeguard peace and stability in the world; on environmental issues, they should assist and cooperate with each other in conservation efforts to take good care of the Earth, the only home of human beings. This proposal won the immediate support of many peace-loving and human rights-respecting states and people as soon as it was put forward. We have every reason to believe that, with passage of time, it will receive even wider response.

The Chinese people had undergone a tortuous road in the struggle for human rights. The establishment of the PRC laid a solid foundation for the development of legal system of human rights protection in China. Since the Third Plenary Session of the Eleventh Central Committee of the CPC, China, by adhering to the ideological line of emancipating the mind and seeking truth from facts and the strategy of reform and opening up, has achieved unprecedented level of development of socialism with Chinese characteristics and of legal protection of human rights. Nevertheless, we should never become complacent and cease to advance because Chinese people have high expectation for human rights protection. Meanwhile, the development of international protection of human rights will also always raise new demand on China. Therefore, China must make continuous progresses in the field of human rights protection. The political report of the Seventeenth National Congress of the CPC comprehensively explains the guideline of constructing socialism with Chinese characteristics and is a new declaration of human rights construction in China. In accordance with the guideline adopted at the Seventeenth National Congress of the CPC, the CPC and the Chinese government have already recognized the respecting and safeguarding human rights as one of the important principle of ruling the country. As long as we adhere to this principle and to the people-oriented scientific outlook on development, deepen our understanding of the importance of human rights, and make continuous efforts on a new starting point, we will be able to push the protection of the human rights of 1.3 billion Chinese people to a higher level, thereby making greater contribution to the cause of international protection of human rights.

Safeguarding Human Rights and the Struggle for and Development of Socialist Democracy:

the Chinese Practice and Experience[①]

Respecting and safeguarding human rights is the objective of the Universal Declaration of Human Rights and human rights conventions as well as a basic principle of the Chinese Constitution. Practice shows that, in order for human rights to be respected and safeguarded, it is necessary to struggle for democracy and develop socialist democracy. Carrying out careful research on and correctly understanding the relationship between human rights and democracy is of great significance to promoting the construction of socialism with Chinese characteristics and to the effective protection of human rights.

I. Marxist Theory on Human Rights and the Full Development and Emancipation of Human Beings

The so-called human rights are the rights of human beings, namely the rights all human beings enjoy or should enjoy by virtue of their natural or social attributes. The slogan of human rights was put forward by bourgeois enlightenment thinkers, but the concept of human rights has been gradually enriched and developed through the long-term struggle by the masses of people under the guidance of Marxist theory on the full development and emancipation of human beings. The subjects of human

---

① Originally a paper submitted to the Seminar on the Development and Innovation of Human Rights Theory and Practice in China, organized by China Society for Human Rights Studies and held in Beijing in August 2011.

rights are all human beings, including not only individuals, but also collectives, not only nationals, but also foreigners and stateless persons. The objects of human rights are all rights, including both fundamental rights and non-fundamental rights, both legal rights and moral rights, both civil and political rights and economic, social and cultural rights—namely all rights that should be enjoyed by all human beings.

The struggle over rights have never ceased ever since their emergence in human history. Italian Poet Dante, a pioneer of the Renaissance in Europe, was the first person in history to put forward the term "human rights" and linked it to political system and the development of a country. However, it was bourgeois enlightenment thinkers who elaborated on the concept of human rights and used it as weapon to fight against divine and monarchical powers. They maintained that freedom, equality and independence are inherent and inalienable "human rights" or "natural rights" of every individual. This theory was used to unit members of the bourgeoisie and other oppressed people at that time to fight against feudal autocratic rule and, after the victor of bourgeois revolution, became a constitutional and legal principle in capitalist countries.

The Marxists fully recognize the historical progressiveness of bourgeois democracy and human rights. Carl Marx called the American Declaration of Independence "the first declaration of human rights" in human history. ①Frederick Engels held that the U. S. Constitution, although incomplete, was "the first constitution to recognize human rights". ②The Resolution of the CPC Central Committee on the Guiding Principles for Building a Socialist Society with an Advanced Level of Culture and Ideology points out that: "The ideas of democracy, freedom, equality, and fraternity formed during the struggle carried out by the emerging bourgeoisie and working people against feudal autocratic system represents a major emancipation of the mind in the human history." Marxists recognize the historical progressiveness of bourgeois democracy, freedom and human rights while at the same time also point out their class limitations. They point out that the bourgeoisie built the capitalist social

① *Complete Works of Marx and Engels* (Chinese Edition), vol. 10, People's Publishing House, 1964, p. 20.

② *Selected Works of Marx and Engels* (Chinese Edition), vol. 3, People's Publishing House, 1995, p. 447.

system on the ruins of the feudal system, realized the political emancipation of the state, and allowed workers and other working people to enjoy certain political rights on the condition of not endangering the basic interests of the bourgeois. However, political rights are inseparable from economic, social and cultural rights. Capitalist society is a kingdom of owners of commodities. The bourgeoisie controls social wealth and, by relying on their wealth, controls powerful state organs. The working class and other working people remain in a exploited and oppressed position. Without economic, social and cultural rights, they cannot truly enjoy political rights. Therefore, the equality and freedom declared by the bourgeois law can only be said to be the equality and freedom of the bourgeoisie before the law and human rights are the rights of the bourgeoisie. After achieving the victor of revolution, the bourgeoisie not only treacherously abandoned its former allies—the working class and other working people—but also deprived the right to vote and the right of political participation of broad masses of women, including the female members of its own class. As for the black people, Indians, indigenous people, and people in the colonies and semi-colonies, they are not regarded as human in the bourgeois concept of human rights. The rights of the oppressed people of different races, ethnic groups, classes and genders are recognized by law only after long and hard struggle. Some of their rights are not recognized even today.

The over 200-year history of struggle has shown that human rights have been developed through the struggle by the working people. Although the bourgeoisie abandoned their former allies after the success of the revolution, Marxists hold that the working class should not reject the limited political rights provided by bourgeois democratic system, but should exercise and expand them to the maximum extent possible to struggle for economic, social and cultural rights. Carl Marx pointed out that, the struggle for these rights "is feasible only within a democratic republic" . [①]It was exactly because of the persistent and dauntless by the working class and other working people that some capitalist countries, in order to avoid the collapse of their own rule together with the society, were forced to enshrine economic, social and cultural rights into their constitutions and laws and implement them conditionally. It was also as a

---

① *Selected Works of Marx and Engels* (Chinese Edition), vol. 3, People's Publishing House, 1995, p. 314.

result of the struggle by the working class and broad masses of working people and the promotion by socialist countries that economic, social and cultural rights have become the focus of attention of countries around the world. In December 1966, the UN adopted the International Covenant on Economic, Social and Cultural Rights which, together with the International Covenant of Civil and Political Rights, adopted at the same day, and the 1948 Universal Declaration of Human Rights, become known as the International Bill of Human Rights.

The Marxists hold that human rights and the full emancipation of human beings are consistent with each other. As far as individuals are concerned, the full development of human beings means that, under the condition of gradually eliminating the manual labor and mental labor, people can choose the professions they like and engage in various health-giving activities, such as artistic, cultural and sports activities in their increasingly growing spare time. As far as collectives are concerned, the full development of human beings means that people are able to follow the objective law of social development, establish a scientific outlook of development, "work according to one's ability", conscientiously develop economic, political, social and cultural undertakings, continuously satisfy their growing material and cultural needs, and ultimately build a society which will be an association in which the free development of each is the condition for the free development of all. [①]The meanings of "the free development of each" and "the free development of all" stressed by Marx are clear. The day of the establishment of such an association is the day of the complete emancipation of and the full enjoyment of human rights by all human beings.

We say that human rights and the comprehensive development and emancipation of human beings are consistent with each other because both of them take human beings as their subjects and rights as their objects. Development itself has been recognized by international human rights instruments as a right. The right to development is a comprehensive and inalienable fundamental right. A precondition for the realization of both human rights and the comprehensive development and emancipation of human beings is the continuous and high-level development of social production force. Marx and Engels had once said that: "Right can never

① *Selected Works of Marx and Engels* (Chinese Edition), vol. 1, People's Publishing House, 1995, p. 294.

be higher than the economic structure of society and its cultural development conditioned thereby."① The development of the production force is the basis of the comprehensive development and emancipation of human beings. In order to develop this basis, people must realize that certain obstacles to development once regarded as "secret limits" must be continuously eliminated. Marx pointed out straightforwardly that: "'Liberation' is an historical and not a mental act, and it is brought about by historical conditions, the development of industry, commerce, agriculture, the conditions of intercourse."② In a word, they believed that the elimination of class oppression and exploitation that impede the development of the production force, the establishment of socialist democracy and the realization of high-level of development of productive force are the necessary conditions for the safeguarding of human rights, as well as for the comprehensive development and total liberation of the mankind.

II. Democracy: a Precondition for the Realization of Human Rights

Although all people strive for liberation and human rights, historical development shows that no exploiting class who is in a dominant position is willing to hand over rights to the exploited class without a struggle. For this reason, Marx and Engels pointed out that "the first step in the revolution by the working class is to raise the proletariat to the position of ruling class to win the battle of democracy."③ Here, the term "democracy" is used at the level of people's sovereignty and political system and "struggle for democracy" means to seize state power and establish a state of the sovereignty of the working class and other working people. Although the above comments mentioned only the working class, they have universal theoretical significance. Under the feudal autocratic system, the

① *Selected Works of Marx and Engels* (Chinese Edition), vol. 3, People's Publishing House, 1995, p. 305.

② *Complete Works of Marx and Engels* (Chinese Edition), vol. 42, People's Publishing House, 1964, p. 368.

③ *Selected Works of Marx and Engels* (Chinese Edition), vol. 1, People's Publishing House, 1995, p. 293.

bourgeoisies was in an oppressed position and their rights were subjected to many restrictions. In order to realize its own freedom, equality and human rights, it must overthrow feudal autocratic rule and establish a bourgeois republic. The bourgeois republic, under the disguise of democracy, safeguards only the human rights of the bourgeoisie while imposes dictatorship on the working class and other working people. Therefore it is only another form of fetters to the latter. It is exactly for this reason that the working class, in order to realize its own rights and liberation, must establish its own political power. Before that, however, the working should struggle for civil rights wherever such rights do not exist. It was exactly under the guidance of the Marxist theory that working class and other working people have adopted the strategy of taking the seizure of state power as their general objective while at same time actively struggle for democratic rights in bourgeois states so as to blaze a trail for their own liberation and enjoyment of human rights. Take the socialist revolution in Russia as an example. Russia had been an impoverished backward agricultural country ruled by the tsar and people were under severe oppression and exploitation. In order to fight for their own rights, the proletarian party headed by Lenin first formed an alliance with the bourgeoisie and overthrew the rule of the Tsar in February 1917 and then formed an alliance with the peasants and overthrew the bourgeois government through the October Revolution and established a socialist state. As soon as it was established, the Bolshevik government promulgated the Decree on Land, which abolished the feudal land ownership system and distributed land to peasants. In January 1918 the first Soviet Constitution was promulgated. Chapter one of the Constitution, "Declaration of the Rights of the Working and Exploited People", recognized the extensive rights of the broad masses of people, expanded the scope of the subjects enjoying democracy, thereby truly making the working people the masters of their own country. Lenin pointed out that the Soviet political power: "Soviet organisation has developed incomparably farther and deeper that feature of bourgeois democracy which marks historically its great progressive nature as compared with medieval times, i. e. , the participation of the people in the election of individuals to office... Soviet power has, at the same time, swept away those negative aspects of bourgeois democracy. "① The proletarian democracy is a million time more democratic than bourgeois democracy. The success of the Russian socialist revolution and construction not only benefited all the Russian people, but also pointed out the direction of development for the neighboring nations and quickly formed a powerful socialist Soviet confederation, which became the mainstay in the fight against the aggression by Nazi Germany and, by making tremendous national sacrifices, save the mankind from even greater disaster.

The new democratic revolution in China was carried out in a semi-feudal and semi-colonial country and was similar to the Russian Revolution in some aspects. It first overthrew the feudal monarchy through bourgeois revolution (the Revolution of 1911) . However, since the fruit of the revolution was usurped by warlords, the Republic of China that established after the revolution was a republic only in name and no fundamental change in the nature of the society have taken place. A new democracy revolution began with the May 4th Movement in 1919. In old China, Chinese people were under the oppression of imperialism, feudalism and bureaucratic capitalism and had no rights to talk about. The advanced elements of the Chinese society learnt from their personal experience that: "In order to deliver themselves from ignorance and catch up with western nations, the Chinese people must attach equal importance to science and human rights. "② In order to realize national independence and liberation of the people, the Communist Party of China (CPC) has written the struggle for human rights in his banner ever since its establishment in 1921. In 1922, accordance with the resolution of its second national congress, the CPC established alliances for human rights in Beijing, Guangzhou, Shanghai, Shandong and Jiangxi. In early 1923, the CPC led a major strike by Jinghan (Peking-Hankou) Railway workers in 1932, during which it put forward the slogan of "Fight for freedom and human rights; march forward and never retreat" . After the Mukden Incident in 1931, Japanese forces entered the Shanhaiguan Pass. On August 1, 1935, at the time of when the Chinese nation was its crucial moment of life and death, the CPC issued the Appeal to All Fellow

① Collected Works of Lenin, (Chinese edition), People's Publishing House, 1984, vol. 36, p. 84.

② Chen Duxiu, "A Letter to Youth", in *La Jeunesse*, vol. 1 No. 1, September 15, 1915.

Countrymen to Resist Japanese Invasion and Save the Chinese Nation, called upon all Chinese compatriots to "Fight for our homeland! Fight for the survival of the Chinese nation! Fight for national independence! Fight for territorial integrity! And fight for human rights and freedom!" In the process of fighting for human rights, the Chinese were brutally suppressed and slaughtered by feudal warlords, KMT reactionaries and Japanese invaders. Under the leadership of the CPC, the Chinese people defied brutal suppression. On the one hand, they carried out democratic patriotic movement in KMT controlled areas to mobilize the public to oppose dictatorship and civil war and resist Japanese invasion; on the other hand, they took up weapons to resolutely fight against Japanese invaders and KMT reactionaries in the war of national independence and people's war of liberation. Countless revolutionaries advanced wave after wave, many of them had lost their precious lives, in the struggle for national independence and democracy, and ultimately defeated the Japanese invaders in 1945 and won the great victory of people's revolution and founded the People's Republic of China in 1949, thereby ended the history of being trampled upon at will, and achieved democracy and freedom.

III. Safeguarding Human Rights Requires the Development of Socialist Democracy

Under the leadership of the proletariat, Chinese people had achieved democracy and freedom and established their own state. However, this was only the first step in the historical process of full realization of human rights. China still need to make long period of arduous efforts go in order to realize total liberation and full enjoyment of human rights. The establishment of the People's Republic of China marked a new stage in the development of the socialist human rights cause. After over half a century's efforts, the Chinese people, under the leadership of the CPC and the guidance of the following principles, have made remarkable achievements in the field of human rights protection:

1. Strengthening the Construction of Democracy and the Rule of Law and Transforming Due Rights into Legal Rights

Human Rights are universal. Initially they manifest themselves as moral rights or due rights. Historical experience shows that due rights can be actually enjoyed by people only after they are transformed into legal rights. This is because, after the emergence of states, people have always lived in a given state and the improvement of human rights needs to be guaranteed by law. For this reason, the newly-founded government of the PRC had, on the basis of negotiations with various democratic parties, non-party personages, and representatives from all sectors of society, adopted the Common Program of the Chinese People's Political Consultative Conference, which served as a temporary constitution at that time. And on the basis of the Common Program and a nationwide discussion, the Constitution of the PRC was adopted at the first session of the First National People's Congress on September 1954. The Explanations on the First Draft of the Constitution, examined and approved by Mao Zedong, stated that: "The socialization of the state fundamentally guarantees the democratization of the state and requires further democratization of the state. The provisions on the state organs and people's rights in the Draft Constitution provide legal guarantee for the democratization of the state."① The Constitution provides that the People's Republic of China is a state of people's democratic dictatorship led by the working class and based on the alliance of workers and peasants. All state power belongs to the people. The Organs through which the people exercise power are the National People's Congress and the local people's congresses. The people's congress system is the basic state system in China. The objective of state construction is to ensure, by means of socialist industrialization and socialist transformation, the gradual abolition of systems of exploitation and the building of a socialist society and to safeguard the economic, political, social and cultural rights of citizens. Although, due to the mistakes made by the CPC leaders in late 1950s, especially during the Cultural Revolution in during the 1960s, the principles established by the 1954 Constitution and the laws adopted in accordance with the 1954 Constitution were abandoned and people's rights were trampled upon. A fundamental change of situation took place with the convening of the Third Plenary Session of the Eleventh Central Committee of the CPC in 1978, in which the CPC summarized the historical experience since the founding of the PRC and established the policy of liberating the mind, reform and opening up. Deng Xiaoping pointed out that: "It is also essential to ensure the democratic rights of the

---

① Pang Xianzhi and Jin Chongji (eds.), *Biography of Mao Zedong (1949—1976)*, Part I, Central Literature Press, 2003, p. 323.

workers and peasants, including the rights of democratic election, management and supervision." "To ensure people's democracy, we must strengthen our legal system. Democracy has to be institutionalized and written into law, so as to make sure that institutions and laws do not change whenever the leadership changes, or whenever the leaders change their views or shift the focus of their attention."①

In order to truly safeguard people's democratic rights, Deng Xiaoping stated in a speech on the revision of the Constitution that "the Central Committee will submit proposals for revising the Constitution of the People's Republic of China to the Third Session of the Fifth National People's Congress. Our Constitution should be made more complete and precise so as to really ensure the people's right to manage the state organs at all levels as well as the various enterprises and institutions, to guarantee to our people the full enjoyment of their rights as citizens."② In accordance with the spirit of the Third Plenary Session of the Eleventh Central Committee of the CPC, the 1982 Constitution, adopted at the Fifth Session of the Fifth National People's Congress, preserves the advantages of the 1954 Constitution, contains comprehensive provisions on the rights of citizens, and changes the "Fundamental Rights and Duties of Citizens" from Chapter III to Chapter II, thereby putting it on a more prominent position in the Constitution. After the promulgation of the 1982 Constitution, in light of the deepening of the reform and the development of situation, the NPC adopted revised to the Constitution in 1988, 1993, 1999 and 2004. Most of these revisions involve the development of socialist market economy and safeguarding of democratic rights. Especially the principles of "ruling the country by law and constructing a socialist state under the rule of law" and "the state respects and safeguards human rights" have been enshrined in the Constitution, which is of great significance to the development of the socialist democracy and the safeguarding of human rights in China. Both the guiding ideologies of the CPC Central Committee and the content of the Chinese Constitution have show that China has attached great importance to socialist democracy and human rights protection during the half a century and more since the founding of the PRC. This can be seen not only in the Constitution, but

---

① *Selected Works of Deng Xiaoping*, Vol. II (1975—1982), People's Publishing House, 1994, p. 146.

② Ibid., p. 339.

also in the basic laws, administrative regulations, local regulations and rules adopted in accordance with the Constitution in the economic, political, social and cultural fields. It was announced at the Fourth Session of the Eleventh NPC that China had already established a socialist system of law with Chinese characteristics, which is an effective guarantee for socialist democracy and human rights.

2. Strengthening Solidarity among Different Ethnic Groups and Upholding National Unity and Independence

China is a unified multi-national state. As mentioned above, China degenerated into a semi-colonial, semi-feudal country after the Opium War of 1840. During more than 100 year between 1840 and 1949, the British, French, Japanese, US and Russian imperialist powers waged hundreds of wars on varying scales against China, and forced upon the Chinese government over 1,100 unequal treaties.[①] Chinese territories were occupied, Chinese humiliated, and tens of millions of them slaughtered, by imperialists. Large number of Chinese cities and ports were divided up foreign powers as concessions in which "extraterritoriality" was exercised. Foreigners committed all kinds of evils with any restraint. Those who committed crimes were not subjected to the jurisdiction of Chinese administrative or judicial organs whereas the Chinese people had become second-class citizens in their own country. historical facts demonstrated again and again that human rights cannot be safeguarded without state sovereignty and national independence. This is the reason why the Common Program, the 1954 Constitution and the current Constitution all take the strengthening of national solidarity and unity, and opposition of imperialist aggression as one of the important of their content. The Common Program provided that: "The great victories of the Chinese people's war of liberation and of the people's revolution have put an end to the era of the rule of imperialism, feudalism and bureaucratic capitalism in China." The People's Republic of China "strives for independence, democracy, peace, unity, prosperity and strength of China." The current Constitution provides that: "The People's Republic of China is a unitary multi-national state created jointly by the people of all its nationalities... The state will do its utmost to promote the common

① See Information Office of the State Council of the People's Republic of China, *Human Rights in China* (1991), available at: http://www.china.org.cn/e-white/7/index.htm.

prosperity of all the nationalities." "China consistently carries out an independent foreign policy and adheres to the five principles of mutual respect for sovereignty and territorial integrity, mutual non-aggression, non-interference in each other's internal affairs, equality and mutual benefit, and peaceful coexistence... consistently opposes imperialism, hegemonism and colonialism."

In the past 50 years and more, the Chinese government, in accordance with the Common Program and the Constitution, has implemented the policy of equality and unity of all ethnic groups in the country and adhering to the principle of national regional autonomy in dealing with the relationship between ethnic groups, thereby upholding the unity of the country. Mao Zedong once pointed out that the national unity and solidarity is the guarantee for all our victories. It was on the basis of the national unity and solidarity that the Chinese government had, at a difficult time when the People's Republic was just established and the Chinese people were still recovering from the trauma of the war, sent volunteer army to Korea to fight against U. S. aggression and ultimately drove the invading army led by the U. S. back to the 38th Parallel, effectively assisted North Korea and protected Chinese territory. Meanwhile, the Chinese government resolutely fought against the invasion of Taiwan by the U. S. army and defeated its harassment of the Chinese coastal areas. Later, the Chinese government gave large amount of human and material support to the Vietnamese people in support of their fight against the U. S. aggressors, and generously offered the vast Chinese territory to the Vietnamese people as the home front until the total defeat of the American aggressors. During the past half a century and more, western countries headed by the U. S., reluctant to admit their failure in China, have tried every means to instigate ethnic separatist activities in China and to launch wars of aggression and enact blockade against China. Even today, they still have not ceased sanctions against and containment of China. However, all these have failed to prevent the peaceful rise of China, but, on the contrary, aroused the patriotic feelings and enhanced national cohesion of the Chinese people, who, under the leadership of the CPC, rose up with great vigor, and through their hard work, promoted the rapid development of the socialist cause and greatly increased the overall national strength of China. The Chinese nation has finally washed off the mortal shames imposed on it by imperialists and colonialists during the past a century and more, upheld its national dignity, and taken its due place in the family of nations. Facts have proved beyond any question that, for a semi-colonial and semi-feudal country like China, which has long being subjected to imperialist aggression, national independence is a precondition for its survival as well as an important content of human rights.

3. Developing Socialist Economy, and Transforming Legal Rights into Actual Rights

The purpose of socialist construction is to develop socialist economy, so as to satisfy the growing material and cultural needs of the people. Development provides material safeguard for the realization of economic, social and cultural rights, as well as civil and political rights. Human rights are interdependent and indivisible. The International Covenant on Economic, Social and Cultural Rights points out that: "the ideal of free human beings enjoying freedom from fear and want can only be achieved if conditions are created whereby everyone may enjoy his economic, social and cultural rights, as well as his civil and political rights". Due to the limited understanding, human rights had not been mentioned in the Chinese Constitution or any Chinese law for a long period of time after the establishment of the People's Republic. And because of the ideological mistakes made by the CPC leaders and the blockade and sanctions imposed on China by the U. S. and other western countries as well as by Japan, China has taken a tortuous course in the development of the country, which has had a negative impact on the cause of human rights protection. However, the Constitution of the CPC, the Chinese Constitution and Chinese laws, and policies have all made it clear that the objective of the CPC and socialist construction is to promote interest of the people. For this reason, the broad masses of Party members and people had not lost their spiritual support and the socialist cause maintained its momentum of improvement even during this period of time. At the Third Plenary Session of the Eleventh Central Committee, the CPC summarized the historical experience, realized that "development is of overriding importance" and decided to implement the policy of reform and opening up, take the development of the socialist market economy as the central task of the CPC and the state, and closely linked it with the right to subsistence. During the past thirty years or more, the socialist cause has developed rapidly, creating material and cultural conditions for the enjoyment of human rights.

With respect to economic, social and cultural rights, since the implementation of the policy of reform and opening up, especially since Chinese government decided to develop socialist market economy in 1992, the GDP in China has been growing at an annual rate 10% and reached 39.8 trillion yuan. Economic growth has brought about the rise in people's income and living standard. In 2010, the urban per capita disposable income and rural per capita net income were 19, 109 yuan 5, 919 yuan, respectively, which 9.7% and 8.9% higher than the previous year. Economic growth has also guaranteed the employment of laid-off employees and incoming labor force, as well as the development of social security, cultural and educational undertakings. In order to deal with the problems caused by the transformation of enterprises and laying-off of enterprises employees, the government promulgated the Employment Promotion Law in 2007 and since then has adopted various measures to promote employment. An average of 57 new jobs had been employed each year during the period of Eleventh Five-year Plan. By the end of 2010, the total number of employed persons in urban and rural areas had reached 790 million. Employment is a thing of the first importance in safeguarding people's livelihood. On the basis of solving the employment problem, China has raised the level of pension and medical insurance of employees and further expanded the coverage of new rural cooperatives medical service system. Meanwhile, the state has increased the investment in educational undertakings. Beginning from 2006, tuition and miscellaneous fees have been exempted for all children undergoing compulsory education in rural and urban areas. By 2010, the nine-year compulsory education had covered 99% of the population in the country and the gross enrollment rate of senior high school and colleges has reached 79.2% and 25%, respectively. The expansion of the coverage of education and the improvement of the quality of education both embody the raise in the level of human rights protection, and indicate that the development of the socialist cause and human rights protection is based on a solid foundation and will enter into a stage of virtuous cycle. With respect to civil and political rights, the establishment of the People's Republic of China in 1949 marked the emancipation of the broad masses of Chinese people. The Third Plenary Session of the Eleventh Central Committee of the CPC further liberated people's mind. Under the guidance of the policy of reform and opening up, China improved the people's congress system and the system of multi-party cooperation and under the leadership of the CPC, the political consultation system, the system of national regional autonomy, and the system of rural and urban self-governance at the grassroots level. With the development of socialist market economy and the dissemination of legal knowledge among the general public, the subject consciousness, rights-protection consciousness and the consciousness of political participation of Chinese people have been greatly enhanced. The turnout of general election in the whole country has been steadily over 90%, and people's enthusiasm for the participation in the election of grassroots organizations of self-government is even higher. In recent years there have been steady decrease in the average age of newly elected deputies to the NPC and members of urban and rural grassroots self-governing organizations, gradual improvement of their ideological, cultural and professional qualities and the raise in their ability of democratic decision-making, democratic management, and democratic supervision, which have effectively safeguard people's right to know, right to political participation, right of expression and right to supervision, strengthened the relationship between the Party and the people, and consolidated and expanded the basis of state power. Meanwhile, various mass organizations carry out economic, political, cultural and scientific activities and put forward their own demands and suggestions in accordance state laws and their own constitutions, and the broad masses of people can also express their opinions through new media and the Internet, thereby further strengthening the supervision over state functionaries. Generally speaking, the current level of human rights protection in China is the highest in history, although a lot of improvements still need to be made in the field of civil and political rights.

The above facts have shown that human rights are genuinely protected in China. Although, because of social and economic backwardness and the continuous wars, had lagged far behind western countries in human rights protection before the establishment of the PRC, the establishment of the New China has given full play to the advantages of socialist system and promoted the rapid development of the human rights cause. It can be said that today the Chinese people are full of confidence in their future, their material conditions have been improving steadily, their cultural life is becoming increasingly rich and colorful, the level of their physical and psychological health is rising continuously, and their life expectancy has reached the level of that of the developed countries. All these are solid evidences of the development of human rights protection in China.

IV. Principles to Be Adhered to in Developing Democracy and Human Rights System with Chinese Characteristics

By summarizing the experience of the progress of human civilization and its own historical experience, China recognizes the universality of human rights. This recognition has been embodied in China's participation in the UN Charter, the Universal Declaration of Human Rights, and its accession to a series of international human rights conventions. Meanwhile, we also confirm the particularity of human rights. The human rights safeguarding system will inevitably show different characteristics in countries with different historical and cultural background, ethnic groups, social systems and levels of development. Although it is important to promote the protection of human rights in accordance with the codes of conduct established by international human rights conventions, the realization of human rights mainly depends on the efforts made by nation states themselves and on the construction of democratic system in a country. At the eve of the national-wide victory of the New Democratic Revolution in China, Mao Zedong summarized the revolutionary experience in the previous 28 years by stating that: "To sum up our experience and concentrate it into one point, it is the people's democratic dictatorship under the leadership of the working class (through the Communist Party) and based upon the alliance of workers and peasants. This dictatorship must unite as one with the international revolutionary forces. This is our formula, our principal experience, our main program."① Although this statement was made over 60 years ago, it has been proved to be correct by the development of democracy and human rights protection system since the establishment of the PRC and today still serves as an important guidance in the determination of the direction of future development of the human rights safeguarding system in China. It is because the socialist system was established in accordance with the will of the Chinese people under the leadership of the CPC. For this reason, China must adhere to the following principles in domestic and international

① *Selected Works of Mao Zedong*, one-volume edition, People's Publishing House, 1964, p. 1485.

protection of human rights:

1. Striking a Balance between State Power and Rights of Citizens

China is a socialist state of people's democratic dictatorship, in which "All state power belongs to the people." The socialist state power, which is aimed at serving the people, is essentially different from the state apparatus of capitalist state, which places itself above society. If we fail to realize this basic fact, we will be confused by bourgeois ideology and blindly treat the state as the obstacle to the realization of human rights. China's experience of past half a century and more has proved that, in order to uphold national independence, state power must be strengthened; and the transformation of people's due rights into legal rights and, ultimately, actual rights depends on the improvement and implementation of the state law. It can be imagined that, were it not for the CPC, which consolidated its political power and upheld social stability on the basis of national unity, achieved victory of the Korean War in the 1950s, and supported Vietnam in defeating the U. S. aggression in the 1970s, the Chinese people would not have enjoyed peace and stability today, but would still be bullied by foreign powers, and face much more severe international situation than that of today. And were it not the implementation of the policy of reform and opening up and the development of the socialist market economy by the CPC since the Third Plenary Session of its Eleventh Central Committee, China's national defense and comprehensive national strength wouldn't have been as strong as they are today and the level of protection of people's economic, social, personal and political rights wouldn't be as high as it is today. Of course, historical and current experience has also shows that the strengthening of the state power must be based on national unity and democracy and the construction and operation of the state power must be conducted in accordance with the principle of socialist democracy and legally prescribed procedures and strictly supervised by the people. Only in this way the state power will not be placed above the people like in capitalist countries and becomes the opposite of society. Of course, the CPC and the Chinese government have made mistakes in the historical process. Nevertheless, the political system in China is different in nature from that of capitalist countries. Those mistakes should be severely criticized. However, the purpose of the criticism is to promote the reform and improve the system so as to harmonize the exercise of the state power with the protection of citizens' rights.

2. The Right to Existence and the Right to Development Being the Primary Human Rights

Human rights are interdependent and indivisible. However, in the process of realization of human rights, different countries are faced with different main problems and therefore have different priorities in human rights protection. Taking the right to existence and the right to development as the primary human rights is a correct policy adopted by China in light of the current national situation. As mentioned above, during the past a century and more, China had suffered a great deal from aggression and oppression by imperialists and colonialists. Wars and famines had impeded social development, resulted in economic stagnation and social desolation, and posed great threat to the survival of people of all ethnic groups. After the establishment of the People's Republic, although China has gained national independence, it has been blockaded, sanctioned, and contained by western countries. Even today, the ban on the sale of high-technologies to China is still not lifted, and the containment policy is continuing, and the external threat to the survival of the Chinese nation still exists. As far as domestic situation is concerned, after over thirty years of development, China has become a comparatively well-off society. However, because of weak economic basis, the level of the living standard of Chinese people is till not high: according to the UN standard, 150 million Chinese people are still living below the poverty line. Generally speaking, China still has a long way to go in order to truly safeguard the right to existence of the Chinese people. Development is the key to solving the problem of existence. In order to realize scientific development, the Central Committee of the CPC has adopted the strategy of adhering to the people-oriented, comprehensive, coordinated and sustainable development, which is in essence consistent with the principle that "The human person is the central subject of development and should be the active participant and beneficiary of the right to development", put forward by the UN Declaration on the Right to Development. The realization of the scientific development provide genuine guarantee for the full enjoyment of the right to existence, the right to development and all other human rights.

3. Combing Individual Human Rights with Collective Human Rights

The subjects of individual human rights are individual nature persons. Individual human rights are the foundation of human rights protection. The purpose of realization of individual human rights is to ensure the comprehensive and free development of human beings. The subjects of collective human rights are groups of people determined according to a certain standard. Individual human rights are components of collective human rights whereas collective human rights are the conditions for the extension, existence and realization of individual human rights. If the rights of a group, a nation or a state cannot be guaranteed, there will be no individual human rights to talk about. This is keenly felt by states and nations that have experience imperialist aggressions and colonialist rules in history and proved by contemporary examples of ethnic groups and races being driven away from their own home or faced with extinction. Based on its national cultural tradition and socialist system, China attaches equal importance to the protection of both individual and collective human rights. Apart from implementing the system of national regional autonomy within the unified state, it has also adopted special laws on the protection of such vulnerable groups as women, children, the elderly and the disabled, so as to realize the dialectic unity of individual and collective human rights and promote mutual development and harmonious coexistence of all ethnic and social groups.

V. Upholding the Unity of Rights and Obligations

Generally speaking, rights and obligations are unified. There is no is right without corresponding obligation and vice versa. The separation of rights from obligations is the result of the separation of laborers from the means of production. Engels pointed out that since the advent of "civilization", a state ruled by the exploiting class "gives one class practically all the rights and the other class practically all the duties."① In the old society, the exploiting class profited from other people's toil by replying on their property, power, and influence and enjoyed rights without fulfilling any obligations while the broad masses of the laboring people had to work hard all year round, and perform obligations without enjoying any rights. After the establishment of the People's Republic, China has eliminated the root cause of the separation of rights from

① *Selected Works of Marx and Engels* (Chinese Edition), vol. 4, People's Publishing House, 2009, p. 197.

obligations both in terms of economic basis and in terms of state system and basically realized the unity of rights and obligations. The Chinese Constitution provides that: "Every citizen is entitled to the rights and at the same time must perform the duties prescribed by the Constitution and the law." However, the enjoyment of human rights depends on the corresponding material and cultural conditions. To ensure the full enjoyment of human rights, the state must mobilize the all citizens to create material and cultural wealth. Of course, we should be full aware that China will be at the primary stage of socialism and implement socialist market system for a long period of time. The system of "from each according to his ability and to each according to his work" is implemented during the socialist stage of social development whereas the system of "taking distribution according to work as the main form while at the same time allowing different forms of distribution to coexist" is implemented at the primary stage of socialism. Although, with the development of production, the state will continuously raise the levels of social security and the income of urban and rural residents, and ultimately realize common prosperity, the so-called "three major differences" (namely, those between workers and peasants, between city and countryside and between manual and mental labor) will exist for a long period of time. Therefore, each individual must pay attention to both the rights he or she aught to enjoy, and his or her contribution to society.

VI. Strengthening International Exchange and Cooperation in the Field of Human Rights

The protection of human rights is essentially a matter that falls within the sovereignty of each state. It is against the basic principle of human rights to wantonly interfere in the internal affairs of other states under the pretense of protecting human rights. However, in the contemporary time, the rapid development of science and technology and the acceleration of economic globalization have unprecedentedly shortened the distance between peoples around the world, who share many common interests and face many common challenges, such as global warming, the protection of the ecosystem, ethnic and religious conflicts, international fight against terrorism, the international economic crisis triggered by the financial storm, the proliferation of weapons of mass destruction and the order of outer space, etc., all of them related to the protection of human rights. The Tackling of these challenges requires the exchange and cooperation between different states. It is for this reason that China has actively participated in international human rights protection in accordance with the principles of the International Bill of Human Rights. With respect to the differences in human rights concept, human rights protection system and human rights policy between different states resulting from their differences in historical and cultural backgrounds and social system, China advocates that they should be solved through carrying out peaceful dialogue, enhancing mutual understanding, eliminating misunderstanding and learning from each other's experiences and opposes the practice of some states of ideologicalizing and politicizing human rights, imposing their own values and systems on others, using double standard to demonize other states or provoke confrontation. In the past 20 years, China's correct proposition has won the support of most countries in the world, including many western countries, and led to positive results. We believe that, with the passage of time, this proposition will be able to win support from more and more countries and people, and play an even more important role in international human rights exchange and cooperation.

Protection of human rights and socialist democracy are inseparably interconnected and supplementary to each other. Although the CPC has made some mistakes and taken some wrong paths in the process of struggle for and the development of socialist democracy in the 90 years since its founding in 1927, it has taken a healthier path and greatly raised the level of human rights protection in China since the establishment of the People's Republic, especially since the Third Plenary Session of the Eleventh Central Committee of the CPC. This is not only a blessing for the Chinese people who make up one-fifth of the world population, but also a great contribution to the international protection of human rights. It can be expected that, with the further development of the socialist democracy and the socialism with Chinese characteristics, Chinese people will enjoy human rights to a fuller extent and make greater contribution to the international protection of human rights.

Cultural Self-Consciousness and Safeguarding of Human Rights[①]

The safeguarding of human rights is based on social, economic, political and cultural conditions and therefore cannot but be restricted by the level of social, economic, political and economic development. To examine the various factors conditioning the safeguarding of human rights from the cultural perspective and to carry out study on the relationship between oriental culture and human rights is conducive to the academic exchange, mutual understanding and cooperation between different countries in the field of human rights.

If it can be said that the universality of human rights is determined by human nature and the inherent rights of every human being, then the particularity of human rights is determined by different social, economic, political and cultural backgrounds of different people. Attaching equal importance to the universality and particularity of human rights is an inherent requirement of the UN Charter, the Universal Declaration of Human Rights and various human rights conventions. The Vienna Declaration and Program of Action, adopted at the World Human Rights Conference in June 1993, points out that: "All human rights are universal, indivisible and interdependent and interrelated. The international community must treat human rights globally in a fair and equal manner, on the same footing, and with the same emphasis." Here, the terms "all human rights" and "to treat human rights globally in a fair and equal manner" naturally refer to human rights of countries, cultures and groups of people. Therefore, the Program of Action continues to point out that: "the significance of national and regional particularities and various historical, cultural and religious backgrounds must be borne

---

① Originally published in China Society for Human Rights Studies, Oriental Culture and Human Rights Development, Beijing: The Oriental Press, 2004.

in mind."[1]

The so-called "oriental culture" is a very broad concept, covering at least Confucian culture, Buddhist culture, Islamic culture, and Indian culture. The basic spirit of these cultures are punishing the evil, promoting the good, and pursuing human happiness, which are basically in line with the western concept of human rights. Of course, the oriental culture, like the western culture, is not perfect and contains elements that are contradictory to modern requirements of human rights. Under this circumstance, we should enhance our cultural self-consciousness. That is to say, we should find out the strong and weak points of our own culture and those of other cultures in a scientific way, so as to draw on the strong points of others and overcome the weak points of our own and find out a correct direction for the development of our own national culture. In today's world, examples of countries with approximately the same economic, political and cultural conditions but having very different human rights conditions can be found in both the West and the East, and among both developing and developed countries. A careful examination of the root causes of such differences shows that this phenomenon is directly related to culture self-consciousness. This is why all states and nations must continuously raise their cultural self-consciousness so as to realize the purpose of the International Bill of Human Rights, to embody the spirit of Vienna Declaration and Programme of Action, according to which "it is the duty of States, regardless of their political, economic and cultural systems, to promote and protect all human rights and fundamental freedoms", and to ensure the full enjoyment of human rights by all people in the world.

Of course, China should treat its own traditional culture in the same spirit. The so-called traditional China culture was created by ancient sages on the basis of rural natural economy and patriarchal legal system, and has been continuously developed by thinkers throughout the ages from the ancient to modern times in light of the concrete conditions in their own times and by taking Confucianism as the mainstay and integrating the doctrines of various schools of thoughts, including Daoism, Legalism, Military Strategist School, and Buddhism. To sum up, this extensive and profound culture takes "benevolence" as its basis, "propriety" as its

---

① Wang Jiafu and Liu Hainian (eds.), *Human Rights Encyclopedia of China*, Encyclopedia of China Publishing House, 1998, p. 845.

main thread, and such ethnical norms as "righteousness" and "the golden mean" as its supplements.

Benevolence, as explained by Confucius, means "to love all human beings"①, that "the man of benevolence is one who, desiring to sustain himself, sustains others, and desiring to develop himself, develops other"②, and that "not doing to others what you would not done to your self"③. Therefore, the concept of benevolence in traditional Chinese culture is similar to the concept of humanity in western culture in that they are both based on the love of people.

The concept of propriety is more complicated. Its development can be divided into two stages. During the period of West Zhou (1957—771 BC), it was a state system backed by coercive power of the state, family bond, and the pressure of public opinion, and covered the political, economic, military, and every other aspects of social life. "The course (of duty), virtue, benevolence, and righteousness can not be fully carried out without the rules of propriety; nor are training and oral lessons for the rectification of manners complete; nor can the clearing up of quarrels and discriminating in disputes be accomplished; nor can (the duties between) ruler and minister, high and low, father and son, elder brother and younger, be determined; nor can students for office and (other) learners, in serving their masters, have an attachment for them; nor can majesty and dignity be shown in assigning the different places at court, in the government of the armies, and in discharging the duties of office so as to secure the operation of the laws; nor can there be the (proper) sincerity and gravity in presenting the offerings to spiritual Beings on occasions of supplication, thanksgiving, and the various sacrifices."④ It can be said that propriety was omnipresent and omnipotent. Therefore, the Book Zuo Zhuan claimed that: "propriety is what is used to guide the state, stabilize the society, put people in order, and benefit the posterity."⑤ After the Spring and Autumn Period, the system of propriety, as the pillar that supported the state, collapsed. However, its basic principles and some of its concrete rules of

① See *The Analects*, Yanyuan.

② See *The Analects*, Yongye.

③ See *The Analects*, Yanyuan.

④ See Liji, Quli Part I.

⑤ See Zuo Zhuan, The Eleventh Year of the Reign of Duke Yin.

conduct have been carried forward by the later generations. These principles and rules include:

First, rites and ceremonies, including ceremonies of coming-of-age, getting married, having audience with a monarch, hosting or attending a banquet, playing music at court, staging archery and wrestling contests, holding funeral services, worshiping and making sacrificial offerings to gods and ancestors, etc. ; second, ethics, including those regulating the relationships between the monarch and ministers, between the father and the son, between elder and younger brothers, between the husband and the wife, and between friends. They require the monarch to be benevolent to his subjects, the ministers to be loyal to their monarch, the father to love his children, the son to be filial to his father, the elder brother to be kind to his younger brother, the younger brother to be obedient to his elder brother, the husband to lead his wife, and the wife to follow his husband. The system of propriety and the system of ethics are interdependent: the latter is the basis of the former whereas the former is the concrete form of the latter. Later, the Emperor Wu of the Han Dynasty (206 B C—220 A D) established the Confucianism as the state orthodoxy and Dong Zhongshu, a famous minister in the Han Dynasty, established the practice of taking the Confucian classics as basis for settling difficult lawsuits, thereby incorporating many norms of propriety into law and greatly increasing their influence.

Also closely related to the doctrine of propriety are the doctrine of righteousness and the doctrine of the golden mean. The doctrine of righteousness is advocated by traditional Chinese culture as the code of conducting oneself in society and the basis for wining popular support and achieving success in any undertaking. Confucius said that "Righteousness is appropriateness". ①Mo Zi also held that: "with righteousness the world lives and without it the world dies; with it the world becomes rich and without it the world becomes poor; with it the world becomes orderly and without it the world becomes chaotic."② Propriety and righteousness are closely related to each other because they both originated from the Chinese patriarchal clan society and serve the purpose of ensuring the stability and the continuation of such a society. The "golden mean" means equilibrium, impartiality or moderation. Confucius spoke highly of the

① See Liji: the *Golden Mean.*

② See Mozi: the Will of Heaven, Part I.

doctrine of the golden mean. He said: "Perfect is the virtue which is according to the Golden Mean!" The general principle of the golden mean is not to go too far either in deed or in word: "to go beyond is as wrong as to fall short."① In practice, propriety and righteousness must be taken as the guideline for action. Xun Zi said: "What is the mean? It is propriety and righteousness."② To a monarch, the golden mean has great bearing on the harmony of his rule: "The mean is the great root from which grow all the human acts in the world, and harmony is the universal path which they all should pursue."③ To realize the mean, "it is most important to uphold harmony"④ and follow the doctrine of "harmony in diversity",⑤ namely to allow the existence of different characteristics and opinions while adhering to the fundamental principles.

From the above we can see that the traditional Chinese culture has the following characteristics: firstly, taking the respect for the seniors and love for the family as its main thread, it has a strong color of hierarchical social ethics; secondly, it values duties over rights and the collective over the individual; thirdly, it designs a set of code of conduct to be strictly observed by everyone according to their roles in family, society and the state, so as to maintain domestic harmony, social stability and peace of the country; fourthly, it incorporates important ethical norms into the law, thereby greatly enhancing the role of ethical norms; fifthly, it takes Confucianism as its main body, integrates the doctrines of different schools of thought, and continuously enriches itself in light of the actual situations and needs of different times and therefore has strong adaptability.

The strong points of the traditional Chinese culture include: it emphasizes overall harmony, takes "the world for all" as its ideal, cultivates in people the sense of responsibility to the state and society and advocates such virtues as putting public interest before private interest, respecting the old and cherish the young, solidarity and mutual assistance, the love of the motherland, and dying for a just cause. As such, it is a bond that connects people belonging to different ethnic groups and religions in China and enables them to live together in peace and

---

① See *The Analects*: Xianjin.

② See Xun Zi: Xiaoru.

③ See Liji: Zhongyong.

④ See *The Analects*: Xue'er.

⑤ See *The Analects*: Zilu.

harmony. Although there are five major religions in China, there had never been a religious war in Chinese history. Traditional Chinese culture is a spiritual pillar that has supported the Chinese people in the resistance against foreign aggressions. In the past 100 years, foreign imperialist powers have launched over 100 wars of aggression against China. However, the Chinese people have never yielded, but continuously strengthened themselves in the struggle against these aggressions. It has been in such a cultural atmosphere that the Chinese civilization has been able to last and continuously develop for thousands of years.

In modern times, the philosophies contained in traditional Chinese culture have caught the attention of international organizations and the people in western countries. The followings are a few examples.

Example 1.

I. During a visit to Canada as the leader of a Chinese delegation in 1991, I met Mr. John Peters Humphrey, a human rights expert who had participated in the drafting of the Universal Declaration of Human Rights. He told us that during the drafting of the Declaration, the representatives of different countries were often at loggerheads with each other over some issues and none of them would compromise. As a result, the drafting work often went into an impasse. At such times, the Chinese representative, Mr. Peng Chun Chang, would propose to the members of the drafting group that they temporarily stop their work at hand and spend some time to study such Confucian doctrine of "the golden mean", so as to reconcile different opinions and find out practical solution to the problems. For this, he was highly praised by Mrs. Roosevelt who presided over the drafting work. She said that Mr. Chang had a good sense of humor, always looked at issues from philosophical point of view, and was able to quote witty Chinese proverbs to cope with any situation. She called Mr. Chang "a master of coordination". ①

Example 2.

During a visit to the Museum of the International Committee of the Red Cross in Geneva, I spotted a rock placed in a prominent position in the hallway the Museum and inscribed on the rock is a famous Confucian motto: "Do not do to others what you do not want to be done to yourself."

① Gudmundur Alfredsson & Asbjørn Eide, *The Universal UN Declaration of Human Rights: A Common Standard of Achievement* (Chinese edition), Sichuan People's Publishing House, 1999, p. 6.

Example 3.

In recent year, some western countries, in the process of judicial reform, have attached great importance to mediation, a form of non-litigious dispute resolution mechanism which is originated in China and has a strong color of traditional Chinese culture. It is believed by some reformers to be a low-cost, high-efficiency method of resolving social conflicts and strengthening social solidarity.

Like all other cultures, the traditional Chinese culture has both strong points and weak points. The latter include: the emphasis on social hierarchy, privileges, and the absolute obedience by ministers and subjects to the monarch and by juniors to the seniors, the unnecessary and over-elaborate formalities that constrain people's freedom of action, and the doctrine of "looking not at what is contrary to propriety; listening not to what is contrary to propriety; speaking not what is contrary to propriety; and making no movement which is contrary to propriety"[①] that fetters people's mind. All these have prevented the Chinese people from giving full play to their initiative and creativity and were directly related to the stagnation in social development in the late period of ancient Chinese history.

On the question of culture, we should neither improperly belittle our own culture and thus losing confidence in ourselves, nor become self-conceited and stop making further progress. The reason why traditional Chinese culture has become a unique and brilliant culture in the world is that it has been continuously integrating and absorbing the good elements of other cultures in the process of self-development. To carry forward this fine tradition, we must make an objective and scientific assessment of all cultures, including the western culture. As far as the protection of human rights is concerned, the western culture has paid early attention to individual rights. Lenin also pointed out that: "Compared to feudalism, capitalism was an historical advance along the road of 'liberty", "equality', 'democracy' and 'civilization'" .[②]Although various crises have been lurking within the capitalist system from the date of its births, it is undeniable that during the past 300 years, capitalist countries, while developing production, creating new jobs, improving the livelihood of

① See The Analects: Yanyuan.

② V. I. Lenin, *Complete Works of Lenin*, Chinese edition, People's Publishing House, 1986, p. 109.

workers and other laborers, have also attached importance to the recognition of some of the rights won by the workers through struggle, so as to prevent the capitalist rule from collapsing as a result of fierce social conflict and class struggle. These measures have been proved to be successful under most circumstances. They should be regarded as a part of the fine culture of mankind that should be borrowed boldly by China for reference.

In the struggle for the full enjoyment of human rights in the past more than 100 years, the Chinese people have been continuously summarizing historical experience, enhancing their own cultural self-consciousness, striving hard to rid themselves of the bondage of old traditions and to carry forward the fine Chinese culture, and by doing so, have gathered huge national strength: it was under the banner of Three Principles of the People (namely, the principles of nationalism, people's livelihood and people's sovereignty) that Dr. Sun Yat-sen launched the 1911 Revolution that overthrew the feudal monarchy that had ruled China for thousands of years and it was under the banner of democracy and science that the Chinese people started the New Democratic Revolution with the May Fourth Movement in 1919, and, after 30 years of arduous struggle, won the victory of the revolution in 1949, thereby putting an end to the days of humiliation, regaining their human dignity and standing up before the people of the whole world.

Since 1978, Chinese people, by further eliminating the influence of the feudal patriarchal system, have again made great progress in emancipating the mind, developing democracy, and safeguarding human rights and freedoms: with respect to the construction of constitutional government, China has introduced modern idea of constitutionalism and established the constitutional principle of ruling the country by law and building a socialist state under the rule of law; with respect to legislation, China has attached importance to the balance between rights and obligations and between individual rights and collective rights, to the check and balance between various state powers and to the building of a legal system compatible with the modern market economy; with respect to law enforcement, China has adopted the clear policy of administration by law and increasing the transparency of and strengthening the supervision over administration; and with respect to administration of justice, China has carried out the judicial reform aimed at realizing judicial fairness, expanding the scope of judicial review, and achieving the independence of the judiciary. The unprecedented openness of legal culture embodied in the above measures have provided reliable safeguard for the enjoyment by the Chinese people of various fundamental rights and freedom provided for in Chinese Constitution and laws. All these are conducive to giving full play to the enthusiasm and creativity of the Chinese people of all nationalities and have contributed to the rapid development of the national economy in China in the past more than twenty years, which have caught world-wide attention.

Today, taking people as the basis and respecting and safeguarding human rights have become the starting point as well as the ultimate goals of all aspects of work and all undertakings in China. It should be pointed out that, with the progress of economic globalization and rapid development of high-technology, with China's accession to the WTO and signing of the two international human rights covenants (China has already ratified the International Covenant on Economic, Social and Cultural Rights), with the further development of the modern market economy, and with the increase of foreign exchange and common codes of conduct, the human rights consciousness of the Chinese people will continue to rise. In order to adapt to the new domestic and international situations, we must further raise our culture self-consciousness. While developing and carrying forward the fine traditional Chinese culture in the spirit of "taking the essence, discarding the dregs", we must boldly draw on the beneficial elements of western and other cultures. I believe that, in this process, the traditional Chinese culture will exert greater influence in broader scope with each passing day and make new contributions to the safeguarding of human rights, not only in China, but in the whole world.

Safeguarding Human Rights: the Special Role of the State[①]

The Chinese Constitution clearly points out that "This Constitution affirms the achievements of the struggles of the Chinese people of all nationalities." In this sense, the Chinese Constitution is a bill of rights of Chinese people. The amendment to the Constitution adopted at the Second Session of the Tenth National People's Congress enshrined in the Constitution the principle that: "The state respects and protects human rights." Under the new situation, further emphasizing the respect and protection of human rights is of great importance to the construction of socialist political civilization, to the coordinated development of material, political and spiritual civilizations, and to building a well-off society in an all-round way. The adoption of this amendment is a great event whether in the development of human rights course or in the development constitutionalism in China.

Human rights are rights that human beings are entitled to by virtue of their natural and social attributes. Here, human beings refer to all human beings and rights refer to all rights. This concept fully demonstrates the universality of human rights. However, human rights take certain social, economic, political, cultural, scientific and technological developments as the conditions for their emergence and realization and therefore cannot but subjected to the restrictions of these conditions and have particularity. In real life, some people in western countries only emphasize the universality of human rights without recognizing the particularity of human rights. They are unrealistic to demand that the formal colonies and semi-colonies of western countries achieve in 10 or 20 years what had taken western countries 200 or 300 years to achieve in the field of human

---

① Originally published in *Chinese Yearbook of Human Rights*, vol. 2, Social Science Documentation Publishing House, 2006.

rights. Some others who make unwarranted charges against and put pressure on developing countries have ulterior motives. China recognizes both the universality and the particularity of human rights, determines its objectives of struggle in accordance with universal human rights standard, improves its human rights protection system in light of the particular conditions in the country, and adopts appropriate measures to continuously improve the human rights conditions. This is the scientific approach to human rights that should be adopted by a state.

Both historical development and current situation show that human rights exist in three forms: due rights, legal rights and actual rights. Due rights are the rights a person ought to enjoy by virtue of his human nature at a certain historical stage of social development; legal rights are the legalized and institutionalized due rights; and actual rights are the rights actually enjoyed by people under a given law or system. The transformation of human rights from due rights to legal rights and to actual rights is a complicated process of struggle. In modern history, the bourgeoisie, who first put forward the slogan of human rights, realized this transformation through revolution or reform and improvement of the existing system. However, even the adoption in of the Bill of Rights by the British parliament in 1689, the Declaration of the Rights of Men and Citizens by the French National Assembly in 1789 and the Bill of Rights by the U. S. Congress in 1971 only marked the beginning of the legalization of human rights. These countries had gone a long way to embody in relevant laws and institutions the principles declared by these documents and turning them concrete and operable measures. For a long period of time, there had been inequalities between white and black people, men and women, the rich and the poor in the enjoyment of political, economic, social and cultural rights in these countries and many problems remain to be resolved even today. In China, a new state was established in 1949 in which people became the maters of their own country. If we take the establishment of the People's Republic of China and the promulgation of the 1954 Constitution as the milestones of human rights construction in China, the transformation of human rights from due rights to legal rights has also gone through a process of practice—understanding—practice again—better understanding. In this process, the state and the nation have paid their prices, some of them (such as the Cultural Revolution) are very high. Since its Third Plenary Session of the Eleventh Central Committee of the CPC, the Chinese government has further raised the consciousness of human rights construction through the implementation of the ideological line of seeking truth from facts: it rectified with great courage unjust, false and erroneous cases, strengthened democracy and the legal system, implemented the socialist market economy, improved people's livelihood, put forward the basic policy of "ruling the country by law, constructing a socialist state under the rule of law" at the Fifteenth National Congress of the CPC, reiterated the principle of "respecting and safeguarding human rights" and promoting the comprehensive development of human beings at the Sixteenth National Congress of the CPC, and enshrined in the Constitution the principle of "The state respect and protect human rights" at the Second Session of the Tenth National People's Congress. On the basis of long period of development, the human rights construction has now entered into a new stage.

From the development of human rights we can see that the state plays a special role in the protection of human rights, whether in the West or in the East. It is especially true in China because the Chinese state is supported by the people and consists of huge system of state organs. It wields legislative, administrative and judicial powers. Only through the operation of state organs can people turn their due rights into legal rights; and only by establishing mechanisms of legal regulation and corresponding systems and by developing democratic political system, and economic, social, cultural and scientific undertakings, can they provide the institutional and material safeguards for the enjoyment of human rights and turn legal rights into actual rights. Emphasizing the role of the state in respecting and safeguarding human rights means that the state must strengthen the regulation of and supervision over state organs and their staff and to ensure that they must strictly follow the law in their legislative, administrative or judicial work, especially prohibit them from violating human rights. Besides, the state has also the obligation to supervise over the implementation by enterprises and public institutions of their social responsibilities, which is of great importance to the protection of human rights. The reason for emphasizing the respect and protection of human rights by the state is that the state has the obligation to provide remedies to the victims of human rights violations, whether such violations are committed by state organs, public officials, enterprises, public institutions, mass organizations or individuals, and to ensure that they receive proper compensation for such violations.

Imperialist aggression and colonial rule in the past and international terrorism, hegemonism, destruction of the ecological system, and the pollution of the environment in contemporary time are all serious threat human rights at the international level. Experience shows that in order to safeguard human rights, states must strengthen their international cooperation. The reason for emphasizing the role of state in safeguarding human rights is that states, as the subjects of international cooperation, play an irreplaceable role in international cooperation and struggle in the field of human rights.

The role played by the state in the protection of human rights is very important. Although the human rights principles have already been embodied in Chinese Constitution and laws and the Constitution has clearly stated that "the state respects and protects human rights", since the theoretical research on human rights started late in China and had been under the influence of "left" ideology for a long period of time, the understanding of some human rights issues among cadres and the general public still needs to be improved. In order to implement the constitutional principle of respecting and safeguarding human rights, China must strengthen theoretical research on as well as publicity and education of human rights, especially among public officials and civil servants. The relevant state organs should take the dissemination of and education on human rights knowledge as one of the important content of their law-popularization work so as to promote the enhancement awareness, the renewal of ideas, and improvement of legal system. Only in this way can the constitutional principle of "The state respects and protects human rights" be truly implemented and various fundamental rights and freedoms of citizens written in the Constitution become the rights actual enjoyed by Chinese people.

Integrating Chinese and Foreign Cultures and Jointly Building a Harmonious World[①]

An ancient Chinese thinker once said: "A sage was able to survey the motive influences working all under the sky. He contemplated them in their common action and special nature, in order to bring out the standard and proper tendency of each."[②] It means that and outstanding person with high morality is able to integrate different cultural ideas in light of changing social conditions and adopt codes of conduct, laws and regulations that meet the needs of the general public, so as to promote social development. The insight and philosophy contained in this comment can be used to review history, observe current situation and look into the future.

I

Sixty years ago, in December 1948, the UN General Assembly adopted the Universal Declaration of Human Rights (UDHR), which is a normative instrument with major historical significance formulated through the integration of the ideas of state representatives from different cultural backgrounds. Before the adoption of this historical instrument, mankind had experienced two world wars in the first half of the 20th century. Especially in the Second World War, Germany Nazis and Japanese militarists had committed terrible atrocities in Asia and Europe, destroying civilizations, slaughtering tens of millions of innocent people

---

① This article was originally a paper submitted to the Academic Seminar Commemorating the Sixtieth Anniversary of the Adoption of the Universal Declaration of Human Rights. An abstract of this paper was published in the *Journal of Chinese Academy of Social Sciences*on May 8, 2008. It was published in full in the book: *Chinese Culture and the Construction of a Harmonious Society*: Guangzhou: Jinan University Press, 2011.

② See Zhou Yi (Book of Change): Xi Ci.

and wreaked unprecedented havoc on mankind. At that time, hundreds of millions of people in Asia, Africa and Latin America were still suffering from the exploitation and oppression by colonialists and leading a miserable life. People of these countries, baptized by the flames of war and long-termed struggle against colonialism, fully understood the importance of independence, freedom, and human rights. It was against this background that the UDHR, drafted by Mrs. Eleanor Roosevelt in accordance with purpose of the UN Charter, and adopted by the UN General Assembly after repeated discussion, provides at its very beginning that:

> "Whereas recognition of the inherent dignity and of the equal and inalienable rights of all members of the human family is the foundation of freedom, justice and peace in the world,
>
> Whereas disregard and contempt for human rights have resulted in barbarous acts which have outraged the conscience of mankind, and the advent of a world in which human beings shall enjoy freedom of speech and belief and freedom from fear and want has been proclaimed as the highest aspiration of the common people,
>
> Whereas it is essential, if man is not to be compelled to have recourse, as a last resort, to rebellion against tyranny and oppression, that human rights should be protected by the rule of law,
>
> Whereas it is essential to promote the development of friendly relations between nations,
>
> Whereas the peoples of the United Nations have in the Charter reaffirmed their faith in fundamental human rights, in the dignity and worth of the human person and in the equal rights of men and women and have determined to promote social progress and better standards of life in larger freedom,
>
> Whereas Member States have pledged themselves to achieve, in cooperation with the United Nations, the promotion of universal respect for and observance of human rights and fundamental freedoms,
>
> Whereas a common understanding of these rights and freedoms is of the greatest importance for the full realization of this pledge.
>
> Now, therefore, the General Assembly, proclaims this Universal Declaration of Human Rights as a common standard of achievement for all peoples and all nations, to the end that every individual and every organ of society, keeping this Declaration constantly in mind,

shall strive by teaching and education to promote respect for these rights and freedoms and by progressive measures, national and international, to secure their universal and effective recognition and observance, both among the peoples of Member States themselves and among the peoples of territories under their jurisdiction."①

The Declaration especially stressed in Article 2 that: "Everyone is entitled to all the rights and freedoms set forth in this Declaration, without distinction of any kind, such as race, color, sex, language, religion, political or other opinion, national or social origin, property, birth or other status."②

The UDHR is the result of the integration of different ideas of representatives of different nation states in the world and the process of its adoption also embodied the spirit of integration and adaptation of different cultures. During a visit to Canada in 1991, I met with Mr. John Peters Humphrey, the Honorary President of Canadian Human Rights Foundation, who had participated in the drafting of the UDHR. He told us that during the drafting of the Declaration, the representatives from different countries were at loggerheads with each other over some issues and none of them was willing to compromise. As a result, the drafting work went into an impasse. At that time, the Chinese representative, Mr. Peng Chun Chang, proposed to Mrs. Roosevelt that the drafting group temporarily stop their work at hand to study such Confucian ideas as tolerance and moderation. This suggestion lightened the atmosphere and enabled drafting work to go on smoothly. For this, he was highly praised by Mrs. Roosevelt and representatives of many other countries.

The UDHR has won the support of people around the world because it integrates different cultures and reflects the aspirations of different nations. In order to give full play and legal binding force to the spirit of the Declaration in different fields, the UN has adopted a series of human rights instruments, including the two international covenants on human rights, the Convention relating to the Status of Stateless Persons, the Supplementary Convention on the Abolition of Slavery, the Slave Trade and Institutions and Practices Similar to Slavery, the Declaration on the Granting of Independence to Colonial Countries and Peoples, the

① Preamble of UDHR.

② Article 2 of UDHR.

International Convention on the Elimination of All Forms of Racial Discrimination, the Convention on the Elimination of All Forms of Discrimination against Women, the Convention on the Rights of the Child, the ILO Convention on the Right to Organize and Collective Bargaining, the Convention against Torture and Other Cruel, Inhuman or Degrading Treatment or Punishment, the Basic Principles on the Independence of the Judiciary, the Standard Minimum Rules for the Treatment of Prisoners, and the Protocol Relating to the Status of Refugees. Among these instruments, the International Covenant on Economic, Social and Cultural Rights and International Covenant on Civil and Political Rights, adopted in December 1966, are of special importance. Together with the UDHR, they form the International Bill of Human Rights. After over half a century of joint efforts by peoples around world who have been inspired by the spirit of the UDHR, the material and spiritual civilizations damaged and poisoned by German Nazis and Japanese militarists have been basically restored and colonial countries and peoples have gained independence and freedom (the victory of Chinese revolution in 1949, which put to an end to the semi-feudal and semi-colonial rule in China and liberated Chinese people who made up one fourth of the world population, had become the most important historical event at that time); the barbarous system of racial segregation has become history; the situation of gender discrimination and inequality has been greatly improve; the rights of minorities and vulnerable groups of society have been safeguarded in most countries; the freedoms of thought, conscience and religious belief and other freedoms provided for in the UDHR have already realized or are becoming reality; strengthening democracy and the rule of law and safeguarding the dignity, the personal rights, the property rights and other rights of human beings has become the trend of the times; with the raise in rights consciousness, violations of human rights by states are not only opposed by the people in their own countries, but also denounced by the international community; and after the establishment of the Human Rights Council, the supervision over the human rights situation in various countries have been strengthened. Protection of human rights, international peace and security, and economic and social development have become three pillars of the UN. The practice of the past 60 years has proven that the UDHR, as the general principles of the International Bill of Human Rights, has become the most influential instruments in the field of international human rights protection.

II

Thirty years ago, the Communist Party of China, after extensively solicitation of opinions both within and outside the Party and under the guidance of the ideological line of "emancipating the mind and seeking truth from facts", adopted the policy of "reform and opening up" at the Third Plenary Session of its Eleventh Central Committee in December 1978. The abolition of the feudal system in 1911 and the victory of New Democratic Revolution in 1949 were the results of drawing on advanced cultures of mankind by China in light of its own national conditions. However, because of various subjective and objective reasons, China had been closed to the outside world for a long period of time after 1949, which seriously impeded the social development in the country. The adoption of the policy of "reform and opening up" at the Third Plenary Session of the Eleventh CPC Central Committee put to an end to this closed condition. The so-called "reform" is to change the old institutions and systems that are no longer compatible with the development of socialist cause; "opening up" means to open the doors of the country to the outside world, to learn from developed countries advanced science, technology, management methods, and other knowledge and culture that are beneficial to China. Deng Xiaoping once pointed out that: "every people or country has something to learn from other peoples and countries"① and that "if we want socialism to achieve superiority over capitalism, we should not hesitate to draw on the achievements of all cultures and to learn from other countries."② It was by basing itself on the actual situation in China, adhering to the principle of independence and self-reliance, and integrating Chinese and foreign cultures that China has been able to find a correct road to the building of socialism with Chinese characteristics, and achieve rapid progress in the development of human rights cause in the country.

After 30 years of unremitting efforts on the basis of the previous achievements in socialist construction, China has built a relatively

① Deng Xiaoping, *Selected Works of Deng Xiaoping*, vol. 2, People's Publishing House, 1994. p. 91.

② Deng Xiaoping, *Selected Works of Deng Xiaoping*, vol. 3, People's Publishing House, 2001. p. 373.

complete system of laws and institutions on the protection of human rights. "Ruling the country by law and building a socialist state under the rule of law" and "the state respects and safeguards human rights" have become important constitutional principles in China. The Chinese Constitution and laws have provided for extensive rights and freedoms of citizens.

With respect to political rights, China has further improved the people's congress system, which embodies the principle of popular sovereignty. The state has attached great importance to the improvement of grassroots democracy, expanded the scope of competitive election, and extensively implemented the system of consultative democracy in state organs and civil society. To safeguard people's right to know, the government has strengthened the supervision over state organs and state personnel, increased the transparency of the operation of state organs, and established the system of government spokesman for governments above the county level. Citizens and legal persons whose rights have been violated by a state administrative organ may apply for administrative reconsideration at the administrative organ at next higher level or bring administrative lawsuit against the administrative organ at a people's court.

With respect to the protection of citizens' personal rights in administrative law enforcement and administration of justice, the Constitution and laws provide that the freedom of the person of citizens is inviolable. No citizen may be arrested except with the approval or by decision of a people's procuratorate or by decision of a people's court, and arrests must be made by a public security organ. Both the Criminal Law and the Criminal Procedure Law have recognized the principle of legally prescribed punishment for a specified crime and the principle of presumption of innocence. The Chinese Constitution and laws also provide that people's procuratorates and people's courts shall exercise adjudicative and procuratorial powers independently; that, except in special circumstances as specified by law, all cases in the people's courts are heard in public and that the accused has the right to defence. The newly revised Lawyer's Law has further improved the criminal defense system. Citizens who have suffered losses as a result of violation of their rights by state organs or state personnel have the right to compensation in accordance with law.

With respect to the protection of the rights of minorities and vulnerable groups of society, the government has adopted a series of laws, including the Law on Regional National Autonomy, the Law on the Protection of

Women's Rights and Interests, the Law on the Protection of Minors, and the Law on the Protection of Disable Persons, and corresponding policies in the areas of economic construction, development of the western parts of the country, culture, education, labor and employment. Many ethnic minority areas are enjoying faster growth of the GDP and rise in people's living standard than central areas. There have also been rapid rises in employment rates and the welfare of women, disabled persons and vulnerable groups.

With respect to the protection of the freedoms of religion, of speech, of the press, of assembly and of association, all these freedoms are been well protected in China: Buddhist and Daoism temples, churches, and mosques have been renovated; a harmonious relationship has been developed between believers of different religions, and between religious people and non-religious people; there has been drastic increase in the numbers of various publications and of NGOs; and the healthy development of civil society is playing an important role in invigorating social life.

With respect to economic, social and cultural rights, the Constitution and laws provide that, at the primary stage of socialism, China will adhere to the basic economic system in which the public ownership is dominant and diverse forms of ownership develop side by side and the distribution system in which distribution according to work is dominant and diverse modes of distribution coexist, that citizens' lawful private property is inviolable, and that the state protects by law the right of citizens to own private property and the right to inherit private property. With the establishment and development of socialist market economy, there has been rapid development in industry, agriculture, science, technology, and cultural undertakings. The GDP has been growing steadily at a rate of more than 9% and reached 11.4% in 2007, making China the fourth biggest economy in the world. China has not only succeeded in feeding a population that makes up 20% percent of the world's total population with only 7% percent of the world's total cultivated land, but also been able to continuously improve the living standard of urban and rural residents, which is a great achievement as well as a remarkable contribution made by China to the cause of international protection of human rights.

Thirty years of practice has shown that the key to sustainable development in China is to take the policy of reform and opening up as guidance, to draw on the outstanding cultural achievements of other civilizations, and continuously blaze new trails in a pioneering spirit. The "people-oriented" scientific outlook on development and the objective of building a well-off and a harmonious socialist society, put forward by China on the basis of development of various undertakings, are exactly the product of integration of Chinese and foreign cultures under the new situation. As far as its content is concerned, the recent Report to the 17th National Congress of CPC is nothing short of a bill of human rights with Chinese characteristics. We have every reason to believe that by achieving the objectives put forward in the report, we will be able to raise the human rights protection in China to a higher level.

III

A review of the contemporary world shows that because of the joint efforts made by and the cultural exchange and mutual emulation carried out between peoples around the world, historical changes have taken place in the fields of human rights construction and social development in countries around the world. Peace and development have become the global trend of development. However, opportunities are always accompanied by challenges. Today peoples of world are still faced with many unsolved problems. These problems include: the destruction and shortage of resources, which has impeded the social development and the realization of the right to development; soil, water, and air pollutions, which are endangering the safety of food; the greenhouse effect and other problems and natural disasters resulting from global warming, which are posing continuous threat to the survival of mankind; the incessant ethnic and religious conflicts in some regions; the growing number of incidents of killing of innocent people by terrorists and religious fanatics; the war launched by the U. S. against the sovereign state of Iraq in the name of eliminating weapons of mass destruction; the imbalance in development between the North and the South, as a result of which hundreds of millions of people are still living in poverty and their right to existence is not guaranteed; the disparity between the rights enjoyed by peasant workers in Chinese cities and migrant workers in Europe and North American and their contribution to the development of the local economy; further measures yet to be taken by governments to strengthen the supervision over the implementation by enterprises of their legal obligations and social responsibilities, especially to avoid the occurrence of accidents that endanger the life and health of the people; and the objectives of safeguarding the rights of both victims of crime and criminal suspects in the administrative law enforcement and judicial process and realizing fairness and justice in the whole society have not yet been achieved.

The development of modern science and technology has greatly reduced the distance between peoples. Things that used to take years or months to complete can be completed in one day, a few hours, or even a few minutes. If the earth can be called a village, the residents of the "global village", while enjoying common rights and interests, are also faced with common risks. Under many circumstances, no country can manage alone or stand aloof. Therefore, in order to ensure its own sustainable development, China must create a good international environment; in order to ensure full enjoyment of human rights by people around the world, representatives of various countries must pool the wisdoms of different nations and establish a social and international order in which the rights and freedoms set forth in the UDHR can be fully realized. Basing itself on its own national conditions and adhering to the basic principles of the UN Charter and the UDHR, China further enriched and developed the idea of "a social and international order" envisaged in the UDHR by proposing that "people of all countries should join hands and strive to build a harmonious world of lasting peace and common prosperity". The basic points of this proposal are peace and security, development and prosperity and universal enjoyment of human rights.

1. International Peace and Security Are the Preconditions of the Construction of a Harmonious World

Without peace and security, people will be living in the fear for their life and property in the chaos caused by war and there will be no world harmony to talk about. Integrating different cultures is conducive to international peace and security. Just as the UN Charter points out: "to save succeeding generations from the scourge of war, which twice in our lifetime has brought untold sorrow to mankind" the people of the United Nations must "practice tolerance and live together in peace with one another as good neighbors." Peace and security are also the goal that has been persistently pursued by Chinese people since the ancient times. The ancient Chinese people believed that harmony is the "basis and the source of all things in the world" and the "utmost importance of the maintenance of harmony" has been a creed of Chinese nation passed on from generation to generation. At the earliest days of the People's Republic, China had advocated together with India the "five basic principles of peaceful coexistence", which later becomes the guiding principles always adhered to by China in its inter-state relationship. In the past more than half a century, China has adopted in accordance with these principles the foreign policies of never seeking hegemony, mutual trust, mutual benefit, equality and cooperation, making friends and making peace with neighboring countries, establishing new international order, and promoting the democratization of international relations. Faced with different cultural backgrounds and different social systems in different countries, China has maintained that no country may impose its own value or social system on another country, which will inevitably intensify contractions and trigger conflicts, even wars. Currently, terrorism and religious fanaticism, by unscrupulous destruction of public facilities and killing of innocent people, have become a major threat to international security and peace. In order to eradicate terrorism and religious fanaticism, it is necessary to carefully study the causes for their existence, and adopt the approach of "comprehensive treatment", rather than meeting violence with violence, to solve this problem. Even for the purposes of "prevention and removal of threats to the peace and the suppression of acts of aggression or other breaches of the peace", they must "take effective collective measures" "in conformity with the principles of justice and international law" and the relevant procedures of the UN Security Council. [①]Unilateralism, by acting arbitrarily in disregard of others' opinions, will only pose greater threat to people's life and property. 2500 years ago, Confucius had proposed "harmony in diversity" as a way of dealing with the relationship between people: "A gentleman is affable but not adulatory whereas a small man is adulatory but not affable."[②] It means that a reasonable man attaches great importance to 'harmony" and reconciliation of differences without denying the existence of differences or imposing uniformity on others whereas an unreasonable man blindly pursues "uniformity" without recognizing the existence of differences or knowing how to reconcile differences and, as a result, will never be able to achieve harmony. This profoundly philosophical teaching, if applied to the relationship between states, means tolerance, harmony, mutual respect, equal consultation in international relationship, resolution of

① See Article 1 of the UN Charter.

② See The Analects: Zi Lu.

international disputes in a peaceful way, rather than benefiting oneself at others'expense, overwhelming others by one's power, or imposing one's own value or system on others.

2. Development and Prosperity Are the Bases of the Construction of a Harmonious Work

Development is a comprehensive economic, social, cultural and political process. It has proven that the integration of different economic, political, social, and cultural systems is conducive to development. In view of the importance of development, the UN Charter provides the following as one of the purposes of the United Nations "To achieve international cooperation in solving international problems of an economic, social, cultural, or humanitarian character." In order to emphasize the importance of development to mankind, the UN General Assembly proclaims in the Declaration of the Right to Development that "The right to development is an inalienable human right" and that "The human person is the central subject of development and should be the active participant and beneficiary of the right to development." The Declaration stresses the obligations of states and the international community in promoting development: "States have the right and the duty to formulate appropriate national development policies that aim at the constant improvement of the well-being of the entire population and of all individuals." "States have the primary responsibility for the creation of national and international conditions favourable to the realization of the right to development", "the duty to co-operate with each other in ensuring development and eliminating obstacles to development" and "the duty to take steps, individually and collectively, to formulate international development policies with a view to facilitating the full realization of the right to development."① The Declaration on the Right to Development promotes development by providing for the guiding principles for the solution of problems relating to development by states and international community.

China has always attached great importance to development and the realization of people's right to development. As an ancient Chinese saying goes "Food is the paramount necessity of the people." Although the

① See Law Institute of Chinese Academy of Social Sciences (ed.), *Instruments of International Human Rights and Institutions of International Human Rights*, Beijing: Social Sciences Documentation Publishing House, 1993. pp. 483—484.

Chinese people, in order to create a better life for themselves and to realize the prosperity of the state and the nation, has always been making unremitting efforts in promoting development, it was only thirty years ago when they truly realized that "development is of overriding importance" and began to explore the objective laws of development. "Poverty is not socialism." In order to shake off poverty, China must first develop the economy. The policy of "reform and opening up" adopted at the Third Plenary Session of the Eleventh CPC Central Committee in 1978 and the development of the socialist in the past thirty years have enabled over 250 million people to shake off poverty and 1.3 billion people to become moderately well off. Of course, just as the UN Charter points out, development is more than mere economic development. It is exact based on the understand of this inherent relationship between economic, social and cultural developments that the Chinese government, while vigorously promoting economic development and building socialist material civilization, has also put forward the objectives of constructing spiritual, political and social civilizations and building a well-off society in a comprehensive way. And it is based on the realization of the importance of development to the right to survival that the Chinese people have listed the right to development and the right to subsistence among the most important human rights for the present time and for a long time to come. To ensure a healthier development, China puts forward the scientific outlook on development, namely "people-oriented, comprehensive, coordinated and sustainable development". With the implementation of this outlook on development, China will be able to take firmer and faster steps on the road of development.

In today's world of rapid technological development and economic globalization, the resources of development and markets for products have been closely linked to each other. Economic problems in one country can affect not only neighboring countries, but also countries in far away regions, even the entire world. The Asian Financial Crisis several years ago and the current Sub-prime Lending Crisis in the U. S. are two examples in this respect, whereas the production and consumption of petroleum, the world's main source of energy, is constantly touching the nerve of the world economy. To ensure the steady and sustained development of the world economy, states must adhere to the principles of cooperation, balance, win-win relationship, generalized preferences, complementary advantages, and joint promotion. Developed countries should give more capital and technological support to developing countries and shoulder more responsibilities in promoting development and in eliminating some of the adverse consequences of development. Because of the imbalance in development, frictions and disputes between states in the process of development are inevitable. Such frictions and clashes should be resolved through equal negotiation; those that cannot be solved through negotiation should be submitted to the dispute resolution mechanisms of the WTO for mediation or arbitration, so as to avoid the outbreak of trade wars, which harm of not only the interests both parties to the dispute, but also those of other countries.

3. The Purpose of Constructing a Harmonious World Is to Safeguard Human Rights

The construction of a harmonious world is the aspiration of mankind. Its ultimate objective is to ensure that everyone can fully enjoy human rights. This is one of the important reasons why China has put forward the people-oriented scientific outlook on development, further improved the system for the safeguarding of social rights, and won the whole-hearted support of the people in the process of building a harmonious society. It can be imagined that the construction of a harmonious world will lose its halo if its goal is to promote the rights or interests of only one state, one nation, one religion or persons of one gender. By bearing in mind the realization of human rights as the goal of constructing a harmonious world, we will be able to highlight the subject status of human beings in the construction, attract more people to participate in this process, and ensure that individual rights do not harm the rights of others or of the public, and the fruits of the construction are shared by all people; to get a better understanding of the universality of human rights and the interdependence between various human rights and apply such understanding in practice to promote the comprehensive development of economic, social, cultural and political rights; attach equal importance to the protection of both individual rights and the collective rights of women, children, the elderly, and disabled persons; to pay attention to both the universality and the particularity of human rights and to enable each country to determine its own priorities in the development of human rights cause in a given period of time in light of the cultural characteristics and level of development and establish a human rights protection system suited to its own national conditions. Human rights laws and institutions are also a kind of culture. The conflicts between different ideas and institutions of different countries are inevitable. They should be solved through exchange and dialogue on an equal basis, so as to achieve the goal of common progress.

The world is colorful and complicated. In today's world, in which each country has its own historical process, national culture, religious belief, ideology, social system and level of economic development, and science and technology are advancing rapidly and weapons of mass destruction are emerging continuously and are becoming accessible to more and more states and individuals, a universally recognized international order cannot be established through the practice of unilateralism based on the selfish interest of only one nation or country. There are still some people in western countries who, with their unique prejudices and the "naivety" of a teenager girl, are convinced that their own values are universal truth and painstakingly advocate their own system as the only model for all other countries and try to impose it on them. As such, they cannot but get into trouble on all sides. Under this circumstance, only harmony can maintain peace and security in the global village.

Since the construction of a harmonious world is a long-term and arduous task, we must set targets and start implementing them as soon as possible. As long as we correctly gasp the spirit of the UDHR, continue to implement the policy of reform and opening up, make an unremitting effort in mobilizing the people both in China and abroad and in drawing on wisdoms of different nations and cultures, we will be able to gather huge strengthen in the construction of a harmonious world and ultimately achieve our expected objectives.

Building a Social and International Order in Which Human Rights Can Be Full Realized①

The goal of building a harmonious socialist society, put forward at the Fourth Plenary Session of the Sixteenth CPC Central Committee, and the decision on major issues relating to the building of a harmonious society, adopted at the Sixth Plenary Session of the Sixteenth CPC Central Committee, will forcefully promote economic, political, cultural and social developments in China and provide more effective safeguards for the full enjoyment of human rights by the Chinese people.

I

The Full enjoyment of human rights is a lofty ideal of mankind as well as an objective of long-term struggle of the Chinese people. However, continuous efforts must be made and necessary conditions created in order to turn this ideal and objective into reality. 58 years ago, the Universal Declaration of Human Rights was adopted after mankind had experienced the holo causts of two world wars. While setting forth various human rights, Declaration calls for the establishment of "a social and international order in which the rights and freedoms set forth in this Declaration can be fully realized."② In 1966, eighteen years after the promulgation of the Declaration, the UN General Assembly adopted on the basis of thorough discussion the International Covenant on Economic, Social and Cultural

---

① Originally published in *Journal of Chinese Academy of Social Sciences* on January 16, 2007.

② Article 28 of the Universal Declaration of Human Rights. Law Institute of Chinese Academy of Social Sciences (ed), *International Instruments of Human Rights and International Institutions of Human Rights*, Social Sciences Documentation Publishing House, 1993, p. 8.

Rights and the International Covenant on Civil and Political Rights, thereby transforming the basic principles recognized in the Declaration into binding international codes of conduct. The Declaration and the two international covenants on human rights—the so-called " International Bill of Human Rights" —become the basic instruments of international human rights law and a new milestone in the development of the cause of international protection of human rights.

Through the joint efforts by the peoples of all countries in the world over the past half a century and more, the cause of human rights protection has developed in breadth and depth with the International Bill of Human Rights as the standard and today the slogan of human rights has become deeply rooted in people's mind. Statistics show that, up to date, the UN has adopted over 60 conventions and other instruments of human rights. Meanwhile, human rights principles have been embodied in the constitution and laws of most countries in the world, including China. To realize these principles, the UN and its subsidiary organs have strengthened the supervision over the implementation of human rights conventions, which have played an important role in abolishing the system of racial segregation, ending colonial rules, achieving ethnic and gender equality, improving work conditions, protecting the rights and interests of the elderly, children, the disabled and other disadvantaged groups of society, realizing judicial fairness, and promoting the development of the entire human rights cause, thereby vividly reflecting the progress of human civilization.

In 2007, the United Nations established the Human Rights Council during the process of reform of the UN system, so as to further promote the development of the cause of international protection of human rights on the existing basis. It is believed that the newly established Human Rights Council will be able to summarized the experience of many years of activities of the UN Commission on Human Rights, put to an end the abnormal practices of some countries of introducing ideology into the discussion on human rights issues and turning the regular sessions of the Commission on Human Rights into a political arena for pursuing the policy of double standard on human rights, truly implement the principles of the UN Charter and international human rights conventions, and play its due role in safeguarding human rights and establishing a social and international order in which the rights and freedoms provided for in the Universal Declaration of Human Rights can be fully realized.

II

Human rights principles are universal. However, in establishing human rights protection system, each state must take into consideration its own particular conditions, national characteristics and level of development. In the process of establishing and improving human rights protection system, the Chinese people, under the leadership of the CPC, have been attaching equal importance to basing themselves on the reality in China and carrying forward the fine Chinese cultural traditions and drawing on the achievements of human civilization and useful experiences of other countries, abiding by the Marxist principles of seeking the emancipation and comprehensive and free development of mankind, and continuous eliminating those obstacles to the development of social productive forces once considered "sacred boundaries", such as outdated social system, outdated economic, political, cultural institutions and outdated ideologies. It is exactly by following Marxist principles that China has been able to find a development path and establish a human protection system with Chinese characteristics.

First, overthrowing the old system through revolution. In 1949, through long revolutionary struggle and war of liberation, Chinese people had overthrown the rules of imperialism, feudalism and bureaucratic capitalism and established the People's Republic, thereby eliminating the social institutional obstacles to their enjoyment of human rights.

Second, the establishing new systems through reform. After the Third Plenary Session of the Eleventh CPC Central Committee held in 1978, China has summarized the positive and negative experiences gained since the late 1950s, established the ideological line of emancipating the mind and seeking truth from facts, implemented the policy of reform and opening up, strengthened democracy and the rule of law, realized the gradual transition from the planned economy to the socialist market economy and, after 30 years of efforts, made remarkable achievements in developing the economy safeguarding human rights.

China is a socialist country and the purpose of developing market economy is to satisfy the growing material and cultural needs of the broad masses of people. In the transition from the planned economy to the socialist market economy, the CPC Central Committee, based on the traditional Chinese culture and for the purpose of mobilizing the Chinese people to participate in development, has used vivid languages to describe the objectives of each stage of socialist development. At the beginning of the reform and opening up, due to the shortage of supplies, over 200 millions Chinese people were still living in poverty and food, cooking oil and meat were rationed and could be bought by urban residents only with coupons. In view of this situation, the CPC Central Committee made the "adequate food and clothing for the Chinese people" the objective to be achieved at this stage of socialist development, which, although seemed to be very low according to the standard of western developed countries, was realistic in light of the level of development in China at that time.

In early 1990s, when most of the people in China had been lifted out of poverty, the CPC Central Committee set the new goal of "striving for a relatively comfortable life", which was a very attractive slogan to the Chinese people. According to this goal, China would raise its per capita GNP to 800—1, 000 US dollars, which would enable the Chinese people to cast off poverty, have adequate food and clothing, and enjoy social assistance at time of childbirth, old age, illness and death. Although this standard was still very low, according to which China would rank beyond 100 in the world in terms of per capital income, it was nevertheless a very difficult objective to achieve for a country with a population of over 1. 2 billion. However, through the joint efforts made by Chinese people under the leadership of the CPC, China's GDP had reached 959. 33 billion yuan by 2001, thereby realizing a historical leap of people's general living standard from that of "having adequate food and clothing" to that of "leading a relatively comfortable life". [①] On this basis, the CPC Central Committee set the new goal of "building a well-off society in an all-round way" in 2002.

The objectives of "having adequate food and clothing" and "realizing a relatively comfortable life" mainly focused on economic development and took the level of economic development as their standard. In contrast, the objective of "building a well-off society in an all-round way", while continues to take economic development as its center and requires that "efforts be made to quadruple the GDP of the year 2000 by 2020", also requires the state "to improve democracy, advance science and education, enrich culture, foster social harmony and upgrade the texture

---

① *Collection of Documents of the Sixteenth National Congress of the CPC*, People's Publishing House, 2002, p. 19.

of life for the people."[①] This shows that "building a well-off society in an all-round way" consists of not only the objective of economic development, but also new objectives of political, cultural, scientific, technological and social developments. The realization of this goal will be a major leap forward in the development of human rights safeguarding system in China.

Third, being people-oriented and building a harmonious society. A harmonious society is a social condition of benign development. To build a harmonious society is to build a society of common prosperity, in which all people do their best and find their proper places, on the basis of healthy and sustainable development of the economy and in accordance with the general requirements of a society of democracy, the rule of law, fairness and justice, sincerity, amity, vitality, stability, orderliness, and harmony between man and nature. This is a process of not only economic development, but also of the improvement of political and legal institutions, the rise of citizens' cultural, ideological and moral qualities, as well as of the maintenance of the social security system and ecological system. The objective of building a harmonious society was put forward in the process of, and is closely connected to, building a well-off society in an all-round way. It is the further development of the theory and practice of building a well-off society in an all-round way: the latter is the objective of a certain phase of socialist construction, while the former is the overall strategic objective of socialist construction. It has been proved in practice that it is important to establish targets in the process of development. However, the key to the successful achievement of targets is to guide the development with the right ideology after the establishment of the targets. The scientific outlook on development was put forward by the CPC Central Committee on the basis of summarization of historical experiences and in response to the many problems emerged in the process of development, such as putting too much emphasis on the growth of GDP, ignoring the conservation of resources, protection the environment, the safety of production, and social security, the imbalance in development and the income gap between urban and rural areas and between different regions in the country, the problems in the settlement of laid-off workers and the employment of incoming labor force, high

① *Collection of Documents of the Sixteenth National Congress of the CPC*, People's Publishing House, 2002, p. 18.

educational and medical costs, and violations of law by and corruption of some government officials, so as to better construct a well-off and harmonious society and realize "people-oriented, comprehensive, coordinated, and sustainable development". Here, "people" is the same as the "human" in the concept of "human rights", which refers to all human beings as compared to "god" and "things". Being "people-oriented" means taking the people as the starting point, the basis and the ultimate goal of development. "Comprehensive development" means the development of not only the social and economic bases, but also the various parts of the superstructure; "coordinated development" means the coordination of relations between economic, political, cultural and social developments, between various parts of each of the above-mention fields of development, and between various departments of the Central Government, between the Central Government and local governments, and between local governments of different regions; "sustainable development" requires not only the conservation of resources and the protection of the environment, but also the cultivation of talents and improvement of the relevant systems. Being "people-oriented" is the core of the scientific outlook on development. Only by adhering to scientific outlook on development will we be able to eliminate ideological obstacles to development and construction of a harmonious society, and truly ensure the full realization of human rights.

III

In building a harmonious society, China needs the support of the international community and a favorable and peaceful international environment. For this purpose, the Chinese government puts forward the proposal of building a harmonious world. External policy is the extension internal policy. China puts forward the proposal of building a harmonious world for the benefit of not only itself, but also all the nations in the world. In today's world, although peace, development and cooperation are the mainstream, there still exist many factors of instability and uncertainty that affect peaceful development. Various countries and peoples in the world are faced with common opportunities as well as common challenges in development. Some of these challenges, such as the global warming, large-scale natural disasters, serious contagious diseases, the destruction of the environment, financial crises and shortage of energy, cannot be successfully dealt with by any one state alone. Moreover, ethnic and religious conflicts, the imposition of ideological and institutional models on others, and international terrorism also frequently lead to large-scale bloodsheds, even wars. It should be pointed out that, although it is necessary to punish acts of terrorism, in doing so, we must never lose our head, violate generally recognized principles of international law, meet violence with violence, adopt the policy of unilateralism, or arbitrarily start a war. History has showed again and again that war will always cause greater harms to innocent people and never bring any good to any state, even a big economic or military power. As Sun Zi, a military strategist in ancient China, pointed out: "A protracted war exhausts the resources of the State... There is no instance of a country having benefited from prolonged warfare."① In order to save the life, property and freedom of mankind from natural disasters, human conflicts, and especially wars, it is imperative to advocate the principle of peaceful co-existence and to call on all states to joint hands in building a harmonious world.

To promote the building of a harmonious world, the Chinese government puts forward a four-point proposal which calls for the peaceful solution of international political, economic, and cultural conflicts. Based on the basic principles of the UN Charter and relevant international conventions, this proposal represents the new development of the "five principles of peaceful co-existence" put forward by China and India in the 1950s, and reflects the objective demands of the contemporary times. Its main content include: "respecting the social system and development path chosen by people of each country", which is the embodiment of the principle of sovereign equality recognized by the UN Charter and a basic principle governing international relations; "common development, mutual benefit, and co-prosperity", which is the embodiment of the objective of "promotion of the economic and social advancement of all peoples"② provided for in the UN Charter and a huge driving force behind the development of a harmonious world; "strengthening the exchange between different cultures, advocating the diversity of the world, and promoting the progress of human civilization", which is the

① See Sun Zi, The Art of War: Waging War.

② Dong Yunhu (ed.), *World Documents of Human Rights*, Sichuan People's Publishing House, 1990, p. 929.

further development of spirit of "promoting international cooperation in the economic, social, cultural, educational, and health fields"① advocated by the UN Charter, and represents the inevitable trend of development of human civilization; and "strengthening cooperation, resolving international disputes in a peaceful way, and upholding world and regional security", which is a basic principle of the UN Charter and the fundamental guarantee for the building of a harmonious world. The building of a harmonious society requires the concerted efforts of all countries of the world and necessitates the adoption of more international codes of conduct. It demands states to respect the UN Charter and the relevant international conventions and actively participate in the making of new international codes of conduct as well as in the activities of the UN and other international organizations. China must prepare itself for and take active actions to adapt itself to these new demands.

It can be expected that the construction of a harmonious society in China and the building of a harmonious world will push the human rights protection in China and the international protection of human rights to a higher level.

① Dong Yunhu (ed.), *World Documents of Human Rights*, Sichuan People's Publishing House, 1990, p. 931.

Several Questions Concerning the Construction of a System of Human Rights Theory with Chinese Characteristics[①]

The Seminar on the Construction of a Theoretical System of Human Rights with Chinese Characteristics, jointly sponsored by the Seventh Bureau of the State Council Information Office and the Editorial Board of the magazine Human Rights, is of great importance. Theory provides guidance to practice. A correct theory can be transformed into huge material force that propels social development. China has a tradition of attaching importance to theories. Since ancient times, Confucianism had been taken as the guidance for ruling the country by the rulers of various dynasties in Chinese history. Quotations from Confucius had frequently appeared in the writings of scholars and government officials, even in the memorials submitted to the imperial court by ministers and in imperial edicts. Karl Marx, Friedrich Engels and other writers of Marxist classics were often quoted by modern Chinese writers. Works of Mao Zedong and other Party and state leaders have also been frequently quoted after the birth of New China in 1949. This habit stems from a pursuit by the Chinese people, including myself, of a theoretical basis or guidance for their activities and actions. I think that Chinese legal scholars should quote more provisions of the Constitution and laws, in addition to Marxist classics, in their writings or speeches, which will be conducive to the dissemination of the policy of ruling the country by law and to the construction of a socialist state under the rule of law. I believe that today's discussion will have a positive impact on the development of human rights theory and the establishment of human rights protection system in China.

Of course, the establishment of a theoretical system of human rights is

---

① Originally published in *Human Rights* No. 2 (2011).

not an easy task. I remember that soon after President Jiang Zemin issued the instruction on carrying out study on human rights in 1991, the relevant state organs and research units had put forward various proposals on establishing China's own theoretical system of human rights—a "Marxist theoretical system of human rights" as it was called back then. To this end, the Theory Bureau of the Publicity Department of the CPC Central Committee organized the compilation and publication of a large book series entitled "Materials for Human Rights Studies", which consists of eight book, including two collections of international instruments on human rights— "World Documents of Human Rights" and "Supplement to World Documents of Human Rights" —compiled by Dong Yunhu and Li Wuping, and two books compiled by the Institute of Law of the Chinese Academy of Social Sciences— "Human Rights Construction in China" and "Developing Countries and Human Rights" . Later, the work of establishing a Marxist theoretical system of human rights with Chinese characteristics has not been carried out in an all-round way due to various reasons, such as shortage of human rights researchers, weak theoretical basis, and insufficient time. Nevertheless, a lot of work has been done in accordance with plans of the Central Committee of the CPC and major achievements made in human rights theoretical research, policy-making, publicity and education. One of such work is the first white paper published by the Information Office of the State Council—Human Rights in China, which served as an important guidance for human rights research and practice in China.

Compared to that of early 1990s, now the theoretical basis of human rights research in China is much more solid and the time is appropriate to discuss the establishment of a theoretical system of human rights with Chinese characteristics. Nevertheless, it is still not an easy task and further efforts need to be made on the research on fundamental issues of human rights theory. Moreover, a theoretical system must be established on the bases of summarization of practical experiences, tested by practice and accepted by the broad masses of people. By saying so, I do not mean that we will not be able to accomplish anything important in this seminar. What I mean is that we should take the opportunity of this seminar to bring the relevant issues to the attention of state leaders concerned and to the theoretical circle, carry out basic investigation and research work in a down-to-earth manner and, on that basis, proceed to develop a theoretical system.

Enlightened and inspired by the speeches of many scholar and experts at today's seminar, here I would also like to share with you some of my own views on this subject.

Firstly, the establishment of a theoretical system of human rights with Chinese characteristics requires a careful study of the relevant concepts, including species concepts, parallel concepts and generic concepts. The theoretical system of human rights with Chinese characteristics is a component part of the theoretical system of socialism with Chinese characteristics. As far as parallel concepts are concerned, human rights theory is parallel to political theory, the theory of the rule of law, social theory, and cultural theory; and as far as generic concepts are concerned, human rights theory is in a generic relationship with economic rights, social rights, cultural rights, personal rights, political rights and environmental rights. In order to establish a theoretical system of human rights, we must carry out basic research on the above-mentioned rights and their inter-relationships. A study cannot be systematic if attention is paid only to general theoretical concepts. As for the "Chinese characteristics" of human rights theory, it is a comparative concept relative to human rights provisions in the laws of other countries and in international conventions. Careful studies need to be carried out on exactly what these characteristics are. Only on the basis of a clear understanding of the above-mentioned issues can the boundaries and the direction of our research be accurately determined.

Secondly, the establishment of a theoretical system of human rights with Chinese characteristics requires a careful study of the Marxist human rights theory. Marxism is the basic theory guiding the socialist cause in China. In order to use Marxist theory on human rights to guide the construction of a theoretical system of human rights with Chinese characteristics, we must first of all carry out careful study on the Marxist human rights theory, which has been a weak link in our human rights research work for a long time in the past. Based on the need of struggle at their time, Karl Marx and Friedrich Engels devoted much space in their works to the denunciation and the exposure of the essence and hypocrisy of bourgeois democracy, freedom and human rights. However, they had never negated human rights themselves. On the contrary, Marx described the American Declaration of Independence as the "first-ever declaration of human rights in the world history" and Engels pointed out that the U. S. Constitution was "the first constitution in the world to recognize human rights" . By saying so, they had positively affirmed human rights. So have all leaders of the Chinese Communist Party, including Mao Zedong, Zhou Enlai, Deng Xiaoping, Jiang Zemin and Hu Jintao. The idea of Marx and Engels about the complete emancipation of mankind and the free development of every human being is consistent with the idea of full enjoyment of human rights; the socialist construction aimed at the elimination of the differences between the urban and rural areas, between industry and agriculture and between mental and physical labor is also compatible with the task of creating material and cultural conditions necessary for the full enjoyment of human rights. Now respecting and safeguarding human rights has been enshrined in the Chinese Constitution and become an important principle for ruling the country by the Party and the state. This requires us to carry out in-depth study on and give comprehensive interpretation to the Marxist theory on human rights.

Thirdly, the construction of a theoretical system of human rights with Chinese characteristics requires a careful study of the relationship between the state power and citizens' rights. China is a socialist country, in which the purpose of the state power is to serve the people, which is fundamentally different from the purpose of a capitalist state power. China must strengthen the state power in order to uphold human rights and to translate due rights into legal rights and ultimately into actual rights. During the past 100 years of modern history, China had suffered oppression and exploitation by imperialists and colonialists. After the establishment of the People's Republic of China, although the Chinese people had won national independence and liberation, hostile foreign forces continue to try everything they can to constrain and contain China. Therefore, China must strengthen its political power so as to uphold national independence. On the other hand, of course, the state power in China shares a common characteristic with that in capitalist countries, namely they are both public power. However, the capitalist public power is above the law and is antagonistic to the rights of citizens. Based on historical experiences and in order to alleviate the contradictions with the laboring people, capitalist states have adopted measures for and achieve some results in restricting public power. In contract, the public power in China is essentially consistent with rights of citizens. But in real life, sometimes conflicts may arise between public power and the rights of citizens. To ensure that public power is exercised in accordance with law, it is necessary to carry out strict supervision over the whole process of establishment and operation of political power and especially to prevent the state power from alienating into the opposite of citizens' rights. Only in this way, can the state power continuously improve the human rights protection system in accordance with the principle of "respecting and safeguarding human rights" and the strategy of building socialism with Chinese characteristics. To this end, it must uphold the right to existence and the right to development as the primary human rights, implement the principle of national equality, strengthen national unity and uphold national independence, correctly deal with the relationship between individual and collective rights, strike a balance between rights and obligations, attach equal importance to civil and political rights and economic, social and cultural rights, and strengthen international exchange and cooperation in the field of human rights.

Fourthly, the construction of a theoretical system of human rights with Chinese characteristics requires the carrying out of comparative studies on the human rights theories of different countries, especially the western countries. Human rights theories were first advanced by enlightenment thinkers during the bourgeois revolution to oppose feudal theocracy and monarchy. After wining the victory of revolution, the bourgeoisie enshrined the human rights principle in the constitution and established corresponding systems. The struggles by workers and other laboring people have contributed to the establishment and improvement such systems. After the Second World War, the international community, to save succeeding generations from the scourge of war that "has brought untold sorrow to mankind", established the United Nations and adopted the UN Charter, the International Bill of Human Rights, and a series of other human rights conventions—27 of which have already been ratified by China. The human rights protection systems in many countries and the human rights conventions adopted by the UN are the products of interactions between various factors in the process of historical development and embody the outstanding achievements of human civilization. Human nature is universal. We recognize both the universality and particularity of human rights. The theoretical system of human rights we are trying to construct should have Chinese characteristics. However, it is not appropriate or possible for this system to reject universal principles of human rights. In the construction of such a system, we should take Marxism as our guidance and the actual situation in China as our starting point, and boldly absorb all those which are beneficial to us through comparative studies.

Fifthly, the construction of a theoretical system of human rights with Chinese characteristics requires the strengthening of the publicity of and education on human rights theories. I full agree with my colleagues who have stressed in their speeches the importance of publicity of and education on human rights theories. However, for many years the mainstream media and the relevant educational institutions have failed to keep up with publicity of and education on human rights laws. As a result, the human rights consciousness of some government officials can no long meet the need of new situation and many avoidable incidents of human rights violation have occurred in practice. Here I will give you a few example examples: because of the slack government supervision, industrial accidents in manufacturing and mining enterprises occur frequently, resulting in large number of death and injury; counterfeit and shoddy food and medicine and other products closely related to people's livelihood are continuously flowing into the market, endangering the life and health of broad masses of consumers, including children; the social insurance policies adopted by the government have not been implemented in practice and the wages of peasant workers have not been paid in time; some enterprises use unlawful means to infringe upon the rights and interests of homeowners in the process of housing demolition and relocation, thus intensifying social conflicts, even resulting in mass disturbances; some sate personnel fail to correctly deal with the reasonable demands of the people, and intercept petitioners, even brutally violate their personal rights, in the name of maintaining stability; incidents of serious violation of human rights of criminal suspects, such as extorting a confession by torture and parading them through the streets to expose them before the public, continue to occur in some places despite repeat prohibition by law, resulting in very bad influence, both in China and abroad. The above examples have fully demonstrated the importance of strengthening human rights education and enhancing human rights consciousness. In the past several decades, governments at various levels have done a large amount of work and made huge achievements in safeguarding human rights. However, faced with domestic and foreign news media, many government officials are unwilling to link such work and achievements with the safeguarding of human rights. Before the occurrence of ten consecutive incidents of suicide committed by employees in the plants of Taiwanese enterprise Foxconn in the Mainland, many organizations responsible for upholding the rights and interests of workers did not dare even to mention "protecting workers' rights", let alone upholding the human rights of workers. All these show that for a long time the term "human rights" had been avoided by many people in China for being too "sensitive". Human rights education should be first carried out among Party and government officials. A few years ago, the Organization Department of the CPC Central Committee compiled a Human Rights Readers for Cadres, which was prefaced by President Hu Jingtao. However, as far as I know, the publication of this reader has failed to achieve its intended goal of starting a campaign of human rights education among Party and government cadres, which is imperative in light of the current human rights situation in China. Human rights education is readily acceptable to the broad masses of Chinese people because human rights touch upon their personal interests. If the human rights consciousness of Party and government cadres lags behind that of the general public, the government would be unable to correctly handle, even intensify, human rights related conflicts, which will seriously affect social stability and harmony in the country.

Human rights education seems to have little to do with the construction of the theoretical system of human rights discussed at today's seminar. Actually, this is not the case. Practice-based theories are always the forerunners of the development of relevant undertakings. The ultimate purpose of establishing a theoretical system of human rights is to raise the human rights consciousness of cadres and the broad masses of people, improve human rights safeguarding systems, and enable the people to enjoy fuller human rights. In this sense, it is also very important to take the opportunity this seminar to discuss the question of how to strengthen human rights education.

Part II

Specific Human Rights

The Right to Health: Responsibilities of the Government[①]

To a human being, health is as important as life itself. For this reason, people are willing to try every means, including seeking helps from medical personnel, gods, immortals and other supernatural beings, and pay any price to obtain good health and states also take various legal and institutional measures to secure citizens' health; and the International Covenant on Economic, Social and Culture Rights (ICESCR) and other international human rights instruments all contain specific provisions on the right to health. Nevertheless, currently the research on and promotion of the right to health are still very inadequate as compared to the research on and promotion of economic, social, cultural and political rights. Therefore, the discussion of the right to health as a central topic of this seminar will certainly attract more attention from scholars in the fields of law, anthropology, sociology and human rights to this issue and is conducive to enhancing people's consciousness of the right to health, and therefore is conducive to promoting the effective implementation of state's obligations relating to the right to health.

I. Health and the Right to Health

Before discussing the right to health, we should firstly have a clear understanding of what is meant by health. The traditional definition of health is "absence of illness", which is oversimplified. In the first half of the 20th century, a definition of health was put forward from purely biological perspective, namely the normal functioning of the physical body

① Originally published in The Steering Committee of the EU-China Human Rights Network (ed.), *Chinese Yearbook of Human Rights* (vol. 2, 2004), Beijing: Social Sciences Academic Press, 2006.

and organs and absence of damage to human tissues. In 1947, the World Health Organization proposed the following definition of health: "a state of complete physical, mental and social well-being and not merely the absence of disease or infirmity."[①] This definition deepens people's understanding of health by expanding the meaning of concept from mere physiological condition to include also mental and social conditions. In 1989, the World Health Organization defined heath as "a good physical, psychological and moral condition". This definition further reveals the nature of health, indicating that health must be analyzed from physiological, psychological as well as social perspectives and that health is the absence of not only physiological disorders, but also subjective inadaptability and generally recognized unhealthy behaviors.[②]The evolution of the definition of health shows the gradual deepening of the people's understanding of health and the rise of their self-consciousness in the face of objective world and is conducive to the adoption of measures for the promotion of human health.

Based on deepened understanding of health and by summarizing relevant historical experiences, the concept of the right to health was created. The so-called the right to health is the embodiment in law of people's demand for the guarantee of their health. As mentioned above, people have gradually realized that health is a matter that concerns everybody and, therefore, both the state and society should provide the necessary conditions to ensure people's health. These conditions are first of all directly related to the safeguarding of health, such as control of diseases, medical treatment, public health and improvement of living conditions and so on. Moreover, there are other conditions related to the safeguarding of health, such as sufficient clothing, quality foods, comfortable habitation, favorable social order, good morale and custom, and harmonious human environment. All these conditions, although idealistic to some extent, are necessary to safeguard health. Precisely because of this, these conditions have been laid down in the constitutions and laws of all countries as well as in the ICESCR and other international instruments on human rights and right to health. Clearly, if we regard all the conditions mentioned above as contents of the right to health to be

① Gu Yuqi and Liu Kejian (eds.), *Health Psychology*, Beijing Science and Technology Press and Anhui University Press, 2004, p. 21.

② *Ibid.*

discussed in this seminar, the right to health would become all-embracing and our discussions will lose its focus. Therefore, it is appropriate to limit the scope of the right to health to a certain area, and to do so, it is necessary to quote the relevant provisions of the ICESCR:

Article 12 of the ICESCR provides that:

> 1. The States Parties to the present Covenant recognize the right of everyone to the enjoyment of the highest attainable standard of physical and mental health.
>
> 2. The steps to be taken by the States Parties to the present Covenant to achieve the full realization of this right shall include those necessary for:
>
> (a) The provision for the reduction of the stillbirth-rate and of infant mortality and for the healthy development of the child;
>
> (b) The improvement of all aspects of environmental and industrial hygiene;
>
> (c) The prevention, treatment and control of epidemic, endemic, occupational and other diseases;
>
> (d) The creation of conditions which would assure to all medical service and medical attention in the event of sickness.

This provision is generally in keeping with the definition of health given by the World Health Organization in 1947: according to both instruments, health has three aspects, namely good physiological, psychological and environmental conditions. Good moral character is not included in this provision as a condition of health, as it is in the definition given by the World Health Organization in 1989. This is because people had not yet fully realized that good moral character is an indicator of good heath when the ICESCR was adopted and "good moral character" has already been embodied in other provisions of the Covenant.

II. The Right to Health and the Obligations of States

When people's claim for health is affirmed by law and becomes the right to health, the state becomes the bearer of the obligation to safeguard citizen' health. Even in ancient China, when people's demand for health had not been recognized by law as the right to health, all enlightened rulers had always attached great important to safeguarding the health of their people. This was because they knew that "the people are the root of the country. As long as the root is firm, the country would be peaceful"① and that "only those who protect the people will become kings" . ②If they wanted to make their countries rich and build up their military power and establish a stable reign, they had to care for their people, pay attention to their health and provide them with adequate food and clothing. Historical records show that Chinese rulers would take measures to meet emergencies when there were natural disasters and epidemic diseases, and many rulers in past dynasties would lead members of the royal family to personally engage in the cultivation of farm land every year, so as to show that they loved the people not only in words, but also in action. In modern times, the health condition of the people is an indicator of a nation's condition of peace and prosperity. The Chinese people will never forget the shame they had experienced in the end of the 19th century and the beginning of the 20th century, when western powers, with their gunboats, turned China into an their opium market, and the Chinese people, poisoned by opium, were sneered at as the "Sick Men of East Asia", and Chinese territories were invaded and divided into spheres of influence by western powers. In modern times, people's health is also closely related to the attraction of talents, moral coherence, market competition, economic, social, cultural and technological development, and the enhancement of comprehensive national power. This is the reason why every country is increasing the investment in people's health.

In order to safeguard people's right to health, the state must, first of all, respect people's right to health. The word "respect" was used in the relevant human rights provisions in both the international human right covenants and the Chinese Constitution and is very important to human rights in general and the rights to health in particular. It reflects the democratic essence of the state and the equal relationship between the state and the citizen. In the protection of human rights or the right to health, the state, public servants and citizens are in an equal relationship with each other. The state is entrusted by citizens to perform certain duties, rather than to grant charity and favor to citizens from a commanding position. Such a relationship is conducive to upholding people's dignity and raising work efficiency. The one who respects others is always respected by others. Only

---

① See *Shang Shu*: Songs of the Five Sons.

② See *Mencius-King Hui of Liang*, vol. 1.

by respecting the people, can the government and public servants win the respect from the people.

Secondly, to fulfill its obligation of safeguarding the right to health, the state must attach importance to the education of citizens on health and the right to health, namely to carry out education by schools, mass media and other means with a view to providing individuals and groups with the knowledge of health, cultivating in them healthy behaviors and lifestyles, enhancing their consciousness of health and the right to health, and promoting their participation in health protection activities, in the adoption of health related legislation and policies, as well as in the supervision over the implement of such laws and policies.

Thirdly, to fulfill its obligation of safeguarding the right to health, the state must carry out health promotion activities in light of the actual situation and needs of citizens. According to the WHO, health promotion refers to "a process of enabling people to increase control over and to improve their health... a mediating strategy between people and their environment, synthesizing personal choice and social responsibility in health"① According to the definitions of health and the right to health, the environment here should include economic, political, cultural and natural environments. To create such environments, the state must support social mobilization with legal, policy, and financial supports. Only with good legislation and policy, can scientific medical and health service systems be established; only with sufficient financial support, can modern equipment be acquired; and only through social mobilization, can the enthusiasm of social organizations, community grassroots organizations and individuals be given full play to under the guidance of government agencies and the government be able to control the situation and safeguard people's health in time of emergency. In this whole process, transparency and freedom of information are very important. In April 2003, SARS, a previously unknown vicious epidemic disease broke out in China. At the beginning, the failure of the government to disclose the information and mobilize the people in time had resulted in the spread of the disease. However, once the government took decisive measures to mobilize the people, SARS was quickly brought under control. In the Spring of 2004, bird flu broke out in some Asian and American countries,

① Lu Zizhi, *Health Education and Health Promotion*, Beijing: Beijing Medical University Press, 1998, pp. 8—9.

including China. Because this time the Chinese government took decisive measures to disclose the information, the epidemic disease was promptly brought under control and no serious damage was caused by it.

Fourthly, to fulfill its obligation of safeguarding the right to health, the state must also take measures to prevent the violations of the right to health by individuals and punish in accordance with law those who violate the right to health of others. Here I stress "others" because, although a person's unhealthy habit or lifestyle may harm his own health, the state has only the obligation to prevent such habit or lifestyle through education. The emphasis of the state's obligation is on preventing violations of the right to health of others, namely behaviors that result in direct or indirect, apparent or potential damages to other people or to society as a whole, such as production and sale of unhygienic food, unqualified medicine, and vegetables and fruits with pesticide residue exceeding the relevant standards, air and water pollution, etc. Such behaviors, motivated only by material gains and constituting serious threat to the health of people, can be controlled only by the coercive power of the state. Some of these behaviors can be stopped only if the state takes forceful actions against them. For example, the Huaihe River has been seriously polluted by many small paper mills in recent years. Although the Central Government has repeated ordered these mills to close down, little results has been achieved. Now the water in some stretches of the river is so polluted that it is not only undrinkable, but also unsuitable even for irrigation. For another example, it is reported that Tuojiang River in Sichuan Province was polluted by a certain chemical plant. As a result, the tap water in Jianyang, a city of 170, 000 residents on bank of the river, had been cut off for 13 days, and the normal life and production of close to a million people in the middle and lower reaches of the river were interrupted. (The responsible persons in this case have been given administrative punishments and are currently under investigation for criminal responsibilities.)[①] These examples have sufficiently shown that, in order to safeguard citizens' right to health, the state must strictly implement the relevant laws on the prevention and punishment of acts endangering citizens' right to health.

① *Beijing Youth Daily*, April 6, 2004, p. A9 and 8 April 2004, p. A10.

III. China's Achievements and Challenges

As early as in 1949, when the People's Republic of China was just founded, the government had taken the promotion of the health of Chinese people as its own mission, although the concept of the right to health was not used back then. At that time, China had just ended more than a century of foreign aggression and civil wars, and people were experiencing all kinds of hardship. A quarter of the population in the country was suffering from hunger. Many were forced to live on tree leaves and wild plants. The most important task of the government at that time was to help people to recover from the war and provide them with sufficient clothing and food. As a result of the concerted efforts by the government and the Chinese people, it took only three years for the national economy to reach the highest level in history. At the same time, the government adopted a series of guiding principles on safeguarding people's right to health, such as "to suit the needs of workers, peasants and soldiers, to take prevention as the main strategy, and to combine traditional Chinese medicine with Western medicine." The government called on medical personnel to educate the people on disease prevention and to mobile the people in the struggle against diseases, superstition, ignorance and unhealthy habits. A patriotic public health campaign of unprecedented scale was launched with the slogan of "mobilizing the people to pay more attention to hygiene, so as to control diseases and improve health". Meanwhile, the government had also established a national network of health services. Thanks to the hard work of medical personnel who had a strong sense of responsibility and enthusiastic participation by the broad masses of people, these policies and measures had achieved great results within a few years. Epidemic diseases that had ravaged variously parts of China for many years, such as smallpox, cholera, pestis, venereal disease, tetanus of new-born infants, and schistosomiasis, were brought under effective control. When Mao Zedong learned the news that the schistosomiasis had been eradicated in Yujiang County of Jiangxi Province, he was "too excited to fall asleep" and wrote a poem to express his happiness.

In the period that followed, because of the huge population, poor economic foundation, shortage of doctors, and outdated medical equipment in China, the government, in order to safeguard people's health, had trained a large number of primary health workers, commonly known as "barefoot doctors", through short-term training, internship, and apprenticeship. Although their title might sound inelegant, these "barefoot doctors" were very effective in treating common diseases. Together with the urban medical services and rural cooperative medical system, they had played a crucial role in safeguarding the health of the broad masses of Chinese people. Since the reform and opening up in 1978, with the fast growth of the economy, there have been rapid developments in medical education, production of medical equipment and propagation of health knowledge. A large number of medical personnel with doctor's and master's degrees and senior paramedics have been trained, hospitals and sickbeds have increased rapidly, and difficult and complicated diseases had been conquered one after another. After many years' effort, the infant mortality rate in China has decreased from 20% in 1949 to the current 2.84%; the mortality rate of pregnant women dropped from 1.5% in 1949 to the current 0.0432%; and the average life expectancy of the Chinese people increased from 35 years in 1949 to the current 71.4 years. All the above indicators have reached and exceeded the levels of developed countries.

China has made remarkable achievements, but at the same time is also faced with tremendous challenges, in safeguarding the right to health. During the past 10 years, the national economy of China has been developing rapidly, with the GDP growing at an average rate of 9.1% per year. However, social development has been lagging behind economic development. Social security system in cities covers only employees of state-owned enterprises, thus excluding a large number of employees in collective, private or foreign-invested enterprises, freelance workers, self-employed persons and peasant workers. Social security system in small towns and rural areas is still at the experimental stage and non-existent in most of the areas. Because of the high price of medicine and medical treatment, many patients can not afford the necessary treatment. Another sign of slow social development is the shortage of hospitals and sickbeds and outdated medial technology and equipment in many hospitals in rural areas, especially in remote rural areas. Because enterprises often attach too much importance to work efficiency and ignore the health and safety of workers, industrial accidents happened one after another, resulting in many unnecessary deaths as well as disabilities and occupational diseases. Even after medical treatment, victims of industrial injuries and occupational diseases, especially those who are peasant workers, will be faced with difficulties for the rest of their lives.

According to official reports of the relevant government departments, among the 27 notifiable infectious diseases, no cases of pestis, cholera, poliomyelitis, diphtheria, and SARS had been reported in the first quarter of 2004. However, there had been 604, 119 new cases of hepatitis B, tuberculosis, gonorrhea, bacillary dysentery and bacteria dysentery, and hepatitis A in the whole country, resulting in a total of 976 deaths, during this period of time. The five epidemic diseases with highest mortality rate are: rabies, tuberculosis, hepatitis B, epidemic cerebrospinal meningitis, and AIDS. [①]For some of these diseases, such as AIDS and hepatitis B, no effective treatment has been found.

The fierce competition under the socialist market economy has put many people under constant pressure and resulted in a drastic increase of cases of mental illness. Due to the influence of traditional culture, many people with mental illness are not aware of their illness or, even if they are aware of it, are too ashamed of it to seek medical treatment. The problem is further compounded by the shortage of qualified psychologists. As a result, many mental patients can not get timely treatment and the suicide rate has increased by a big margin in recent years.

Despite the great importance the state attaches to the protection of natural environment, environmental degradations, such as water and air pollutions, desertification, deforestation, destruction of wetland, and rapid drop of ground water level, have so far not been brought under control. These problems have posed serious threats not only to the present generation, but also to the future generations and, therefore, need to be solve as soon as possible.

Faced with these challenges, the Chinese government has put forward the ideas of "taking people as the foundation of government" and "government for the people", more specifically, "to take the full development of human beings as the ultimate goal of the government and the basic interest of the broad masses of people as the starting point of development, to make continuous efforts to meet people's increasing material and cultural demands, to conscientiously safeguard economic, political and cultural rights and interests of the people, and to enable

① *Beijing Evening News*, 12 April 2004, p. 16.

everyone to benefit from development."[1] This idea comes down in one continuous line from Mao Zedong's idea of "serving the people whole-heartedly" and is the declaration of government policy under new historical condition.

We are confident that, as long as the Chinese government adheres to the principle of "government for the people" and the scientific outlook on comprehensive, coordinated, and sustainable development, it will be able to overcome one by one the obstacles to the realization of the right to health, and truly safeguard the right of health of the Chinese people.

IV. The Right to Health and International Co-operation

Safeguarding the right to health is mainly an internal affaire of a country. However, international exchange and cooperation is also indispensable to safeguarding the right to health and constitutes an important content of the international protection of human rights.

First of all, international cooperation is necessary for the prevention and treatment of epidemic diseases. Some epidemic diseases come from the natural world, but some others are created by men. The natural ones are usually mutations of certain harmless species. Some of them have been understood by men while for many others, more research is still needed. The man-made ones are deliberately created by certain individuals, organizations, even states, with evil intentions. Natural epidemic diseases are disseminated through the movement of population and trade in goods; the man-made ones are released through various channels. The former need to be prevented while the latter must be strictly prohibited.

Secondly, international cooperation is necessary for the protection of the environment. Many environmental problems, such as the greenhouse effect, desertification, recession of glaciers, shrinkage of wetlands, pollution of oceans and rivers, deforestation, increase of acid rains, extinction and reduction of animal and plant species, and depletion of natural resources, directly threaten the health and the survival of mankind. These problems can not be resolved by one country alone or by some countries only.

---

① Hu Jintao, "Speech on the Conference on Population, Resources and Environment", *People's Daily*, 4 April 2004, p. 16.

Besides, good mental condition and moral quality are also indices of human health. Therefore, a good international order, codes of civilized international conduct, peaceful living environment, freedom from the threat of war and terror have become social conditions of human health. Acts such as dumping harmful nuclear or industrial wastes in other countries or advocating mistrust and hatred between nations, instigating national separatism, or provoking conflicts between states pose great danger to people's physical, mental and moral wellbeing throughout the world.

Moreover, since international cooperation is necessary for the prevention and treatment of epidemic diseases, the protection of the natural environment, and the creation of good social environment, states should also abide by the principle of "do not do to others what you would not have them do to you". ①They should not take advantage of other people's misfortune and made money out of their misery. Take the AIDS medicine for example, we should, on the one hand, protect the intellectual property and reasonable profit of the pharmaceutical companies while, on the other hand, prevent the price from rising to the point that the medicine is beyond the reach of most people, especially those in developing countries. Therefore, the developed countries should adopt a more tolerant and sympathetic attitude towards the demand of South Africa and other countries to produce generic AIDS medicine.

As far as the international protection of the right to health is concerned, we believe that the world we are living in will become much better if only governments can show a little more love and a little less hatred towards each other, and divert a small fraction of the money spent on the research and development of weapons of mass destruction to health promotion undertakings.

① See *The Analects*: *Yanyuan*.

Safeguarding People's Livelihood in China: Opportunities and Challenges[①]

People's livelihood refers to matters relating to people's basic necessities of life, such as food, clothing, housing and transportation, namely matters covered by the United Nations' 1966 International Covenant on Economic, Social and Cultural Rights. People's livelihood affects the survival of the people and the stability of the state and therefore is an issue that no social system or state could ignore. Summarizing the relevant historical experiences and carrying out research on the opportunities and challenges faced by China in this respect are of both theoretical and practical significance.

I. Historical Experience

China had been an agricultural society under the natural economy for the most part of its several-thousand-year history. According to historical records, during the Warring State Period more than 2000 years ago, the king of the State of Wei once asked Mencius for his advice on ruling the country. The followings were the advices given by Mencius: "If the seasons of husbandry be not interfered with, the grain will be more than can be eaten. If close nets are not allowed to enter the pools and ponds, the fishes and turtles will be more than can be consumed. If the axes and bills enter the hills and forests only at the proper time, the wood will be more than can be used. When the grain and fish and turtles are more than can be eaten, and there is more wood than can be used, this enables the people to nourish their living and mourn for their dead, without any feeling against any. This condition, in which the people nourish their living and bury their dead without any feeling against any, is the first step

① Originally published in the Journal *Citizen and Law*, No. 11, 2010.

of royal government." This was a general principle on ruling a country proposed by Mencius. As for each household, Mencius' advice was: "Let mulberry trees be planted about the homesteads with their five mu, and persons of fifty years may be clothed with silk. In keeping fowls, pigs, dogs, and swine, let not their times of breeding be neglected, and persons of seventy years may eat flesh. Let there not be taken away the time that is proper for the cultivation of the farm with its hundred mu, and the family of several mouths that is supported by it shall not suffer from hunger. Let careful attention be paid to education in schools, inculcating in it especially the filial and fraternal duties, and grey-haired men will not be seen upon the roads, carrying burdens on their backs or on their heads. It never has been that the ruler of a State, where such results were seen, -persons of seventy wearing silk and eating flesh, and the black-haired people suffering neither from hunger nor cold, -did not attain to the royal dignity." He believed that social stability could be achieved only if people are allowed to own permanent property and to have means to support their family: "As to the people, if they have not a certain livelihood, it follows that they will not have a fixed heart. And if they have not a fixed heart, there is nothing which they will not do, in the way of self-abandonment, of moral deflection, of depravity, and of wild license. When they thus have been involved in crime, to follow them up and punish them-this is to entrap the people. How can such a thing as entrapping the people be done under the rule of a benevolent man? Therefore an intelligent ruler will regulate the livelihood of the people, so as to make sure that, for those above them, they shall have sufficient wherewith to serve their parents, and, for those below them, sufficient wherewith to support their wives and children; that in good years they shall always be abundantly satisfied, and that in bad years they shall escape the danger of perishing. After this he may urge them, and they will proceed to what is good, for in this case the people will follow after it with ease."①

Although the above advices, put forward under the condition of agricultural natural economy, were only some ideals, they contained some elements of truth. For example, the ideas of not interfering with farming, allowing people to own permanent property, attaching importance to education, respecting and being filial to the elderly, supporting parents,

---

① See *Mencius*: *Liang Hui Wang*, Vol. I.

and taking measures to prevent natural disaster, all had had a profound influence on later generations.

Basically speaking, people's livelihood is closely related to the development of social production. However, the development of social production does not happen naturally, but depends on sound social institutions. This is especial true in societies with private ownership and industrialized mass production. The safeguarding of the livelihood of the whole society requires great efforts by all the people. The relationships of capitalist production grew gradually within the feudal society. In the 16th century Britain, the proportion of commodity production in the agriculture began to increase, the manufacturing industry developed gradually, and commerce started to expand overseas. Between mid 16th century and early 17th century, export made up 80—90% of the total production of woolen goods in the country. Meanwhile, new developments had been made in the shipbuilding industry, the wine-making industry, the glass manufacturing industry, the sugar making industry, the paper-making industry, and gun powder-manufacturing industry. Overseas trade was expanding and overseas plunder accelerated. In order to accelerate the accumulation of capital, the Great Britain first carried out trading activities with and then waged wars of aggressions against many countries around the world, from the Baltic Sea to Africa, and from China to the West Indies, and turned them into its own colonies. After the industrial revolution in the 17th century, capitalism developed at even faster speed in the European Continent. In order to increase their strength and further build wealth, the bourgeoisie ruthless exploited workers in their own countries and waged wars of aggression against foreign countries so as to turn them into their raw materials bases and commodity markets. In doing so, they threw the European Continent, even the entire world into great turmoil. Faced with violent class struggle, the bourgeoisies realized that, in order to ensure normal production and avoid the mutual destruction of opposing classes and the collapse of the whole society, and to ensure their own peace and development, they must enable workers and other laborers to make a living and amend and improve their existing methods of ruling and exploitation. The restriction on monopoly and the social security system emerged against this background. Historical records show that German Prime Minister Otto von Bismarck was a pioneer in the establishment of the social security system. However, social security as a system has taken a long time to develop and is still in the process of improvement even today. An example in this respect was the adoption by the U. S. Congress of the health care reform plan proposed by the Obama Administration. The current situations in Greece and other European countries are also manifestations of the difficulties in balancing the relationship between social welfare and economic development and state revenue. Both historical facts and current situation have demonstrated that people's livelihood has always been an important issue whether in the ideas put forward by ancient Chinese philosophers under the condition of agricultural natural economy or in the practices of modern industrialized European societies. We should not expect rulers in high positions and their spokesmen to take the safeguarding of human rights, rather than the interests of their own class, as their sole starting point when putting forward theories, adopting measures or establishing institutions. From historical perspective, however, it should not be denied that these ideas and measures had benefited the masses of people and therefore could be regarded as progressive. Especially the truth contained in ideas they put forward and the positive and negative experiences gained by them in relevant practices are valuable assets of human civilization that should be taken as reference by China in the construction of socialism.

II. The Reform in China

National independence, freedom and happiness are always the objectives of struggle for Chinese people.

The establishment of the People's Republic of China in 1949 marked the independence of the Chinese nation. Since then, the people's government has been striving for the realization of the freedom and happiness of the Chinese people. In 1950, in accordance with the Common Program of the Chinese People's Political Consultative Conference, which served as the temporary constitution at that time, China adopted the Marriage Law, which freed hundreds of millions Chinese people from the bondage of feudal marriage system, and Land Reform Law, which enabled landless peasants all over the country, with the exception of a few ethnic minority areas, to become owners of land. Meanwhile, the democratic reform carried out in urban areas freed workers from the oppression and exploitation by feudal bosses. The reform in rural and urban areas had greatly aroused the enthusiasm of broad masses of people, with whose strong support the Chinese government eliminated over one million armed bandits in the first three years of the People's Republic, thereby upholding people's right to a peaceful living environment. After the victory of the Korean War, in which the Chinese people defended their own homeland by assisting North Korea to resist the U. S. invasion, China rapidly restored the severely damaged national economy. By the end of 1952, the total industrial and agricultural production in the whole country had hit a record high. This was the first stage of reform carried out since the establishment of the new China.

On the basis of the above reform, China began large-scale socialist economic construction in 1953. According to the general line for the transitional period, the Central Committee of the CPC decided to "gradually realize the long-term objectives of socialist industrialization of the country and the socialist transformation of agricultural, handicraft industry, and capitalist industry and commerce."① The government realized the socialist transformation of the agriculture and handicraft industry by means of collectivization and the socialist transformation of capitalist industry and commerce was achieved by means of placing state orders with private enterprises, unified purchase and sale, public-private partnership, and other forms of state capital. By 1956, the socialist transformation of the private ownership of means of production had been completed in most parts of the country. During the latter part of this period, due to the eagerness the Chinese leaders for quick results, some problems had emerged in the socialist transformation and construction, resulting in adverse consequences for the development of the socialist cause. Generally speaking, however, China had made major achievements in the development of socialist economy during the period from 1953 to 1956: a number of large infrastructural projects necessary for the industrialization of the country had been completed; the gross industrial and agricultural output values had been increasing at an annual rate of 19.6% and 4.8% respectively; the market had been brisk and the prices stable; people's living standard had been rising continuously; and social order had been good. This was the second stage of reform in China since 1949.

The completion of the basic socialist transformation and the realization of

---

① See *Resolution on Certain Questions in the History of the CPC since the Founding of the People's Republic of China*, adopted at the Sixth Plenary Session of the Eleventh Central Committee of the Communist Party of China on June 27, 1981.

the public ownership of the means of production laid a foundation for the implementation of socialist planned economy. The 20 years between 1956 and 1976 was a period in which China had strictly implemented the planned economy and could be regarded as the third stage of the social reform in China. This period can be further divided into two parts—the first decade and the second decade. During the first decade, the Chinese leaders, blockaded by western countries and eager to uphold national independence and realize national unification, became too ambitious in economy development and launched the movements of "Great Leap Forward" and "People's Commune", which were serious mistakes in violation of objective laws of development. In 1964 and 1965, the Chinese leaders, after summarizing experiences and lessons of the first decade, adjusted its economic policy, thus enabling China to enter into a period of economic development. Before long, however, they made another big mistake by launching the so-called "Cultural Revolution". During the "Cultural Revolution", which lasted for 10 years, some Chinese leaders, under the banner "to rebel is justified", encouraged students in schools and colleges "to suspend classes to carry out revolution" and workers in some factories "to stop production to carry out revolution", thereby disrupting the orders of production, study and daily life of the Chinese people, and leading to great social chaos. "Practice has shown that the 'Cultural Revolution' did not in fact constitute a revolution or social progress in any sense, nor could it possibly have done so."① During the 20—year period, despite a series of mistakes, especially the serious mistake of launching the "Cultural Revolution", the CPC and its leaders still enjoyed high prestige among Chinese people because of the great achievements they had made in the democratic revolution and in the democratic reform and socialist transformation in the 1950s. A large number of CPC cadres and ordinary CPC members still adhered to the correct direction, and the broad masses of Chinese people still had confidence in the CPC and the people's government. Thanks to the concerted efforts by all CPC members, the masses of workers, peasants, commanders and fighters of the Chinese People's Liberation Army, intellectuals, educated youth and cadres, China continued to make

① See *Resolution on Certain Questions in the History of the CPC since the Founding of the People's Republic of China*, adopted at the Sixth Plenary Session of the Eleventh Central Committee of the Communist Party of China on June 27, 1981.

progress in the socialist construction during this period of time: "By 1966, the value of fixed industrial assets, calculated on the basis of their original price, was 4 times greater than in 1956. The output of such major industrial products as cotton yarn, coal, electricity, crude oil, steel and mechanical equipment all recorded impressive increases. Beginning in 1965, China became self-sufficient in petroleum. New industries such as the electronic and petrochemical industries were established one after another. The distribution of industry over the country became better balanced. Capital construction in agriculture and its technical transformation began on a massive scale and yielded better and better results. Both the number of tractors for farming and the quantity of chemical fertilizers applied increased over 6 times."① Meanwhile, there had also been major developments in the field of education, with marked improvement of the quality of education. The backbone force in later economic and cultural construction was trained during this period.

During the ten years of "Cultural Revolution", some progress was made in the development of the national economy despite tremendous losses: "Grain output increased relatively steadily. Significant achievements were scored in industry, communications and capital construction and in science and technology. New railways were built and the Changjiang River Bridge at Nanjing was completed; a number of large enterprises using advanced technology went into operation; hydrogen bomb tests were successfully undertaken and man-made satellites successfully launched and retrieved; and new hybrid strains of long-grained rice were developed and popularized."②

The main problem with people's livelihood during this period was that, because of the tremendous losses suffered by the national economy, the rapid growth of the population, and the improper treatment of the relationship between accumulation and consumption, there was no marked rise in people's living standard. Grains, edible oil, meat, cloth, and other necessities of life had always been rationed at a low level. The health level of some people in disaster-stricken areas was low and in some areas there was a high rate of unnatural death among population. There was no

---

① See *Resolution on Certain Questions in the History of the CPC since the Founding of the People's Republic of China*, adopted at the Sixth Plenary Session of the Eleventh Central Committee of the Communist Party of China on June 27, 1981.

② Ibid.

major improvement in people's living conditions. Forests and lakes were turned into farmland, resulting in serious desertification of land and destruction of the environment. Nevertheless, even during the period in which there were serious problems in national development and no marked improvement in people's livelihood, the CPC and Chinese leaders had led the Chinese people in establishing a rural cooperative medical care system based on the public ownership system; in light of the actual need, the government trained a large number of so-called "barefoot doctors" who provided basic medical services in rural areas while engaging in agricultural work and, on the basis of the "barefoot doctor system", established a rural medical care network; a system of "five guarantees" was established for the old people in rural areas who had no family to support them, so as to provide them with guarantees of food, clothing, medical care, housing and burial expenses; and a healthcare system for urban employees and a medical aid system for employees of enterprises and public institutions had been established in urban areas. These systems had guaranteed the basic livelihood of the people and upheld social stability at that time.

In 1978, the Third Plenary Session of the Eleventh Central Committee of the CPC summarized the historical experiences both in China and abroad and decided to implement the policy of emancipating the mind, reform and opening up, thereby beginning the fourth stage of the reform in China since the establishment of People's Republic. This stage of reform, which began more than 30 years ago, can be further divided into the following periods: first, the period between 1978 and 1992, in which China was groping the way forward in economic reform, first in rural areas, then in urban areas. Second, in 1992, China set the goal of developing socialist market economy, thereby further determining the direction of the reform. The Outline of the Ninth Five-Year Plan for National Economic and Social Development and the Long-Term Goals to the Year 2010, adopted at the Fourth Meeting of the Eighth National People's Congress, set the goal of quadrupling the GNP of 1980 by the year 2000, basically eradicating poverty, raising people's living standard to a relatively comfortable level, and quadrupling the GNP of 2000 by the year 2010. The first part of this goal had already been realized at the end of 2000, when China's GNP reached 8.9 trillion yuan. Third, in 2002, after reaching the goal of raising people's living standard to a relatively comfortable level, the CPC and the Chinese government decided that, in the first two decades of the 21 century, namely before the year 2020, China would concentrate on building a well-off society of a higher standard in an all-round way, to the benefit of well over one billion people, and that it would "further develop the economy, improve democracy, advance science and education, enrich culture, foster social harmony and upgrade the texture of life for the people."① Now the Chinese people are making concerted efforts towards this goal. According to the Report on the Work of the Government given by Premier Wen Jiabao in March 2010, China's GDP reached 33.5 trillion yuan in 2009. On the basis of the achievement already made, the Chinese government has set the goal of increasing GDP by approximately 8% in the year 2010. ②

III. Opportunities and Challenges Faced by China in Safeguarding People's Livelihood

During the 60 years since the founding of the People's Republic, although China has experienced many frustrations and setbacks in the reform and socialist construction, generally speaking, it has been advancing along the socialist road. Especially since the reform and opening up in 1978, there has been sustained and rapid development of the socialist construction and all-round improvement of people's political, social and cultural life. However, in addition to the rare opportunities, China is also faced with severe challenges in safeguarding people's livelihood.

The practice in the past 30 years has proved that the socialist system with Chinese characteristics is superior to other social systems and that it is a correct approach to let some people get rich first on the basis of continuously developing socialist economy and then let those who have already become rich help those who are still poor to achieve common prosperity. The system has stood the test of not only domestic practice of economic development, but also the crisis of the real economy triggered by

---

① See Jiang Zemin, "Build a Well-off Society in an All-Round Way and Create a New Situation in Building Socialism with Chinese Characteristics", Report to the 16th National Congress of the Communist Party of China (CPC) on Nov. 8, 2002.

② See Report on the Work of the Government, Presented by Premier Wen Jiabao on March 5, 2010 and adopted by the National People's Congress on March 14, 2010.

international financial crisis. China has been advancing rapidly towards its established goals. However, the socialist market economic system is a new system whether compared to Soviet socialism, the strict planned economic system implemented by China before 1978, the American-style free market economic system, or the German-style socialist market economic system. Therefore, it is necessary for China to further summarize its experiences and carry out exploration, both in theory and practice, on how to combine socialism with market economy. Today, the market economic system in China is still at a stage of adjustment in many fields. The main problems at this stage include:

Development is of overriding importance. During the past 30 years, China has always been taking economic construction as its central task. This policy is very correct and will continue to be implemented in the future. However, for a period of time, China has put too much emphasis on the growth of the GDP and on the quantity and speed, rather than the quality, of development, resulting in waste of natural and human resources, pollution of the environment, production of defective products, even foods and medicine that are harmful to people's health.

In the process of development, attention has been paid to the accumulated public funds and state revenue, which brought fast increase in foreign exchange reserves, rapid development of infrastructure, a major change in the appearance of the country, and marked rise in the income of urban and rural residents. However, there is a problem of lack of coordination between accumulation and consumption. The increase of employees' wages has been slow. Those of employees in some areas have remained at the same level for years, even for over a dozen years, without being increased along with the growth of the national economy and the rise in commodity prices. The widening income gap between ordinary employees and some senior managerial personnel and seriously unequal distribution of social wealth have caused discontent among ordinary employees. Another aspect of the problem of lack of coordination between accumulation and consumption is the insufficient state input in such areas as education, medical care, and social pension. At a time the state even tried to commercialize education and medical service, resulting in negative ideological and institutional impacts on society which have not yet been totally eliminated even today.

Expanding employment is a matter of primary importance to the safeguarding of people's livelihood. Currently China is still at the peak of the growth of urban and rural labor force. Although over the years the Chinese government has made every effort in expanding employment, kept the unemployment rate at around 4. 5%, and arranged work for over 100 million migrant peasant workers, it is still faced with tremendous employment pressures. It is predicted that, during the 12th Five-Year Plan period between 2011 and 2015, "the number of people needing employment in urban areas will be around 25 million each year, while the number of new jobs and jobs made available as a result of natural reduction of staffs will be only 12 million each year. China is now faced with the triple difficulty of reemployment of laid-off workers, employment of youth, and employment of workers migrating from rural areas to urban areas. And there will be a significant increase in the complexity of the problem of employment of migrant workers from rural areas."[①] Under this circumstance, further researches need to be carried out on how to ensure the sustainable development of production, expand employment, and raise the quality, increase the scientific and cultural knowledge, and improve the entrepreneurial ability of the labor force.

In accordance with the Constitutional provision of "adhering to the basic economic system in which the public ownership is dominant and diverse forms of ownership develop side by side", both the public sector of the economy and sectors of the economy with different types of ownership, including private ownership, have developed rapidly in recent years and made their contributions to the socialist construction. However, some enterprises, especially Hong Kong and Taiwan enterprises and private enterprises, do not conscientiously implement the relevant state laws or their social responsibilities, ignore the safety in workplace, and refuse to pay the medical, unemployment or old-age insurances for their employees. Some factories in the manufacturing industry have even become sweatshops. Some local governments, in order to protect local interest, failed to supervise and regulate these enterprises in accordance with law. Some government officials even collude with business owners to engage in unlawful acts for personal gains, resulting in frequent occurrence of accidents in factories and mines, thereby seriously endangering the personal safety and the life of employees.

---

① Wu Ting and Guo Xiaoya, "Employment in China: Dilemma and the Way Out", in *Chinese Social Sciences Weekly*, June 17, 2010.

In 2003, in order to improve the socialist market economic system, the Chinese government decided to "adhere to the people-first principle, and establish the concept of comprehensive, coordinated and sustainable development", thereby rectifying the erroneous tendency of overemphasizing the growth of the GDP. After the crisis of real economy trigged by the financial crisis in the U. S., the implementation of the scientific outlook on development became even more urgent. For this reason, the Chinese government strengthened macroscopic regulation. However, because of the decentralization and individualization of interests caused by the development of the market economy, there emerged unprecedented amount of game-playing between the central and local governments, between the government and enterprises, between enterprises, and between the government, enterprises and the general public in the process of such regulation. There are always people who openly violate laws, exploit loopholes in laws and policies, or abuse power for personal gains, whether in the use of land and resources, in credit origination, in the use of fund, in the setting of commodity prices, or in the recruitment of employees. All these have increased the difficulties of the problems and endangered the people's livelihood.

Nevertheless, China is also faced with many favorable opportunities and conditions that enable it to meet these challenges.

Firstly, as mentioned above, the purpose of the construction of socialism with Chinese characteristics is to meet people's growing material and cultural needs and the purpose of the development of socialist market economy is to achieve common prosperity. The above purposes provide guarantee in terms of guiding ideology and basic system for the resolution of the problems.

Secondly, the efforts made by China in the past 60 year, especially in the past 30 years since 1978, have laid a sound material foundation for the solution of the problems relating to the people's livelihood, such as the so-called "three rural problems" (problems relating to agriculture, rural areas and farmers), urban employment problem, problems in educational and medical care systems, and problems in the social assistance system.

Thirdly, the ideas of "people first" and "harmonious society" in traditional Chinese culture have already provided guiding ideology for the construction of the system of safeguarding people's livelihood. Other concepts in traditional Chinese culture, such as "benevolence", "respecting the aged and taking good care of children", "being considerate to others", "kindheartedness and justice", "benevolent government", "peace", "harmony", etc., also have profound influence among the Chinese people, and, together with socialist ideological resources and theories, will play an important role in the construction of the system of guaranteeing the people's livelihood.

Fourthly, the rights consciousness of both government officials and ordinary people in China has been greatly enhanced. The changes in domestic and international situation have enabled them to realize that the improvement of people's livelihood is necessary not only for increasing domestic demand and promoting the healthy development of the economy, but also for the full protection of human rights. Such an understanding will further enhance people enthusiasm for participating in the construction of the system of safeguarding people's livelihood.

Fifthly, when implementing the policy of reform and opening up, China needs not only to continuously summarize it own experience, but also to draw on the useful experiences of EU countries and other countries in the world. EU countries have rich experience in safeguarding people's livelihood: they have encountered many of the problems now encountered by China and they are also facing some of the same problems faced by China today, such as unemployment. Strengthening international exchange and cooperation will be conducive to mutual development and mutual benefit.

IV. Further Strengthening the Human Rights Safeguarding Mechanism

In order to strengthen the safeguarding of human rights, including people's livelihood, the UN adopted in December 1993 the "Paris Principles", which require member states to establish national human rights institutions. This instrument was adopted at the requests raised at human rights conferences in Africa, Latin America and Asian and therefore is broadly based. Its intention is good and its objective correct. China will implement the "Paris Principles" in light of its own national conditions.

Although currently China has not yet established a specialized national human rights institution with extensive powers, it has established a human rights protection mechanism in light of the actual need in the country, namely the mechanism of complaint letters and visits. Complaint bodies have been established under state administrative, legislative, and ruling-party organs at various levels throughout the country to receive such letters and visits. Although the 2005 Regulation on Complaint Letters and Visits was promulgated by the State Council, they are to be taken as reference by other government organs in the handling of complaint letters and visits. The Regulations point out in the General Provisions that the purpose of the Provisions is "to keep the people's governments at all levels in close contact with the masses, and protect the legitimate rights and interests of those who complain by letters and visits." They provide that "the people's governments at all levels or working departments of the people's governments at or above the county level shall properly handle complaint letters and visits, carefully deal with such letters, receive such visitors, listen attentively to the opinions, proposals and requests of the masses, subject themselves to the supervision by the masses and exert themselves to serve the masses"; that "when handling complained matters, an administrative organ and its functionaries shall fulfill its duties scrupulously, be impartial, find out facts, distinguish liabilities, propagandize the legal system, make ideological education, duly and properly settle matters and may not shift responsibilities to others or do their work in a perfunctory or delayed manner"; that "a hearing may be held for a major, complicated or difficult matter. The hearing shall be held publicly in an effort to find out facts and differentiate responsibilities by way of interrogation, debate, discussion and collegial deliberation. The scope, presiding hearer, attendees and procedures for the hearing shall be prescribed by the people's governments of each province, autonomous region or municipality directly under the Central Government"; and that "a complaint which is based on clear facts and in line with the laws, regulations, rules or other relevant provisions shall be supported; a complaint which is short of facts or not in line with any law, regulation, rule or any other relevant provision shall not be supported". An accountability system is implemented in the work relating to complaint letters and visits: "In case any organ in charge of dealing with complaint letters and visits oversteps or misuse its authority, conducts nonfeasance when it shall take actions, is erroneous in applying laws or regulations, or breaches the statutory procedures, thus impairing the legitimate rights and interests of complaint makers, the principal and any other person held to be directly responsible shall be imposed with administrative sanctions pursuant to the provisions in relevant laws and administrative regulations; in case any crime is constituted, the offender shall be investigated for criminal liabilities."

In China, the law has also given such social organizations as trade unions, women's federations, and committees for the wellbeing of the youth the power of protecting the rights of workers, women and children. A National Working Committee on Women and Children has been established under the State Council and women's federations have been praised as women's "mother's home" for their effective work in protecting women's rights and interests. And, as the recent development in Guangdong Province has shown, trade unions will strengthen its work of upholding workers' rights and interests.

The experiences of EU countries and other countries in the world show that a society will enter into a social conflict-prone period when its per capita GDP reaches the level of 1,000 to 3,000 U.S. dollars. From the problems discussed above we can see that today's China is in exactly such a period of development: the numbers of social conflicts, of problems to be solved by the government, and of complaint letters and visits are on the rise; strikes by workers have emerged in some enterprises; crime rate is high; some government officials do not strictly follow the law in their work, even abuse their power for personal gain, or violate human rights. Currently the Chinese government is making great efforts in strengthening the rule of law, resolving social conflicts by various means, and speeding up the construction of human rights protection mechanism.

As to the question of whether to establish a national human rights institution, discussions have been carried out in the Chinese academic circle and proposals submitted by some members of China Society for Human Rights Studies. Personally I believe that establishing such an institution is conducive to strengthening human rights protection. However, because the establishment of such an institution involves the allocation of state power, careful study is needed on its legal status, on the scope of its functions and powers, and on its relationship with existing relevant state organs. In 2007, I proposed that a human rights coordination mechanism be established under the direct leadership of the highest state decision-making organ to be responsible for coordination of policymaking, dissemination and education, theoretical research, liaison with social organizations, and international exchange and cooperation in the field of human rights and that researches be carried out on specialized national human rights institution with a view to establishing such an institution when the condition becomes ripe.

Protection of the Rights of Disabled Persons from the Perspective of International Human Rights Conventions[①]

The rights of disabled persons are an important content of human rights and the level of protection of these rights is an indication of the level of civilization and of human rights protection in general in a country. The international community has always attached special importance to the protection of the rights of disabled persons. The Convention on the Rights of Persons with Disabilities, adopted by the UN General Assembly in 2006, is a new milestone in the development of the cause of protection of the rights of disabled persons.

I. Disabled Persons and the Protection of Their Rights

The Convention on the Rights of Persons with Disabilities defines persons with disabilities as "those who have long-term physical, mental, intellectual or sensory impairments which in interaction with various barriers may hinder their full and effective participation in society on an equal basis with others."[②] The Law of the People's Republic of China on the Protection of Disabled Persons defines a disabled person as "a person who suffers from the loss or abnormity of a certain organ or function, psychologically, physiologically or in human structure, and has lost all or in part of the ability to normally carry out certain activities."[③] According to a drafter of the UN Convention on the Rights of Persons with

① Originally published in *Global Law Review*, 2009, No. 4.

② Article 1 of the Convention on the Rights of Persons with Disabilities.

③ Article 2 of the Law of the People's Republic of China on the Protection of Disabled Persons.

Disabilities, the Convention, in view of the fact that disability is an evolving concept, does not give a strict definition to "persons with disabilities", so as to leave some room for future development. The Chinese Law on the Protection of Disabled Persons, while giving a definition to "disabled person", also leaves plenty room for future development by providing that: "The criteria for the classification of disabilities shall be formulated by the State Council. "① A review of the laws of different countries in the world shows that the criterion for the determination of disability varies from country to country. According to a sampling survey, disabled persons make up about 6. 34% of the Chinese population. In other countries, the percentage is between 8% and 10% or even higher than 10%. The difference in the percentage of disabled persons in the population is mainly caused by the different criteria on disability adopted by different states in light of their national conditions. Let's assume disabled persons make up 8% of the world population. Then there will be a total of 520 million disabled persons in today's world, which has a total population of 6. 2 billion. Let's further assume that each of these disabled persons belongs a family of four persons. Then there will be 520 million families with 2 billion persons affected by disability. This calculation may be not very accurate or scientific, but it does reveal the scale of the problem. Just as Mencius pointed out: "All men have natural sympathies. "② The protection of the rights of disabled persons has an extensive and profound impact on society. If disabled persons are unable to have their rights safeguarded or properly safeguarded, and if some of them are left without any means to support themselves, become homeless, or even die on the street or in the wilderness, more people will be disheartened by the misery and apathy of the society they live in; on the other hand, in a society that truly safeguards the rights and interests of disabled persons, enables disabled persons to integrate themselves into society and live with other people in equality, provide them with social security, and respect their human dignity, then not only the disabled persons, but also their families and all members of society will feel the warmth and safety of society, and be inspired to devote themselves to the construction of a more harmonious society.

---

① Article 2 of the Law of the People's Republic of China on the Protection of Disabled Persons.

② See *Mencius*: *Gaozi*.

II. The Convention on the Rights of Persons with Disabilities: from Formal Equality to de facto Equality

The UN Charter, the Universal Declaration of Human Rights, the InternationalCovenant on Economic, Social and Cultural, and the International Covenant on Civil and Political Rights are great historical instruments that formally incorporate the protection of human rights into international law. The Universal Declaration of Human Rights proclaims at its very beginning that: "recognition of the inherent dignity and of the equal and inalienable rights of all members of the human family is the foundation of freedom, justice and peace in the world". ①A similar proclamation can be found in the two 1966 international human rights covenants. This proclamation highlights the universality of human rights, which is embodied in the relevant provisions of the Declaration and the two covenants: all the provisions on specific human rights in these three instruments begin with such terms as "everyone", "anyone", "all human beings". In a world in which exploitation, oppression, discrimination and hunger are still facts of life and the right to life and the right of existence of many people are not guaranteed, such proclamations of binding codes of conduct is very heartening. However, the promulgation of these instruments is still not enough to guarantee the rights of vulnerable groups of society, such as women, children, and especially disabled persons. If they are treated the same as healthy persons, it would be impossible for them to enjoy de facto equality. Therefore, the state must adopt laws and establish institutions to provide them with special protection to compensate for their mental and physical disabilities, so as to enable them to enjoy actual equality with other members of society. This is an important aspect of the particularity of human rights protection.

Soon after the promulgation of the two international human rights covenants in 1966, the international community has adopted a series of instruments that provide special protection to disabled persons: the UN adopted the Resolution on Prohibiting All Social Conditions Disregarding Persons with Disability in 1969, the Declaration on the Rights of Mentally Retarded Persons in 1971, the Declaration on the Rights of Disabled

① See the Preamble of the Universal Declaration of Human Rights.

Persons in 1975, the World Programme of Action Concerning Disabled Persons in 1982, and the Standard Rules on the Equalization of Opportunities for Persons with Disabilities in 1993. Moreover the ILO has adopted Vocational Rehabilitation and Employment (Disabled Persons) Convention and Recommendation in 1983. Of course, the most important instrument in this field is the Convention on the Rights of Persons with Disabilities, adopted by the UN General Assembly in 2006. When commenting on the current situation of the rights of persons with disabilities, the Convention points out in its Preamble: "despite these various instruments and undertakings, persons with disabilities continue to face barriers in their participation as equal members of society and violations of their human rights in all parts of the world". To change this abnormal situation, the Convention reaffirms "the universality, indivisibility, interdependence and interrelatedness of all human rights and fundamental freedoms and the need for persons with disabilities to be guaranteed their full enjoyment without discrimination". It recognizes that "discrimination against any person on the basis of disability is a violation of the inherent dignity and worth of the human person" and emphasizes "the need for persons with disabilities to be guaranteed their full enjoyment without discrimination" and "the importance of mainstreaming disability issues as an integral part of relevant strategies of sustainable development". The purpose of Convention, which consists of 50 articles with clear and detailed contents, is "to promote, protect and ensure the full and equal enjoyment of all human rights and fundamental freedoms by all persons with disabilities, and to promote respect for their inherent dignity." To this end, the Convention provides for the following eight general principles: "(a) Respect for inherent dignity, individual autonomy including the freedom to make one's own choices, and independence of persons; (b) Non-discrimination; (c) Full and effective participation and inclusion in society; (d) Respect for difference and acceptance of persons with disabilities as part of human diversity and humanity; (e) Equality of opportunity; (f) Accessibility; (g) Equality between men and women; and (h) Respect for the evolving capacities of children with disabilities and respect for the right of children with disabilities to preserve their identities. The above principles are comprehensive, involving both ideological and institutional issues, and each of them is very important. The most important among these principles are the principles of equality and non-discrimination and respect for difference and acceptance of persons with disabilities as part of human diversity and humanity. "Respect for difference" does not mean treating persons with disabilities as different, but to adopt special measures to reduce the differences and narrow the gap between persons with disabilities and healthy people, and adopt different preferential measures for persons with different disabilities and for each individual in the group of persons with same disability in light of their special needs. Accessibility includes both accessibility in movement and audio and visual accessibility. To realize accessibility, the state should create necessary conditions and provide necessary facilities and equipments. The purpose of the provisions on equality between men and women and on children with disabilities is to enable people to realize that women, children and elderly with disabilities are vulnerable groups within the vulnerable group of society and, as such, need to be paid special attention. In order to realize the principle of equality and non-discrimination, measures must be taken to ensure "the full and effective participation and inclusion" of persons with disabilities in society under the condition of equality of opportunity. In the protection of disabled persons, attention must be paid to respecting their own choices, and their inherent dignity and autonomy. The above principles are indispensable to the protection of the rights of disabled persons and the realization of de facto equality between disabled persons and other members of society.

III. The Comprehensiveness of the Protection of the Rights of Disabled Persons

Human rights are comprehensive. After the World War II, the comprehensiveness of human rights was further recognized by international community through the summarization of the historical experience and confirmed by various international human rights instruments. More detailed explanations of this concept were given by the Proclamation of Tehran, adopted at the International Conference on Human Rights in Teheran in 1968, and the Resolution on New Concepts of Human Rights, adopted by the UN General Assembly in 1997. the Resolution points out that: "All human rights and fundamental freedoms are indivisible and interdependent; equal attention and urgent consideration should be given to the implementation, promotion and protection of both civil and political, and economic, social and cultural rights; the full realization of civil and political rights without the enjoyment of economic, social and cultural rights is impossible, as recognized by the Proclamation of Teheran of 1968. "① This conclusion fully demonstrates the comprehensiveness of human rights, which is very important to the construction of human rights system in a country and to the safeguarding the rights of all persons, especially those of disabled persons. It is exactly based on this understanding that the Convention on the Rights of Persons with Disabilities points out in its Preamble the importance of "a comprehensive and integral international convention to promote and protect the rights and dignity of persons with disabilities". This comprehensiveness is embodied not only in the confirmation by the Convention of the close relationship between economic, social and cultural rights and civil and political rights, but also in the detailed provisions on each of the rights of disabled persons in the Convention, formuated in light of the special needs of disabled persons. The followings are a few examples:

First, "equality and non-discrimination". Article 5 of the Convention not only confirms "equal before and under the law" as a principle applicable to every person and prohibits "all discrimination on the basis of disability", but also provides that "In order to promote equality and eliminate discrimination, States Parties shall take all appropriate steps to ensure that reasonable accommodation is provided." The Convention contains detailed provisions on such accommodations, including ten provisions on "accessibility", which include accessibilities with respect to buildings, roads, transportation and other indoor and outdoor facilities, including schools, housing, medical facilities and workplace and outdoor facilities, as well as information, communications and other services, including electronic services and emergency services.

Second, habilitation, rehabilitation and health. Enabling disable persons to restore as much as possible their functions and health, and enhancing their self-care ability and their ability to integration themselves into society by providing them with medical treatments and habilitation and rehabilitation services in light of their particular conditions is the precondition for their equal participation and inclusion in society. The Convention contains detailed provisions on the health services needed by persons with disabilities specifically because of their disabilities, including early identification and intervention as appropriate, assessment

---

① Dong Yunhu (ed.), *World Documents of Human Rights*, Sichuan People's Publishing House, 1991, p. 991.

of individual needs and strengths, habilitation and rehabilitation, the development of initial and continuing training for professionals and staff working in habilitation and rehabilitation services, as well as the range, quality and costs of health care for disabled persons.

Third, education. The article on education in the Convention contains five paragraphs and more than ten subparagraphs. Their purpose is to provide disabled persons with individualized, inclusive and lifelong education, so as to enable them to fully develop their potential and their sense of dignity and self-worth, and truly participate in society. To this end, the state should provide reasonable accommodation so as to enable persons with disabilities to access an inclusive, quality and free primary education and secondary education on an equal basis with others in the communities in which they live; and it should provide special education, including educational in sign language and/or Braille to persons, especially children, suffering from blindness, deafness and mental disabilities, and train qualified professionals and staff for such education. On the above basis, the state should provide disabled persons with reasonable accommodation to ensure that they are able to access general tertiary education, vocational training, adult education and lifelong learning without discrimination and on an equal basis with others.

Fourth, work and employment. The right to work and the right to employment are the fundamental rights of all people, including disabled persons. These rights enable disabled persons to improve their living conditions, participate in society and enjoy the material and cultural achievements of social progress on an equal basis with other members of society. To realize these rights, the Convention requires states parties to: prohibit discrimination on the basis of disability with regard to all matters concerning all forms of employment, including conditions of recruitment, hiring and employment, continuance of employment, career advancement and safe and healthy working conditions; protect the rights of persons with disabilities, on an equal basis with others, to just and favorable conditions of work; including equal remuneration for work of equal value and safe and healthy working conditions; ensure that persons with disabilities are able to exercise their trade union rights; and enable persons with disabilities to have effective access to placement services and vocational and continuing training. Moreover, the Convention also requires states parties to promote opportunities for self-employment, entrepreneurship, the development of cooperatives for persons with disabilities, employ persons with disabilities in the public sector, promote the employment of persons with disabilities in the private sector, and ensure that persons with disabilities are not held in slavery or in servitude, and are protected, on an equal basis with others, from forced or compulsory labor.

Fifth, civil and political rights. In view of the fact that the civil and political rights of disabled persons are more likely to be ignored or violated, the Convention contains separate articles on various civil and political rights of persons with disabilities, including the right to life, right to physical and mental integrity, liberty and security of the person, situations of risk and humanitarian emergencies, freedom from torture or cruel, inhuman or degrading treatment or punishment, and access to justice. To ensure the realization of these rights, the Convention requires states parties to adopt relevant laws and policies, and "promote appropriate training for those working in the field of administration of justice, including police and prison staff".

The above examples of the comprehensiveness of the Convention reflects the good intention of UN human rights organs to protect the rights of disabled persons, as well as the actual need for truly safeguarding of the rights of disabled persons.

IV. The Obligations of Family, Society and the State in Safeguarding the Rights of Disabled Persons

The Convention on the Rights of Persons with Disabilities emphasizes the obligations of family, society, and especially the state, to implement the various provisions in the Convention.

1. The Family

The Convention points out in its Preamble that: "the family is the natural and fundamental group unit of society and is entitled to protection by society and the State, and that persons with disabilities and their family members should receive the necessary protection and assistance to enable families to contribute towards the full and equal enjoyment of the rights of persons with disabilities. This provision first explains the nature of family and its important role in safeguarding the rights of disabled persons. The family and its members bear many responsibilities in the support, education, daily life and inclusion in society of disabled persons. To enable family to make its due contribution to the safeguarding of the rights of disabled persons, the state should provide the necessary protection and support to disabled persons and their family members. Article 23 of the Convention contains detailed provisions on such protection and support, including: to prevent concealment, abandonment, neglect and segregation of children with disabilities; to ensure that a child shall not be separated from his or her parents against their will; to render appropriate assistance to persons with disabilities in the performance of their child-rearing responsibilities; to ensure that, in the establishment of the systems of guardianship, wardship, trusteeship, adoption of children or similar institutions, the best interests of the child shall be paramount; and to respect the rights of persons with disability in matters relating to marriage, family, and parenthood and to provide them with necessary accommodation to facilitate their exercise of these rights. The Convention also provides that: "States Parties shall take all appropriate and effective measures to ensure the equal right of persons with disabilities to own or inherit property". Facts have shown that, under normal circumstance, parents usually show more care and love to their disabled children in family life. However, when parents lose their ability to support their children or themselves, especially when they are old and suffer from disabilities, their healthy children often fail to show enough love or care to their disabled parents or siblings. To solve this problem, the state should improve the relevant laws and institutions and at the same time hand strengthen the education on traditional ethnics of being filial to parents and caring for brothers and sisters.

2. The Community

The community is component part of society, where disabled persons carry out most of their activities outside their homes and prepare for their inclusion in society. The Convention attaches great importance to the role played by the community in safeguarding the rights of disabled persons and imposed on it many duties and obligations in this respect. First, the duty to care for disabled children. The Convention provides that: "States Parties shall, where the immediate family is unable to care for a child with disabilities, undertake every effort to provide alternative care within the wider family, and failing that, within the community in a family setting." This is because disabled children can be better and more conveniently taken care of by their close neighbors in the community whom they are familiar with and trust. The community also plays an important role in the education, medical care and development of inter-personal skills of disabled persons. The Convention provides that: "States Parties to this Convention recognize the equal right of all persons with disabilities to live in the community, with choices equal to others". This include the right to access an inclusive, quality and free primary education and secondary education on an equal basis with others in the communities in which they live; the right have access to health services as close as possible to their own communities, including in rural areas; the right to learn life and social development skills to facilitate their full and equal participation in education and as members of the community; and the right to receive support and help from the community and society when necessary, including the right to sufficient food, clothing, housing, clean water and other low-cost services. The Convention especially stresses that participation and inclusion in the community and all aspects of society should be voluntary, and available to persons with disabilities as close as possible to their own communities. A representative of disabled persons who participated in the deliberation on the Convention pointed out that measures for the protection of disabled persons should be formulated from the point of view of disabled persons and take into consideration their actual needs and circumstances. Otherwise, such measures will only harm the dignity of the disabled persons and further restrict their freedom. Therefore, such protection should be individualized in light of the actual needs of disabled persons and should never take the form of compulsion.

3. The State

States parties are the bearers of the obligations under the Convention on the Rights of Persons with Disabilities and are responsible for the implementation of these obligations. Apart from the Preamble, three articles (articles 1—3) on the "Purpose", "Definitions" and "General Principles" of the Convention, and 18 articles (articles 34—50) on the "Committee on the Rights of Persons with Disabilities", namely the deliberation of state party reports on the implementation of the Convention, and relevant procedural matters, the rest of the articles (articles 4—33) are all about the obligations of states parties to the Convention. According to these provisions, "States Parties undertake to ensure and promote the full realization of all human rights and fundamental freedoms for all persons with disabilities without discrimination of any kind on the basis of disability." To this end, they should adopt all appropriate legislative, administrative and other measures for the implementation of the rights recognized in the Convention, to modify or abolish existing laws, regulations, customs and practices that constitute discrimination against persons with disabilities, to eliminate discrimination on the basis of disability by any person, organization or private enterprise, and to undertake or promote research and development of universally designed goods, services, equipment and facilities suitable to be used by persons with disabilities. In the process of implementing the Convention, special care should be given to disabled women, children and elderly persons. To reduce the resistance to the implementation of the Convention, states parties must carried out effective public awareness campaigns in the whole society so as to promote awareness of the capabilities and contributions of persons with disabilities, promote recognition of the skills, merits and abilities of persons with disabilities; foster at all levels of the education system, including in all children from an early age, an attitude of respect for the rights of persons with disabilities; and encourage all organs of the media to portray persons with disabilities in a manner consistent with the purpose of the Convention. On the above basis, the state should supervise over the implementation of laws and policies on the protection of disabled persons by its subsidiary organs, public institutions, and corporations, and pay special attention to the protection of the rights of disabled persons to participation in political and public life, to liberty and personal security, to freedom from exploitation, violence and abuse, and to access to justice. Safeguarding the rights of disabled persons is mainly a domestic obligation of the state. However, after ratification of the Convention, a state must also fulfill its international obligations, strengthen international exchange and cooperation and draw on the useful experiences of other countries. It must also submit periodical report on the implementation of the Convention to the Committee on the Rights of Persons with Disabilities and accept its supervision, and while improving the domestic system of protection of the rights of disabled persons, promote the development of the cause of international protection of disabled persons.

According to an investigation by some EU scholars, currently only a few EU member states have already ratified Convention on the Rights of Persons with Disabilities, while most of the others are still in the process of ratification or preparation for the ratification of the Convention.

According to this investigation, in order to truly ensure the implementation of the Convention, attention should be paid not only to various special treatments given to disabled persons, but also to "social repair", so as to eliminate conscious or unconscious ideological and institutional discrimination against disabled persons. Some representatives of disabled persons used their personal experiences to show that some people or organs do not take the interest of the disabled persons, but rather their own interests, as the starting point of the special treatments they given to disabled persons: the purpose of these special treatments is either to avoid liability in case some problems arise, or to flaunt them as the charities they have done or achievements they have made. Deep in their mind, they still regard disabled persons as burdens to themselves or to society and the protections of the interests of disabled persons as the charities given to them by others, rather than inherent rights of disabled persons or the obligations of society or the state to the disabled persons. In fact, the drafters of the Convention also noticed this problem: almost each article of the Convention, while providing for the rights of the disabled persons, prohibits various possible discriminations based on disability in the enjoyment of these rights. The purpose of "social repair" proposed by those scholars is to truly implement these provisions in the Convention through the building of a sound society.

V. Convention on the Rights of Persons with Disabilities and the System of Protection of Disabled Persons in China

In the early years of the People's Republic of China, industry made up only a very small part of the national economy, commerce was very underdeveloped, and the dominant economy in the country was agricultural natural economy. In order to lay a foundation for the development of modern industry, the state quick carried out agricultural collectivization and socialist transformation of industry and commerce on the basis of land reform. A "five-guarantee" system was implemented whereby the basic livelihood of disabled and elderly persons of no family was guaranteed by grassroots social organizations in urban and rural areas. Such social security system was compatible with the socialist planned economic system implemented at that time. After implementation of the policy the reform and opening up in 1978, China began the transition from the planned economy to socialist market economy. The 1982 Constitution clearly provides that: "Citizens of the People's Republic of China have the right to material assistance from the state and society when they are old, ill or disabled. The state develops social insurance, social relief and medical and health services that are required for citizens to enjoy this right." The Constitution especially stipulates that: "The state and society ensure the livelihood of disabled members of the armed forces, provide pensions to the families of martyrs and give preferential treatment to the families of military personnel. The state and society help make arrangements for the work, livelihood and education of the blind, deaf-mutes and other handicapped citizens."① To implement these provisions of the Constitution, the Chinese Government has adopted in accordance with the Constitution the Election Law, the Civil Law, the Civil Procedure Law, the Contract Law, the Marriage Law, the Inheritance Law, the Law on Maternal and Infant Health Care, the Adoption Law, the Law on Compulsory Education, the Education Law, the Law on Higher Education, the Sports Law, the Law on the Protection of the Rights and Interests of the Elderly, the Insurance Law, the Employment Promotion Law, the Partnership Business Law, the Individual Income Tax Law, the Product Quality Law, the Law on the Protection of Consumer Rights and Interests, the Law on Donations for Public Welfare, the Law on Administrative Penalty, the Law on Administrative Reconsideration, the Law on Prevention and Control of Occupational Diseases, the Military Service Law, the Law on Officers in Active Service, the Law on National Defense, the Public Security Administration Punishments Law, the Criminal Law, the Criminal Procedure Law, the Law on People's Police, and the Prison Law, which contain concrete provisions on the protection of various rights of disabled persons. More importantly, China adopted in 1990 the Law on the Protection of Disabled Persons and the State Council has promulgated a series of special administrative regulations on the protection of the rights of disabled persons, including the Regulations on the Employment of Disabled Persons and the Regulations on the Education of the Disabled Persons. These laws and regulations form a legal system of protection of rights of disabled persons compatible with socialist market economy, which has greatly improved the conditions of rehabilitation, education, labor and employment,

① Article 45 of the Chinese Constitution.

guarantee of livelihood, cultural life and social status of disabled persons.

However, due to the regional imbalance in development and other problems emerged in the process of development, many problems still need to be solved in the protection of the rights of disabled persons in China. These problems include: the living standard of disabled persons in general is much lower than the average in the country; there is no institutional guarantee for the rehabilitation of disabled persons; the educational level and employment rate of disabled persons are lower than those of other members of society; and there is a lack of barrier-free facilities in rural as well as in urban areas. ①To facilitate the solution of the above problems and truly safeguard the rights of disabled persons, the Standing Committee of the National People's Congress revised the Law on the Protection of Disabled Persons in April 2008. The revised law, by summarizing the historical experience since the promulgation of the Law, incorporating the content of Convention on the Rights of Persons with Disabilities, and taking into consideration of the actual conditions in China, further strengthens the protection of the various rights of disabled persons on the existing basis. The revised Law first reaffirms the principles that disabled persons shall enjoy equal rights with other citizens in political, economic, cultural, social, family and other aspects of life, that their personal dignity shall be protected by law, and that it shall be prohibited to discriminate against, insult and injure disabled persons, or derogate the personal dignity of disabled persons through mass media or by other means. To embody the essential characteristics of socialism, the revised Law especially stresses the right of disabled persons to "participate in the administration of the state, economic, cultural and social affairs according to law and through various channels". In the formulation of laws, regulations, rules and public policies, the opinions of disabled persons and of their organizations shall be heard on significant issues involving the rights and interests of disabled persons and the cause of disabled persons. The Law contains systematic and comprehensive provisions on the rights of disabled persons with respect to such matters as rehabilitation services, education, labor and employment, culture and sports, social security and barrier-free environment. With respect to

---

① *The Law of the People's Republic of China on the Protection of Disabled Persons* (*annotated edition*), Law Press China, 2008, pp. 1—2.

rehabilitation, the Law provides that the people's governments at all levels shall adopt measures to create favorable conditions for the rehabilitation of disabled persons, establish and improve disabled persons rehabilitation service system, and establish a sound mechanism for the prevention, early detection and early treatment of birth defects; with respect to education, the people's governments at all levels shall provide gratuitous textbooks to disabled students and students from poor families of disabled persons receiving compulsory education and provide aids to those receiving education other than the compulsory education; with respect to labor and employment, the state shall adopt the pro rata employment arrangement system for disabled persons. Employing units that fail to reach the prescribed proportion shall perform the obligation to ensure the employment of disabled persons under the relevant provisions of the state; with respect to cultural life, the government shall organize and support the compilation and publication of Braille readers, talking books for visually impaired persons and other readers for disabled persons, set up reading rooms of Braille readers and talking books for visually impaired persons in a public library, and promote the adding of captions or narrations to television columns and film and television works; with respect to social security, disabled persons and their employers shall participate in the social insurance under the relevant provisions of the state. Social insurance subsidies shall be granted to disabled persons living with real hardships under the relevant provisions of the state. People's governments at and above the county level shall take other measures to ensure the basic life of families of disabled persons which enjoy the treatment of minimum living guarantee but still live with some particular hardships. To ensure the implementation of the above provisions, the revised Law contains a special chapter on "Legal Liabilities" which provides that: "where any of the lawful rights and interests of a disabled person is infringed upon... the relevant department shall investigate and deal with the case"; that "the organization of disabled persons shall have the right to require the relevant departments to investigate and deal with any conduct of infringing upon the interests of a specific group of disabled persons"; and that: "where a state functionary fails to perform his legal duties and timely stop the conduct infringing upon any of the rights and interests of a disabled person or provide necessary assistance to the victim, causing severe consequences, his employer or the superior organ shall impose sanctions to the directly liable person in charge and other directly liable persons."

The Chinese Law on the Protection of Disabled Persons is well linked up to the UN Convention on the Rights of Persons with Disabilities and its content is comprehensive and complete. However, the realization of any right is dependant on social development and needs to be based on certain economic, political, cultural and social conditions. Although China has achieved rapid development during the past thirty years of reform and opening up, and is expect to become the second largest economy in the world this year, it is a country with a large population, low per capita GDP, a large number of disabled persons, and big gaps in development between different regions and between urban and rural areas. Currently the medical, rehabilitational, and educational services for disabled persons are outdated can no longer meet their actual needs, the employment situation of disabled persons is very grim, auxiliary appliances for disabled persons are in short supply and very expensive, and barrier-free facilities are still far from meeting the actual needs in both urban and rural areas. Especially in a period of transition, the implementation of the legal protection of disabled persons requires greater efforts to be made by the state, enterprises and society. We should all take humanitarianism and human rights as the starting point of our actions, show more love, kindness and tolerance towards others, carry forward the fine traditions of the Chinese nation of respecting the old and cherishing the young and helping those in distress and aiding those in peril, and jointly find solutions to the problems encountered in the process of development. In early 1980s, Mr. Hu Yaobang, a famous Chinese statesman, in an effort to make children's books and stationeries more affordable, appealed to entrepreneurs they should not always try to make money from kids. Today, here I would like to use this forum of EU-China Human Rights Dialogue to make an appeal to entrepreneurs and inventors:, please lower the prices of new scientific and technological products and the transfer of new technologies related to persons with disabilities out of humanitarian considerations, that more disabled persons will be able to receive the help they need and better and more harmonious world can be created.

Protection of Woman's Rights: from the Perspective of International Human Rights Conventions

Women make up half of the world total population. Whether as wife or mother, they always play a very important role in the wellbeing of the family, in the raising of children and in the development of society. However, for some physiological, social and historical reasons, women have become the largest disadvantaged group in society. It has been proved that the significance of protecting the rights and interests of women far exceeds the significance of women's proportion in the total population.

I

Both Chinese legend of creation of the world by Pan Gu and the western myth about the creation of human beings by God and the Garden of Eden in the Bible show that men and women were equal in the beginning of human history. The research on Iroquois tribes described by Lewis H. Morgan in his book Ancient Society and the investigation by anthropologists on the ethnic minorities in Southwestern part of China show that women once occupied a dominant position in society in certain periods of human evolution and this phenomenon still exists in Lake Lugu of Dali Prefecture in China's Yunnan Province. Later, women's dominant position was replaced by men only because of some physiological and social reasons. And this change was a social progress caused the development of the productive force. There is no evidence to show that it was a process of violence struggle like the life-or-death class struggles that followed it. However, gradually the situation had changed. With the transfer of their dominant position to men, women became dependent on men, and then were turned into their appendants. Some even become men's exclusive or common sex toys.

The traditional Chinese code of moral conduct advocates the Three Cardinal Guides (ruler guides subject, father guides son and husband guides wife) and Five Constant Virtues (benevolence, righteousness, propriety, knowledge and sincerity) and women's Three Obediences (namely, obedience to their fathers before marriage, to their husbands during married life and to their sons in widowhood) and Four Virtues (fidelity, physical charm, propriety in speech, and efficiency in needle work) . From the above we can see that, in ancient China, women's status, whether in society or in family, was the lowest—even lower than that of their own children. The above traditional ethics were confirmed by law and enforced by the coercive power of the state during the period of Western Zhou Dynasty, about 3, 000 years ago, so as to strengthen the dominant position of men and the feudal patriarchal hierarchical order which took the blood relationship as its linkage and monarchical power as its center. Although such legal system was abolished along with the last emperor of China during the 1911 Revolution, its influence has not been totally eradicated from people's mind even today.

Western countries do not have such a long history of feudal system asthat in China and other oriental countries and therefore are less severely influenced by ideas of traditional ethics. In ancient times and in the Middle Ages, the restraint on women was mainly manifested in the areas of property rights and inheritance, which determined that women were inevitably dependent on men and that their status in family and society was low. Even after the ideas of freedom, equality and human rights were put forward by modern Enlightenment thinkers and embodied in laws through the Bourgeois Revolution, women had still been in a powerless position for a long period of time. It was only after the adoption and implementation of the UN Convention on the Political Rights of Women in 1952 that women in major western countries began to enjoy the right to vote and other political rights. In some western countries, such rights were not realized until the 1970s.

Examples of the low status of women in Chinese and western societies include: in traditional Chinese society, after a girl is marriage to a man, her own name loses significance and she is only called by her husband's family name, such as Mrs. Zhang, Mrs. Wang or Mrs. Li. To avoid mix-up, in formal occasions, her own family name is added to that of her husband's, for example, Mrs. Zhang-Sun, Mrs. Wang-Zhao and Mrs. Li-Zhou. And this change of family name has implications to property rights and personal rights. Today, this phenomenon still exists in some rural areas. I am not sure whether the practice in today's western countries and Chinese regions of Hong Kong and Taiwan of women using their husbands' family name is influenced by traditional ideas, because some of the women there have very high social status and it is possible that they use their husband's family name only to show their love for their husbands. In general, however, the low status of women is an undisputable fact.

II

To change this situation and uphold women's rights, international organizations represented by the UN strengthened the protection of the rights and interests of women after the World War II and put the adoption of international conventions and promotion of domestic legislation in this field on their agenda. Although the progress has not been very fast, the coverage of the relevant laws have gradually expanded and the safeguards for women's rights developed from those of general principles to those of specific and concrete safeguards.

1. Gradual Improvement of International Treaties on Women's Rights

On 26 June 1945, in view of the massacres committed during the World War II, especially the systematic and brutal slaughter of innocent people, including women and children, committed by German Nazis and Japanese militarists, the UN Charter declares at its very beginning that the purpose of the UN is: "to save succeeding generations from the scourge of war, which twice in our lifetime has brought untold sorrow to mankind, and to reaffirm faith in fundamental human rights, in the dignity and worth of the human person, in the equal rights of men and women and of nations large and small." Article 1 (3) of the Charter provides that one of the objectives of the UN is: "to achieve international co-operation in solving international problems of an economic, social, cultural, or humanitarian character, and in promoting and encouraging respect for human rights and for fundamental freedoms for all without distinction as to race, sex, language, or religion."① On 10 December 1948 the UN adopted the Universal Declaration of Human Rights (UDHR), which, as the first world instrument specialized in safeguarding human rights, greatly expanded and enriched the human rights con-

① *Collection of Human Rights Instruments in the World*, Sichuan People's Publishing House, 1990, pp. 928—928.

tents in the UN Charter. In addition to its Preamble, the UDHR contains a total of thirty articles. It reiterates the above-mentioned the principle in the UN Charter: "Everyone is entitled to all the rights and freedoms set forth in this Declaration, without distinction of any kind, such as race, colour, sex, language, religion, political or other opinion, national or social origin, property, birth or other status."① The Declaration explicitly lists sex as a prohibited ground for discrimination and in the subsequent articles uses the terms "everyone" or "all" to describe the subjects of human rights, so as to emphasize gender equality.

In order to give binding legal force to the principles established in the UDHR, the UNset up a Human Rights Commission to be responsible for the drafting of an international human rights covenant. At the beginning, the Human Rights Commission, guided by the ideology of western countries, drafted a human rights covenant centred on the civil and political rights in the UDHR and submitted it in 1950 to the UN General Assembly for deliberation. The General Assembly was of the opinion that the draft covenant failed to fully reflect the content of the UDHR and therefore needed to be revised and supplemented. Through the efforts made by socialist states and developing countries, the General Assembly began to deliberate on the two draft covenants submitted by the Human Rights Commission in 1962. On 16 December 1966, after over 10 years of deliberation, the General Assembly adopted the International Covenant on Economic, Social and Cultural rights (ICESCR) and the International Covenant on Civil and Political Rights (ICCPR) with a vote of 105 for and 0 against.

During the drafting and deliberation of the human rights covenants, the UN General Assembly, in order to adapt to the new situation, adopted the International Convention on the Political Rights of Women in 1952, the Convention on the Nationality of Married Women in 1957, and the Convention on Consent to Marriage, Minimum Age for Marriage and Registration of Marriages in 1962. Moreover, the ILO also adopted the Convention on Equal Pay for Work of Equal Value of Men and Women Workers in 1951. The adoption and implementation of the above conventions played a positive role in safeguarding women's rights and the contents of these conventions were embodied in the two international human rights covenants adopted in 1966.

---

① See *International Human Rights Instruments and International Human Rights Bodies*, Social Sciences Documentation Publishing House, 1993.

The adoption of the two international human rights covenants was of great significance: firstly, the covenants gave legal binding force to the various principles provided for in the UDHR and, together with the UDHR, they form the core of the International Bill of Human Rights; secondly, it further emphasized the indivisibility and interdependence of human rights. For example, the Preamble of the ICESCR points out: "in accordance with the Universal Declaration of Human Rights, the ideal of free human beings enjoying freedom from fear and want can only be achieved if conditions are created whereby everyone may enjoy his economic, social and cultural rights, as well as his civil and political rights"; thirdly, it took a step forward from the UDHR in safeguarding women's rights. For example, the UDHR only provides in article 25 that: "Motherhood and childhood are entitled to special care and assistance", whereas the ICESCR provides in article 10 (2) that "Special protection should be accorded to mothers during a reasonable period before and after childbirth. During such period working mothers should be accorded paid leave or leave with adequate social security benefits." The same Covenant also provides that the States Parties shall ensure "Fair wages and equal remuneration for work of equal value without distinction of any kind, in particular women being guaranteed conditions of work not inferior to those enjoyed by men, with equal pay for equal work."① And the ICCPR provides that: "The States Parties to the present Covenant undertake to ensure the equal right of men and women to the enjoyment of all civil and political rights set forth in the present Covenant;" and that "Sentence of death shall not be imposed for crimes committed by persons below eighteen years of age and shall not be carried out on pregnant women;"② and fourthly, the two covenants each set up a special body to be responsible for the supervision over its implementation and provides that state parties shall submit to such body periodical reports on their implementation of the covenant, thereby providing institutional safeguards for the implementation of the covenant.

Although the two international human rights covenants of 1966contain special provisions on the protection of women's rights in light of women's physiological characteristics and social responsibilities, the majority of the provi-

---

① See *International Human Rights Instruments and International Human Rights Bodies*, Social Sciences Documentation Publishing House, pp. 12 and 14.

② *Ibid.*, pp. 23 and 25.

sions in the two convents still apply the same standards to different groups and individuals. Needless to say, the two covenants represent historical progresses and their objectives are not easy to achieve. However, these objectives can only be said to be formal equality. In order to achieve equality in reality, it is necessary to adopt special provisions suited to the special needs of different groups of people, including women. In order to safeguard women's rights in light of their special needs, the UN General Assembly adopted in 1967 the Declaration on the Elimination of Discrimination against Women, which points out that: "despite the Charter of the United Nations, the Universal Declaration of Human Rights, the International Covenants on Human Rights and other instruments of the United Nations and the specialized agencies and despite the progress made in the matter of equality of rights, there continues to exist considerable discrimination against women;" that "discrimination against women is incompatible with human dignity and with the welfare of the family and of society" and that "All appropriate measures shall be taken to abolish existing laws, customs, regulations and practices which are discriminatory against women, and to establish adequate legal protection for equal rights of men and women."① Propelled by this Declaration and the First World Conference on Women, held in Mexico City in 1975, the UN General Assembly adopted in 1979 the Convention on the Elimination of All Forms of Discrimination against Women (CEDAW), which came into force in 1981.

The Convention, apart from the Preamble, consists of six parts. In the Preamble it is pointed out that, despite the principles provided for in the UN Charter, the UDHR and a series of other human rights instruments, "extensive discrimination against women continues to exist."② Such discrimination violates the principles of equality of rights and respect for human dignity, is an obstacle to the participation of women, on equal terms with men, in the political, social, economic and cultural life of their countries, hampers the growth of the prosperity of society and family and makes more difficult the full development of the potentialities of women in the service of their countries and of humanity. In view of this situation, the General Assembly is determined to implement through the Convention "the principles set forth in the Declaration on the Elimination of Discrimination

① See *International Human Rights Instruments and International Human Rights Bodies*, Social Sciences Documentation Publishing House, p. 120.

② *Ibid.*, p. 125.

against Women" . The first part of the Convention defines the term "discrimination against women" as "any distinction, exclusion or restriction made on the basis of sex which has the effect or purpose of impairing or nullifying the recognition, enjoyment or exercise by women, irrespective of their marital status, on a basis of equality of men and women, of human rights and fundamental freedoms in the political, economic, social, cultural, civil or any other field," and provides for the general obligations of state parties with respect to the elimination of discrimination against women, including adoption of corresponding legislative, publicity and educational measures. In the second part, state parties are required to adopt all appropriate measures to eliminate discrimination against women in the political and public life of the country and, in particular, to ensure to women, on equal terms with men, the right to vote, to hold public office, to represent their Governments at the international level and to acquire, change or retain their nationality. In the third part, the Convention requires state parties to eliminate discrimination against women in the field of education, employment, social security and health care. They must ensure that women have equal rights with men in pre-school, general, technical, professional and higher technical education, as well as in all types of vocational training; that they are not discriminated against in the field of employment, especially on grounds of marriage, pregnancy, and child birth; and that they have the right to protection of health and to safety in working conditions, including the safeguarding of the function of reproduction; state parties must prevent discrimination against women on the grounds of marriage or maternity and to ensure their effective right to work; prohibit, subject to the imposition of sanctions, dismissal on the grounds of pregnancy or of maternity leave and discrimination in dismissals on the basis of marital status; introduce maternity leave with pay or with comparable social benefits without loss of former employment, seniority or social allowances; and provide special protection to women during pregnancy in types of work proved to be harmful to them. This part of the Convention also provides for the elimination of discrimination against rural women, and for the preferential treatment for rural women in such matters as health care, family planning, cultural and vocational training, and access to agricultural credit and loans. The fourth part of the Convention requires state parties to prohibit discrimination against women in the areas of family, marriage, property rights, and education of children, and accord to women a legal capacity identical to that of men in the movement of persons and the freedom to choose residence and domicile, management of family and other civil matters. In case of dispute, men and women shall be treated equally in all stages of procedure in courts and tribunals. Part five of the Convention establishes a Committee on the Elimination of Discrimination against Women, to be responsible for the supervision over the implementation of the Convention. The members of the Committee shall be elected for a term of four years. According to article 18 of the Convention, States Parties undertake to submit to the Secretary-General of the United Nations, for consideration by the Committee, a report on the legislative, judicial, administrative or other measures which they have adopted to give effect to the provisions of the Convention and on the progress made in this respect: (a) Within one year after the entry into force for the State concerned; (b) Thereafter at least every four years and further whenever the Committee so requests. Part six of the Convention deals with matters relating to the ratification of the procedure of the Convention. It is noteworthy that article 23 of the Convention provides that: "Nothing in the present Convention shall affect any provisions that are more conducive to the achievement of equality between men and women which may be contained: (a) In the legislation of a State Party; or (b) In any other international convention, treaty or agreement in force for that State."[①]

The CEDAW is a specialized Convention on the protection of women's rights adopted by the UN after the adoption of the two international human rights covenants in 1966. On the basis of the principle of the equal rights of men and women provided for in a series of international human rights instruments, the CEDAW provides some positive measures in light of the fact that women are more likely to be subjected to various forms of discrimination because of their physiological characteristics and their low status in family and society, thereby taking an important stepforward towards the realization of not only *de jure* equality but also *de facto* equality between men and women. In December 1993, the UN General Assembly, in order to strengthen and supplement the CEDAW, adopted the Declaration on the Elimination of Violence against Women, which requires governments to adopt effective measures to eliminate the physical and psychological violence against women occurring in public or in private life and to punish perpetrators of such violence.

---

① See *International Human Rights Instruments and International Human Rights Bodies*, Social Sciences Documentation Publishing House, p. 126—136.

2. Vigorous Promotion by World Conferences on Women

Promoted by the UN and people around the world, especially by women in different countries, the system of international instruments on the protection of women's rights becomes increasingly complete. Historical process and current practice show that the four world conferences on women held since 1975 have played an important historical role in improving the international instruments on the protection of women's rights and in enriching the theory and practice of protection of women's rights.

The First Word Conference on Women, held in the Mexico City in 1975, adopted the Declaration of Mexico on the Equality of Women and Their Contribution to Development and Peace, which points out that the problems of women, who constitute half of the world's population, are the problems of society as a whole and that women played an important role in-the history of humanity, especially in the struggle for national liberation, the strengthening of international peace, and the elimination of imperialism, colonialism, neo-colonialism, foreign occupation, Zionism, alien domination, racism and apartheid, stressing that greater and equal participation of women at all levels of decision-making shall decisively contribute to accelerating the pace of development and the maintenance of peace; that discrimination against women has prevented and will continue to prevent women from giving full play to their role; and that the changes in the economic structure of the societies, although are the prerequisites for resolving practical problems and improving women's conditions, "cannot of themselves ensure an immediate improvement in the status of a group which has long been disadvantaged", therefore, specific measures need to be undertaken in order to eliminate all forms of discrimination against women. The Mexico City Declaration requires that urgent consideration be given to the full, immediate and early integration of women into national and international life. To achieve this goal, further efforts must be made to eliminate discrimination against women in areas of family life, property relations, child-raising, cultural and vocational education, employment, promotion, wage and welfare, so as to realize the equal rights of man and woman in family, society, and in every areas of national and international life. The Declaration especially points out that: "Equality between women and men means equality in their dignity and worth as human beings as well as equality in their rights, opportunities and responsibilities."① It was based on this understanding that the Declaration of the Mexico City played an important role in promoting the 1979 UN Convention on the Elimination of All Forms of Discrimination against Women. At the Conference it was decided to establish two special bodies on women's affairs within the UN: Research and Training Institute for the Advancement of Women and United Nations Development Fund for Women. The Conference also adopted Programme of Action for the United Nations Decade for Women (1976—1985): Equality, Development and Peace, which provided a blue print for women's participation in national and international activities and the comprehensive development of society.

The Second World Conference on Women was held in Copenhagen in 1980. The main task of this Conference was to evaluate the progresses made in implementing the Declaration of the Mexico City and the Programme of Action and adjust various programmes in of the Programme of Action for the United Nations for the second half of the Decade for Women in light of new situations. The Conference adopted the Programme of Action for the Second Half of the United Nations Decade for Women: Equality, Development and Peace, which pointed out that the principles and goals of equality, development and peace established at the First World Conference on Women were feasible and constituted the basis of the activities of the UN Decade for Women. It especially pointed out that equality means not only legal equality or elimination discrimination in law, but also the right, responsibility and opportunity of women to participate in the development process as agents and beneficiaries of development. The so-called development refers to the comprehensive development of politics, economy, society, culture and human life, including the development of economic resources and the physical, moral, intellectual, and cultural growth. In order to realize comprehensive development, actions must be taken at the national, local and family levels. And peace and stability are also indispensable to development. The dialectic relations between development, equality and peace are as the following: without development, it is not possible to eliminate discrimination and realize equality or lasting peace; the realization of equality, development and peace is also conducive to the struggle against imperialism, colonialism and neo-colonialism, Zionism,

① See Declaration of the Mexico City on the Equality of Women and Their Contribution to Development and Peace.

racism, apartheid, hegemonism, foreign domination and oppression; although development is important, it should be regarded not as a goal in itself, but as an important means for maintaining peace and promoting equality between men and women. Its ultimate objective is to achieve gender equality. The Second World Conference on Women, based on the summarization of the experience in the implementation of the Programme of Action for the United Nations Decade for Women in the first five years, adopted Programme of Action for the Second Half of the United Nations Decade for Women, which urged governments to adopt laws and policies to increase women's participation in political and other decision-making processes, speed up the implementation of the strategy for women's full participation in economic and social development, and solve their problems in employment, health care, education and training. Special attention was paid to the special problems faced by rural women, migrant women, unemployed women and young women. ①

The Third World Conference on Women was held in Nairobi in 1985 and was participated by representatives from 157 countries. The final document adopted by the Conference, the Nairobi Forward Looking Strategies for the Advancement of Women, pointed out that the inequality of women in most countries stems to a very large extent from mass poverty and the general backwardness of the majority of the world's population caused by underdevelopment, which is a product of imperialism, colonialism, neo-colonialism, apartheid, racism, racial discrimination and of unjust international economic relations. And the unfavourable status of women is aggravated in many countries, developed and underdeveloped, by *de facto* discrimination on the grounds of sex. One of the fundamental obstacles to women's equality is that *de facto* discrimination and inequality in the status of women and men derive from larger social, economic, political and cultural factors that have been justified on the basis of physiological differences and result in the denial of equal access to the power structure that controls society and determines development issues and peace initiatives. Ultimately, society is the loser if the talents of women are under-utilized as a result of discrimination. The Nairobi Forward Looking Strategies pointed out that, law-making is a crucial factor in the realization of gender equality because it provides legal basis for the adoption of actions and promotes social chan-

① For the above contents and citations, see *Programme of Action for the Second Half of the United Nations Decade for Women: Equality, Development and Peace.*

ges. However, it should be noted that the sharp contrast between legislative changes and effective implementation of these changes is a major obstacle to the full participation of women in society. Therefore, governments should strengthen the implementation of relevant laws. The Conference once again showed concern for disadvantaged women, including rural and urban poor women, women in areas affected by natural disaster; women deprived of their traditional means of livelihood, women who are sole supporters of families, physically and mentally disabled women, women in detention and women who have committed crimes, refugee and displaced women, migrant women, etc. Among the various measures for safeguarding women's rights, the Nairobi Forward Looking Strategies laid special emphasis on the equal participation by women in public affairs at the national and international levels and further developed the ideological understanding that had gradually taken form since the First World Conference on Women, namely: although solving the practical problems faced by women and improving their status are the prerequisite for the solution of women's problem, the most fundamental solution is to enable women to participate in public life at national and international levels. The objectives of equality, development and peace can be achieved only through equal participation by women. Thus, the Strategies clearly changed the past approach of only taking social welfare as the main measure for supporting women and improving their status, emphasized women's role as the participants, decision-makers, contributors and beneficiaries of social development, and enabled them to enter into the mainstream of social, economic, political and cultural development. ①

The Fourth World Conference on Women was held in Beijing in 1995, on the occasion of the 50 years anniversary of the establishment of the United Nations. It was a grand event of unprecedented scale, participated by government and NGO representatives from 189 countries. Meanwhile, about 30, 000 people participated in NGO forums with a wide range of topics, including women and poverty, education and training of women, women and health, women and armed conflicts, women and economy, women in power and decision-making, institutional mechanism for the advancement of women, women and human rights, women and the media, and women and the environment. The Beijing Declaration and Platform for

① For the above contents and citations, see *Nairobi Forward-Looking Strategies for the Advancement of Women to the Year 2000.*

Action adopted at the Conference reviewed the progresses made in the implmentation of the United Nations Decade for Women (1976—1985) since the First World Conference on Women in 1975, evaluated the implementation of the Convention on the Elimination of All Forms of Discrimination against Women adopted by the UN General Assembly in 1979, and especially examined the achievements made and obstacles encountered by governments in the implementation of the Nairobi Forward Looking Strategies for the Advancement of Women, which was adopted at the Third World Conference on Women in 1985. The Platform for Action confirmed that, through the efforts made by governments and the international community, "there has been important progress in achieving equality between women and men. Many Governments have enacted legislation to promote equality between women and men and have established national machineries to ensure the mainstreaming of gender perspectives in all spheres of society. International agencies have focused greater attention on women's status and roles." Meanwhile, the Platform for Action pointed out various obstacles to the further realization of equality between women and men. They mainly include: the imbalance in the development of rights between different groups of women; continuing environmental degradation that affects all human lives, especially women; more than one billion people in the world today, the great majority of whom are women, living in unacceptable conditions of poverty; armed conflicts and terrorism that resulted in large number of casualties, especially among women; the legislation on the equality between men and women in many countries need to be further improved and, whether in family or society, traditional or customary practices incompatible with law still exerting serious influence on people's mind and systems; women having much less cultural and technical training than men; serious inadequacies in health care available to women, etc. The Platform of Action expounded on the manifestations and causes of problems relating to "women and poverty", "education and training of women", "women and health care", "violence against women", and "mechanisms for the advancement of women", as well as measures to be adopted for the solution of these problems. It also raised demands on and made appeals to governments and the UN with regard to these issues. The Beijing Declaration and Platform for Action, after summarizing the historical process in the 20 years since the First World Conference on Women, further strengthened and developed the idea that gender perspectives should be mainstreamed in all spheres of society so that a declaration can be made to the world that "women's rights are human rights." The human rights of women and girl children are an inalienable, indispensable and inderogable part of human rights and fundamental freedoms of all human beings. Only by safeguarding women's rights, realizing gender equality and transforming the relationship between men and women into that of an equality partnership can the mankind meet the challenges of the 21st century and fully realize political, social, economic, and cultural rights. ①

3. The Important Role Played by a Series of Special International Conferences and Declarations

In the process of organizing the four world conferences on women, the UN and the relevant international organizations had held a series of conferences and adopted a series of resolutions and declarations on the relevant human rights, which have played an important role in safeguarding women's rights. These declarations and conferences include: Resolution on the New Concepts of Human Rights, adopted by the UN General Assembly in 1977; the Declaration on the Elimination of All Forms of Intolerance and of Discrimination Based on Religion or Belief, adopted by the UN General Assembly in 1981; the Convention concerning the Promotion of Collective Bargaining, adopted by the ILO in 1983; the Employment Promotion and Protection against Unemployment Convention, adopted by the ILO in 1988; the Convention concerning Indigenous and Tribal Peoples in Independent Countries adopted by the ILO in 1989; the World Summit for Children, held in New York in 1990; the United Nations Conference on Environment and Development, held in Rio de Janeiro in 1992; the Vienna Declaration and Programme of Action, adopted by the World Conference on Human Rights in Vienna in 1993; and the World Summit for Social Development, held in Copenhagen in 1995. All of them have greatly promoted, either directly or indirectly, the realization of women's rights and the equality between men and women.

III

Promoted by the adoption and implementation of international human rights conventions, especially by conventions and other instruments on

① For the above contents and citations, see *The Beijing Declaration and Platform for Action*, adopted at the Fourth World Conference on Women in 1995.

women's rights, China has made great progress in improving its legal system for safeguarding women's rights. Since Chinese women make up about 1/5 of the total population of women in the world, the perfection of the legal system for the safeguarding the rights of Chinese women is not only of great importance to human rights protection in China, but also a great contribution to international protection of women's rights.

As mentioned before, in history, Chinese women had very low status both in family and in society. They suffered from multiple oppressions and led a miserable life. In 1911, in a revolution led by Dr. Sun Yat-sen, the feudal system that had lasted for over 2, 000 years was overthrown and the last emperor abolished. The Provisional Constitution of the Republic of China, adopted in 1912, provided that: "All people in the Republic of China are equal"① and this provision was retained in the 1913 (Draft) Constitution of the Temple of Heaven, the 1914 Provisional Constitution of the Republic of China and the 1923 Constitution of the Republic of China. However, it is not clear whether the concept of "people" in these constitutions covered women at that time, or whether this constitutional provision was implement in real life. It was not until in 1930 and 1931 that the equality between men and women was specifically provided for in the Draft Constitution of Republic of China, adopted at the Taiyuan Enlarged Conference, and in the Provisional Constitution of the Republic of China during the Period of Tutelage. It was the "Red Political Power" established by the Chinese Communist Party after 1927 that had made real efforts in promoting the protection of women's rights in China. The Outline Constitution of the Soviet Republic of China of 1931 and the Draft Outline of the Basic Law (Constitution) of the Soviet Republic of China adopted before that contained unprecedented specific and clear provisions on women's rights. The Draft Outline provided that: one of the constitutional principles of the Soviet Republic was: "not only to completely realize the liberation of woman, adopt laws on reasonable gender and family relationships that are not restrained by patriarchal feudal relations and religious superstition, and recognize the freedom of marriage and divorce, but also implement measures to protect women and mothers, develop science and technology, so as to create the material basis that can enable women to

① See The Provisional Constitution of the Republic of China, in *supra* note 1, p. 740.

truly free themselves from household duties and take job in society. "① And the Outline Constitution provided that: "The Chinese Soviet political power takes the complete liberation of women as its objective, recognizes the freedom of marriage, implement various measures for the protection of women, and enable women to obtain the material basis to be free from household duties and take part in the economic, political and cultural life of society. "② Although the provisions in these constitutional documents adopted by the political power of red revolutionary bases during the Second National Revolutionary War were not fully implemented due to such factors as the war situation, the lack of material conditions, and the small scale of the revolutionary bases, their spirit was later embodied in the relevant laws of anti-Japanese bases and liberated areas. It was exact this spirit and the laws made in accordance with this spirit that ensured the liberation of the broad masses of women in China, who became a major force in China's struggle against western powers, Japanese militarism and domestic reactionaries, and made great contribution to the independence of the Chinese nation and the liberation of Chinese people.

With the establishment of the new China in 1949, a new chapter was opened in the safeguarding of women's rights in China. The 1949 Common Programme of the Chinese People's Political Consultative Conference, which served as temporary constitution at that time, provided that: "The People's Republic of China abolishes the feudal system that has fettered Chinese women. Women enjoy equal rights with men in political, economic, cultural, educational and all other aspects of social life. The system of freedom of marriage shall be implemented. "③ On the basis the Common Programme, the 1954 Constitution of the People's Republic of China provided that: "All citizens of the People's Republic of China shall be equal before the law;" and that: "All citizens who have reached the age of 18, regardly of their ethnic origin, race, sex, occupation, birth, religious belief, level education, property, or year of residence, have the right to vote and the right to stand for election. " The principle of equality between men and women confirmed in the Common Programme was later embodied in the Marriage Law and the Land Reform Law adopted in 1950 and the

---

① See the Draft Outline of the Basic Law (Constitution) of the Soviet Republic of China, in *supra* note 1, p. 777.

② *Ibid.*, p. 779.

③ Ibid., p. 811.

Election Law adopted in 1953. To implement these laws, the Chinese government lauched large-scale publicity and education campagins and mass movements of great momentum, which drastically improved the status of women. The implementation of the 1954 Constitution further strengthened and promoted this strend of development. However, during the 1960s and 1970s, the development women's rights, like that of all the other rights of Chinese people, was impeded by such factors as historical conditions, the levels of social, economic, political and cultural development, and political movements.

After 1978, in the process of reform and opening up, the strengthening of socialist democracy and the legal system, the development of socialist market economy, and the construction of socialism with Chinese characteristics, China has made significant progresses in safeguarding women's rights and human rights in general in China. Based on the 1954 Constitution, the 1982 Constitution further strengthened the protection of human rights: it gave "The Foundamental Rights and Duties of Citizens" a more prominent position by moving it from Chapter Three to Chapter Two and, through a constitutional amendment, recognized the principles of "ruling the country by law and construction of a socialist state under the rule of law" and "The state respects and protects human rights". During this period, the Marriage Law was amended twice in 1980 and 2001, the Inheritance Law was adopted in 1985, and the Trade Union Law was revised in 1992. These laws contain clear provisions on the freedom of marriage, the equality between men and women in marriage relation, the equal right between men and women in such matters as inheritance, raising of children, support for the elderly, division of property at divorce, equal employment opportunity and special protections for women in light of their special physiological conditions. It should be specially pointed out that, after the ratification of the UN Convention on the Elimination of All Forms of Discrimination against Women, China has actively improved its legal system for the safeguarding of women's rights: the Law on the Protection of the Rights and Interests of Women was adopted by the National People's Congress in April 1992 and amended by the Standing Committee of the National People's Congress in 2005.

The Law on the Protection of the Rights and Interests of Women, by summarizing the domestic and foreign experiences in the protection of the rights and interests of women, contains comprehensive stipulations on the protection of women. The Law points out at its very beginning that: "Equality between men and women is a basic State policy." The state promotes the equality between men and women, safeguards the lawful rights and interests of women, protects their special rights and interest, eliminates all forms of discrimination against them, and prohibits maltreatment, abandonment, and physical abuse of women. Under the guidance of this general principle, the Law provides in various chapters the political, cultural, educational, labour, social security, property, personal, marriage and family rights that women should enjoy on an equal footing with men. Firstly, women enjoy equal political rights with men. Women have the right to conduct state affairs, manage economic and cultural undertakings and administer social affairs through various channels and in various ways and they enjoy the equal right, with men, to vote and to stand for election. To realize these rights, the Law provides that there shall be an appropriate number of women deputies among deputies to the National People's Congress and local people's congresses at various levels and there should be appropriate number of women among the members of the residents 'committees and villagers' committees. The state shall actively train and select female cadres. State organs, public organizations, enterprises and public institutions must, in training, selecting and appointing cadres, adhere to the principle of equality between men and women, and create condition for women to participate in the making of laws and public policies. Secondly, women enjoy equal rights with men in the fields of culture and education. Schools and departments concerned shall, by implementing the relevant regulations of the state, guarantee that women enjoy equal rights with men in such matters as starting school, entering a higher school, job assignment upon graduation, conferment of academic degrees and dispatch for study abroad and in their participation in scientific, technological, literary, artistic and other cultural activities. The government, society and schools shall take effective measures to solve the actual difficulties for female school-age children to receive education and shall create chances to ensure female school-age children among the poor, disabled and migrant population to finish compulsory education and technical training. Thirdly, women enjoy equal labour and social security rights with men. These rights include equal employment right, right to equal pay for work of equal value, rights relating to promotion in post or in rank, evaluation and determination of professional and technological titles, the right to safe and healthy work environment, the right to social security, the right to special labour protection during menstrual period, pregnancy, obstetrical period and nursing period; no entity may, for the reason of matrimony, pregnancy, maternity leave or breast-feeding, decrease a female employee's wage, dismiss her or unilaterally terminate her labour (employment) contract or service agreement; and no entity may discriminate against women for the reason of gender when implementing the retirement system of the state. Fourthly, women enjoy the equal right, with men, to property. In joint property relationship derived from marriage or family, the rights and interests enjoyed by women according to law may not be infringed upon. Widowed women shall have the right to disposed of the property they have lawfully inherited and no one may interfere with such right. Women shall enjoy equal rights with men in the contracted management of rural land, distribution of proceeds of collective economic organizations, use of land, requisition and occupation compensations and use of house sites. No organization or individual may infringe upon a woman's rights and interests in the rural collective economic organization on the ground that she hasn't got married, is married, is divorced or has lost her spouse. Fifthly, women enjoy equal right of person with men. Women's rights to life, health, personal freedom, reputation, honour, and portrait shall not be violated; drowning, abandoning or causing any harm to female babies, abduction of and trafficking in, or kidnapping of women, sexual harassment or indecent acts against of women, and prostitution and whoring are prohibited; and it is prohibited to organize, force or induce women to engage in obscene performances. Sixthly, women enjoy equal rights with men in marriage and family. Women shall enjoy the freedom of marriage and divorce. A woman shall enjoy equal rights with her spouse in possessing, utilizing, profiting from and disposing of their joint property. Domestic violence against women is prohibited. Both parents shall enjoy the same right to guardianship of their minor child (children). At the time of divorce, the husband and the wife shall seek agreement regarding the disposition of their jointly possessed houses; if they fail to reach an agreement, the people's court shall make a judgment in light of the actual circumstances of both parties and according to the principle of showing consideration for their child (children) and for the rights and interests of the wife. ①

Through the summarization of relevant domestic and international laws

---

① The above contents are cited from the Law on the Protection of the Rights and Interests of Women.

and practices, China has been continuously improving its laws on the protection of the rights and interests of women. The State Council Working Committee on Women and Children is responsible for the supervision over the implementation of these laws. Many foreign friends admire the Chinese government for carrying on its glorious tradition of the revolutionary era by establishing women's federations—powerful organizations responsible for the safeguarding of women's rights and interests—at the central and various local levels. The Law on the Protection of the Rights and Interests of Women provides that "the All-China Women's Federation and women's federations at various levels shall, in accordance with the relevant laws and the charter of the All-China Women's Federation, represent and uphold the rights of women of all nationalities and all walks of life, and strive for the protection of women's rights and interests;" that "when a woman's lawful rights and interests are infringed upon, she may file a complaint with a women's organization, which shall require the relevant department or entity to investigate and deal with the case;" and that "a women's organization shall support the women victims who need help in litigation." Apparently, the above legally prescribed powers of women's federations exceed those of ordinary social organizations. Because of the legal support, these organizations are playing an important role in protecting women's rights and interests and consequently are affectionately called by the broad masses of Chinese women their "parents' home".

From the above we can see that, after long period of struggle, the women's issue has been mainstreamed in the public policy and state life in China. Not only the state has adopted national programme for the development of women, but the law also requires local governments at various levels to adopt programmes for the development of women in their respective administrative areas in accordance with the national programme and incorporate them into national economic and social development plan. The effective measures adopted by the state have created the necessary condition for women to exercise their rights in accordance with law. Governments at all levels should attach importance to and strengthen the work of safeguarding women's rights and interests. The Law on the Protection of the Rights and Interests of Women provides in many articles for the legal responsibilities for violations of women's rights and interests. Anyone who infringes upon women's rights and interests shall, in light of the severeness of the consequences of the violation, bear legal responsibilities. Those whose acts of violation constitute crimes shall be investigated for criminal responsiblities. An accountability system for state organs and their staff have also been established: "If a state organ or any of its staff members fails to perform its (his) duties, fails to stop an infringements upon the rights and interests of a woman or fails to give necessary help to a woman victim and thus causes any serious consequences, the entity of the aforesaid staff member or the superior organ shall give an administrative sanction to the directly liable person-in-charge and other directly liable persons."①

Thanks to a complete system of laws and effective implementation of these laws, China has been making continuous progress in safeguarding women's rights and interests. However, there are still gaps between the actual situation of women's rights in China and the requirements of international human rights conventions and the relevant Chinese laws. Take the right to social security as an example. Because of the differences in the level of development between different regions, between rural and urban areas, and between different social strata in rural and urban areas, there exist big gaps in the level of social security enjoyed by women in different areas and different strata of society. The tradition of son preference still affects a large number of people, resulting in frequent family conflicts and huge social problems related to gender imbalance. The drop-out rate among school-age girls is higher than that among school-age boys, especially in rural, remote and mountainous areas, where some girls are still unable to finish the nine-year compulsory education. Low educational level has affected women's employment opportunity and their further development in the fields of science and technology: currently the proportion of women is lower than that of men among senior scientists, technicians, and civil servants. Although the coverage of medical security is gradually expanding throughout the country, the situation of low level of medical security still can not be changed in a short period of time and many women are still faced with difficulties in acquiring qualified medical care. Moreover, with respect to personal rights, the number of women subjected to sexual harassment and violence, including domestic violence, is still very large.

The existence of the above problems affects not only the realization of women's rights and interests, but also domestic happiness, social harmony, and socialist construction and, therefore, must be attached great importance by the whole society. The solution to this problem is of course the rule of law. Governments at various levels and the relevant social

① See article 57 of the Law on the Protection of the Rights and Interests of Women.

organizations should take further steps to truly implement the relevant laws so as to gradually raise the level of the protection of women's rights and interests in China.

Legal Protection of Personal Rights in China[1]

Personal rights are basic human rights as well as important constitutional rights. All the other fundamental rights provided for in the Constitution take the enjoyment of personal rights as the precondition of their realization. Without personal rights, there will be no political, economic, social, and cultural rights to talk about and, just as has been show by countless examples in the process of historical development, human beings will be treated as tools or things. In a sense, the recognition, respect and protection of personal rights is an important indicator of the level of social development. After the "Cultural Revolution", with the rise of Chinese people's awareness of the importance of protection of personal rights, the system of legal protection of personal rights in China has been gradually improved and the amount of literatures on the legal protection of personal rights and its importance has also increased. Although there is no lack of real knowledge and deep insights in these literatures, as far as I know, most of them focus on civil law or certain aspects of the criminal law and there is a lack of comprehensive and in-depth research on personal rights as important human rights and constitutional rights. In view of this fact, this article will not confine itself to a certain branch law, but will conduct a comprehensive discussion on the protection of personal rights.

I. The Concept and Main Content of Personal Rights

Personal rights are rights relating to the non-property aspects of human person and personality. Generally speaking, they mainly include the right to life, the right to health, personal freedom, sexual freedom, freedom of marriage, right to human dignity, right to name, right to portrait,

---

① Originally published in *China Social Sciences*, No. 4 (1996).

right to reputation and honor, and right to privacy.

In view of the fact that there are different opinions in international and Chinese academic circles on the concept and content of personal rights, neither the 1948 Universal Declaration of Human Rights (HDHR) nor the 1966 International Covenant on Civil and Political Rights (ICCPR) gives a definition of the concept of "personal rights", but only contains provisions on specific personal rights, for example, articles 3, 4, 5, 12, and 16 of the UDHR and articles 6 to 11 of the ICCPR. The current Chinese Constitution has used only the concept of "personal freedoms" (Article 37), but not the concept "personal rights"; the current Chinese Criminal Law uses the concept of "personal rights" (Article 10), but there are different interpretations of the connotation and extension of this concept. Therefore, it is necessary to give some brief interpretations and definitions to these concepts.

1. Right to Life

From biological point of view, life is a phenomenon exhibited by living organism composed of nucleic acid protein complex. Only a person who has life can be regarded as human being and a subject of law. It is because of the importance of life, the right to life of every person, regardless of his race, ethnicity, gender or health condition, is protected by the constitution and laws and violation of the right to life is regarded as the most serious crime in all countries. Even the act of voluntary giving up one's own right to life or taking one's own life is not accepted or protected by society or law under most circumstances. It is for this reason that euthanasia and abortion are still controversial topics in international academic circle.

2. Right to Health

The right to health refers to the right to healthy development and functioning of various organs of the body, and to physical and mental well-being. To a rights holder, the importance of the right to health is second only to that of the right to life. Without the guarantee of the right to health, even if one's life is sustained, he will only be lingering on in a steadily worsening condition, losing the functions of the main organs of his body and ultimately the capacity to act. Infringements upon citizens' right to health include causing physical injuries by violent means or mental harms by non-violent means, as well as endangering people's health by various kinds of pollution produced by modern industry.

3. Personal Freedom

Personal freedom refers to the right of a person to autonomously decide his own daily life and action. The scope of personal freedom should be limited. Some authors classify some participatory rights, such as the freedoms of speech, of the press, of assembly, of association, and of procession and demonstration, into the category of personal freedom. I think this definition of personal freedom is too broad and therefore inappropriate. A person without person freedom has not legal rights to talk about, even if he has life and health. Such a person is at best a salve or prisoner.

4. The Right to Sexual Freedom

The right to sexual freedom refers to the right of men and women to independently and freely choose their sex partners. Sex is an instinctive desire and need of the human body. It is the expression of love between men and women based on the need of mankind for self-reproduction. Violation of sexual freedom, which can not only cause physical and mental sufferings to the victims of such violation, but also tramples upon their human dignity, refers to the act of having sex with another person against his or her will, including rape, having sex with an underage girl, forcing others into prostitution, sexual molestation, sexual harassment, buying an abducted woman as wife, and forcing a woman into cohabitation. In the exercise of the right to sexual freedom, one may not violate social morals or transmit venereal diseases. Otherwise, such exercise of sexual freedom may constitute crime.

5. Freedom of Marriage

Here I discuss the freedom of marriage as a separate right because it is connected but not identical to sexual freedom. Marriage normally refers to the establishment of the husband-wife relationship and formation of a family between a man and a woman. Since love is the basis of marriage, whether there is true love between husband and wife is the only criterion for judging whether a marriage is free or not. The freedom of marriage is an important personal freedom because it has an important bearing on the happiness of each man and woman as well as on the harmony of marriage and family life. The freedom of marriage also includes the freedom of divorce, without which a freedom cannot be truly freedom. In China the main forms of violation of the freedom of marriage include arranged marriage, mercenary marriage, and interference in marriage by a parent, a son, a daughter or other family members. Factors impeding the exercise of the right to divorce include influence of traditional ideas and pressure of public opinion.

6. Right to Human Dignity

The right to human dignity refers to the social respect a subject of right is entitled to enjoy psychologically or spiritually. It is recognized by law as a personal right because protection of personal right means protecting a subject of right from harms in both biological sense and in social psychological or mental sense. Psychological and mental harms can often lead to depression, fear, sadness, anger, anxiety, or despair, which may in turn lead to physiological dysfunction, the reduction of the capacity for social activity, even insanity and the loss of capacity for act. The legal recognition of the right to human dignity is an important indicator of the progress of human civilization. According to the relevant legal provisions, acts of defamation, false accusation, and framing up constitute violation of human dignity.

7. Right to Name

A name consists of two parts: family name and given name, which together form an exclusive symbol that distinguishes one person from another. The exclusive use of name is an ancient as well as a fundamental right. The exclusiveness of the right to name distinguishes the subject of the right to a specific name from other subjects of rights, so as to determine his rights and obligations. The subjects of the right to name include not only nature persons, but also legal persons. Violations of right of name mainly include interfering in another person's use of his own names, and unauthorized use or counterfeiting another person's name.

8. Right to Portrait

Portrait is a reproduction of a person's true image by drawing, photography, sculpture or other means. It is an exclusive graphic symbol of a person. Modern technology makes its possible to reproduce high-fidelity portrait of a person on a physical carrier, which can become the proof of a person's identity or his participation in certain activity. Therefore, infringement upon the right to portrait often constitutes fraud and results in harms to the subject of the right. Moreover, the physiological features of some people can give pleasant feeling to other people, thereby bringing commercial profit whereas those of some others can give disgusting feeling to other people and the publicity of them can result in huge psychological trauma and suffering to the persons concerned or their family members. Therefore, the right to portrait is an indivisible part of personal right. In real life, the right to portrait is often closely connected to the right to human dignity.

9. Right to Reputation and Honor

The reputation of a natural person is the social evaluation of his moral quality and behavior; the reputation of a legal person is the social evaluation of its behavior and prestige. The reputation of a citizen or a legal person is formed on the basis of his or its behavior during a long period of life experience or practice. In contrast, honor is awarded by the state or society to a citizen or a legal person who has made major contributions or remarkable achievements in a certain field, including non-material rewards, such as the titles of hero, model, person who has rendered outstanding service, or expert who has made outstanding contribution, etc. , and a material reward in the form of bonus, trophy, etc. Good reputation and honor are similar in that, once formed or awarded, they will produce corresponding social influences and social benefits, thereby becoming an inseparable part of the personal right of a citizen or right of a legal person. Infringement upon the right to reputation or honor of a citizen or legal person mainly takes the form of defamation, frame-up, and counterfeiting, which can cause mental or reputational harms to a citizen or legal person and affect their norm life or operation.

10. Right to Privacy

Privacy refers to some facts in a citizen's personal life which he does not want others to know, such as living habits, sexual life, diary, photos, banking information, and correspondence. The trade secrets of a legal person, such as information concerning business negotiation, investment, operation, and communications with clients, also belong to privacy. As a result of the development of modern state system, privacy has become an important personal right and is protected by law. Under normal circumstances, the legal protection of privacy focuses on the prohibition of unlawful disclosure of citizens' private information by civil servants, or by such media as publications, films, TV or radio programs without the consent of the persons concerned. As for the act of one citizen disclosing the private information of another citizen to the third citizen, such act is normally regulated by moral code, rather than law, as long as it does not result in major losses to the person concerned. The private information of a deceased person no longer belongs to privacy if its disclosure is agreed upon by the deceased before his death and by his family members after his death. The practice of some countries shows that the disclosure of certain kinds of privacy of some members of parliament and civil servants by mass media for the sake of public interest is allowed by law and the higher their position, the more prominent their status and the more public attention they receive, the less privacy they enjoy. The presidents of the United States and the royal family in the U. K. are examples in this respect.

Logically, the above-listed ten aspects of personal rights can be roughly divided into four categories: first, the right to life and the right to health; second, the freedom of the person, including sexual freedom and freedom of marriage; third, right to personality, including right to human dignity, right to name, right to portrait, right to reputation and right to honor; and fourth, right to privacy.

II. Historical Development of the System of Protection of Personal Rights

The concept of personal rights, as an important content of human rights, was put forward during the bourgeois revolution in modern history. However, like other human rights, they originate from the natural attribute of human beings and are the products of development of social relationships. The right to life is an inherent right; the right to health is based on the human need for survival; sexual freedom comes from the human instinct of love of the opposite sex; and all other rights have been gradually formed, recognized, and developed on the basis of the natural attributes of human beings in the long process of evolution of human society.

At the early stage of development of human society, people had no idea of rights. All their activities were based on their need for survival. The protection of the person was an instinctive reaction to external attacks. Later, people learnt from practice that the safety of an individual had a bearing on the safety of the family and a great group of people as a whole and gradually established social order and institutions on the basis of this common understanding. The personal safety of each individual was protected by the whole group. As a result, "blood revenge" and "revenge of the same state" became recognized means of punishment for the violation of personal safety. Thus, the vague idea and the loose system of respecting the personal rights of others in exchange for the respect by other of one's own personal rights had gradually taken form. This was the earliest form of personal rights and method for their protection.

After mankind entered into a civilized society, personal rights were given unprecedented sanctity and become rights of social nature protected by the coercive power of the state and the law. Violation of the person of an individual is regarded not only as the violence against a particular individual person or against the interest of a particular family or clan, but also as an attack against class society as well as against the existing social order and social relationships. Therefore, the state, as the embodiment of public power, must take decisive, rapid and forceful measures to punish such acts. However, it needs to be pointed out that, at that time, only aristocratic slaveholders, who made up a very small percentage of the population, could enjoy full protection of their personal rights. Under the hierarchical social system, small and medium-sized slaveholders could enjoy their personal rights only to the extent that the enjoyment of these rights would not harm the interests of aristocratic slaveholders. Although the common people could have their family and property, they were not only under the heavy burden of taxes and corvee, but also frequently forced to join the army to fight wars for aristocratic slaveholders. As for the slaves who were at the bottom of society, they were treated both in people's mind and in law as livestock and goods that had no personality and could be slaughtered or sold by slaveholders at will, whether in ancient Greece, ancient Rome, and ancient Babylon, or in the Xia, Shang and Zhou dynasties in ancient Chinese history. Among the inscriptions on bones or tortoise shells of the Shang Dynasty were records about the pursuit and execution of escaped slaves. In the archaeological excavation of tombs of that period, many beheaded remains of slaves were found in these tombs along with the remains of their masters. All these have proved that slaves at these times were not treated as human beings and had no personal right to talk about.

The Spring and Autumn and Warring States Period was a period of major reform, major restructuring and major development in Chinese history, in which the development of the productive force had promoted social transformation. The patriarchal clan system represented by the kings of the Zhou Dynasty, based on blood lineage, and characterized by hierarchical social order, could no longer meet the demands of social development. With the emergence of the private ownership of land and the delegation of power, more and more people were demanding for their share of rights. A group of laws of the Qin Dynasty inscribed on the bamboo slips found in an ancient tomb in Yunmeng County of Hubei Province excavated in 1975 show that the "soldiers" and their family members who lived in urban and rural areas and made up the majority of the population were actually freemen who possessed certain amount of land, houses and other properties. These people were tied to the land, pay taxes and corvee to the state according to the land they cultivate and the number of people in their family. In law, they had already become subjects of civil rights and their rights, including some personal rights, were protected by the state and the law. In the group of laws mentioned above, acts of murdering, injuring, bringing false charges against, and sending anonymous letters about others were regarded as crimes for which corresponding punishments were provided. [①]Most surprisingly, a law at that time required government officials not to use torture or intimidation in interrogating criminal suspects under normal circumstances. Torture was allowed on a criminal suspect who had changed his statement many times or lied, but it should be written in the interrogation record that "torture was used on the suspect because he changed his statement several times but was still unable to explain himself."[②] Another law of that time provided that: "an official who, in arresting a person suspected of a crime punishable only by confiscation of property or fines, intentionally attacks him with weapon, resulting in the death of such person, shall be sentenced to long-term hard labor; if the attack has resulted in the injury of such person, he shall be sentenced to short-term hard labor."[③] This shows that, as early as in the Qin Dynasty more than 2, 000, the law had provided for the protection of criminal suspects. Of course, these newly-discovered laws also show that there were

① See *Qin Dynasty Bamboo Slips Unearthed in Suidihu: Questions and Answers on Issues of Law*, Cultural Relics Publishing House, 1978.

② See *Qin Dynasty Bamboo Slips Unearthed in Suidihu: Criminal Interrogation*, Cultural Relics Publishing House, 1978.

③ See *supra* note 1.

still many slaves at that time. But these slaves were different from those in the Zhou Dynasty in that their life and health were already partial protected by law. Although the phenomenon of illegal killing and injuring by fathers and slaveholders of their sons and slaves still existed, these acts were defined as "family crimes" by the law of that time. According to the Qin Code, the victims of "family crimes" had no right to bring charges against their father or masters. It is not clear whether other people could bring charges against such crimes. However, the Qin Code listed two cases in which a slaveholder brought one of his slaves to a court for "being insolent" towards their master and requested the court to punish the slave. In one of the cases, the slaveholder was a viscount who was in a very high position in society. This shows that the slaveholders' power to punish slaves had already been restricted at that time. The Qin Code reflected the situation at the early stage of development of feudal society in China. During the more than 2, 000 years that followed, although China had experienced countless changes of dynasty, foreign invasions, and political turmoil, the society had been developing continuously. In this long process, economically, the state, represented by the emperor and his agents throughout the country, took control over a large amount of land and became the largest landlord in the country. Other land in the country was owned by medium and small landlords and land-holding peasants. Although land-holding peasants were large in number, the land owned by them was very limited. The state, represented by the emperor, apart from exploiting the peasants through taxes and corvee, also lent out the land under its control to peasants for cultivation, just like other landlords; politically, a highly centralized system was implemented; and ideologically, the Confucian idea of "great unity" and the supremacy of the monarch was taken as the orthodoxy and the patriarchal ethics of the Three Cardinal Guides (ruler guides subject, father guides son and husband guides wife) and Five Constant Virtues (benevolence, righteousness, propriety, knowledge and sincerity) were advocated. From the relatively well-preserved ancient Chinese law codes, such as the Tang Code, the Criminal Code of Song Dynasty, the Code of the Great Ming Dynasty, and Code of the Great Qing Dynasty, we can see that peasants, whether land-holding peasants or tenant peasants, who made up the majority of the population in feudal society in ancient China, were in a relationship of personal bondage with the state and landlords. They were tightly bond to the land and suffered from super-economic exploitation, although compared to the serfs in medieval Europe, who could be bought and sold together with the land, they seemed to enjoy more personal freedom. However, under the patriarchal clan system, the Chinese peasants were under the oppression of not only the feudal state, but also clan leaders and family heads. And women were also under the oppression of their husbands. In the study of the protection of personal rights in ancient China, we should not ignore the fact that clan leaders and family heads in such society actually had the power over the life and death of other family members.

Beginning from mid—19th century, with the introduction of western learning, China began to prepare for the reform of its legal system. After the failure of the Hundred Days Reform, the Qing government established the Bureau for Compilation of Law in 1903. Shen Jiaben and others began to revise the existing laws according to the principle of "striving to make Chinese law effective not only in China but also abroad". ①In 1910 the Contemporary Criminal Code of the Great Qing Dynasty was promulgated, which separated civil law from the criminal law by abolishing criminal punishments for civil disputes over inheritance, division of family property, marriage, and debt and abolished cruel corporal punishments, such as flogging, whipping, *lingche* (put to death by dismembering the body), hanging up the head of an executed prisoner as warming to others, posthumous execution, and tattooing the face, as well as the practice of extorting a confession by torture, so as to show respect for personal rights. Between 1906 and 1908, the New Criminal Code of the Great Qing Dynasty was drafted with the help of a Japanese advisor, Dr. Okada. The new law embodied many new reforms, including the recognition of the principle of nulla poena sine lege, the systems of probation and parole, the abolition of the system of inequality in the protection of rights based on social status. The 1911 Revolution led by Dr. Sun Yat-sen was a great revolution in any sense. After the revolution, the Senate of the Temporary Government of Najing promulgated in March 1912 the Temporary Constitution of the Republic of China, which for the first time in Chinese history affirmed citizens' personal rights as constitutional rights. A series of presidential decrees promulgated afterwards prohibited corporal punishments, extorting a confession by torture, discrimination based on

① See Shen Jiaben, "Memorial on Abolishing Cruel Punishments in the Code of the Great Qing Dynasty", in Shen Jiaben, *Collected Works of Shen Jiaben*, 1907.

social hierarchy, human trafficking, indenture by which one sells oneself or a member of one's family, and servitude and other slave-like practices. ①

The above-mentioned temporary constitution, laws and decrees opened a new chapter in the protection of personal rights in Chinese history. Although the 1911 Revolution met with setbacks because of the treacheries of Yuan Shikai and the laws promulgated in the revolution were not implemented, the revolution and the laws on the protection of personal rights promulgated during it had inspired the Chinese people and given them hopes. During the 1930s and 1940s, Dr. Sun Yat-sen's ideas were put into practice in the New Democratic Revolution led by the Communist Party of China (CPC) headed by Mao Zedong. Apart from the Outline Constitution of the Chinese Soviet②, which contained a large number of provisions on the protection of human rights, the CPC had also promulgated a series of regulations on the protection of human rights in anti-Japanese bases in Shaanxi-Gansu-Ningxia Border Region, Heibei-Shandong-Henan Border Region, Northwest Shaanxi Province, and Shandong province since November 1940, including Regulations of Shangdong Province on the Protection of Human Rights and the Rules for the Implementation of Regulations of Bohai District on the Protection of Human Rights. ③The victory of New Democratic Revolution in 1949 showed a beautiful prospect and created corresponding conditions for the full enjoyment of personal rights by Chinese people.

It should be said the situation in China at the early days of the People's Republic was satisfactory: Chinese people had driven imperialist powers out of the country, thereby putting to an end to the days when foreigners did whatever they wanted and oppressed the Chinese people at will and achieved the success in suppressing bandits and local despots who have bullied the people in many areas for hundreds of years; the victory of land

① See Presidential Decree on the Prohibition of Extorting a Confession by Torture; Presidential Decree on the Prohibition of Corporal Punishments, Presidential Decree on the Equality of All Citizens in the Enjoyment of Rights in Public and Private Laws, and Presidential Decree on the Prohibition of Human Trafficking, all promulgated in March 1912.

② Han Yanlong and Chang Zhaoru (eds.), *Selection of Legal Documents Promulgated by the Revolutionary Bases During the Period of New Democratic Revolution in China*, vol. 1, Beijing: China Social Sciences Publishing House, 1981, pp. 8—12.

③ Ibid., pp. 89—100.

reform in rural areas and the democratic reform in urban areas had thoroughly overthrew the feudal rule of oppression and enabled the broad masses of laboring people in rural and urban areas to rid themselves of their relationship of personal bondage with landlords, feudal bosses, and gang leaders; the adoption and implementation of the marriage law provided citizens with legal safeguards for the realization of the freedom of marriage and family happiness; and the 1954 Constitution affirmed in many ways the personal rights of Chinese citizens. During the period before and after the adoption of the Constitution, a situation of peaceful prosperity, in which "if aught was dropped upon the road, none picked it up, nor were the doors of houses locked at night", did appeared in the vast territory of China and Chinese citizens had gained unprecedented sense of personal safety. Of course, there is no denying that there had been incidents of violation of citizens' human dignity and personal freedom by means of "special cases for investigation", "interrogation in incommunicado", and "mass debate and denunciation". In the expansion of the "Struggle against Rightist" in 1957, the "Great Leap Forward" Movement in 1958, the "Anti-rightist Movement" in 1959, and a series of movements of "rectification of communes", many innocent citizens had been framed up, thrown into prison, even met with violent death. The trend of development at that time showed that the "Great Proletarian Cultural Revolution" that was launched in 1966 and lasted for ten years was inevitable. The "Ten-Year Catastrophe" had pushed many things to the extreme: the sacred constitution and laws were openly trampled upon, the President of the People's Republic and many highly decorated marshals and generals had been persecuted to death, and countless intellectuals, model workers, patriotic democratic personages, returned patriotic overseas Chinese, and cadres and ordinary citizens had been persecuted and tortured. As an ancient Chinese saying goes, "every cloud has a silver lining", it were exactly catastrophes like the "Anti-Rightist" Movement, especially the "Cultural Revolution", that wakened the people up, thereby creating opportunity and motive force for the progress of the system of legal protection of personal rights in China.

III. Progresses in the Development of the System of Legal Protection of Personal Rights in China during the Past Thirty Years

The lesson of the "Ten-Year Catastrophe" enabled people to realize that, in order to safeguard socialist democracy, it is necessary to strengthen the socialist legal system and to ensure that everyone is equal before the law and that no one has privileges above the law. With the development of socialist legal system in the more than ten years after the Third Plenary Session of the Eleventh CPC Central Committee, China has adopted comparatively comprehensive and systematic laws on the safeguarding of personal rights and established corresponding institutions.

1. Legal Protection of the Right to Life and the Right to Health

The Preamble and especially Chapter Two of the Chinese Constitution contain extensive provisions on the protection of various rights of citizens, including the right to life and the right to health. Some of these provisions do not directly mention the right to life or the right to health not because of any omission by legislators, but because these two rights are self-evident in these provisions. The Chinese Criminal Law, the General Principles of the Civil Law and other laws adopted in accordance with the Constitution contain a series of concrete provisions on the protection of the right to life and the right to health. Firstly, the Chinese law has provided for severe criminal punishments and necessary civil liabilities for the violation of the right to life. The Chinese Criminal Law provides that: "Whoever intentionally commits homicide shall be sentenced to death, life imprisonment or fixed-term imprisonment of not less than ten years; if the circumstances are relatively minor, the offender shall be sentenced to fixed-term imprisonment of not less than three years and not more than ten years." and that: "Whoever negligently kills another shall be sentenced to fixed-term imprisonment of not more than five years; if the circumstances are especially flagrant, the offender shall be sentenced to fixed-term imprisonment of not less than five years."① The General Principles of Civil

① For the provisions in the Chinese Criminal Law and other Chinese laws quoted in this article, see *Compilation of Laws of the People's Republic of China*, Changchun: Jilin People's Publishing House, 1994.

Law stipulates that "citizens have the right to life and the right to health" and provides for liability for compensation for the violation of these rights: "if the victim dies, the infringer shall pay the funeral expenses, the necessary living expenses of the deceased's dependents and other such expenses." In September 1983, the Standing Committee of the National People's Congress adopted the Decision Regarding Severe Punishment of Criminals Who Seriously Endanger Public Security, which provided that: "Punishment above the maximum punishment stipulated in the Criminal Law, up to and including death sentences, may be imposed on seven categories of criminals who seriously endanger public security, including "those who intentionally inflicts serious bodily injury upon another person or causes the person's death" . One form of violation of the right to life is killing of infants, who have the same right to life as adults. The Chinese Marriage Law stipulates in Article 15 that: "Parents shall be under the obligation of upbringing and educating their children", that "underage children and dependent children shall be entitled to demand their parents to pay aliments", and that "It shall be forbidden to drown or desert infants or commit any kind of infanticide." In view of the fact that the phenomenon of drowning of female infant still exists in some remote rural areas, it is necessary to provide for a separate crime of infanticide and corresponding punishment for this crime in the Criminal Law, so as to more effectively protect the right to life of infants.

The law forbids anyone to take the life of another person. But what about someone who takes his own life, or consciously ask someone else to help him end his own life in order to spare himself the suffering from illness? The Chinese law contains no provision on this issue. As for those who commit suicide, apart from expressing compassion and regret, people often give them different appraisals in light of the reasons for the suicide and the moral character of such persons. As for those who help others to commit suicide, namely "euthanasia", the issue is still under debate and no consensus has been reached. However, from the point of view of judicial practice, a very cautious approach should be taken before clear legal provision on this issue is adopted.

Second, Chinese laws also contain specific and comprehensive provisions on the protection of the right to health. Violation of the right to life will inevitably result in the violation of the right to health whereas violation of the right to health may also lead to the violation of the right to life. Therefore, life and health are often mentioned together in the criminal law. The Chinese Criminal Law provides in Article 134 that: "Whoever intentionally inflicts bodily injury upon another person shall be sentenced to fixed-term imprisonment of not more than three years or criminal detention. Whoever, by committing the crime mentioned in the preceding paragraph, causes severe bodily injury to another person shall be sentenced to fixed-term imprisonment of not less than three years and not more than seven years; if he causes a person's death, he shall be sentenced to fixed-term imprisonment of not less than seven years or life imprisonment." and in Article 135 that: "Whoever negligently injures another person and causes him severe bodily injury shall be sentenced to fixed-term imprisonment of not more than two years or criminal detention; if the circumstances are especially flagrant, the offender shall be sentenced to fixed-term imprisonment of not less than two years and not more than seven years." As mentioned above, the 19383 Decision of the Standing Committee of the National People's Congress Regarding the Severe Punishment of Criminals Who Seriously Endanger Public Security provided that punishment above the maximum punishment stipulated in the Criminal Law may be imposed on those who intentionally inflicts serious bodily injury upon another person or causes serious harms to the health of others. The General Principles of Civil Law provides in Article 119 for the civil compensation for the violation of the right to health: "Anyone who infringes upon a citizen's person and causes him physical injury shall pay his medical expenses and his loss in income due to missed working time and shall pay him living subsidies if he is disabled." To protect citizens' right to health from infringements in the name of achieving "lawful" purposes, the Criminal Law provides in Article 136 that: "It shall be strictly forbidden to extort a confession by torture. Any state functionary who extorts a confession by torture shall be sentenced to fixed-term imprisonment of not more than three years or criminal detention. Whoever causes injury or disability to a person through corporal punishment shall be charged with the crime of injury and given a heavier punishment."

Third, in a modern society, there are many factors that can endanger human right and health, such as working conditions, infectious diseases, food hygiene, product quality, and air, soil, water and noise pollutions. Therefore, after the promulgation of the Criminal Law and the General Principles of the Civil Law, China has also adopted the Law on Labor Protection, the Law on Product Quality, the Law on the Protection of Consumers' Rights and Interests, the Environmental Protection Law, the Law on the Protection of Disabled Persons, and the Law on the Protection of Minors, and the Law on the Protection of the Rights and Interests of Women. By the time of promulgation of the State Compensation Law, China has established a relatively complete system of law on the protection of the right to life and the right to health.

2. Legal Protection of Personal Freedoms

Personal freedoms, as the precondition for citizens to participate in various social activities and enjoying other rights, have always been paid close attention to by society and affirmed by the Chinese Constitution. The current Chinese Constitution provides in Article 37 that: "Freedom of the person of citizens of the People's Republic of China is inviolable. No citizen may be arrested except with the approval or by decision of a people's procuratorate or by decision of a people's court, and arrests must be made by a public security organ. Unlawful detention or deprivation or restriction of citizens' freedom of the person by other means is prohibited, and unlawful search of the person of citizens is prohibited." and in Article 39 that: "The residences of citizens of the People's Republic of China are inviolable. Unlawful search of, or intrusion into, a citizen's residence is prohibited." The Constitution also provides that marriage, family, the mother, and the child are protected by the state and it is prohibited to restrict the freedom of marriage. To ensure the effective protection of personal freedoms, a series of concrete legal provisions have been made in accordance with the Constitution.

The Chinese Criminal Law provides in Article 143 that: "The unlawful detention of another person or the unlawful deprivation of his personal freedom by any other means shall be strictly prohibited. A violator shall be sentenced to fixed-term imprisonment of not more than three years, criminal detention or deprivation of political rights. In circumstances where battery or humiliation has occurred, the violator shall be given a heavier punishment. Whoever commits the crime mentioned in the preceding paragraph and causes serious bodily injury shall be sentenced to fixed-term imprisonment of not less than three years and not more than ten years; if he causes a person's death, he shall be sentenced to fixed-term imprisonment of not less than seven years." and in Article 144 that: "Whoever unlawfully subjects another person to public surveillance, unlawfully subjects another person to a body search or a search of his residence or unlawfully intrudes into another person's residence shall be sentenced to fixed-term imprisonment of not more than three years or criminal detention."

Kidnapping and trafficking in human beings is a serious crime of violation of personal freedom. The Criminal Law provides in Article 141 that: "Whoever abducts and traffics in human beings shall be sentenced to fixed-term imprisonment of not more than five years; if the circumstances are serious, the offender shall be sentenced to fixed-term imprisonment of not less than five years." and in Article 184 that: "Whoever abducts a boy or girl under the age of 14, thereby cutting the child off from his family or guardian, shall be sentenced to fixed-term imprisonment of not more than five years or criminal detention." To suppress and punish this kind of serious crimes against vulnerable groups of society, the Standing Committee of the National People's Congress adopted in September 1991 Decision on the Severe Punishment of Criminals Who Abduct and Traffic in or Kidnap Women or Children, which listed the most severe form of the crime of abducting and trafficking in human being, namely abducting and trafficking in a woman or a child, as a separate crime. Thus, the crime of abducting and trafficking in human beings in the Criminal Law refers only to the abduction and trafficking in male human beings over the age of 14. Decision of the Standing Committee of the National People's Congress Regarding the Severe Punishment of Criminals Who Seriously Endanger Public Security stipulates in Article 1 that: "Punishment above the maximum punishment stipulated in the Criminal Law, up to and including the death penalty, may be imposed on" "ringleaders of groups who abduct and traffic in human beings, or whoever abducts and traffics in human beings when the circumstances are especially serious". According to this Decision, the punishments for the crime of abducting and trafficking in women and children can be divided into three grades in light of the circumstances the crime: (1) fixed-term imprisonment of up to five years if the circumstances of the crime are not serious; (2) fixed-term imprisonment of not less than five years and not more than fifteen years if the circumstances are serious; (3) life imprisonment or death penalty for ringleaders of groups who abduct and traffic in human beings or if the circumstances are especially serious.

Sexual freedom is an important aspect of personal freedoms. The Criminal Law provides for severe punishments for the rape or gang rape of a woman and for forcing a woman into prostitution. The crime of rape refers to the act of having sexual intercourse with a woman against her will by force, threat or other means. Article 139 of the Criminal Law provides that: "Whoever rapes a woman by force, threat or other means shall be sentenced to fixed-term imprisonment of not less than three years and not more than ten years. Whoever has sexual relations with a girl under the age of 14 shall be deemed to have committed rape and shall be given a heavier punishment. If the circumstances of a crime mentioned in the preceding two paragraphs are especially serious or a person's serious bodily injury or death has been caused, the offender shall be sentenced to fixed-term imprisonment of not less than ten years, life imprisonment or death. If two or more persons commit rape and violate the same victim in succession, they shall be given a heavier punishment." As for the crime of forcing a woman to engage in prostitution, the 1979 Criminal Law provides for the punishment of "fixed-term imprisonment of not less than three years and not more than ten years". The 1983 Decision of the Standing Committee of the National People's Congress Regarding the Severe Punishment of Criminals Who Seriously Endanger Public Security provides for severer punishment for this crime: "Punishment above the maximum punishment stipulated in the Criminal Law, up to and including death sentences, may be imposed on" "whoever lures or forces a woman into prostitution or shelters her in prostitution, when the circumstances are especially serious." Broadly speaking, many acts of insulting a woman also constitute the violation of sexual freedom. They come under the crime of hooliganism in the 1979 Criminal Law. Insulting a woman refers to humiliating and acting indecently towards a woman (including an underage girl) by force, threat or other means. Such acts are punishable by up to seven years of fixed-term imprisonment under the Criminal Law. The 1983 Decision of the Standing Committee of the National People's Congress Regarding the Severe Punishment of Criminals Who Seriously Endanger Public Security has also increased the severity of the punishment against the crimes of hooliganism, including the crime of insulting a woman.

The freedom of marriage, which includes both the freedom to marry and the freedom to divorce, is closely connected to sexual freedom. Under normal circumstances, it is impossible to truly enjoy sexual freedom without the freedom of marriage. The Chinese Marriage Law provides that: "Marriage shall be based on the complete willingness of both the man and the woman. No party may coerce the other party to enter into marriage, and no third party may interfere with the marriage." The Law also protects the freedom of divorce. General Principles of the Civil Law provides in

Article 103 that: "Citizens shall enjoy the right of marriage by choice. Mercenary marriages, marriages upon arbitrary decision by any third party and any other acts of interference in the freedom of marriage shall be prohibited." The Criminal Law also regards the act of forcibly interfering with another person's freedom of marriage as crime and provides for corresponding punishment: "Whoever forcibly interferes with another person's freedom of marriage shall be sentenced to fixed-term imprisonment of not more than two years or criminal detention. If anyone committing the crime mentioned in the preceding paragraph causes his victim's death, he shall be sentenced to fixed-term imprisonment of not less than two years and not more than seven years." In practice, apart from one party to the marriage, those who forcibly interfere with another person's freedom of marriage are usually the parents, elder brothers or other elder members of the family of one or both parties to the marriage. And the reasons for the interference are mainly old traditions. It is probably based on the consideration of the above-mentioned factors that the punishment for the crime of forcibly interfering with another person's freedom of marriage that results in the death of the victim is not very severe as compared to other crimes that result in the death of the victim.

3. Legal Protection of the Right to Personality

The respect for and protection of the right to personality is an indicator of modern civilization. Here, the right to personality includes the right to name, the right to portrait, the right to reputation, the right to honor and the right to human dignity. In accordance with the relevant provisions of the Constitution, the General Principles of the Civil Law, the Criminal Law and other laws in China contain more detailed provisions on the protection of the right to personality. Article 38 of the Constitution provides that: "The personal dignity of citizens of the People's Republic of China is inviolable. Insult, libel, false accusation or false incrimination directed against citizens by any means is prohibited." The General Principles of the Civil Law provides in Article 99 that: "Citizens shall enjoy the right of personal name and shall be entitled to determine, use or change their personal names in accordance with relevant provisions. Interference with, usurpation and false representation of personal names shall be prohibited", in Article 100 that: "Citizens shall enjoy the right of portrait. The use of a citizen's portrait for profits without his consent shall be prohibited", in Article 101 that: "Citizens and legal persons shall enjoy the right of reputation. The personality of citizens shall be protected by law, and the use of insults, libel or other means to damage the reputation of citizens or legal persons shall be prohibited", and in Article 102 that: "Citizens and legal persons shall enjoy the right of honor. It shall prohibited to unlawfully divest citizens and legal persons of their honorary titles." The Criminal Law provides in Article 145 that: "Whoever, by violence or other methods, including the use of "big character posters" and "small character posters", publicly insults another person or fabricates facts to defame him, if the circumstances are serious, shall be sentenced to fixed-term imprisonment of not more than three years, criminal detention or deprivation of political rights" and in Article 138 that: "It shall be strictly forbidden to use any method or means to implicate cadres or the people on false charges. Whoever fabricates facts to implicate another person (including a criminal) on false charges shall be given a criminal sanction in light of the nature, circumstances, consequences and sentencing standards of the crime that he falsely accused the other person of committing. A state functionary who commits the crime of false accusation shall be given a heavier punishment."

The above legal provisions on the protection of the right to personality involve both criminal responsibilities and tort liabilities. With respect to criminal responsibilities, the subject as well as the object of crime must be a natural person, rather than a state organ, enterprise, public institution or mass organization. As for any journal or magazine that publishes an article that insults or libels another person, the Interim Regulations on the Administration of Periodicals, promulgated by the State Press and Publication Administration in November 1988, provide in Article 5 and Article 36 that any periodical that publishes any content that constitutes insult or libel against another person in violation of these Regulations shall be given the following administrative sanctions by the competent department in charge of administration of the press and publication in light of the circumstances of the violation: warming, fine, suspension of the selling the publication, confiscation and destruction of periodicals that contain illegal content, suspension of publication for a fixed period of time, suspension of business operation for rectification, and cancellation of registration. The object of crime in the above-mentioned laws can only be a nature person. The Opinions on Several Questions Concerning the Implementation of General Principles of the Civil Law of the People's Republic of China, promulgated by the Supreme People's Court in

November 1988, provides in Article 16 that: "In case anyone be spatters or slanders the reputation of a legal person in writing or orally, which results in damages to the legal person, such act shall be determined as act of infringing the right of reputation of the legal person." This shows that insult or libel against a legal person constitutes only a tort, not a crime.

As far as the crimes committed against a nature person is concerned, the above-mentioned legal provisions have provided for three kinds of crimes that are both connected to and different from each other: insult, libel and false charge or frame-up. Their commonalities include: the subject of the crime is a natural person who has attained the age for criminal liability; the object of crime is the right to personality of another person; and the crime is directly intentional. Their differences include: the crime of insult is the act of publicly humiliating of another person's personality by violence or other methods; the crime of libel is the act of damaging the personality of another person by fabricating or spreading certain false story about him; the crime of false charge or frame-up also involves the fabrication of a false story about another, only that the story fabricated is a story of crime and it is provided to the relevant state organs for the purpose of framing up another person.

The above-mentioned acts, if they have not resulted in serious consequences, do not constitute a crime and should be punished by a public security organ in accordance with Regulations on Administrative Penalties for Public Security. Article 16 of the Regulations provides that: "Whoever openly insults other persons or fabricates stories to slander other persons, if such act is not serious enough for criminal punishment, shall be detained for a maximum of fifteen days, fined a maximum of two hundred yuan or given a warning."

4. Legal Protection of the Right to Privacy

In modern countries, correspondence has become an important part of individual life. Therefore, the right to privacy covers both secret of individual life and the secret of correspondence. Although Chinese Constitution and Criminal Law contain no provision that specifically mention the right to personal secret or the right to privacy, the Constitution provides Article 40 that: "Freedom and privacy of correspondence of citizens of the People's Republic of China are protected by law. No organization or individual may, on any ground, infringe upon citizens freedom and privacy of correspondence, except in cases where, to meet the needs of state security or of criminal investigation, public security or procuratorial organs are permitted to censor correspondence in accordance with procedures prescribed by law." In accordance with this provision, the Criminal Law provides in Article 149 that "Whoever conceals, destroys or unlawfully opens another person's letters, infringing upon the citizen's right to freedom of correspondence, if the circumstances are serious, shall be sentenced to fixed-term imprisonment of not more than one year or criminal detention." and in Article 191 that "Any postal and telecommunications worker who opens, conceals or destroys mail or telegrams without authorization shall be sentenced to fixed-term imprisonment of not more than two years or criminal detention." As for those who commit the acts of hiding, destroying, discarding or illegally opening another person's postal articles or telegrams, but the circumstances are not serious enough to constitute a crime, Article 22 of the Regulations on Administrative Penalties for Public Security provides that they shall "be detained for a maximum of fifteen days, fined a maximum of two hundred yuan or given a warning". With respect to the protection of privacy of individual citizens, although there is no specific provision in the Criminal Law and the General Principles of the Civil Law, the 1991 Civil Procedure Law has made up for this deficiency to some extent by providing that cases involving the private affairs of individuals must be tried in camera and divorce cases may be tried in camera upon application of the parties. Besides, the Opinions of the Supreme People's Court on Several Issues concerning the Implementation of the General Principles of the Civil Law of the People's Republic of China stipulates in Article 140 that in case anyone propagates the privacy of any other person in writing or orally, such act shall be determined as act infringing the citizen's right of reputation. Of course, the above provisions are far from enough to safeguard the right to privacy. Nevertheless they show that legislative and judicial organs in China are paying attention to the protection of this right.

5. Compensation to Victims of Violation of Personal Rights

The adoption of legal provisions on the compensation to victims of violation of personal rights marked a major progress in the protection of personal rights in China. In the past, influenced by the ideology of the planned economic system, people believed that the harms to a person's life, health and personality could not and should not be measured or compensated by money. Thus, in cases of violation of citizens' rights to life and health, attention was paid only to the criminal or administrative punishments on the perpetrators of such crimes, while the compensation to the victims of crimes had been neglected. As a result, the victims of crimes and their family members often had to endure not only mental and physical sufferings, but also financial difficulties resulting from the crimes, even were driven into a desperate situation. A major change in this situation occurred with the promulgation in September 1986 of the General Principles of the Civil Law, which provides for the compensation not only for the damages to state, collective or individual properties, but also for the violation of citizens' personal rights. The General Principles provide in Article 119 that "Anyone who infringes upon a citizen's person and causes him physical injury shall pay his medical expenses and his loss in income due to missed working time and shall pay him living subsidies if he is disabled", in Article 120 that "If a citizen's right of personal name, portrait, reputation or honor is infringed upon, he shall have the right to demand that the infringement be stopped, his reputation rehabilitated, the ill effects eliminated and an apology made; he may also demand compensation for losses. The above paragraph shall also apply to infringements upon a legal person's right of name, reputation or honor", and in Article 121 that: "If a state organ or its personnel, while performing its duties, encroaches upon the lawful rights and interests of a citizen or legal person and causes damages, it shall bear civil liability." Moreover, articles 122 to 127 of the General Principles also provide for civil liabilities for the property or personal damages to others caused by substandard products, operations that are greatly hazardous to the surroundings, pollutions to the environment in violation of state provisions for environmental protection and the prevention of pollution, construction in a public places without setting up clear signs and adopting safety measures, collapse of a building or any other installation or detachment or dropdown of an object placed or hung on a structure, or attack by a domesticated animal. The main methods of bearing civil liability include: (1) cessation of infringements; (2) removal of obstacles; (3) elimination of dangers; (4) return of property; (5) restoration of original condition; (6) repair, reworking or replacement; (7) compensation for losses; (8) payment of breach of contract damages; (9) elimination of ill effects and rehabilitation of reputation; and (10) extension of apology. The above methods of bearing civil liability may be applied exclusively or concurrently.

In order to implement the above-mentioned provision on the bearing of civil liabilities by state organs and state personnel for the infringement of the lawful rights and interests of citizens and legal persons in the performance of duties, the Standing Committee of the National People's Congress adopted the State Compensation Law in May 1994. The Law consists of six chapters with a total of 35 articles, which mainly provides for administrative compensation, criminal compensation, and forms and assessment of compensation. According to this law, the victim shall have the right to administrative compensation if an administrative organ or its functionaries, in exercising their administrative functions and powers, commit any of the following acts infringing upon the right of the person of a citizen: detaining a citizen in violation of the law or unlawfully taking compulsory administrative measures in restraint of his personal freedom; unlawfully taking a citizen into custody or depriving him of his right of the person by other unlawful means; using or instigating violence such as beating one up, thereby causing bodily injury or death to a citizen; unlawfully using weapons or police restraint implements, thereby causing bodily injury or death to a citizen; or other unlawful acts causing bodily injury or death to a citizen. The victim shall have the right to criminal compensation if an organ in charge of investigatory, procuratorial, judicial or prison administration work, or its functionaries, infringe upon his right of the person in the exercise of its functions and powers in any of the following circumstances: wrongful detention of a person without incriminating facts or proof substantiating a strong suspicion of the commission of a crime; wrongful arrest of a person without incriminating facts; innocence is found in a retrial held in accordance with the procedure of trial supervision, but the original sentence has already been executed; extortion of a confession by torture or causing bodily injury or death to a citizen by using or instigating the use of violence such as beating one up; or causing bodily injury or death to a citizen by the unlawful use of weapons or police restraint implements.

Article 6 of the Sate Compensation Law stipulates that: "Victimized citizens, legal persons or other organizations shall have the right to demand compensation. In case of death of a victim, his heirs or other relatives in maintenance relationship with him shall have the right to demand compensation." As for the organs responsible for the compensation, the Law clearly provides they should be the state organs that have infringed upon the lawful rights and interests of the victim or the state organ whose functionaries who have infringed upon the lawful rights and interests of the victim; if reconsideration of a case has been made, the administrative organ that first did the tortuous act shall be the organ liable for compensation; and if a person is adjudged not guilty in a retrial, the people's court passing the originally effective sentence shall be the organ liable for compensation. The Law also contains concrete provisions on the forms of compensation and standard for the calculation of compensation.

The Chinese State Compensation Law, with its complete and comprehensive content, is among the best of the similar laws adopted by major countries in the world, and marks a historical progress in the legal protection of personal rights in China.

6. Protection of Personal Rights by Procedural Law

Recently the Eighth National People's Congress adopted at its fourth session major amendments to the 1979 Criminal Procedure Law, which strengthened the judicial protection of citizens' personal rights. These revisions mainly include: (1) recognizing the principle of "presumption of innocence" by providing that no person shall be found guilty without being judged so by a people's court in accordance with law and correspondingly referring all persons suspected of committing a crime as "criminal suspects" before they are brought to the court for trial; and providing that the time for interrogation through summons or forced appearance shall not exceed 12 hours and that a criminal suspect shall not be detained under the disguise of successive summons or forced appearance. (2) Highlighting the role of the lawyer in safeguarding the personal rights and other rights of the defendant. The Law allows the lawyer to intervene in criminal proceedings at an earlier time by providing that after the criminal suspect is interrogated by an investigation organ for the first time or from the day on which compulsory measures are adopted against him, he may appoint a lawyer to provide him with legal advice and to file petitions and complaints on his behalf, and further providing that a criminal suspect in a case of public prosecution shall have the right to entrust persons as his defenders from the date on which the case is transferred for examination before prosecution; a defendant in a case of private prosecution shall have the right to entrust persons as his defenders at any time; and if the criminal suspect is arrested, the appointed lawyer may apply on his behalf for obtaining a guarantor pending trial. Meanwhile the Law also provides for the corresponding responsibilities of judicial organs: a people's procuratorate shall, within three days from the date of receiving the file record of a case transferred for examination before prosecution, inform the criminal suspect that he has the right to entrust persons as his defenders. A people's court shall, within three days from the date of accepting a case of private prosecution, inform the defendant that he has the right to entrust persons as his defenders. (3) If the evidence is insufficient and thus the defendant cannot be found guilty, he shall be pronounced innocent accordingly on account of the fact that the evidence is insufficient and the accusation unfounded. (4) Strengthening the protection of victims of crimes by making them the parties to the criminal proceedings and giving them the right to apply for the withdrawal of a judge or other judicial officer, to entrust agents *ad litem*to participate in the proceedings, or to request the people's procuratorate to present a protest if he refuses to accept a judgment of first instance made by a people's court. (5) Reforming the relevant systems. By providing for a longer time limit for filing an request for the arrest of persons suspected of committing crimes from place to place, repeatedly, or in a gang, the revised Law incorporates the reasonable elements of the system of " detention for interrogation" into the criminal procedure law, thereby abolishing this coercive administrative measure that had been implemented for several decades. (6) Improving litigation efficiency and reducing the litigation burden of parties by providing that the people's court may apply summary procedure to cases of public prosecution where the defendants may be lawfully sentenced to fixed-term imprisonment of not more than three years, criminal detention, public surveillance or punished with fines exclusively, where the facts are clear and the evidence is sufficient, and for which the people's procuratorate suggests or agrees to the application of summary procedure; cases to be handled only upon complaint; and cases prosecuted by the victims, for which there is evidence to prove that they are minor criminal cases. (7) Further improving the judicial system by abolishing the system of exemption from prosecution and providing that, with respect to a case that is minor and the offender need not be given criminal punishment or need be exempted from it according to the Criminal Law, the people's procuratorate may decide not to initiate a prosecution. (8) Reforming the mode of court trial by transforming it from an inquisitional mode to an adversarial mode, giving full play to the role of the public prosecutor and the defender in court trial, as well as the role of the collegial panel, so as to change the past practice of " making the judgment before trial" and treating court trial a mere formality.

The above-mentioned reforms represent a major progress in the protection of personal rights in China.

IV. Challenges Faced by China in the Construction of the System of Legal Protection of Personal Rights

During the past decades, China has made remarkable progresses in the construction of the system of legal protection of personal rights: we have successfully resolved many historical problems resulting from the violation of personal rights of cadres and ordinary citizens; through the summarization of historical experience, we have abandoned forever both in terms of ideology and in terms of institution the past abnormal practices of setting up working groups on specific cases outside the existing state organs and legal procedures and interrogating people in incommunicado. The new laws and systems of protection of personal rights attach importance to the maintenance of social stability while at the same time are adapted to the need of socialist market economy. The following consensus has been reached in Chinese law circle: although China has made rapid progresses in the laws and institutions relating to the protection of personal rights, further improvement of these laws and institutions still urgently need to be made; in the future, attention should be paid to making legislation more scientific and more compatible with international standard, to strengthening the enforcement of law, and to ensure that there are laws to go by, the laws are observed and strictly enforced, and lawbreakers are prosecuted.

1. Violation of Personal Rights Is Still a Relatively Widespread Phenomenon in China

Because of the influence of the traditional patriarchal ideas, there is an apparent lack of respect for the personal rights of the juniors by seniors in some families and in some clans in certain areas. Parents often verbally and physically abuse their children, and force them into arranged, even mercenary marriage. The direct consequences of these kinds of violation of personal rights are normally not very serious: under most circumstances, they ended with the submission of the children and the juniors to their parents or seniors in the family. However, such violations often leave deep wounds on their souls that are difficult to heal. To children, family is the first classroom and parents and elders are their first teachers. The consequences of above-mentioned violations of personal rights are often manifested in the relationship between generations within the family as well as in the interpersonal relationship in society.

In recent years, the rates of various crimes, including various crime of serious violation of citizens' personal rights, such as murder, intentional injury, kidnapping, abducting and trafficking in women and children, rape, gang rape, molestation of women, defamation, violation of the home of another person, insult, libel, false charge, and frame-up, are on the rise. To deal with this situation, the state adopted the policy of comprehensive treatment, but the main approach is to increase the severity of criminal punishment, which although produced some results, has ultimately failed to achieve the objective of curbing the rising crime rate. In the relationship between government officials and ordinary citizens, some cadres, especially those at the grassroots level in rural areas, influenced by the traditional idea of social hierarchy and the ideology of the exploiting class, have abandoned the principle of serving the people and the modest and prudent work style and place themselves high above and ride roughshod over the people. Some of them even verbally and physically abuse other people on a regular basis. And there have been incidents of village cadres killing villagers who file complaints against them. Some public security and judicial officials abuse the power in their hand not only to extort by torture a confession from law breakers or criminal suspects, but also to get even with another person for a private grudge, sometimes even resulting in the death of their victims.

According to statistics published in the *Law Yearbook of China*, between 1987 and 1993, the numbers of cases of violation of citizens' personal rights and democratic rights accepted by people's courts at various levels in Mainland China were: 89, 156 in 1987; 83, 771 in 1988; 100, 265 in 1989; 121, 096 in 1990; 128, 804 in 1991; 137, 582 in 1992; and 135, 517 in 1993. Besides, during this period of time, the numbers of same kind of cases in which the people's Procuratorates at various levels had made a decision of exemption of prosecution were: 4, 006 in 1987; 4, 737 in 1988; 4, 780 in 1989; 6, 203 in 1990; 6, 484 in 1991; 7, 164 in 1992; and 6, 591 in 1993. ①The majority of these cases involved violations of personal rights.

---

① See "Statistics on the Cases Accepted and Concluded by the People's Courts at Various Levels in China" and "Statistics on the Cases in Which the Decision on the Exemption from Prosecution Is Made by the Procuratorate", in *Law Yearbook of China*, Beijing: Law Yearbook of China Press, 1988—1994.

Another prominent problem in the legal protection of personal rights in China is the lack of labor protection in some enterprises, especially in foreign-funded enterprises and individually-owned enterprises. In the past, under the planned economic system, there had been a relatively complete system of labor protection in sate-owned and collective enterprises. Later, as the efficiency-pursuit mechanism was initiated by market-oriented reform, some enterprises, in the pursuit of profit, have raised labor quota, extended working hours, increased labor intensity, while at the same time reduced labor protection, resulting in the increase in the number of industrial accidents and in the number of industrial injuries and deaths. This problem is especially serious in foreign-funded enterprises and individually-owned enterprises, as evidenced by many serious fire accidents in factories that have resulted in the death of dozens of workers. Moreover, violation of the personal rights of workers is also very common in the daily administration of these enterprises. For example, workers in these enterprises are often forced to work more than ten hours a day and not allowed to take a rest even during the weekends and holidays and any disobedience is met with deduction of wages or even physical abuse.

The continuous rise in the crimes against personal rights fully demonstrates the arduous and long-term nature of the fight against such crimes.

2. The Need for Further Improvement of the System of Legal Protection of Personal Rights

In the field of constitutional law, the 1982 Constitution contains comprehensive provisions on the fundamental rights of Chinese citizens. The Chinese government issued the white paper Human Rights in China in 1991, which fully affirms the concept of human rights and gives a comprehensive introduction to the past, the present and the future of human rights conditions in China. Some scholars suggest that, in the future amendment of the Constitution, the concept of human rights should be formally used in the Preamble and the chapter on General Principles. Moreover, the right to life and the right to privacy should also be clearly provided for in the Constitution. In the field of criminal law, the Criminal Law and the Criminal Procedure Law adopted at the early years of reform and opening up had played a huge role in safeguarding the socialist construction in China during the past ten years and more. However, with the passage of time, some of the contents of these two laws had become outdated and urgently need to be revised. In fact, since the adoption of the Decisions Regarding the Severe Punishment of Criminals Who Seriously Sabotage the Economy in March 1982 and the Decision Regarding the Severe Punishment of Criminals Who Seriously Endanger Public Security in September 1983, the Standing Committee of the National People's Congress had adopted more than ten supplementary provisions to the Criminal Law, which had made drastic changes to the original provisions of the Criminal Law, including increasing the severity of criminal punishments and imposing the death penalty on many crimes. ①

---

① Among these separate laws and regulations, the following have provided for the application of the death penalty:

1. Interim Regulations on Punishment of Servicemen Who Commit Crimes Contrary to Their Duties;
2. Decision on the Severe Punishment of Criminals Who Seriously Endanger Public Security;
3. Decisions on the Severe Punishment of Criminals Who Seriously Sabotage the Economy;
4. Supplementary Provisions on the Punishment of the Crimes of Smuggling;
5. Supplementary Provisions on the Punishment of the Crimes of Embezzlement and Bribery
6. Supplementary Provisions on the Crime of Divulging State Secret
7. Supplementary Provisions on Cracking Down on the Crime of Killing Rare and Endangered Wildlife That Are Selectively Under the State's Protection;
8. Decision on Prohibiting Drugs;
9. Decision on Punishing Criminal Elements Committing Smuggling, Producing, Selling, or Disseminating Obscene Materials;
10. Decision on Strictly Prohibiting Prostitution and Whorehouse Visiting;
11. Decision on Punishing Criminal Elements Committing Abduction and Selling or Kidnapping of Women or Children;
12. Supplementary Provisions on Cracking Down on the Crime of Robbing Ancient Cultural Ruins or Ancient Tombs;
13. Supplementary Provisions on Cracking Down on the Crime of Evading Taxes or Refusing to Pay Taxes;
14. Decision on Punishing Criminal Elements Hijacking Aviation Vehicles;
15. Decision on Cracking Down on the Crime of Producing or Selling Counterfeit or Inferior Commodities;
16. Supplementary Provisions on Severely Cracking down on the Crime of Organizing People to Illegally Cross National Borders (Frontiers) or of Illegally Shipping People across National Borders (Frontiers).

Originally, there had been seven death penalty clauses in the 1979 Criminal Law, providing for 28 capital crimes. This number was already high compared to the criminal laws in other main countries in the world. By the time the Standing Committee of the National People's Congress promulgated the Supplementary Provisions on Severely Cracking Down on the Crime of Organizing People to Illegally Cross National Borders (Frontiers) or of Illegally Shipping People Across National Borders (Frontiers) in March 1994, there were already 40 death penalty clauses in the criminal law, providing for 68 capital crimes, which made China one of the countries with the largest number of capital crimes in the world. The purpose of increasing the severity of criminal punishment and the number of capital crimes is to curb crimes. However, people have different opinions on whether these measures can achieve this objective. In the past more than ten years, the numbers of both economic crimes and of crimes of endangering public security have been on the rise. The increase in the number of major and serious cases of economic crimes and vicious crimes of endangering public security, such as murder, intentional injury and rape, have shown that the most effective way of curbing crimes is not to increase the severity of punishment, but to ensure that anyone who has committed crimes are punished according to law. Some scholars hold that in the revision of the criminal law, the severity of criminal punishment should be reduced, rather than increased. Moreover, the principle of "legally prescribed punishment for a specific crime" should be provided for in the General Provisions of the Criminal Law, so as more accurately and effectively punish crimes.

In the field of public security and judicial administration, which cover a wide range of issues, but mainly minor crimes or violations of law, attention should be paid to the problems relating to the system of "detention for interrogation" and the system of "rehabilitation through labor". The legal bases of the system of "detention for interrogation" are the Notice to Unify the Measures of Compulsory Labor and Detention for Interrogation into the System of Rehabilitation through Labor, promulgated by the State Council in February 1980 and the Notice on Strictly Controlling the Use of Detention for Interrogation, adopted by the Ministry of Public Security in 1985. From their titles we can see that these two notices have only confirmed an existing system, rather than establishing a new system. In fact, the system of "detention for interrogation" originates from the measures adopted in the 1950s and 1960s and aimed at repatriating rural residents who blindly migrated into cities. Later the target of this measure were defined as: "persons who have been found to have committed minor crimes or violations of law and refuse to give their real names and address and are of dubious background or those who have been found to have committed minor crimes or violations of law and are suspected of committing crimes from place to place, repeatedly, or in a gang and therefore need to be detained for further interrogation"① and "persons who are suspected of committing crimes from place to place, or are found to have committed a crime but refuse to give their real name and address and are of dubious background"②.

In view of the above-mentioned two notices and the situation of their implementation, attention should be paid to the following two issues with respect to the system of "detention for interrogation": firstly, as a system, detention for interrogation does not has sufficient legal basis and there is no clear procedure for its control and supervision; and secondly, in practice there is a tendency of expanding the scope and exceeding the time limit of detention for interrogation. In some places, the system has become the tool for extending the time period of detention. There are different opinions in Chinese law circle on the system of detention for interrogation: one pinion is that, in view of the poor conditions of transportation and communication in China and the short time limit provided for by the laws and regulations on detention, it is necessary to retain this system so as to ensure the punishment of crimes; another opinion is that this system should be abolished because it can easily lead to the violation of personal rights and many problems have already emerged in practice. As the ancient Chinese saying goes: of two evils, choose the less. China should decide whether or not to abolish this system on the basis of careful consideration of its advantages and disadvantages.

The system of "rehabilitation through labor" is an administrative measure that imposes compulsory education through labor on persons who repeatedly commit acts of violation laws and regulations that are not serious

---

① See the *Notice to Unify the Measures of Compulsory Labor and Detention for Interrogation into the System of Rehabilitation through Labor*, promulgated by the State Council in February 1980.

② See the *Notice on Strictly Controlling the Use of Detention for Interrogation*, adopted by the Ministry of Public Security in 1985.

enough to constitute a crime and who have the ability to work. [①]Decisions on the imposition of the rehabilitation through labor are approved by the management committees of rehabilitation through labor of provinces, autonomous regions, municipalities directly under the Central Government, and large and medium-sized cities, which are composed of the leaders of civil administration, public security, and labor administration departments. [②]The time limit of rehabilitation through labor is one to three years, and can be extended for one more year if necessary. During the term of rehabilitation through labor, persons under rehabilitation through labor are organized to study political and cultural knowledge and technologies, trained to develop a good habit of work, and paid wages in light of the type of work they participate in, their skill of work, and the quantity and quality of their work, and allowed to have days off during the holidays and weekends and, after the completion of their term of rehabilitation through labor, they are able to seek employment without discrimination. Since its establishment in the 1950s, the system of "rehabilitation through labor" has been effective in preventing crimes and won the support of the broad masses of the people. Now the main problems with this system are that the overall role of the management committees of rehabilitation through labor need to be further improved and the time limit of the rehabilitation through labor needs to be shortened.

When improving the legal protection of personal rights, we should also give careful consideration to the issue of the equality in the protection of personal rights, namely, how to safeguard the personal rights of both the seniors and of the juniors, of both government officials and ordinary citizens, and of both law-abiding citizens and persons who have committed minor crimes and violations of law. According to the principle of equality before the law, criminals, even those who have committed capital crimes, are entitled to certain rights, which need to be safeguarded. In dealing with this issue, we are faced with not only individual cases of individual persons, but also the society as a whole, certain social relationships, and certain general principles. We have already paid heavy prices in the past

① See *the Trial Measures for Rehabilitation through Labor*, promulgated by the State Council in January 1992.

② See *the Supplementary Provisions of the State Council for Rehabilitation through Labor*, approved by the Standing Committee of the National People's Congress in November 1979.

for not paying enough attention to this issue, and will continue to pay heavy prices in the future if we continue to ignore this issue. The key to dealing with this issue is, first of all, to have a good system of law and then to strictly observe and implement the laws. Here, a good system of law means a scientific system of law. In the protection of personal rights, attention must be paid to the definition of concrete rights, to the measures of protection, as well as to the punishment of perpetrators. In this respect, the scholars in ancient China had put forward the principle of "proportionality between punishment and crime" more than 2, 000 years ago. The current Chinese system of laws on the protection of personal rights is based on the summarization of historical experience and is a good system on the whole. However, careful consideration still needs to be made on how to make ensure that punishment is proportional to crime, namely to ensure that it is neither too lenient nor too severe. Here it should be stressed that the most important thing to do after the adoption of good laws is to development a system that ensure the strict implementation of the law, which has been proved by historical experience to be even harder than the adoption of the laws.

3. Higher Demands Raised by the Development of Socialist Market Economy on the Protection of Personal Rights

The socialist market economy in China is a socialist economy that takes the public economy as its main body and consists of diverse sectors of economy, including state-owned, collective, individual as well as foreign-invested sectors of economy. It emphasizes efficiency, competition, fairness and common prosperity and, in a certain sense, is also an economy under the rule of law. It affirms in accordance with law the status of market entities, protects different types of ownerships, upholds contractual freedom and fair competition, and continuously develops and improves various social security systems. The socialist market economy in China is realized through the reform of the planned economy: firstly, reform was carried out in the rural areas by dissolving the people's communes and the production brigades and production teams under them and establishing the household contract responsibility system, so as to mobilize farmers' enthusiasm for production and promote the development of agriculture; secondly, reform was carried out in the urban areas through the delegation of power to enterprises and within enterprises, and by organizing business operation in the forms of contracts and stock companies. Meanwhile, foreign-invested enterprises have been introduced in many cities and areas, and township enterprise and individual enterprises become active parts of the socialist market economy. The socialist market economy raised new demands for the safeguarding of rights, including the safeguarding of the rights of market entities.

The development of the socialist market economy is accompanied by the individualization of interests and the rise in people's level of scientific and cultural knowledge, which have further awakened people's self-consciousness and their consciousness of human dignity, and enabled them to cherish more and pay more attention to the protection their own life and health. The free competition and fair dealing of the socialist market economy will enable more enterprises to select employees according to their own needs and employees to more freely choose their own profession. This two-way selection mechanism and the accompanying flow of labor force enable people to enjoy more personal freedoms while at the same time have to a certain extent caused some people to lose the safety they used to enjoy. As a result, personal safety becomes an increasingly prominent problem. To sum up, under the new situation, people are demanding more personal freedom as well as better protection of personal rights.

Currently one of the major challenges faced by China is to get a clear understanding the reality of personal rights in the country and the trend of its development, conscientiously keep up with the demands of objective situation, and establish corresponding systems. The realization of rights is conditioned by economic and cultural development. It is impossible for rights to be put forward and enjoyed before the necessary conditions are created. Nor can the development of rights lag behind the economic and cultural development for a long period of time without causing social turmoil.

The development of the system of legal protection of personal rights is a very long process. Although we still have a long way to go and an arduous task to fulfill in this respect, we are confident in bright prospect of the development of personal rights in China because we have already accumulated rich experiences, both positive and negative, and laid a sound foundation in this field.

Legal Protection of Religious Freedom and National Equality[①]

Religious freedom and national equality are the two important components of human rights. Carrying out research on and promoting the improvement of legal protection of religious freedom and national equality is of great significance to the full enjoyment of human rights.

I

Religion is a form of social culture which takes belief as its core. By nature, it belongs to ideology. A nationality (ethnic group) is a stable community of people formed on the basis of common language, common territory, common economic life, and common psychological make-up. Although religion and nationality belong to two different categories, they are both the products of social development at a certain historical stage and are closely related to each other. In the formation and development of a nationality, common religious belief strengthens the various constitutive elements of the nationality and enhances national characteristics, whereas the economic and cultural development of the nationality and the relative stability of the territory of the nationality provide support and create conditions for the development and dissemination of a religion.

Religion and nationality have always been very complicated issues. There are many different religions in the world and there are often many different sects within a religion. Similarly, there are many different ethnic groups in

---

① * This paper was originally submitted to the "Sino-U. S. Seminar on Human Rights and Administration of Justice", held in Washington D. C. in September 1998, and latter published in *Journal of Beijing College of Politics and Law* (2000) 3.

Articles 2 – 7 of the International Convention the Elimination of All Forms of Racial Discrimination, please see the appendix in thio article.

the world, and members of an ethnic group are often scattered in many different parts of a country or of the world. There are many examples of a same religion being believed by members of several, even over a dozen, ethnic groups as well as examples of members of the same ethnic group believing in several, even over a dozen, religions. It is almost impossible to find a country in the world in which there is only one ethnic group or only one religion or religious sect. In addition, the believers of the same religion can belong to different classes and social strata in society and members of the same ethnic may have different economic conditions, interests and demands, thus resulting in ceaseless and complicated contradictions between different religions, between different sects of the same religion, between different ethnic groups, between different classes and strata of the same ethnic group, and between different states. These contradictions are the root causes of many internal disturbances, international disputes and wars, whether in the past or in the present days.

In light of historical experiences and lessons, especially the catastrophes brought about by the atrocities committed by German Nazis and Japanese militarists in Europe, Africa and Asia during the World War II, and in order to safeguard human rights, the international community has adopted a series of international and regional human rights instruments, including the 1945 UN Charter, the 1948 Universal Declaration of Human Rights (UDHR), and the 1966 International Covenant on Economic, Social and Cultural Rights (ICESCR) and International Covenant on Civil and Political Rights (ICCPR), which all fully and clearly recognize religious freedom and national equality. The UDHR provides in Article 1 that: "All human beings are born free and equal in dignity and rights. They are endowed with reason and conscience and should act towards one another in a spirit of brotherhood." and in Article 2 that: "Everyone is entitled to all the rights and freedoms set forth in this Declaration, without distinction of any kind, such as race, colour, sex, language, religion, political or other opinion, national or social origin, property, birth or other status." Here, "everyone" includes believers of different religions as well as people who do not believe in any religion and people of different colors and races as well as people belonging to the same color or race but different ethnic groups. If it can be said that the above provisions of the UDHR are only declarations of general principles, the relevant provisions of the ICESCR and ICCPR are legally binding on state parties to them. Article 2 Paragraph 2 of the ICESCR provides that: "The States Parties to the present Covenant undertake to guarantee that the rights enunciated in the present Covenant will be exercised without discrimination of any kind as to race, colour, sex, language, religion, political or other opinion, national or social origin, property, birth or other status." Article 2 Paragraph 1 of the ICCPR contains a similar provision with only slightly different wording.

In order to realize religious freedom and national equality, the UN General Assembly adopted the Declaration on the Elimination of All Forms of Religious Intolerance and of Discrimination Based on Religion or Belief in 1981, the Declaration on the Granting of Independence to Colonial Countries and Peoples in 1966, the International Convention on the Elimination of All Forms of Racial Discrimination in 1968, the Convention on the Prevention and Punishment of the Crime of Genocide in 1985, and the International Convention against Apartheid in Sports in 1985.

The above declarations and conventions contain comprehensive provisions on safeguarding religious freedom and national equality, which embody the conscience of mankind, reflect historical progresses of human civilization, and demonstrate the important position of religious freedom and national equality in the human rights system: firstly, believers of one particular religion or religious sect in a country are often a minority compared to the rest of the population in the country; so are most ethnic groups in a country, or in the world. A minority, if not in a dominant position in society, is often vulnerable and needs special protection. Secondly, a declaration provides for general moral principles whereas a convention contains detailed provisions on the rights and obligations established according to general principles and aims to establish an order beneficial to all mankind. Those who violate minority rights also violate general principles of human rights, social relations, as well as social order. "In places where minority rights are not recognized, universally recognized human rights are also violated"① and it is impossible to maintain national and international peace and stability. Thirdly, the purpose of providing for special rights for minorities is to enable them to use their own language, to manage their own schools, to enjoy the

① UN Fact Sheet No. 18: Rights of Minorities, Chinese Edition, P. 1.

benefits of various undertakings management by themselves, and to participate in the administration of political, economic, cultural and other affairs in their own country on an equal basis with the majority people in the country. Of course, special rights are not what are usually meant by "privileges" and special attention should be paid in research and practice to the limits of such rights, so as to avoid conflicts resulting from reversed inequality.

The realization of religious freedom, national equality and minority rights, like the realization of all other human rights, ultimately depends on domestic institutions and mechanisms. Therefore, all international conventions attach great importance to the obligations of state parties. For example, the International Convention on the Elimination of All Forms of Racial Discrimination provides for detailed obligations of state parties to the Convention in articles, 2, 3, 4, 5, 6, and 7. With respect to religious freedom, Article 4 of the Declaration on the Elimination of All Forms of Intolerance and of Discrimination Based on Religion or Belief provides that: "All States shall take effective measures to prevent and eliminate discrimination on the grounds of religion or belief in the recognition, exercise and enjoyment of human rights and fundamental freedoms in all fields of civil, economic, political, social and cultural life." In order to supervise the implementation of the International Convention on the Elimination of All Forms of Racial Discrimination, the UN established, in addition to the Commission on Human Rights, the Special Committee against Apartheid, the Sub-committee on Prevention of Discrimination and Protection of Minorities and other subsidiary bodies. These international human rights bodies, apart from periodically reviewing the implementation of relevant conventions by state parties, also accept complaints from and provide remedies to the victims of violation of some human rights who have exhausted all domestic remedies.

II

China is a country with a long history, a vast territory, and a huge population. There are 56 nationalities in China. Apart from the Han nationality, which is the majority in the country, all the remaining 55 are minority nationalities, which have a total population of over 100 million. In the process of long historical evolution and development, various nationalities in China have been continuously getting into contact, mingling, and integrating with each other and ultimately developed into a diversified unity of the Chinese nation. [1]Diversified unity means a unified Chinese nation formed through economic, political and cultural integration of various ethnic groups in China, each of them having its own unique cultural and historical characteristics: "The Chinese nation is basically a historical and cultural concept... As a self-conscious ethnic entity, it emerged in the antagonism between China and western powers in the past century (more specifically, the term 'Chinese nation' refers to the 1.2 billion people now living within the Chinese territory who share the same sense of national identity.)"[2]

Long period of national integration and many years of joint struggle for survival have enabled various nationalities in China to recognize their common interests and to form an unprecedentedly intimate relationship between them. In this sense, we should thank the western and eastern big powers, who since the Opium War in 1840 had used strong gunboats and powerful cannons to turn China into a semi-colonial society, for the transformation of the Chinese nation from a national entity "in itself" into a self-conscious nation entity.

China is both a multi-national country and a multi-religious country. According to their historical and contemporary influences, religions in China can be divided into traditional patriarchal religions, witchcraft religions, Taoism, Buddhism, Islam, and Christianity. Traditional patriarchal religions are based on the religions of primitive tribal clans and have gradually improved and strengthened themselves in the long process of historical evolution. They take the worship of deities and ancestors as their cores, the worship of nature—such as soil, grain, mountains and rivers—as their wings, and the worship of various ghosts and spirits as their supplements, and have a relatively stable system of ceremonies for worshiping the heaven and the earth, ancestral temple system and other systems of worshiping ceremonies. Before the first century, traditional patriarchal religions in China had been the largest religion in the world. Witchcraft religions are a primitive form of religion which has a strong clan color. Although the witchcraft religions practiced by various

① Fei Xiaotong, *The Multiplex and Integrative Structure of the Chinese Nation*, the Central College of Nationalities Press, 1989, p. 1.

② Zhang Zuosheng (ed.), *Religion and Nation*, China Social Sciences Press, 1997, p. 17.

clans and tribes do not have a common scripture, deity or organization, they do share a basic characteristic, namely they all take the worship of nature, ancestors, and spirits as their main content. Daoism is a religion that takes the "Dao" (the Way) as the supreme faith. It originated in ancient witchcraft and took form in the Han Dynasty through the efforts by some scholars and sorcerers on the basis of ancient ideas about gods, ghosts, and supernatural beings, the doctrine of yin-yang and five elements, some religious thoughts of Huangdi and Laozi, and practices for achieving longevity or immortality. Daoism is established by the Han people, but it also has profound influence on other nationalities, especially those in southern China. Apart from the above-mentioned religions, Buddhism was introduced into China in the Han Dynasty and Islam in the Tang Dynasty. Christianity was introduced into China three times, in the Tang, Yuan and Ming dynasties, but each time failed to establish itself in the country "because of its lack of the effort to integrate itself into the Chinese culture."① It succeeded in taking root in the country only after the Opium War. Apart from believers of patriarchal traditional religions and witchcraft religions, there are over 100 million believers of various religions in China.

Although there are many religions in China, these religions, having coexisted within the diversified unity of the Chinese nation and being influenced by the traditional Chinese culture for a long period of time, share many common historical characteristics: firstly, they all contain the patriarchal ideology of "worshiping the heaven and following the examples of ancestors"; secondly, throughout the Chinese history, the imperial power had always been in a dominant position in society and religions had always been dependent on politics; thirdly, because of the dominance of the imperial power in society and the dependence of religion on politics, all religions had tried to connect themselves with the orthodox Confucian ideology and assimilated the Confucian ideas of "the golden mean" and "benevolence" which, combined with the religious doctrines of tolerance and fraternity, enabled them to coexist with each other in peace and harmony and to avoid the cruel religious wars that had occurred frequently in western history; fourthly, throughout the history the Chinese rulers had attached great importance to "using religion to instruct and

---

① Zhang Zuosheng (ed.), *Religion and Nation*, China Social Sciences Press, 1997, pp. 30 and 31.

enlighten the people". As a result, religions in China have a strong humanistic color, and emphasize "this life", ethics, and "practicing what you preach". ①Religion also has a huge influence on the formation and development of a nation. The multi-religious pattern in China not only has strengthened the constitutive elements of the Chinese nation with its belief system, cultural functions and social lifestyle, but also is conducive to the communication and connection between various nationalities. It is for this reason that the multi-religious pattern has become a characteristic and advantage of the diversified unity of the Chinese nation and a vital link that has kept the Chinese nation together at critical moments of national peril.

All successful strategies of revolution, reform and construction in history have been made after careful consideration of specific historical and cultural backgrounds. Religion and nationality are important content of such specific cultural backgrounds. Since China was reduced to a semi-colonial and semi-feudal society after the Opium War in 1840, the most important task of Chinese revolution had been national independence and liberation of the people. Faced with oppression by powerful imperialism, feudalism and bureaucratic capitalism, the revolutionary leaders in China had adopted the external policy of "uniting all nations in the world that treat China with equality"② and the internal policy of establishing a most extensive united front of various nationalities, classes, and religious groups in the country. The united front, the leadership of the CPC and armed struggle are regarded as "the three magic weapons" with which the CPC had won the victory of the democratic revolution in China. The unity of various nationalities had an important position in the united front and correct religious policies played an important role in the unity of nationalities. The Chinese communists are atheists who do not believe in any religion. However, they recognize that religion is a long-standing and universal phenomenon of human society. "Religion will continue to exist as long as the social conditions on which it depends for its existence are not

---

① See Mou Zhongjian, *Chinese Religions and Chinese Culture*, Beijing: China Social Sciences Press, 2005, p. 27; Feng Jinyuan, "Religious Ethics and the Construction of Socialist Spiritual Civilization" in (1997) 1 *Studies in World Religions*.

② Sun Yat-sen, "Last Will and Testament on Sate Affairs", in Sun Yat-sen, *Complete Works of Sun Yat-sen*, vol. 11, Beijing: Zhonghua Book Company, 1986. p. 639.

totally eliminated. "[1] "Respecting and tolerating the religious beliefs of various nationalities is conducive to increasing the trust and communication and reducing confrontation and conflicts between various nationalities and to upholding the political unity of the country. "[2] Therefore, to ensure the success of the socialist revolution, reform and construction in China, it is necessary to adopt correct policies on religion and nationalities as well as laws that safeguard religious freedom and national equality.

With regard to religion, as early as before the nationwide victory of revolution, Mao Zedong declared to the world that: "All religions are permitted in China's Liberated Areas, in accordance with the principle of freedom of religious belief. All believers in Protestantism, Catholicism, Islamism, Buddhism and other faiths enjoy the protection of the people's government so long as they are abiding by its laws. Everyone is free to believe or not to believe; neither compulsion nor discrimination is permitted. "[3] On the eve of the establishment of the People's Republic of China, the Chinese People's Political Consultative Conference adopted at its first session the Common Program of the Chinese People's Political Consultative Conference, which served as temporary constitution at that time. Article 5 of the Common Program provided that "citizens of the People's Republic of China shall have the freedom of religion" . A similar provision is contained in the 1954, 1978, and 1982 constitutions. Article 36 of the 1982 Constitution provides that: "Citizens of the People's Republic of China enjoy freedom of religious belief. No state organ, public organization or individual may compel citizens to believe in, or not to believe in, any religion; nor may they discriminate against citizens who believe in, or do not believe in, any religion. " The same article also provides that: "The state protects normal religious activities. No one may make use of religion to engage in activities that disrupt public order, impair the health of citizens or interfere with the educational system of the state. Religious bodies and religious affairs are not subject to any foreign domination. " In accordance with Article 36 of the Constitution, more detailed measures for the protection of religious freedom have been

---

① Zhou Enlai, *Selected Works of Zhou Enlai*vol. II, People's Publishing House, 1997, p. 308.

② Ibid. , p. 490.

③ Mao Zedong, *Selected Works of Mao Zedong*, vol. 3, People's Publishing House, 1991, 1093.

provided for in the Law on Regional National Autonomy, the Military Service Law, the Law on Compulsory Education, the Electoral Law for the National People's Congress and Local People's Congresses, and the Organic Law of Villagers' Committees. Violation of citizens' religious freedom is a crime to be severely punished under the Chinese Criminal Law.

With respect to the rights of minority nationalities, the Common Program of the Chinese People's Political Consultative Conference, adopted in September 1949, provides that: "All nationalities in China are equal." Article 12 of the 1982 Constitution provides that: "All nationalities in the People's Republic of China are equal. The state protects the lawful rights and interests of the minority nationalities and upholds and develops a relationship of equality, unity and mutual assistance among all of China's nationalities. Discrimination against and oppression of any nationality are prohibited; any act which undermines the unity of the nationalities or instigates division is prohibited." In accordance with the Common Program and the Constitution, China has adopted a series of special laws and regulations on the protection of minority rights, including the 1952 Outline for Implementing Regional National Autonomy, the 1952 Decision on Ensuring the Enjoyment of the Right to National Equality by Members of Minority Nationalities Living in Scattered Groups, and the 1984 Law on Regional National Autonomy. The Constitution and laws also contain special provisions on the political and economic, cultural and educational development, and the implementation of the system of regional autonomy in minority areas in light of the actual situation of inequality in development between minority nationalities and the majority Han nationalities. With respect political participation, Article 59 of the Constitution provides that: "All the minority ethnic groups are entitled to appropriate representation in the National People's Congress"; Article 17 of the Election Law provides that "Nationalities with exceptionally small populations shall each have at least one deputy to the National People's Congress"; and Article 65 of the Constitution provides that: "There should be an appropriate number of representatives of ethnic minorities in the Standing Committee of the National People's Congress". With respect to economic development, the Constitution provides in Article 4 that "The state assists areas inhabited by minority nationalities in accelerating their economic and cultural development in light of the characteristics and needs of the various minority nationalities", in Article 118 that: "In exploiting natural resources and building enterprises in national autonomous areas, the state shall give due consideration to the interests of those areas", and in Article 122 that: "The state provides financial, material and technical assistance to the minority nationalities to accelerate their economic and cultural development." With respect to culture and education, Article 4 of the Constitution provides that: "All nationalities have the freedom to use and develop their own spoken and written languages and to preserve or reform their own folkways and customs"; the Law on Compulsory Education provides in Article 12 that: "The state shall assist areas inhabited by minority nationalities to implement compulsory education by providing them with teachers and funds" and in Article 6 that: "Schools in which the majority of students are of minority nationalities may use the spoken and written languages of those nationalities in instruction." With respect to regional national autonomy, the Constitution provides in Article 4 that: "Regional autonomy is practiced in areas where people of minority nationalities live in concentrated communities; in these areas, organs of self-government are established to exercise the power of autonomy", in Article 112 that: "The organs of self-government of national autonomous areas are the people's congresses and people's governments of autonomous regions, autonomous prefectures and autonomous counties", and in Article 114 that: "The chairman of an autonomous region, the prefect of an autonomous prefecture or the head of an autonomous county shall be a citizen of the nationality exercising regional autonomy in the area concerned."

The system of legal protection of religious freedom and national equality in China is comprehensive, its basic content is consistent with the provisions of relevant international human rights instruments, and it is earnestly implemented by the government in practice. Since the founding of the new China, especially since the reform and opening up, religious freedom has been fully respected and protected. Currently the number of believers of Buddhism, Daoism, Islam, and Christianity has exceeded 100 million. According to incomplete statistics, current there are over 85, 000 places of religious activities, more than 30, 000 religious staff members, over 3, 000 religious organizations, and 74 religious institutions established by religions organizations for the training of religious staff in the whole country. A relationship of solidarity, equality and harmony has been developed between believers of different religions and between religious and non-religious people in China. The laws on the protection of the rights of minority nationalities have also been earnestly implemented. In accordance with the Constitution and the Law on Regional National Autonomy, China has now established 158 areas of regional national autonomy, including five autonomous regions, 30 autonomous prefectures, and 123 autonomous counties (or banners), which cover over 64% of the Chinese territory. Among the 55 minority nationalities, apart from the ten which have exceptionally small population, 45 have established their own regional national autonomous areas. 78% of total population of minority nationalities in the country is exercising regional national autonomy. ①

Moreover, in order to safeguard the equal rights of members of minority nationalities living in scattered groups and minority nationalities with exceptionally small population, over 1, 500 nationality townships have been established throughout the country as a supplement to the system of regional national autonomy. To solve the problem of imbalance in economic, cultural, scientific and technological development between the eastern part of the country and the western part of the country where most minority nationalities inhabit, the state has implemented the strategy of developing the western part of the country. With deepening of the reform and opening up, the sustained development of the national economy, and the implementation of the develop-the-west strategy, the various undertakings in minority areas will continue to develop and prosper and people of minority nationalities will be able to enjoy equal rights with the majority Han people in the political as well as economic, social and other fields.

III

Thanks to the efforts made by various international organizations and the governments of various states, including the Chinese government, the legal protection of religious freedom, national equality and other human rights has received wide public attention and achieved positive results, both internationally and in domestically. However, just as mentioned at the beginning of this article, many religious and ethnic problems are complicated problems deeply rooted in history. The complete solution of

① Su Ming (ed.), *Human Rights Construction in China*, Sichuan People's Publishing House, 1994, p. 751.

these problems takes times, not only because they have deep history roots, but also because they are constantly giving rise to new problems. It has been proven that former imperialists are very font of interfering in the religious and ethnic conflicts of other countries, either overtly or covertly, by various excuses and means, thereby further complicating and intensifying these conflicts. The invasion of the former Yugoslavia, the current situation in the Gulf Region, and the half-a-century-long Arab-Israeli conflict have all been shrouded in the shadow of the interests of some big powers. Faced with the cruel reality of daily bloodshed, the people of the world have every reason to call on the representatives of some big powers, who look every inch a gentleman and talk with eloquence about human rights in international conferences, to indulge less in high-sounding tirades and shoulder more responsibilities in the resolution of religious and ethnic problems, or at the very least, not to further exacerbate the already intense religious and ethnic conflicts in other countries by adding fuel to the fire out of the interests of their own countries.

With respect to the religious and ethnic problems in state parties to an international human rights convention that have not been resolved after all domestic remedies have been exhausted, they may be brought to the attention of the international community, which may provide remedies to the victims of human rights violations under the precondition that thorough investigation on and objective analysis of the facts have been carried out with a view to finding out whether the alleged violation of human rights is an isolated incident or a persistent pattern, and whether it is an act of individual government officials or an act of the state. Special attention should be paid not to politicize purely religious or ethnic issues, complicate simple issues, internationalize domestic issues, or multi-lateralize bilateral issues. International organizations should avoid being manipulated by some big powers and applying double standard the in the dealing of religious and ethnic issues in some countries, so as to embody objectiveness and fairness and win public trust.

Since religion belongs to ideology and takes belief as its core, it has both moral and rational aspects and superstitious and irrational aspects. A major challenge faced by religion is how to rationally suppress religious fanaticism. Meanwhile, since ethnic groups must try to distinguish themselves from others by their territorial, linguistic and cultural characteristics while at the same time seek to develop themselves by communicating and interacting and integrating with each other, a major challenge faced by them today is how to open themselves up to the outside world, continuously draw on the strong points of others, and free themselves from isolation and seclusion. In the relationship between religion and nationality, the moral or rational elements of either one of them are conducive to the development of the same elements in the other; and the fanatic and irrational tendency of either one of them can intensify the same tendency in the other; the harmony of either one of them can promote the harmony of the other while the antagonist tendency of either one of them can lead to the same tendency in the other. A religious or ethnic group must continuously reform and develop itself in order to maintain harmonious relationships within itself, with other religious groups, with non-religious groups, and with other ethnic groups. In today's world of rapid scientific and technological development, a religious or ethnic group, by absorbing elements of other religious or ethnic groups or adopting advanced science and technology, will inevitably bring certain changes to itself. How to preserve one's own national culture while drawing on the cultures and advanced science and technology of other nations is a question to be reflected on and treated seriously by all nations in the world, include the Chinese nation.

Religious freedom and national equality have been attached more and more importance by international community and provided for not only by many UN and regional declarations and conventions, but also by the constitution of many countries. As mentioned above, China has adopted the Law on Regional National Autonomy in light of its own national conditions, implemented the system of regional national autonomy in areas where minority nationalities live in concentrated communities, and established a complete system of legal protection of religious freedom and minority rights. However, there is no denying that China, like many other countries in the world, still needs to make further efforts in improving the system of legal protection of religious freedom and national equality and in reducing the gap between legislation and law enforcement and judicial practice in this field. For this reason, it should pay more attention to the training of government officials, especially those of minority nationalities, so as to enhance their understanding of the relevant policies and laws, improve their cultural and professional qualities, and ensure the effective implement of relevant laws. We should always remember that any right must be conditioned by social, economic and cultural development of the society in which it exist. Today human history has entered into a new stage of peaceful development. I am confident that, with continuous social, economic, scientific and technological development and advancement of human civilization, people of the world, by uniting themselves and making further joint efforts, will be able to realize religious freedom and national equality and make greater progress in the safeguarding of human rights.

The appendix

Article 2

1. States Parties condemn racial discrimination and undertake to pursue by all appropriate means and without delay a policy of eliminating racial discrimination in all its forms and promoting understanding among all races, and, to this end: (a) Each State Party undertakes to engage in no act or practice of racial discrimination against persons, groups of persons or institutions and to en sure that all public authorities and public institutions, national and local, shall act in conformity with this obligation; (b) Each State Party undertakes not to sponsor, defend or support racial discrimination by any persons or organizations; (c) Each State Party shall take effective measures to review governmental, national and local policies, and to amend, rescind or nullify any laws and regulations which have the effect of creating or perpetuating racial discrimination wherever it exists; (d) Each State Party shall prohibit and bring to an end, by all appropriate means, including legislation as required by circumstances, racial discrimination by any persons, group or organization; (e) Each State Party undertakes to encourage, where appropriate, integrationist multiracial organizations and movements and other means of eliminating barriers between races, and to discourage anything which tends to strengthen racial division.

2. States Parties shall, when the circumstances so warrant, take, in the social, economic, cultural and other fields, special and concrete measures to ensure the adequate development and protection of certain racial groups or individuals belonging to them, for the purpose of guaranteeing them the full and equal enjoyment of human rights and fundamental freedoms. These measures shall in no case en tail as a con sequence the maintenance of unequal or separate rights for different racial groups after the objectives for which they were taken have been achieved.

Article 3

States Parties particularly condemn racial segregation and apartheid and undertake to prevent, prohibit and eradicate all practices of this nature in territories under their jurisdiction.

Article 4

States Parties condemn all propaganda and all organizations which are based on ideas or theories of superiority of one race or group of persons of one colour or ethnic origin, or which attempt to justify or promote racial hatred and discrimination in any form, and undertake to adopt immediate and positive measures designed to eradicate all incitement to, or acts of, such discrimination and, to this end, with due regard to the principles embodied in the Universal Declaration of Human Rights and the rights expressly set forth in article 5 of this Convention, inter alia: (a) Shall declare an offence punishable by law all dissemination of ideas based on racial superiority or hatred, incitement to racial discrimination, as well as all acts of violence or incitement to such acts against any race or group of persons of another colour or ethnic origin, and also the provision of any assistance to racist activities, including the financing thereof; (b) Shall declare illegal and prohibit organizations, and also organized and all other propaganda activities, which promote and incite racial discrimination, and shall recognize participation in such organizations or activities as an offence punishable by law; (c) Shall not permit public authorities or public institutions, national or local, to promote or incite racial discrimination. States Parties undertake to prohibit and to eliminate racial discrimination in all its forms and to guarantee the right of everyone, without distinction as to race, colour, or national or ethnic origin, to equality before the law, notably in the enjoyment of the following rights: (a) The right to equal treatment before the tribunals and all other organs administering justice; (b) The right to security of person and protection by the State against violence or bodily harm, whether inflicted by government officials or by any individual group or institution; (c) Political rights, in particular the right to participate in elections-to vote and to stand for election-on the basis of universal and equal suffrage, to take part in the Government as well as in the conduct of public affairs at any level and to have equal access to public service; (d) Other civil rights, in particular: (i) The right to freedom of movement and residence within the border of the State; (ii) The right to leave any country, including one's own, and to return to one's country; (iii) The right to nationality; (iv) The right to marriage and choice of spouse; (v) The right to own property alone as well as in association with others;

(vi) The right to inherit; (vii) The right to freedom of thought, conscience and religion; (viii) The right to freedom of opinion and expression; (ix) The right to freedom of peaceful assembly and association; (e) Economic, social and cultural rights, in particular: (i) The rights to work, to free choice of employment, to just and favourable conditions of work, to protection against unemployment, to equal pay for equal work, to just and favourable remuneration; (ii) The right to form and join trade unions; (iii) The right to housing; (iv) The right to public health, medical care, social security and social services; (v) The right to education and training; (vi) The right to equal participation in cultural activities; (f) The right of access to any place or service intended for use by the general public, such as transport hotels, restaurants, cafes, theatres and parks.

Article 6

States Parties shall assure to everyone within their jurisdiction effective protection and remedies, through the competent national tribunals and other State institutions, against any acts of racial discrimination which violate his human rights and fundamental freedoms contrary to this Convention, as well as the right to seek from such tribunals just and adequate reparation or satisfaction for any damage suffered as a result of such discrimination. Article 7

States Parties undertake to adopt immediate and effective measures, particularly in the fields of teaching, education, culture and information, with a view to combating prejudices which lead to racial discrimination and to promoting understanding, tolerance and friendship among nations and racial or ethnical groups, as well as to propagating the purposes and principles of the Charter of the United Nations, the Universal Declaration of Human Rights, the United Nations Declaration on the Elimination of All Forms of Racial Discrimination, and this Convention.

Transparency and Regulation of the Mass Media[1]

"Transparency and regulation of the mass media" is a very broad topic. Even if we concentration our discussion on the transparency of the operation of state organs in light of the requirement of the two international human rights covenants, we will still have a wide variety of issues to cover. The discussion of this topic is of great theoretic and practical significance because it concerns the obligations of the governments, the rights of citizens and the improvement of democratic system.

I

Transparency, when discussed within the context of the two international human rights covenants, refers to the obligation of state organs to disclose through certain channels information that the public are entitle to know in the process of their operation in accordance with the relevant provisions of the Constitution, laws and international conventions. Transparency of the government is an indicator of the level of development of freedom, democracy and human rights in a country.

In autocratic societies in both western and eastern histories, transparency of the government was out of the question. In ancient China, it was believed that: "the rulers should only let people know what they should do, not the reasons why they should them." According to historical records, in about sixth century BC, there had been a heated debate within the ruling class in China as to whether the law should be made known to the public. At that time, there was a minister in the State of Zhen named Zi Chan (? -522 BC). He was a reformist who attached great importance to the role played by law. In 536 BC, he promulgated

---

① Originally published in *Human Rights*, 2 (2002)

written criminal laws by casting them on quadripods and put them in public places, thereby setting a precedent of promulgation of law in ancient China. This practice was opposed by some conservatives. Shu Xiang, a minister in the State of Jin criticized him in a letter. He wrote that: "the former kings deal with state affairs according to traditions and conventions, rather than laws; laws should be kept a secret to the people. Otherwise, the people will no longer be afraid of their rulers. They will ignore traditions and seek justifications for their actions from laws and, as a result, the State of Zhen will descent into chaos." Zi Chan dismissed such criticism by replying that: "I did this for the better development of the state." The reformists won the debate and, from then on, promulgation of law had become a common practice in various states. The newly discovered Qin Code (cir. 360-210 BC) contained special provisions on the promulgation of laws. In late Warring States Period, the legalists described the laws as something that is made by the government and made known to the common people" . One of the representatives of the legalists, Shang Yang, also advocated that the laws should be "easy to understand", and government officials should carry out publicity of laws, so as to let the common people know what they should do and what they should do in order to avoid harms and seek interests, thereby enabling them to exercise self-government." From the above we can see that major progresses had already been achieved by China at that time in terms of the concept and practice of transparency.

Modern states of representative democracy have much higher standards on transparency. These standards include:

First, electoraltransparency. The multi-party election system requires that the election should be transparent. Political parties and candidates participating in the election must present to their constituents their achievements, their analysis of the current political situation, and their political opinions, so that the voters can decide who can be chosen as the spokesmen of their own interests.

Second, legislative transparency. Modern states implement the rule of law. The government must protect citizens' rights, administer state affairs and maintain social order in accordance with law. It is important that the law embodies the will and the demands of the people. Therefore, the introduction, demonstration and deliberation of bills must all be transparent, so as to facilitate public participation and ensure laws reflect the demand of the time and people's interest and, as such, can be truly implemented in practice.

Third, administrative transparency. Administration by law is the key to ruling the country by law as well as a basic characteristic of the operation of modern states. Since strong administrative power is deeply rooted in history and the expansion the administrative power is a common problem in the actual operation of many modern states, it is especially important to increase administrative transparency. Only in this way can we put the administrative power under effective control, prevent the abuse of the discretional power of administrative organs, facilitate public supervision over administrative power and enable victims of abuse of administrative power obtain effective remedies.

Fourth, judicial transparency. Judicial organs and their exercise of judicial power are the last line of defense for social justice and citizens' rights. The independence and fairness of the judicial power is a goal pursued by people of all countries. Therefore, the exercise of judicial power must be transparent and put under the effective supervision by the public.

II

It is because of the great importance of transparency of the operation of sate organs that the constitutions and laws of all countries as well as in relevant international conventions have all established corresponding systems aimed at ensuring such transparency, include the system of work reports by the parliament and the government, the system of reports on the implementation of state budget, the system of open trial, the system of press release by various state organs, and the system of questioning of members of the cabinet.

Moreover, the Universal Declaration of Human Rights provides in Article 21 that everyone has the right to take part in the government of his country, directly or through freely chosen representatives. The International Covenant on Economic, Social and Cultural Rights provides in Article 2 that "Each State Party to the present Covenant undertakes to take steps, individually and through international assistance and co-operation... to the maximum of its available resources, with a view to achieving progressively the full realization of the rights recognized in the present Covenant by all appropriate means, including particularly the adoption of legislative measures." and that "The States Parties to the present Covenant undertake to guarantee that the rights enunciated in the present Covenant will be exercised without discrimination of any kind". Meanwhile Article 16 of the Covenant provides for the system of state party report on the implementation of the Covenant: "The States Parties to the present Covenant undertake to submit in conformity with this part of the Covenant reports on the measures which they have adopted and the progress made in achieving the observance of the rights recognized herein."

The International Covenant on Civil and Political Rights (ICCPR) provides in Article 19 that "Everyone shall have the right to freedom of expression; this right shall include freedom to seek, receive and impart information and ideas of all kinds." Although this provision is aimed at safeguarding individual rights, it obviously contains an obligation of the government to provide relevant information to citizens. Article 25 of the ICCPR contains a provision on the right of election and the right to political participation with content similar to that of Article 21 of the Universal Declaration of Human Rights. The Covenant also establishes the Committee on Human Rights and the system of state party report on the implementation of the Covenant. The ICCPR provides in Article 28 that "There shall be established a Human Rights Committee", in Article 40 that: "The States Parties to the present Covenant undertake to submit reports on the measures they have adopted which give effect to the rights recognized herein and on the progress made in the enjoyment of those rights: (a) Within one year of the entry into force of the present Covenant for the States Parties concerned; (b) Thereafter whenever the Committee so requests", in Article 41 that: "A State Party to the present Covenant may at any time declare under this article that it recognizes the competence of the Committee to receive and consider communications to the effect that a State Party claims that another State Party is not fulfilling its obligations under the present Covenant", and that "Communications under this article may be received and considered only if submitted by a State Party which has made a declaration recognizing in regard to itself the competence of the Committee. No communication shall be received by the Committee if it concerns a State Party which has not made such a declaration." It is noteworthy that, apart from the two international human rights covenants, the WTO Rules contain requirements on the transparency of the operation of state organs of member states, which are even stricter than those contained the former and are also accompanied by corresponding reporting and deliberation mechanisms. All these show that the transparency of state organs is not only a domestic legal obligation, but also an international obligation undertaken by state parties to the relevant international conventions.

III

The transparency of the operation of state organs is important because it is crucial to the development of democracy and human rights protection. It is also for this reason that transparency is not unlimited. A particular form of transparency will constitute violation of human rights if it infringes upon the privacy and the reputation of an individual or endangers political, economic or national security of the state, resulting in serious harms to the state or other individuals. Therefore, the constitutions and laws of various states as well as international human rights conventions all contain provisions on the restriction of transparency. The constitutions of various states, while affirming the fundamental rights and freedoms of citizens, all provide that in the exercise of rights and freedoms, no one shall harm the interests of the state or society, or the lawful rights and freedoms other citizens. Many countries have also adopted special laws on the protection of national security and state secret. The ICCPR, while providing in Article 19 Paragraph 2 that citizens have freedom to express their opinion and seek, receive and impart information, also provides in Paragraph 3 of the same article that: "The exercise of the rights provided for in paragraph 2 of this article carries with it special duties and responsibilities. It may therefore be subject to certain restrictions, but these shall only be such as are provided by law and are necessary: (a) For respect of the rights or reputations of others; (b) For the protection of national security or of public order (ordre public), or of public health or morals." It should be pointed out that, because different countries have different national cultures, historical backgrounds and levels of development, each state must take into consideration social reaction to and tolerance of transparency in its own country and it is not appropriate to impose a uniform model on countries of different cultural backgrounds or levels of development, such as western and eastern countries. Otherwise it will also lead to chaos and violation of human rights.

IV

In modern states, mass media has a close relationship with transparency. With the development of the Internet, this relationship will become increasingly close. In addition to traditional forms of mass media, such as books, newspapers, magazines, radio, and TV, the Internet is becoming an increasingly important issue in the discussion of transparency and the regulation of mass media.

The so-called regulation refers to not only ensuring by legal means the freedom of speech and the right of new reporting of the media industry and media workers, but also strengthening the administration of the media industry in accordance with law, so as to ensure that their reporting activities meet the public need of the right to know while at the same time do not infringe upon the privacy of individuals and endanger national security, public health and moral and to promote the healthier development of society.

As far as I know, in most countries, the regulation of the mass media takes the form of combination of discipline and self-discipline, or so-called "hunger disciple", and there is no such a thing as absolute freedom. A responsible government must strike a balance between freedom and order in light of the level of social acceptability, so as to ensure the stability and development of the state and society.

V

China attaches great importance to the transparency of the operation of state organs and the regulation of mass media. During the past half a century, it has always been trying to strike a balance between freedom and disciple and between development and stability. During the past 20 years of reform and opening up, it has made new progresses in this respect which have contributed greatly to the rapid economic development and substantial rise in people's living standard. In recent years, China has again made new progresses in this area through the improvement of laws and institutions. These progresses include: the development and operation of grassroots democratic system, the improvement of the system of election of deputies to people's congresses, the system of investigation, research, demonstration of and extensive discussion for the adoption of important laws, the publicity of laws, rules and regulations, the publication of normative government documents, the establishment of system of uniform national examination for the qualification of civil servants, the universal implementation of the system of public notice of appointment and promotion of government officials, the openness of administrative punishment and court trial, the extensive reporting by news media on the operation of state organs, and in-depth reporting on some major and prominent events.

Currently, China needs to further improve the legislation in the above-mentioned areas by adopting corresponding basic laws in accordance with the relevant provisions of the Constitution, so as to change the current situation in which the transparency of the operation of state organs and the mass media are mainly regulated by administrative rules and regulations, rather than laws. While accepting the regulation by law, mass media should adhere to the fine tradition of seeking truth from fact. In the process of improving the relevant laws and institutions, China should summarize its own experience while at the same time draw on the experience of the EU and other countries. This academic seminar is a precious opportunity for Chinese and European scholars to deepen their mutual understanding and learn from each other.

Freedom of Speech and Social Development[①]

Freedom of speech and social development are both very important to mankind. However, the question of how to correctly handle the relationship between the two has always been a perplexing question, whether in history or in the present time. Some people argue that the freedom of speech is an inevitable cost which must be paid by developing country in order to achieve development while some others maintain that freedom of speech is an absolute right, which must be safeguarded at any cost, even to the extent of allowing cultural products with pornographic and violent content to affect the physical and mental development of minors. The above two arguments are embodied in the design and operation of institutions, in legislative, administrative and judicial practices, especially in the mechanisms for the resolution of conflicts of interests or rights in different countries. In the followings I would like to share with you some of my personal views on the freedom of speech and social development in light of the above facts.

I

The freedom of speech is the freedom of everyone to acquire and impart various kinds of information and idea in oral, written or other forms. It includes three aspects of freedom: (1) freedom to seek and receive information. In order to survive and develop, people must understand and transform the subjective and objective worlds, form society and carry out communication with each other. To do so, they must seek and acquire the experiences of their ancestors and other people and exercise the freedom to seek and receive information. Otherwise the survival and development of

① Originally published in *Journal of Zhengzhou University*, No. 5 (1999) and reprinted in *Xinhua Digest*, No. 1 (2000)

mankind would be impossible. (2) The freedom of thought and the freedom to hold opinions. The information sought or received by a person are the materials for his thought, and after processing, become his own ideas, opinions or will. This process should not be interfered with or limited, otherwise the human society will cease to develop and the survival of mankind will be endangered. (3) The freedom to impart various kinds of information, ideas and opinions, which is a basic condition for the cooperation and association between people for the purpose of transforming the natural world and realizing social progress. The freedom of speech is an important way by which people acquire, receive, develop and transmit knowledge, experience and truth. To safeguard the freedom of speech is to show concern for and to respect people. Together with other freedoms and rights, the freedom of speech constitutes the foundation of modern market economy, democracy, and modern state. A review of human history shows many strong evidences of the close relationship between the freedom of speech and social development.

During the Spring and Autumn Period (771—403 BC) and the Warring States Period (403—221 BC), the development of social productive force had enabled people to break the restraint on their mind by old ethics and rites. The "contention of a hundred schools of thought" was the concrete form and manifestation of the freedom of speech in ancient China. Being the product of social transformation itself, it had greatly promoted the transformation of the Chinese society from a slavery society into a feudal society and laid the foundation for the establishment of the feudal system that had lasted for over 2,000 years in China.

In the 19th century, the feudal autocratic system in China became increasingly decadent. However, any criticism of this system was regarded as "great disrespect to state" and punished severely by law. After the Opium War in 1840, China was invaded by western imperial powers, the feudal rulers were forced to forfeit its sovereignty, cede its territory and pay indemnities to the invaders. Nevertheless, they continued to hang on to the old systems and suppress any idea about and call for reform. During the past 100 years, the bourgeois and communist revolutionaries had paid with their blood for the dissemination of the bourgeois ideas of constitutional monarchy and democratic republic and the Marxist ideas of people's democracy. It can be said that the lack of freedom of speech had been one of the reasons for the slow development of Chinese society. After arduously struggles, advanced ideas had ultimately been disseminated in

China and transformed into huge spiritual and materials motive forces that contributed to the overthrow of the feudal system, the victory of democratic revolution and the birth of a new China.

The remarkable achievements made by China in economic and social development since 1978 are inseparable from the ideological line of emancipating the mind and seeking truth from fact adhered to by the Chinese government. The emancipation of the mind has enabled Chinese people to break one theoretical forbidden zone after another and reflect on things they had not been allowed to think and say things they had not been allowed to say in the past. Under the guidance of the policy of "letting a hundred flowers blossom and a hundred schools of thought contend", free discussions have been carried out on many important issues, enabling people's understanding of these issues to be more in line with or closer to truth. The principle of seeking truth from fact requires people not to be bound by book worship, or to take the existing definitions and doctrines as the starting point of their thinking of the relevant issues, but to take practice as the sole criterion for testing their ideas and understandings. As Deng Xiaoping pointed out that: "The chief criterion should be whether it promotes the growth of the productive forces in a socialist society, increases the overall strength of the socialist state and raises living standards." Under new historical conditions, this principle has inspired the Chinese people to emancipate their mind and exercise their freedom of speech and promoted the social development in China and will continue to do so in the future. As numerous examples in western history have shown, freedom of speech is closely related to social development. Apparently, if the theocratic legal system under which Giordano Bruno was burned at the stake were still in existence today, men's landing on the moon and the exploration of the outer space would be impossible. It is because of the great significance of the freedom of speech that it is treated as a creed and confirmed and safeguarded by not only domestic laws, but also international declarations and conventions.

II

The fact that the freedom of speech is very important to social development does not mean that it is an absolute and unrestricted freedom. Montesquieu held that freedom is to do anything not prohibited by law: "If a citizen is free to do what are prohibited by law, he can no longer be free because other people are free to do the same things to him." Therefore, both international instruments and domestic constitutions, while proclaiming the freedom of speech as a fundament human right, have all provided for corresponding restrictions on the exercise of this freedom. The International Covenant on Civil and Political Rights provides in Article 19 that: The exercise of the freedom of speech "carries with it special duties and responsibilities. It may therefore be subject to certain restrictions, but these shall only be such as are provided by law and are necessary: (a) For respect of the rights or reputations of others; (b) For the protection of national security or of public order (ordre public), or of public health or morals." Other international or regional human rights conventions contain similar restrictions on the exercise of this freedom. According to the statistics made by two Dutch constitutional scholars, among the 142 constitutions in the world, 124 have provided for the freedom of speech. While confirming this freedom as one of the fundamental human rights, all these constitutions contain restrictions on the exercise of this freedom in the form of a proviso, so as to prevent the abuse of this freedom. The provisos on the freedom of speech in the U. S. are mostly contained in the constitutions of various states. For example, the Constitution of the State of New York provides that: "Every citizen may freely speak, write and publish his or her sentiments on all subjects, being responsible for the abuse of that right." The Illinois Constitution provides that "All persons may speak, write and publish freely, being responsible for the abuse of that liberty." And the Declaration of the Rights of Man and of the Citizen, which forms part of the Preamble of the French Constitution, provides that: "The free communication of ideas and opinions is one of the most precious of the rights of man. Every citizen may, accordingly, speak, write, and print with freedom, but shall be responsible for such abuses of this freedom as shall be defined by law." From the above constitutional provisions we can see that the restriction on the freedom of speech is as common as the confirmation of the freedom itself. Nevertheless, I believe that, as far as the relationship between the freedom of speech and its restriction is concerned, the former has priority over the latter, just as rights have priority over obligations. The purpose of restricting the freedom of speech is to coordinate the relationship and strike a balance between rights and obligations.

III

The scope and degree of the restriction on the freedom of speech can not be clearly defined by the constitution and laws, but should mainly be determined by the actual situation of judicial and law enforcement practice in each country. The differences in the restrictions on the freedom of speech in different countries result from not only the differences in the gap between constitutional and legal provisions and their implementation, but also some deeper-rooted and more complicated factors, such as historical and cultural backgrounds, religion and customs, level of economic, cultural, scientific and technological development, public security situation of, as well as the international environment faced by different countries.

The objective world is complicated and constantly changing, unlike the abstract doctrines put forward by theorists, which are rigorously logic and consistent. Politicians who bear state responsibilities and are answerable to their constituency and judges are more concerned about the concrete operation of the legal system under specific situations. While safeguard citizens' freedom of speech, they must ensure that the exercise of this freedom will promote, rather than impede, the maintenance of public order and the development of society. To this end, they must strike a balance between guaranteeing the freedom of speech and maintaining social order and stability, which is indispensable for the development of society. This balance can be found in the constitutions and laws of various countries.

When I visited Norway in the winter of 1997, the President of the Supreme Court of Norway, Mr. Karstein Smith, informed me about a case the Court was hearing at that time. In this case, a political party named White Electoral Alliance publicly advocated in its party program the prohibition of marriage between Norwegian people and black people in the name of preserving the Norwegian people's ethnic composition. Because of this section of the party program, the leader of the party was sentenced by a Norwegian court to imprisonment and fine. The defendant appealed the judgment directly to the Supreme Court on ground that it violated the provisions on the freedom of speech in the Norwegian Constitution and the European Convention on Human Rights. In view of the fact that the case touched upon major issues of principle, the Supreme Court decided to make an exception by accepting the appeal and hearing the case with the full members of the Court. After hearing, the Court found that the defendant's argument that the call for the prohibition of the inter-marriage between white and black people in the party program was within the scope of the freedom of speech was untenable and therefore decided to reject the appeal and uphold the original judgment, so as to uphold judicial fairness and social justice. The trial and the final verdict of this case showed that the provisions on the freedom of speech in the constitutions and international conventions should not be abused.

When ratifying the ICCPR, many states have made reservations to or declaration on the provisions on the freedom of expression in Article 19 of the Convention. For example, Austria, Belgium, France and Germany declared that Article 19 of the ICCPR will be implemented in accordance with articles 10, 11 and 16 of the European Convention on Human Rights and Australia, Ireland, Luxemburg and the Netherlands made reservations to Article 19 Paragraph 2 concerning the regulation of radio and television broadcasting and licensing of broadcasting enterprises. These reservations and declarations should be treated with understanding as long as they do not go against the basic principles of the Convention.

IV

Just as pointed at the beginning of the article, in history the Chinese people had carried out long struggle and paid with their blood for the enjoyment of the freedom of speech. After the establishment of the new China in 1949, the Chinese people enshrined their hard-won freedom of speech in the Common Program of the Chinese People's Political Consultative Conference, which served as temporary constitution before the adoption of the 1954 Constitution. Article 5 of the Common Program provided that: "The people of the People's Republic of China shall have freedom of thought, speech, publication, assembly, association, correspondence, person, domicile, change of domicile, religious belief and the freedom of holding procession" . Although the Chinese constitution has been revised many times since its promulgation in 1954, it always contains a clear provision on the freedom of speech. The current Constitution provides that: "Citizens of the People's Republic of China enjoy freedom of speech, of the press, of assembly, of association, of procession and of demonstration. " Meanwhile, citizens also have the "freedom to engage in scientific research, literary and artistic creation and other cultural pursuits." In light of the concrete conditions in China, the Constitution especially provides that: "Citizens have the right to criticize and make suggestions regarding any state organ or functionary and to make to relevant state organs complaints or charges against, or exposures of, any state organ or functionary for violation of the law or dereliction of duty." Like the constitutions of other countries, the Chinese Constitution also provides for restrictions on the exercise of the freedom of speech. Article 51 of the Constitution provides that: "Citizens of the People's Republic of China, in exercising their freedoms and rights, may not infringe upon the interests of the state, of society or of the collective, or upon the lawful freedoms and rights of other citizens." This provision requires citizens to respect the rights and freedoms, including the reputation, dignity, and privacy of others, observe public order, guard state secret, uphold national security, and comply with public morality. To ensure the implementation of the above constitutional provisions, China has adopted the General Principles of Civil Law, the Law on the Protection of Minors, and the Law on Guarding State Secrets, which contain more specific provisions on the restrictions of the freedom of speech. The Criminal Law and the Regulations on Administrative Penalties for Public Security also provide for punishments for violations of these provisions.

Despite the above legal provisions, because of the long history of feudal autocratic rule and the patriarchal system in China, various forms of feudal ethnics and principles, such as the crimes of "lese majesty", "vilifying the emperor", "offending taboos", "being unfilial to parents", and "making charging against parents", and the principles of "mutual concealment of crimes between the relatives" and "obligation to conceal the crimes committed by the seniors in the family", have not been buried together with feudal dynasties, but are still exerting significant influence on Chinese society. In the past several decades, the Chinese people have learnt bitter lessons on the freedom of speech. During the "Cultural Revolution", constitutional principles were trampled upon, and citizens' freedom of speech was not protected and respected at all. On the one hand, the freedom of speech was excessively restrict, "very often, what leaders say is taken as the law and anyone who disagrees is called a law-breaker." On the other hand, the freedom of speech had been abused. Under the pretext of "great democracy" and "revolutionary action", people verbally attacked, vilified, violated the privacy, and insulted the human dignity of each other. Such verbal attacks had later escalated into physical attacks and ultimately into a "full-scale civil war" in which people attacked each other with sticks, knives, guns, even cannons. It was only after 1978 that the CPC, guided by correctly ideological lines, decisively put an end to the "Cultural Revolution" and restored the constitution and legal order.

Just as the emancipation of mind in the late 1870s and early 1980s had promoted the reform and opening up, the social progress brought about by the reform and opening up has also promoted the realization of the freedom of speech. On the one hand, the economic reform carried out since 1978 have given greater freedoms first to the broad masses of farmers, and then to all Chinese citizens, in terms of property relations, status relations and the corresponding behavior choice, thereby encouraging them to better and more truthfully express their interest demands and aspirations; on the other hand, with the progress of social, economic, scientific and technological development, various forms of mass media, such as newspapers, magazines, radio, TV, VCD, and the Internet, have been developing in a breathtaking way, both in speed and in scope, providing unprecedented favorable conditions for the full enjoyment of the freedom of speech by Chinese citizens. To implement the provisions on the freedom of speech in the 1982 Constitution, the National People's Congress and its Standing Committee as well as local people's congresses at various levels and their standing committees have adopted a series of laws and regulations on mass media, publishing industry, patents, trade marks, and copyrights.

Currently China is in the process of building socialist democratic system and implementing the strategy of ruling the country by law, and realizing democratic election, democratic decision-making, democratic administration and democratic supervision of state organs. In this process, there is no ready-made model to be followed. Therefore, in order to realize economic, scientific, technological, educational and political development, the Chinese government must rely on the wisdoms and the initiatives of the broad masses of people. And to do so, it must create the basic conditions for the full enjoyment of various rights and freedoms, including the freedom of speech, by the people. Just as Jiang Zemin pointed out, the Chinese Government must ensure that people enjoy the most extensive rights and freedoms and respect and safeguard human rights.

Currently China is still at the primary stage of socialism and its legal system still needs to be further improved. Many laws on safeguarding the freedom of speech, such as the Press Law, the Law on Publications, the Broadcasting Law, the Law on Motion Pictures and Televisions, and the Law on Performance, and other laws on the dissemination of information, still need to be adopted so as to further clarify the relationship of legal rights and obligations between the practitioners in these fields, and between these practitioners and their audiences, viewers and readers, and enable them to have rules to go by in their daily activities and legal basis to rely on in case of disputes between them. It should bring the protection of various civil and political rights and freedoms, including the freedom of speech, into the orbit of law, so that the victims of violations of these rights and freedoms can obtain timely remedies. However, the imperfections in the legal system of safeguarding the freedom of speech in China do not negate the efforts made and the historical progress achieved by Chinese Government in safeguarding the freedom of speech. It may be fairly stated that today the Chinese people are enjoying the most extensive freedom of speech ever in history and it can be predicted that the full enjoyment of the freedom of speech will further enhance the consciousness of democracy and human rights of Chinese citizens and promote the development of the socialist market economy and social progress in China and, with the development of society, advancement of science and technology, and rise in people's cultural level, the Chinese people will be able to enjoy even fuller freedom of speech.

Adhering to the Prohibition of Torture and Promoting the Development of Civilization[①]

The International Seminar on the Protection of Human Rights and Prohibition of Torture in the 21st Century is now drawing to an end. I am glad to make a concluding remark on the seminar. It can be said without any doubt that this seminar is very successful: it was very well organized; an English-Chinese compendium of all the papers submitted by participants was distributed at the beginning of the seminar; and the discussion at the seminar was very lively. The participants have reached consensus on basic issues of prohibition against torture, exchanged opinions on other relevant issues, deepened the understanding between Chinese and foreign scholars, and laid a sound foundation for further discussions. The followings are my own opinions on some of the issues discussed at the seminar.

I. The Concept of Torture

We have noted from the papers submitted to and speeches made at the seminar that people have different views concerning the concept of torture: some believe torture refers only to an act of judicial personnel, some say it can only be committed by police and other officials responsible for maintaining public security; some think it is an act of state personnel. Still some others expended the scope of torture to include not only the physical, psychological and sexual violence committed by government organs and government officials, but also those committed by military personnel,

① This Paper is based on the author's concluding remarks at the International Seminar on the Protection of Human Rights and Prohibition of Torture in the 21st Century It was originally published in Xia Yong et. al (ed.), *How to Eradicate Torture*, Beijing: Social Sciences Documentation Publishing House, 2003.

public security organizations entrusted by the government, as well as those committed within a family. Ms. Lisbet Ilkjaer from Denmark mentioned in her speech the identification by the ICTY and ICTW of crimes against humanity committed in the territories of the former Yugoslavia and Rwanda; Mr. Basil Fernando from Sri Lanka talked about the identification by the international community of the atrocities committed by the former Chilean president Pinochet. They believed that such identification had shown that torture carried out within the territory of a state has already become one of the most serious crimes under international law. The above facts show that the concept of torture is developing, people's understanding of torture is deepening, and their attention towards the problem of torture is growing. However, in order to grasp the key issues and the trends of development of the prohibition against torture, it is necessary to clarify the concept of torture and distinguish it from other acts prohibited by the law.

Torture has existed since very early in history. The Book of History (Shi Ji) recorded various kinds of torture inflicted by cruel officials on other officials and ordinary people. Such examples are also abundant in history books of other countries. Acts of torture in Chinese history can be divided into two categories: those carried out within the law and those carried out outside the law. Those carried out outside the law were prohibited; those carried out within the law were considered normal performance of functions as long as the law had not been bent.

It was only after the Second World War that torture was regarded as a crime under international law. The Universal Declaration of Human Rights (UDHR), adopted by the United Nations in December 1948 provides in Article 5 that "No one shall be subjected to torture or to cruel, inhuman or degrading treatment or punishment." Although the UDHR is part of the International Bill of Human Rights, it is generally considered to be only morally bindling on state parties to it. Its provisions can be legal binding on state parties only if they are embodied in an international treaty.

It was for this reason that, in December 1966, the UN General Assembly adopted the International Covenant on Economic, Social and Cultural Rights and the International Covenant on Civil and Political Rights, which reaffirmed, in the form of legally binding treaties, the principles provided for in the UDHR. Article 7 of the International Covenant on Civil and Political Rights provides that: "No one shall be subjected to torture or to other cruel, inhuman or degrading treatment or punishment. In particular, no one shall be subjected without his free consent to medical or scientific experimentation." The first sentence of this article is copied word for word from article 5 of the UDHR. The second sentence of the article reflects the new development in this area. However, the concept of torture in both the UDHR and the CCPR is too general, which has inevitably resulted in different interpretations in practice.

In view of the fact that torture continued to exist in many countries of the world after the adoption of the UDHR and the CCPR and with a view to deepening and unifying people's understanding of torture and, more importantly, providing "guiding principles for all states or individuals exercising effective power"① and ensuring that "exceptional circumstances such as a state of war or a threat of war, internal political instability or any other public emergency may not be invoked as a justification of torture or other cruel, inhuman or degrading treatment or punishment."②, the UN Assembly adopted in December 1975 the Declaration on the Protection of All Persons from Being Subjected to Torture and Other Cruel, Inhuman or Degrading Treatment or Punishment. Article 1 of the Declaration has for the first time provided for a definition of torture: "1. For the purpose of this Declaration, torture means any act by which severe pain or suffering, whether physical or mental, is intentionally inflicted by or at the instigation of a public official on a person for such purposes as obtaining from him or a third person information or confession, punishing him for an act he has committed or is suspected of having committed, or intimidating him or other persons. 2. Torture constitutes an aggravated and deliberate form of cruel, inhuman or degrading treatment or punishment." It should be noted that this definition has expended the subjects of torture to include not only judicial officers and policemen, but also public officials or persons instigated by public officials; torture must be inflicted intentionally and for the purposes of obtaining from the victim or a third person information or confession, punishing him for an act he has committed or is suspected of having committed, or intimidating him or other persons; and torture must constitutes an aggravated and deliberate form of cruel, inhuman or

---

① See Preamble of Declaration on the Protection of All Persons from Being Subjected to Torture and Other Cruel, Inhuman or Degrading Treatment or Punishment.

② See Preamble of Declaration on the Protection of All Persons from Being Subjected to Torture and Other Cruel, Inhuman or Degrading Treatment or Punishment. Article 3.

degrading treatment or punishment. This definition has clarified the subject, the intention, the object, the purposes and the methods of torture, thereby further deepened people's understanding of torture and basically met the needs of prohibition against torture.

In December 1984, the UN General Assembly, in order to further develop the law against of torture and "make more effective the struggle against torture and other cruel, inhuman or degrading treatment or punishment throughout the world"①, and on basis of the above-mentioned Declaration, adopted the Convention against Torture and Other Cruel, Inhuman or Degrading Treatment or Punishment. Article 1 of the Convention further clarified the definition of torture, namely the term "torture" means "any act by which severe pain or suffering, whether physical or mental, is intentionally inflicted on a person for such purposes as obtaining from him or a third person information or a confession, punishing him for an act he or a third person has committed or is suspected of having committed, or intimidating or coercing him or a third person, or for any reason based on discrimination of any kind, when such pain or suffering is inflicted by or at the instigation of or with the consent or acquiescence of a public official or other person acting in an official capacity." Compared with the 1975 Declaration on Torture, the Convention changed the subjects of torture from "public officials and persons instigated by public officials" to "a public official or other person acting in an official capacity" or any person who inflicted torture "at the instigation of or with the consent or acquiescence of a public official or other person acting in an official capacity." Apparently the scope of the latter is much wider than the former. In modern society, persons such as security personnel and bodyguards are officially authorized quasi-military personnel who possess great powers. Therefore, it is necessary to include them in the subjects of torture. With regard to the purposes of torture, the Convention added the phrase "or for any reason based on discrimination of any kind". This is very necessary because examples of torture committed for reasons based on racial, ethnic, religious, gender or political discrimination are numerous, both in history and in reality. Very frequently, such discrimination has lead not only to torture, but also to massacres, even armed conflicts and wars. Besides, the second paragraph

① See Preamble of the Convention against Torture and Other Cruel, Inhuman or Degrading Treatment or Punishment, of the definition of torture in the Declaration was deleted in the Convention. This was done partly because the paragraph was unnecessary repetition of provision in the previous paragraph and partly for the purpose of expending the scope of the definition of torture.

II. Torture and the Death Penalty

The death penalty is the criminal punishment of deprivation of life by a special state organ in accordance with criminal procedures. It is also called the capital punishment, which means the severest and harshest criminal punishment. The death penalty, although is the harshest punishment, cannot be equaled to torture. On the other hand, neither can we deny the relationship between the death penalty and torture. The key questions are whether the death penalty is carried out in strict accordance with the law, whether the law according to which the death penalty is carried out is fair and supported by the people, and whether the law has been abused or trampled upon. Even if the law is fair and lenient, if it is abused by judicial officials, resulting in the killing of innocent people, the death penalty still constitutes torture. As to the question of whether the law is fair and lenient, it depends on the actual conditions in a specific country and the will of the people in that country. Even the criminal law of a country has provided for many capital crimes and the death penalty is applied frequently in judicial practice, as long as democratic politics are practiced and the law is supported by the majority of the people, we cannot consider the death penalty as constituting a violation of the prohibition of torture in international law.

Currently, the Chinese criminal law provides a wide variety of capital crimes and the number of death sentences imposed in judicial practice is also relatively high. At a time when many countries in the world have already abolished the death penalty and many others which still retain the death penalty have actually stopped the application or rarely apply the penalty, the issue of death penalty in China becomes very prominent, both in terms of legislation and in terms of judicial practice. However, it should be noted that this problem is determined by the actual conditions in China. Since the reform and opening to the outside world, drug-related crimes have spread throughout the country, from the southwest to northeast, from Hong Kong and Macao to the frontiers of Xinjiang and Inner Mongolia. Drug trafficking, which is spreading rapidly despite repeated prohibition, has become a major threat to the health of the Chinese people, especially the young people. Besides, various kinds of economic crimes, such as embezzlement, bribery and smuggling, have also increased rapidly and often involve high-level government officials. These crimes have caused serious damages to the socialist economic construction and aroused great indignation among the people. Moreover, due to the widening gap of income between different people during the period of transition, some people have lost psychological balance and engaged in various kinds of violent crimes such as robbery, murder, setting off explosions, and organized crimes such kidnapping, blackmailing, and bullying and oppressing the ordinary people. These crimes, which are often extremely cruel and savage, have resulted in serious public security problems and made it impossible for the ordinary people to lead a normal life. As a result, people strongly demand that severe punishment be imposed on these crimes. In a society which is still under the influence of the traditional ideas of "a life for a life and an injury for an injury", and in which the clan system has not yet been totally eliminated, abolishing the death penalty against people's may result not only in a lack of deterrent effect of the punishment but also in incidents of people taking the law into their own hands. In the end, the society and the state will have to pay much higher price. Under these circumstances, China has currently adopted a legislative and judicial policy of maintaining the death penalty, restricting the death penalty, and reducing the number of death sentences.

International law differentiates death penalty from torture. As has been discussed above, torture is prohibited by international law and the scope of prohibition is widening. This is not the case forthe death penalty. Article 6 of the International Covenant on Civil and Political Rights provides that: "in countries which have not abolished the death penalty, sentence of death may be imposed only for the most serious crimes in accordance with the law in force at the time of the commission of the crime and not contrary to the provisions of the present Covenant and to the Convention on the Prevention and Punishment of the Crime of Genocide," and that "this penalty can only be carried out pursuant to a final judgment rendered by a competent court." The main points of this article are the followings: 1. "Death penalty may be imposed only for the most serious crimes"; the most serious crime should be understood as "intentional crimes with lethal or other extremely grave consequences"[①]; 2. "Capital punishment may be imposed only for a crime for which the death penalty is prescribed by law at the time of its commission."[②] 3. "Capital punishment may only be carried out pursuant to a final judgment rendered by a competent court after legal process which gives all possible safeguards to ensure a fair trial, including the right of anyone suspected of or charged with a crime for which capital punishment may be imposed to adequate legal assistance at all stages of the proceedings."[③] The above interpretations are contained in Safeguards Guaranteeing Protection of the Rights of Those Facing the Death Penalty, adopted by UN Economic and Social Council on 25 May 1984. The three "only" s in this document reflect the strict restriction on the death penalty. Although international instruments impose strict restrictions on the death penalty, this does not mean that they prohibit or demand the abolition of the death penalty. This shows that the international community has made a clear distinction between the death penalty and torture. The Chinese policy of retaining and restricting the death penalty is compatible with international law. It is in keeping with the actual needs in China and supported by the majority of the people in the country. The aim of this policy is to create conditions for the ultimate abolition of the death penalty.

III. The Harmful Effects of Torture

The harmful effects of torture are obvious. Although torture had been widely used throughout history as a means of class domination, it had not been used without any restriction. In Chinese history, the restrictions on torture, both in law and in practice, had been most strict in times of peace and prosperity. Even during the Qin Dynasty, which was famous for its harsh laws and cruel punishments, torture was not used without any restriction. In December 1975, some bamboo slips with carved information about the laws of the Qin Dynasty in the period from Shangyang's Reform to

① Article 1 of the Safeguards guaranteeing protection of the rights of those facing the death penalty.

② Article 2 of the Safeguards guaranteeing protection of the rights of those facing the death penalty.

③ Safeguards guaranteeing protection of the rights of those facing the death penalty, article 5.

Emperor Qinshihuang's rule were unearthed from some Qin tombs at Shuihudi, Yunmeng County, Hubei Province. Among these laws, there were two provisions on criminal interrogation. 1. "The best way of conducting criminal interrogation is to get to the truth without resorting to torture; it is not good to use torture during criminal interrogation; and the interrogation shall be considered a failure if intimidation is used against the criminal suspect." 2. "In criminal interrogation, the first step is to ask the criminal suspect to make a statement about the facts and take a written record of the statement. While the suspect is making the statement, the interrogator should not ask him questions even if he knows that the suspect is lying. Only after the suspect has finished the statement and a written record of the statement is taken, can the interrogator begin questioning him... Torture can be used on a criminal suspect in accordance with the law only if he has repeatedly lied and changed his statements, is unable to answer the questions, and yet refuses to admit the crime. Under this circumstance, the following written statement must be added to the case file: 'torture has been used on the criminal suspect, who has repeatedly changed his confession, was unable to answer the questions put to him and yet refused to admit the crime' "① The Qin Code also provided that: "an official who, in the process of making the arrest, intentionally attacks with weapon a person suspected of a crime punishable only by confiscation of property or fines, resulting in the death of such person, shall be sentenced to long-term imprisonment; if the attack has resulted in the injury of such person, he shall be sentenced to short-term imprisonment."② During the rules of Emperor Wen and Emperor Wu in Han Dynasty, the criminal punishments included the tattooing the face, cutting of the nose, and amputating the legs. Emperor Wu issued an edict which read: "I feel pity for the criminals who are punished without being taught what is right and what is wrong and without given a chance to turn over a new leaf. And it is very cruel and inhuman to cut off their limps and tattoo their faces, which will leave them handicapped for life. These kinds of corporal punishments shall be abolished and replaced with other kinds of

---

① See *Bamboo Slips Unearthed from Qin Tombs in Shuihudi: Criminal Interrogation*, Cultural Relic Publishing House, 1982.

② See *Bamboo Slips Unearthed from Qin Tombs in Shuihudi: Questions and Answers on Legal Issues*, Cultural Relic Publishing House, 1982.

punishments. "[1] From then on, all these corporal punishments were replaced with flogging. Later, Emperor Jin decided to make the flogging less cruel and ordered that the number of blows should be limited, the size of the instrument used for flogging be reduced, and only the buttock could be hit during flogging. [2]The law in Tang Dynasty permitted the use of torture during criminal interrogation. However, the Codes of Tang provided that: "Criminal suspects who are over the age of 75 or bellow the age of 15 and those with disability may not be subjected to torture. When it is necessary to torture a suspect, all the officials participating in the trial should be present when the torture is used. A suspect shall not be tortured more than three times. The total number of blows he receives during the torture may not exceed 200 or the number of blows the suspect should received as punishment if convicted of the crime he is suspected of." Officials who violated this provision should be punished according to the circumstances of the case. Like the Han Dynasty during the rules of Emperor Wen and Emperor Jin, the Tang Dynasty during the rule of Emperor Zhenguan was also a period of peace and prosperity in Chinese history. The first Emperor of Tang Dynasty, Taizong, adopting a policy of "ruling the state with benevolence", had reduced the number of capital crimes in the criminal law. He established a system whereby a death sentence must be reviewed three times or even five times before it could be executed. He personally reviewed all death penalty cases and tried as much as possible to find out mitigating circumstances so as to avoid the imposition of the death penalty. These measures had produced good results. "Although the criminal code was very lenient at that time, the number of crimes had dropped drastically. "[3] Soon after the establishment of the Tang Dynasty, the public security conditions improved rapidly, the economy, which had suffered serious damaged during the war, had been recovered, and a situation of "universal peace and prosperity" had emerged. "At that time, property left by the roadside remained untouched till the owners returned for it, doors of houses were never locked at night, traveling merchants slept in open air without the fear of being robbed. "[4]

---

① See *History of Han*: *Biography of Emperor Wen.*

② See *History of Han Dynasty*: *Biography of Emperor Jin.*

③ *History of Tang Dynasty*: *Criminal Law.*

④ *History of Shui Dynasty*: *Criminal Law.*

On the other hand, governments in Chinese history which oppressed their own people with harsh laws and cruel punishments were all short-lived. According to history books, Qinshihuang, the first emperor in China, "abandoned the laws made by the wise kings of the past, persecuted honest ministers, and arbitrarily applied criminal punishments". As a result, "all kinds of evil grew out of control, prisons were as crowded as marketplace, voices of discontent were heard throughout the country and people were forced to revolt against the government."① The situation was seminar at the end of Shui Dynasty: "The emperor launched endless wars of aggression against neighboring states and levied exorbitant taxes against his own people... the law was abandoned and trample upon, corruption and bribery prevailed, and the poor people were forced to engage in various crimes such as theft and robbery."② Under this circumstance, "Emperor Yang imposed increasingly harsh laws and cruel punishments against the people, who were driven beyond the limit of forbearance and raised up in revolt. The dynasty was soon overthrown."③

In China's several-thousand-year-long history, there have been both positive and negative experiences in the field of criminal punishment.

The stability of the state depends on the support of the people. The wise emperors in ancient China had realized that "the monarch is like the boat and the people the water. The water that bears the boat is the same that swallows it."④ And that "a virtuous monarch is always supported by the people and a tyrant will ultimately be abandoned by the people". By taking the people as the basis of the state and being prudent in applying criminal punishment, they had achieved long-term peace and stability in the country.

Today, with the economic, cultural, scientific and technological developments and the advance of the civilization, all modern states are claiming themselves to be based on democracy, the rule of law and human rights. People's consciousness of using the law to uphold their own rights has been greatly enhanced, and torture becomes even more unpopular. Generally speaking, the harmful effects of torture can be

① Old History Book of Tang Dynasty: Criminal Law.

② History of Shui Dynasty: Criminal Law.

③ See *Old History Book of Tang Dynasty: Criminal Law.*

④ See *Essence of Zhengguan's Governance: Teaching of the Princes.*

summarized as the followings:

First, a person who has been subjected to torture will lose his confidence in public officials, the government, the law, even the whole system. The government and public officials are supported by taxpayers. In a modern state, at least according to the law, public officials should be servants and protectors, rather than masters or oppressors, of the people who support them. However, if torture is inflicted by a public official and such torture is supported, tolerated or acquiesced by the state organ to which he belongs, the person subjected to torture will lose his confidence in the public officials and the government and consider the law as mere formality and hypocrisy. Under severe pain, he may provide certain information, which may or may not be true. If such information is true, it may help solve some problems. But the trust between the tortured and the torturer will be permanently damaged and their confrontation will intensify. False information will endanger innocent people and cause even greater harm to the life and property of the people.

Second, torture harms not only the victim of torture, but, more importantly, also social relationships. It violates the legal provision on the prohibition of torture and other relevant laws. According the constitutional principle of a modern state, the law is sacred and the social relations protected by law are inviolable. This principle of the rule of law is an ideological stronghold for the safeguarding of social stability and national security. Once torture is committed by or at the instigation of or with the consent or acquiescence of a public official or other person acting in an official capacity, the dignity of the law will disappear from the mind of those who have been subjected torture and the practice will spread like plague among the people who hold public power or strong private power. As a result, the society will be filled with violence and atrocities and civilization will no longer be able to survive.

Third, torture not only harms the persons subjected to it and damage the social relationship protected by the laws, but also poisons the mind torturers and those who order or condone torture. This is because torturers are first of all the violators of the law. It has been proved that those who disregard or violate the law are dangerous to society, especially if they hold public or military power. Moreover, torturers are also violators of their own conscience. The victims of torture are often persons who have lost their ability of self-defense or vulnerable groups in society. Those who inflict torture on such persons must first of all violate their own conscience. There are many examples of killers and rapists who have ultimately turned into lunatics.

It is for the above-mentioned reasons that torture, especially extorting a confession by torture, is strictly prohibited by the Chinese laws and policies. The Constitution of the People's Republic of China provides in article 37 that: "Freedom of the person of citizens of the People's Republic of China is inviolable" and in article 38 that: "The personal dignity of citizens of the People's Republic of China is inviolable. Insult, libel, false accusation or false incrimination directed against citizens by any means is prohibited." In accordance with the Constitution, the Law on Judges, the Law on Public Procurators and the Law on People's Police all prohibit the use of torture to extort a confession. The Law on People's Police provides in Article 42 that people's police may not: 1. extort a confession by torture or subject criminals to corporal punishment or maltreat them; 2. unlawfully deprive other people of, or restrict, their freedom of the person, or illegally search a person, his or her belongings, residence or place; or 3. beat up other persons or instigate others to do so. The Law provides for legal responsibilities for the violation of these prohibitions. The Criminal Law provides for severe punishments for the crime of torture. According to articles 247 and 248, a judicial officer who extorts a confession from a criminal suspect or defendant by torture or extorts a testimony from a witness by violence or a policeman or other officer of an institution of confinement like a prison, a detention house or a custody house who beats a prisoner or maltreats him by subjecting him to corporal punishment shall be sentenced to fixed-term imprisonment of not more than three years or criminal detention. If the circumstances are especially serious, he shall be sentenced to fixed-term imprisonment of not less than three years and not more than 10 years. If he causes injury, disability or death to the victim, he shall be convicted of murder or intentional injury and sentenced to fixed-term imprisonment of more than 10 years, life imprisonment or death in accordance with article 234 or article 232 of the Law. The above provisions have demonstrated China's determination to fulfill its obligations under the Convention against Torture.

IV. Causes of Torture

Torture, as a very harmful and abhorred practice, is morally condemned and legally prohibited in most countries of the world.

Nevertheless, the phenomenon of torture is still widespread even today. The reasons for this phenomenon are mainly the followings:

First, the influence of the old traditions. Both eastern and western societies have experienced a long period of slavery and feudal rules in history, which were characterized by class oppression and prerogatives. At the top of such societies were the emperors and aristocrats and at the bottom were slaves, surfs and poor peasants. In a slavery society, the slaves were regarded as the tools and the property of slave owners who could sell them and even kill them like animals. In a feudal society, although surfs and poor peasants had a higher status than slaves, they were still dependent on the feudal aristocrats and landlords, who possessed great power over them. In ancient China, emperors and government officials were regarded as "parents" and the ordinary people as "children" or "subjects" . People in such society were divided into different classes according to their birth. Those sprung from noble ancestors were power holders while those sprung from obscurity were obligation bearers. The state was defender of this hierarchical system. In order to suppress the revolt by slaves and surfs, the state adopted harsh laws and cruel punishments. Corporal punishment and the practice of extorting a confession by torture had been prevalent in both eastern and western histories. Although torture was restricted by the law in feudal Chinese society, it had never been prohibited. The practice was handed down from generation to generation and became a part of the system which survived one dynasty after another. The facts that torture still exists in some many countries of the world, that the practice of extorting a confession by torture has resulted in countless unjust, framed-up and wrong cases and that in some countries, police violence is often committed against the black or colored people have provided us with much materials for thought. They remind us of the obnoxious style of work of the feudal government and the slave trade in the 18th century. And they reminded us that event today, 200 years after the overthrown of the feudal system and establishment of the bourgeois system based on "democracy, freedom and equality", it is still necessary to fight against the influence of old traditions and old practices in the field of prohibition of torture as well as in many other fields.

Second, the quality of the relevant personnel. Another important reason for the existence of torture is the low quality of the relevant personnel. Torture is committed by persons. Under the same conditions, the higher the quality of the relevant personnel, the lower the possibility of the occurrence of torture. Quality of personnel includes moral quality and professional quality. Persons with low moral quality tend to abuse their power to pursue fame and personal gains, even to vent personal spite whereas persons with high professional quality are able to strictly implement the relevant policies and laws, abide by professional code of conduct, summarize experience from practice, and find out a proper solution in a difficult situation. China has always attached great importance to the improvement of the quality of judicial and law enforcement personnel and has made great effort in providing judicial and public security organs with excellent and young personnel. In order to strengthen the ranks of judicial and public security personnel and ensure that they perform their functions in accordance with the law, the state adopted in 1995 the Law on Judges, the Law on Public Procurators, and the Law on People's Police. Apart from providing for the powers and functions, obligations, disciplines, supervision and legal responsibilities of such persons, the law also provides for their qualifications and examination systems.

In recent years, the moral and professional qualities of the judicial and law enforcement personnel have been gradually improved and a large number of model judicial and law enforcement personnel have emerged in China. When I visited Denmark in 1998, a friend at a police station in Copenhagen told me that in a recent government survey, the police came out as the public authority which enjoyed the highest degree of public trust in Denmark. We would like very much to learn from the Danish experience in this respect.

Third, the defects in the system. Generally speaking, torture is prohibited by all modern states in terms of institutional design. The constitutions of modern states all contain provisions on the protection of personal freedom and on the prohibition of torture. However, there are often defects and loopholes in the system. For example, some states attach great importance to substantive law but do not pay enough attention to the lawfulness of the procedure. Under circumstances where certain information or confession is urgently needed, the leaders of state organs often condone or even encourage the use of any means, including torture, to obtain such information or confession. Under such circumstance, the policies and laws on the prohibition of torture become mere formalities. Moreover, during the trial of cases, judicial organs often do not pay enough attention to the means by which evidences are obtained and, as a result, often admit evidences which are obtained by unlawful means and by doing so actually legitimized evidences obtained by torture and other unlawful means. Both the Declaration on the Protection of All Persons from Being Subjected to Torture and Other Cruel, Inhuman or Degrading Treatment or Punishment and the Convention against Torture contain specific provisions on evidences obtained by unlawful means. Article 12 of the Declaration provides that: "Any statement which is established to have been made as a result of torture or other cruel, inhuman or degrading treatment or punishment may not be invoked as evidence against the person concerned or against any other person in any proceedings." Article 15 of the Convention provides that: "Each State Party shall ensure that any statement which is established to have been made as a result of torture shall not be invoked as evidence in any proceedings, except against a person accused of torture as evidence that the statement was made." The domestic laws of some western countries contain similar provisions. The implementation of these provisions in practice, however, is another matter. The 1979 Chinese Criminal Procedure Law contained no clear provision on the legal effect of the evidence obtained through unlawful means. After China ratified the Convention against Torture in 1988, some scholars suggested that the Criminal Procedure Law should be revised to include a clear prohibition against the use of evidence obtained through unlawful means as the basis for deciding the case so as to make the law compatible with the Convention. However, this problem was not resolved during the 1996 revision of the Criminal Procedure Law. It was only in 1998 that the Supreme People's Court formally expressed its view on this issue in the document "Interpretations on Several Issues relating to the Implementation of the Criminal Procedure Law of the People's Republic of China". Article 61 of the document provides that: "It is strictly prohibited to collect evidence by unlawful means. Any testimony and statement which is established to have been obtained through torture, threat, inducement, or cheat shall not be invoked as evidence in the court." This interpretation is a great step forward towards making the Chinese law compatible with the Convention against Torture. However, because the Chinese law belongs to the civil law system, the legal effect of judicial interpretation is limited. Further effects should be made to include this principle into the Criminal Procedure Law through legislative process.

Among the above-mentioned three main reasons for the existence of torture in China, the most important and the most basic one is the defective system. By perfecting the system, we can not only stop the loopholes in the system itself, but also change people's attitude towards traditions and enable them to absorb what is good and reject what is bad in Chinese traditions. By perfecting the system, we will be able to improve the quality of relevant personnel through education, to ensure that only qualified persons be recruited by public security and judicial organs and that such organs handle cases in strict accordance with the law.

V. Resolutely Combating Torture

Torture is an important problem of human rights protection faced by the humanity in the 21st century. Despite repeated prohibition by international treaties and domestic laws, the phenomenon of torture is still widespread. This is because, to some people, torture is like stinky fermented bean curd in China, which smells bad, but tastes good. To some other people, it is more like opium or heroine on which they are dependent, not knowing that it will in the end take their own lives. As is mentioned above, torture has existed for thousands of years and has become a chronic illness of mankind. We must resolutely fight against torture, although in order to eradicate torture we have overcome numerous obstacles, even pay high prices. To this end, we must:

First, enhance the consciousness of the prohibition against torture among public officials and the ordinary citizens through education and publicity campaign. To carry out education and publicity campaign is an obligation of the government both under the constitution and other domestic laws and under the international treaties. Article 10 of the Convention against Torture provides that: "1. Each State Party shall ensure that education and information regarding the prohibition against torture are fully included in the training of law enforcement personnel, civil or military, medical personnel, public officials and other persons who may be involved in the custody, interrogation or treatment of any individual subjected to any form of arrest, detention or imprisonment. 2. Each State Party shall include this prohibition in the rules or instructions issued in regard to the duties and functions of any such person." Before the adoption of the Convention, the UN adopted in December 1979 and December 1982, respectively, the Code of Conduct for Law Enforcement Officials and the Principles of Medical Ethics Relevant to the Role of Health Personnel, Particularly Physicians, in the Protection of Prisoners and Detainees against Torture and Other Cruel, Inhuman or Degrading Treatment or

Punishment. The above codes of conducts were adopted to ensure civilized law enforcement and the prohibition of torture and therefore should be included in the training of law enforcement personnel, civil or military, medical personnel, and public officials. In China, the Constitution, the Criminal Law, the Criminal Procedure Law, the Administrative Procedure Law, the State Compensation Law, the Law on Judges, the Law on Public Prosecutors, and the Law on People's Police all contain provisions on the protection of the fundamental rights and freedoms of citizens and on the prohibition against torture. During three consecutive "Five-year National Legal Education and Publicity Campaigns", the above provisions have been widely disseminated among the relevant personnel and very good results have been achieved. However, in carrying out such education and publicity campaign, we must attach equal importance to both teaching by precept and teaching by example. That is to say, law enforcement, judicial and other officials must conscientiously fulfill their obligations under the law and international treaties. They must guard against the practice of saying one thing and doing another thing, which will cause people to lose confidence in the Convention, in the relevant laws, even in the government. The legal provisions and the international treaties against torture are the result of long-term struggle by the people of various countries and the crystallization of the development civilization. The dissemination and the implementation of the laws and the convention against torture will promote the progress of civilization in each country and in the whole world.

Second, further perfect the laws and mechanisms against torture. Since defects in the legal system are the most important and fundamental cause of torture, further perfection of the legal system is the key to the effective prevention of torture. Generally speaking, the domestic laws of each state party to the Convention against Torture should ensure that its domestic law is compatible with the Convention and each government shall fulfill its obligation under the Convention. In fact, article 2 and article 4 of the Convention against Torture have already provided for specific requirements on the domestic legal mechanism in each state party to the Convention. Article 2 of the Convention stipulates that: "1. Each State Party shall take effective legislative, administrative, judicial or other measures to prevent acts of torture in any territory under its jurisdiction. 2. No exceptional circumstances whatsoever, whether a state of war or a threat of war, internal political instability or any other public emergency, may be invoked as a justification of torture." Article 4 provides that: "Each State Party shall ensure that all acts of torture are offences under its criminal law. The same shall apply to an attempt to commit torture and to an act by any person which constitutes complicity or participation in torture." The Chinese law is basically compatible with the Convention, but further improvement is still necessary. For example, with the improvement of the public security situations in the country, the severity of punishment for some kinds of crimes and the number of crimes punishable by death in the Criminal Law should be reduced. The Criminal Procedure Law should clearly prohibit the use of evidence collected by unlawful means, especially by torture, as the basis for deciding the case.

In view of the fact that in many countries judicial activities are often interfere in by administrative organs and other organs and organizations, more efforts should be made in these countries to further safeguard judicial independence. In China, the system related to the appointment of judicial officials must be further perfected. Otherwise, it is not possible to implement the provisions of the Constitution and other laws relating to the independent exercise of functions and powers by judicial organs. Currently, there is an urgent need to promote judicial reform and the relevant political reforms.

Third, conscientiously implement the provisions relating to legal remedies for the victims of torture. Article 11 of Declaration on the Protection of All Persons from Being Subjected to Torture and Other Cruel, Inhuman or Degrading Treatment or Punishment provides that: "Where it is proved that an act of torture or other cruel, inhuman or degrading treatment or punishment has been committed by or at the instigation of a public official, the victim shall be afforded redress and compensation in accordance with national law." Article 14 of the Convention against Torture provides that "1. Each State Party shall ensure in its legal system that the victim of an act of torture obtains redress and has an enforceable right to fair and adequate compensation, including the means for as full rehabilitation as possible. In the event of the death of the victim as a result of an act of torture, his dependants shall be entitled to compensation. 2. Nothing in this article shall affect any right of the victim or other persons to compensation which may exist under national law." The above provisions in the Declaration and the Convention are thorough and comprehensive. One of the criteria for judging a state party's attitude towards torture is whether it has established corresponding judicial mechanism for the implementation of the Convention. There are many examples in which state organs, out of considerations of their own "interests" or "reputation", have adopted an attitude of "no trial without a complaint", "reconciliation" or "officials shield one another" when dealing with cases of torture. By adopting this attitude, they have in fact encouraged the act of torture, whether intentionally or unintentionally, and exerted a negative influence on the training of personnel, on the construction of relevant institutions, as well as on the rule of law in general.

In order to ensure that citizens, legal persons and other organizations whose rights and interests have been infringed by state organs or state personnel receive timely and adequate compensation, China adopted in May 1994 the State Compensation Law. Article 3 of the Law provides that: "The victim shall have the right to compensation if an administrative organ or its functionaries, in exercising their administrative functions and powers, commit any of the following acts infringing upon the right of the person of a citizen: 1. detaining a citizen in violation of the law or unlawfully taking compulsory administrative measures in restraint of his personal freedom; 2. unlawfully taking a citizen into custody or depriving him of his right of the person by other unlawful means; 3. using or instigating violence such as beating one up, thereby causing bodily injury or death to a citizen; 4. unlawfully using weapons or police restraint implements, thereby causing bodily injury or death to a citizen; or 5. other unlawful acts causing bodily injury or death to a citizen." Article 14 of the same Law provides that: "The victim shall have the right to compensation if an organ in charge of investigatory, prosecuratorial, judicial or prison administration work, or its functionaries, infringes upon his right of the persons in the exercise of its functions and powers in any of the following circumstances: 1. wrong detention of a person without incriminating facts or proof substantiating a strong suspicion of the commission of a crime; 2. wrong arrest of a person without incriminating facts; 3. innocence is found in a retrial held in accordance with the procedure of trial supervision, but the original sentence has already been executed; 4. extortion of a confession by torture or causing bodily injury or death to a citizen by using or instigating the use of violence such as beating one up; or 5. causing bodily injury or death to a citizen by the unlawful use of weapons or police restraint implements." Compared with those of other countries, the State Compensation Law in China is very thorough and comprehensive. The conscientious implementation of the law will have a great impact on administration by law, on judicial fairness, especially on the prohibition against torture.

Forth, strengthen the supervision over law enforcement, judicial and all other organs or persons acting in an official capacity. Supervision is an important precondition for ensuring that all public authorities and persons acting in an official capacity strictly observe the Convention against Torture and the relevant domestic laws. Article 11 of the Convention against Torture provides that: "Each State Party shall keep under systematic review interrogation rules, instructions, methods and practices as well as arrangements for the custody and treatment of persons subjected to any form of arrest, detention or imprisonment in any territory under its jurisdiction, with a view to preventing any case of torture." This is a kind of antecedent supervision. Meanwhile, the Convention also provides for post supervision in article 12: "Each State Party shall ensure that its competent authorities proceed to a prompt and impartial investigation, wherever there is reasonable ground to believe that an act of torture has been committed in any territory under its jurisdiction." Apart from providing for the obligation of state parties to carry out supervision, the Convention also establishes the Committee against Torture to carry out international supervision. Article 19 and article 20 of the Convention provide for a system whereby the state parties submit to the Committee against Torture, through UN Secretary-general, periodical and non-periodical reports and a system whereby the Committee may carry out investigations within the territory of a state party. Such kind of international supervision is conducive to the implementation of the Convention, as long as it is carried out objectively and fairly, not manipulated by some big powers with ulterior motives. It has been proved that, among various kinds of supervision, the supervision by mass media is a relatively effective one. The state should make public through the mass media information about the cases of torture that have occurred, their consequences, the handling of such cases, and the remedies. To some states, this kind of supervision may be embarrassing. However, they should welcome it as long as it is required by the principles of humanity and the rule of law, by the safeguarding of the interested of the people, and by the long-term peace and stability of the country.

Torture is a chronic illness of human society that has constituted a serious danger to the civilization. The fact that the international community has jointly adopted measures to combat torture marks the progress of human civilization. Nevertheless, today torture is still a main threat to human society. Practice has proved that combating torture is a complicated and arduous task. The key to combating torture lies not only in the education of the relevant personnel, helping them to change their ideas and freeing them from the influence of the traditional practices, but also in the reforming and perfecting of the relevant systems.

Ladies and gentlemen, it is the opinion of all the participants that the seminar is a success. Before concluding my speech, I would like to express my sincere thanks to the CASS Law Institute and the Danish Center for Human Rights that have successfully organized this seminar and to the experts, scholars, lawyers, procurators and police officials whose excellent speeches, profound ideas and rich knowledge have benefited all of us. Finally, I would like to ask Professor Hatla Thelle to convey our gratitude to the Danish Foreign Ministry, the Ministry of International Co-operation, and the Minister of International Cooperation, who have given generous support to the CASS-DCHR Cooperation Project on the Prevention of Torture. This seminar is a part of that Project.

Influence of Tradition Criminal Law Thoughts on the Modern Death Penalty System in China[①]

Today's reality comes from the past history. As the most severe criminal punishment, the death penalty has its own history of emergence and development. Currently some countries in the world have already abolished the death penalty, some have stopped the application of the death penalty, still some others have not yet abolished the death penalty, but are very cautious in applying this form of punishment. Although China belongs to this last category of countries, discussions have already begun in China on the abolition of the death penalty. In the process of long historical development, the death penalty, as compared to the practice of slaughtering or eating all captured enemies in the age of barbarism, was a historical progress and a symbol of development of human civilization.

Of course, whether or not a country should abolish the death penalty is determined neither by the eloquent talks in the academic circle, nor by the number of countries that have already abolished the death penalty in the world, but mainly by the history, current reality, and the comprehensive political, economic, and cultural conditions in the country. It is for this reason that the International Covenant on Civil and Political Rights, adopted by the UN in 1966 and came into effect in 1976, uses very cautious wording in the provision on the death penalty. I believe that the abolition of the death penalty is a long process that can be completed only when necessary conditions are created. In order to shorten this process, it is necessary to carry out research on the influence of traditional Chinese criminal law thought on the idea and system of death

---

① Originally published in Liu Hainian et. al (eds.), *Human Rights and Administration of Justice*, Beijing: China Legal System Publishing House, 1999.

penalty in contemporary China.

Since very early in history, the Chinese people have believed that thereis another world beyond this world and that when a person dies, his soul does not perish, but would transmigrate into another life. And this other world was described by some people as a wonderful paradise. But even in ancient times, death was still regarded as a terrible thing because every human being has the natural instinct to stay alive. Throughout history, the death penalty, which was originated from the custom of "talion" (an eye for an eye, a tooth for a tooth), have been considered as the severest form of criminal punishment. Historical records show that, although the death penalty was originally used as a means of revenge, it has been applied since ancient Chinese history as a form of punishment. Therefore, its use had exceeded the scope of simple "talion", both in terms of law and in terms of practice.

Among the existing ancient books and records, there is a statement issued by the first ruler of the Xia Dynasty (which is believed by historians as the Chinese dynasty in which the state machinery and the law had first taken form). This proclamation, which is considered to be a military criminal law document, contains the following passage: "I have now received an order from God to send army to exterminate Youhu, who is disrespectful to the Xia Empire and refuses to obey the heavenly laws. Those who obey my orders will be rewarded before the spirit tablets of the ancestors and those who disobey my orders will be put to death before the spirit tablets of ancestors and their families will suffer the same fate."[1] It shows that death penalty was not only imposed on those who had killed other people, but also on people like Youhu, who showed disrespect to the emperor or did not obey the heavenly laws. This was called "severe punishment executed through the act of war" in ancient historical records. Moreover, death penalty was also imposed on those in the emperors own army who disobey his orders, even on their family members. The despotic rule in the end of the Xia Dynasty and the indiscriminate killing of innocent people by Emperor Zhou in the end of Yin Dynasty had resulted in social turmoils and ultimate collapse of both dynasties. Drawing a lesson from the collapse of these two dynasties, the rulers of the Western Zhou Dynasty had adopted the principle of "developing benevolent rule and being cautious in the imposition of

① See Shang shu, Ganshi.

criminal punishment" (Ming De Shen Fa)[1]. Its main content include: to conduct detailed analysis of crimes so as to distinguish those committed intentionally from those committed out of negligence; to differentiate those who had committed crimes repeatedly from those who had no previous criminal record; and to abolish the practices of imposing death penalty on the family members of offenders and the indiscriminate killing of innocent people. Although this principle had not been, nor was it possible for it to be, strictly obeyed, the mere fact that such a principle was adopted at that time was remarkable. It played an important role in stabilizing the political power of the Western Zhou Dynasty and had exerted a profound influence on succeeding dynasties.

The principles of the rule of virtue, the rule of rites (*li*) and the rule of benevolence are the core contents of Confucianism, which is the school of philosophy that had the greatest influence on the traditional legal thoughts in China. These principles were developed on the basis of the principle of "developing benevolent rule and being cautious in the imposition of criminal punishment" of the idealized codes and systems of the Western Zhou Dynasty. The Confucians attached great importance to the "rule of benevolence", which has many different interpretations. Confucius had said that "benevolence is to be humane."[2] Mencius had said that "benevolence is the love of mankind"[3] and that "a benevolent man shows kindness not only to the people he likes, but also to the people he does not like."[4] All these showed that benevolence means the love of human beings and is the opposite of tyranny. Although the Confucian thoughts was later called into question and criticized by the legalists, after long period of debate and practice, the Chinese ruling class had finally reached a consensus on the need for implementing the "rule of benevolence" and the political and legal systems in ancient China, which were based on the natural economy and patriarchal clan system, had apparently embodied the ideas of both the Confucianism and Legalism. Throughout history, the Rule of Benevolence had been the goal pursued by the rulers of various dynasties. It had also been the criterion used to evaluate the achievements of all the rulers.

---

① See Shangshu, Kangku

② See Book of Rites, the Principle of the Mean..

③ See Mencius, Lilou. vol. II.

④ See Mencius, With All My Heart, vol. II.

In order to realize the rule of benevolence and avoid the killing of innocent people, the scholars in ancient China had developed theories on the purposes and principles of criminal punishment. According to these theories, the purposes of criminal punishment was "to reduce and eliminate crimes"①, thereby "gradually reducing and stop the use of criminal punishment". ②This shows that, as early as 2, 000 years ago, some people in China had already put forward the idea of abolition of death penalty. The principle for the application of criminal punishment was based on the understanding of the nature of criminal punishment. Xun Zi said that "the application of criminal punishment, like granting titles, offering official positions or bestowing gifts, is giving a person what he deserves."③ According to him, criminal punishment is a kind of retribution or revenge and "the severity of criminal punishment should not exceed that of the crime to be punished."④ He also pointed out that "If criminal punishments are proportional to crimes, there will be peace and prosperity; if not, there will be chaos."⑤ Xun Zi's philosophy was quite advanced, considering that he lived in a highly hierarchical society during the period between 400—300 BC, when arbitrary punishment against slaves and ordinary people were the prevailing practice.

Since Xun Zi's idea reflected the demand of the times, it had exerted certain influence on the legislation in ancient China. For example, his principles had been embodied in the Qin Code which was adopted after the Shang Yang Reform. The Qin Code provided that only those who had stolen 660 *qian* or more worth of property could be considered as having committed felony and be given severe punishment;⑥ it divided crimes into two categories: intentional crimes and criminal negligence and provided for more severe punishment for the former; the Qin Code also provided that when arresting an offender, the officers should not take a compulsory measure against him that is more severe than the criminal punishment that he may receive for the crime he had committed. When Liu Bang, a famous

① See Zuozhuan, 11th year of Yinggong.

② See Book of Shangjun, Reword and Punishment.

③ See Xunzi, On Justice.

④ See Xunzi, Gentlemen.

⑤ See Xun Zhi, Zhenglun.

⑥ *Bamboo Slips of the Qin Dynasty Unearthed in Shuihudi, Yunmeng County, Answers to Legal Questions.*

emperor in the end of the 3rd century BC, had taken the central China, the first measure he took was to issue a proclamation abolishing the harsh laws of the Qin Dynasty and to provide that "Those who have committed murder shall be punished by death and those who injure others or steal shall be punished according to the severity of their offenses."① Because this measure embodied the principle of social justice, it had won the support of the people and produced good social effects. As a result, Liu Bang not only quickly stabilized the situation in Guangzhong and Sanqin area, but also defeated Xiang Yu, his main competitor, thereby laying a sound basis for a strong Han Dynasty. One of the important results of the influence of the principle of "developing benevolent rule and being cautious in the application of criminal punishment" was that, even under the feudal autocracy, some emperors also used the law to regulate their own behavior and the behaviors of the classes they represent. After the Qin Dynasty, the founders of almost every new dynasty would draw a lesson from the collapse of the previous dynasty and promulgate new laws providing for more lenient criminal punishments than those of the previous dynasty: the Nine-Chapter Code of the Han Dynasty was more lenient than the Qin Code; the codes of Wei and Jin dynasties were more lenient than the Han Code; the Shui Code was more lenient than the codes of Wei and Jin dynasties; the codes of Tang and Song dynasties were more lenient than codes of Shui Dynasty; the codes of the Ming and Qing dynasties were in turn more lenient than the codes of Tang and Song dynasties. Generally speaking, all the open-minded emperors in time of peace and prosperity took strict internal discipline, streamlined administration and lenient criminal punishment as the criteria of good governance.

In order to implement the principle of "developing the rule of benevolence and being cautious in the application of criminal punishment", the rulers of various dynasties, apart from continuously improving substantive laws, also paid attention to the reform of procedural law. The Criminal Law of Lu in the Western Zhou Dynasty provided that "during the trial of a case, the judge should listen to both the plaintiff and the defendant." The Qin Code stipulated that "To obtain confession without the use of torture is the best method of interrogating criminal suspects; the use of torture is a bad method of interrogation; and the use

① Book of History, Basic Annals of Gao Zu.

of terror is a failure in interrogation."[①] The Qin Code also provided that torture could be used only on the criminal suspects who refuse to admit crime or repeatedly change confession. The use of torture should be mentioned in the interrogation records.[②]

The Han Code provided for a system of submitting difficult cases to the judicial organs at the higher level for decision. It prohibited the execution of prisoners in Spring and Autumn and provided for the system of keeping records of all prisoners. The Tang Code provided for a special procedure to prevent mistakes in the execution of criminals: "Within two days of the execution of a death sentence, the case should be reported to the emperor for review. A case in the capital should be reviewed five times and a case in a province should be reviewed three times."[③] In Ming and Qing dynasties, the population in the country had increased and, in order to more carefully review cases in which the death penalty and other severe punishments were imposed, the government followed the system of the Tang Dynasty whereby every year after the Frost's Descent, the emperor would designated three high ranking judicial officers and other officers to review the death penalty cases submitted by the judicial organs in the capital and various provinces. After the review, all the cases were divided into five categories, namely those which have been verified; those in which the death sentence may be suspended; those in which death penalty should be imposed cautiously and leniency may be shown towards the offenders; those in which there were still some doubts; and those in which the offenders may be spared to continue the family line. Apart from the verified cases, the offenders in all the other cases had a chance to be spared of their live.

Mainly influenced by Confucianism, traditionalChinese criminal law thought has a rich color of humanism, which means to take the people as the basis of the state. Ancient Chinese rulers realized that the support of the people was the motive force for the prosperity of the country and the basic guarantee of the security of the state power. Mencius said that "The people are more important than the state and the state is more important

---

① *Bamboo Slips of the Qin Dynasty Unearthed in Shuihudi*, Yunmeng County, Fengzhenshi.

② Ibid.

③ Zi Zhi Tong Jian, Tang Ji Jiu.

than the kings and emperors."① Li Shiming, the first emperor of the Tang Dynasty, also said that "the rulers are like a boat and the people are like the water; Just as the water can carry the boat, it can also capsize the boat."② On the basis of this understanding, he noted that "Only the emperors who follow the Way will be recognized by the people as their rulers; those who do not follow the Way will ultimately be abandoned by the people."③

Such a humanistic idea came from the understanding of the human nature and the lessons learned from real life. According to the Confucian philosophy, "all human beings are kind-hearted in the beginning of their live," whether a person will remain kind-hearted or become evil is determined by the education he receives afterwards. The lessons learned by Chinese rulers from real life were reflected in their fear of the rebellion by the people: it was no coincidence that every major policy change in the Chinese history was related to large-scale wars and peasant uprisings.

All human beings live in specific historical conditions and all ideas and systems, including the ideas and systems of the death penalty, are influenced by historical traditions. The followings are the main manifestations of the influence of traditional criminal law thoughts on the current death penalty system in China:

1. Prudence in imposing criminal punishment. After the founding of the New China, the People's Government, headed by Mao Zedong, issued an instruction that "the death penalty shall not be imposed unless it is absolutely necessary to do so." This guiding principle had given certain discretional power to judges who had the complete power over lives and death of offenders, so that they could be more lenient. This instruction was indeed very important to the judges who were working in an extremely "Left" environment. It was based on this principle that China refrained from taking "an eye for an eye and a tooth for a tooth" measures against the war criminals whose hands were stained with the blood of the Chinese people and the emperor of the Puppet Manchu State. Instead, the Chinese government had made great effort to educate and reform these criminals so as to help them to turn over a new leaf. This policy has been proved very successful in practice and praised by people all over the world.

---

① Mencius. With All My Heart. Vol. II.

② Chronicles of Zhenguan, A Moral Lesson to the Princes and Dukes.

③ Chronicles of Zhenguan, Political System.

2. Leniency in imposing criminal punishment. The balancing between sentiment and the law is one of the important contents of traditional criminal thought in China. This principle is embodied in the handling of juvenile delinquents, especially those who have committed capital crimes. Article 44 of the 1979 Criminal Law provided that the death penalty shall not be imposed on persons who had not reached the age of 18 at the time the crime was committed or on women who are pregnant at the time of trial. The reason why the death penalty is not imposed on persons who have not reached the age of 18 is that before that age they have not yet reached physical and psychological maturity. As a result, they lack the ability of self-control and the ability to distinguish the good from the bad. Therefore, efforts should be made to educate these young people and help them to turn a new leaf. However, the same article also provided that "Persons who have reached the age of 16 but not the age of 18 may be sentenced to death with a two-year suspension of execution if the crime committed was particularly serious." This was contradictory to the previous provision that "death penalty shall not be imposed on persons who have not reached the ago of 18" because death penalty with a two-year suspension of execution is still death penalty, only with a special method of execution. Article 49 of the 1997 Criminal Law abolishes the imposition of death penalty with a two-year suspension of execution on juvenile offenders, thereby better embodying the principle of leniency in criminal legislation.

3. Suspension of the execution of criminal punishment. The suspension of criminal punishment in modern Chinese criminal law embodies the principles of prudence and leniency. It is a system whereby the criminal punishment imposed on an offender is suspended for a prescribed period of time under certain circumstances. These circumstances include: the offender has no previous criminal record and can be reformed through education; the circumstances of the crime is not serious; or the offender has special needs or special difficulties. The death penalty with a two-year suspension of execution, as discussed earlier in this article, belongs to the category of the death penalty. This system, although should not be considered as the continuation of the system of "suspended death by decapitation" or "suspended death by hanging" in ancient China, is certainly influenced by the ancient system and by the traditional criminal law thoughts. At least the subjective and objective conditions in the modern system are similar to those in the ancient system. Namely, both are imposed on offenders who have committed capital crimes but need not to be

executed immediately because there are circumstances for leniency, because the offender could provide important evidence if kept alive, or because he has important social relations, etc. In judicial practice, a person sentenced to death with a two-year suspension of execution generally will not be executed unless he shows no remorse and commits new crime during the period of suspension.

4. The idea of retribution of the same kind. Since Xun Zi put forward the theory that criminal punishment was a kind of retribution and Liu Bang adopted the law of three points that "Those who kill shall be punished by death and those who injure others or steal shall be punished in light of the seriousness of their offenses", the idea of retribution of the same kind had influenced the criminal law in China for over 2, 000 years. "Those who kill shall be punished by death" had become not only a legal principle that guided the judicial practice in China, but also a deep-rooted belief of the Chinese people. "Those who have taken the lives of others should pay back with their own lives just as those who have taken money from others should pay back with their own money" is a well-known saying in China. Under the feudal hierarchical system, this could be considered as a historically progressive idea. Even today, this idea still has important practical significance because it embodies the principle of equality and impartiality under many circumstances. Article 4 of the 1997 Criminal Law provides that "The law shall be equally applied to anyone who commits a crime. No one shall have the privilege of transcending the law." But now the problem is that sometimes the principle of "those who kill shall be punished by death" or "he who takes another's life shall pay back with his own life" is understood by some people in an over-simplified or extreme way. Simply taking "a life for a life" or "the popular indignation cannot be assuaged if the death penalty is not imposed on those who kill others" as the guiding principles in criminal legislation or judicial practice, without taking into consideration such factors as whether the crime is committed intentionally or negligently, whether the acts of the victim had contributed to the commission of the crimes, etc., will result in serious consequences.

To sum up, the traditional Chinese criminal law thought has both positive and negative influences on modern ideas and system of the death penalty in China. What we need to do is to eliminate the negative influences and enhance the positive influences. However, under certain circumstances and in certain cases, a large amount of works need to be done by the government in order to avoid the imposition of the death penalty. Therefore, with regard to the abolition of death penalty, we should not take unduly hasty or radical measures without taking into consideration the objective and subjective conditions, although the issue could be studied by the scholars and discussed among the general public. Otherwise, in the event of the occurrence of vicious criminal cases, it would be difficult to prevent people from taking justice into their own hand or seeking revenge by resorting to the help of Mafia-style social forces; in many urban and rural areas where people belonging to the same clan tend to live together, large-scale fighting with weapons may break out between different clans, resulting in social unrest. If so, the number of people killed and the social losses resulting from the abolition of the death penalty may far exceed those resulting from the application of the death penalty.

Therefore, in dealing with the issue of the death penalty, we should not indulge ourselves in illusion, but proceed from the actual conditions in China. We should first try our best to reduce the provisions in the Criminal Law that impose the death penalty and to be prudent in judicial practice so as to reduce the application of death penalty and eliminate the miscarriage of justice in death penalty cases. By making continuous efforts in tackling the problem in a comprehensive way, creating condition of long-term social stability, and improving public order situations, we will ultimately be able to abolish the death penalty in China.

Restriction, Reduction, and Abolition of the Death Penalty[①]

I

The death penalty is a criminal punishment that has been widely applied throughout the world for thousands of years. The fact that today the experts, scholars and government officials from China and EU countries are sitting together to discuss the retention or abolition of this form criminal punishment once considered to be perfectly justified is an indication of the progress of human civilization. Some European and American friends have doubts about the significance of the human rights dialogue advocated by the Chinese government. I think that the fact that the death penalty is made an important topic of today's seminar itself can dispel their doubts. I believe that this seminar is conducive to the exchange of information and opinions between Chinese and European scholars and to the deepening of their understanding of the issue of death penalty.

II

The so-called death penalty is the criminal punishment whereby state organs deprive the life of criminals through trial procedure in accordance with the relevant provisions of the criminal law. In China, the death penalty is also called capital punishment, as it is the most severe and cruel form of criminal punishment. This is not only because the method of execution is cruel, but also because life, as the carrier of human value, is the most precious thing to a human being. When a person is deprived of his life, all his other values also disappear with it.

---

① Originally the keynote speech given by the author at the Sixth EU-China Seminar on Administration of Justice and Human Rights.

III

Although the death penalty is cruel, it should not be equaled with torture or corporal punishment, which had been applied as a form of legal punishment in ancient times, both in China and in the West, and is still legally applied in some countries of the world even today. Whether the imposition of the death penalty constitutes torture depends on the following three questions:

1. Whether it is imposed in accordance with law?
2. Whether such law embodies the will of the people and the principle of fairness? and
3. Whether such law has been abused or trampled upon?

If the death penalty is imposed by abusing the law, resulting in the harm of innocent people, it should be considered as torture, even under the feudal autocratic system under which whatever the emperor said became law, although under such a system it was impossible to prohibit such act by law. 2100 years ago, the great Chinese historian Sima Qian wrote the Historical Records (Shi Ji), which recorded the implementation of cruel laws by some emperors and government official in the previous dynasties. The book contains a special chapter entitled Cruel Officials, which recorded some high ranking government officials who used various cruel methods to inflict physical and mental torture on and destroy the life of others. These acts of abuse of criminal punishments are still considered constituting torture even today whereas the imposition of the death penalty by emperors and ministers in ancient times in accordance with law is not. Today we do not come here to discuss history, but to use historical examples to show that distinctions have been made between the death penalty and torture since ancient time. In other words, established laws have always generally respected in all countries and times.

IV

In today's world, distinction is also made between torture and the death penalty by a series of international human rights conventions. Torture is strictly prohibited. The Universal Declaration of Human Rights provides in Article 5 that "No one shall be subjected to torture or to cruel, inhuman or degrading treatment or punishment." And the International Covenant on Civil and Political Rights (ICCPR) provides in Article 7 that that "No one shall be subjected to torture or to cruel, inhuman or degrading treatment or punishment. In particular, no one shall be subjected without his free consent to medical or scientific experimentation." To ensure the observance of the above provisions, the UN General Assembly adopted the Declaration on the Protection of All Persons from Being Subjected to Torture and Other Cruel, Inhuman or Degrading Treatment or Punishment in 1975 and the Convention against Torture and Other Cruel, Inhuman or Degrading Treatment or Punishment 1984, and established corresponding supervisory mechanism and the sate party reporting system. This is not the case for the death penalty. The ICCPR provides in Article 6 Paragraph 2 that: "In countries which have not abolished the death penalty, sentence of death may be imposed only for the most serious crimes... This penalty can only be carried out pursuant to a final judgement rendered by a competent court." This provision shows that the death penalty is not prohibited by the Covenant. Today, many countries still apply the death penalty as a punishment for crimes. However, just as pointed out in the above-mentioned provision, the death can be imposed only for the most serious crimes and can be carried out only pursuant to a final judgement rendered by a competent court. After the adoption of the ICCPR, the UN General Assembly adopted in 1989 the Second Optional Protocol to the ICCPR, which pointed out that "abolition of the death penalty contributes to enhancement of human dignity and progressive development of human rights" and that "all measures of abolition of the death penalty should be considered as progress in the enjoyment of the right to life" and calls on all countries that still retain the death penalty to abolish the penalty. The UN Human Rights Commission adopted a series of resolutions in 1997, 1998 and 1999, urging states that have not yet abolished the death penalty to stop executing or abolish the punishment. However, all the above are moral appeals, rather than legally binding provisions. The question of whether or not to abolish the death penalty should be determined by each sovereign state in light of its own national conditions.

V

The debate over the abolition of the death penalty has been going on for many years among law practitioners, legal scholars and social activists both at the international and domestic levels. Although the general trend becomes gradually clear, no universal consensus has been reached. Professor Hu Yunteng from the Law Institute of the Chinese Academy of Social Sciences published a book in 1999 entitled the Death Penalty: Retention or Abolition, which lists 16 arguments for and 16 arguments against the death penalty. Because of the time constraint, here I will not remunerate these arguments. If you have any question about these arguments, please read this book or ask Professor Hu Yuteng himself (he is sitting right here at the rostrum right now). In my opinion, the question of whether a country should abolish the death penalty must be considered in light of the historical and cultural background, the level of social, economic and cultural development, especially the will of the people of that country. In short, this issue should be considered on case-by-case basis, rather in abstract. It is even less desirable to impose one model on all countries. The death penalty is the most severe and costly criminal punishment, which no state should or will readily apply. However, modern states have the primary task of upholding social order necessary for ensuring the free, happy, and peaceful live of the people and safeguarding the security of their life and property. Of course, if such an order can be maintained without the application of the death penalty, China should abolish the death penalty without any hesitation. However, if the abolition of the death penalty will increase vicious crimes and endanger the life, freedom, welfare and peace of the people, then China has to choose to retain the death penalty as the lesser of two evils. Politicians in modern democratic states have to consider the will of the majority of the people when making the above-mentioned choice. This is the reality of most countries in the world, including China. Although, because of the differences in historical and cultural background, social system, and level of economic development, China and EU have different understanding of and adopted different policies and laws on the death penalty, I believe that they have one thing in common: they both have to follow the will of their own people when making decisions on this issue.

VI

China is a country that retains the death penalty and also the country with the largest number of capital crimes in the criminal law. Although, after the revision in 1997, the current Chinese criminal law contains less capital crimes than before the revision, it still contains 68 kinds of capital crimes, including seven crimes of endangering national security, 14 crimes of endangering military interest and the interest of national defense, 16 crimes of disrupting economic order, 14 crimes of endangering public security, eight crimes of obstructing the administration of public order, five crimes of infringing upon citizens' right of the person and democratic rights, and four crimes of embezzlement, bribery and other property violations. Among the countries that have not abolished the death penalty, China has the largest number of capital crimes in the criminal law. However, a close examination of these crimes shows that many of them, such as crimes of endangering national security and military interest, have never or rarely been applied. Among the crimes of robbery and theft, only extremely serious robberies of banks or other financial institutions and extremely serious thefts of precious cultural relics are punishable by death. Moreover, China has imposed strict restrictions on the application of the death penalty both in terms of substantive law and in terms of procedural law.

1. The Chinese Criminal Law provides in Article 48 that: "The death penalty shall only be applied to criminals who have committed extremely serious crimes." This provision is in line with Article 6 of the ICCPR, which provides that: "sentence of death may be imposed only for the most serious crimes", with the term "extremely serious crimes" in Chinese Criminal Law corresponding to term "the most serious crimes" in the ICCPR.

2. Article 48 of the Chinese Criminal Law also provides that: "If the immediate execution of a criminal punishable by death is not deemed necessary, a two-year suspension of execution may be pronounced simultaneously with the imposition of the death sentence." As far as I know, among criminals sentenced to death with two-year suspension of execution, over 99% have their sentences commuted to life imprisonment or fixed-term imprisonment of 20 years upon the expiration of the two-year period.

3. Article 49 of the Chinese Criminal Law provides that: "The death penalty shall not be imposed on persons who have not reached the age of 18 at the time the crime is committed or on women who are pregnant at the time of trial." Here, "women who are pregnant at the time of trial" include women who are pregnant at the stage of criminal investigation, and "the imposition of death penalty" refers to both imposition and execution

of the sentence of death.

4. Of persons who have committed capital crimes, only those whose circumstances of crime are particularly serious, namely those who have committed murder, arson, poisoning, setting off explosion, rape, kidnapping, trafficking in women and children, and drug trafficking and resulted in particularly serious consequences, will be sentenced to death. With respect to the crime intentional killing, if the victim has fault or the perpetrator confesses the crime, voluntarily surrenders himself, or performs meritorious services after commission of the crime, a two-year suspension of execution may be pronounced simultaneously with the imposition of the death sentence or the death sentence may be commuted to life imprisonment.

5. The Chinese law also provides for strict trial and review procedures for the imposition of the death penalty. China implements a trial system whereby the second instance is final. Cases of capital crimes and other major crimes are tried by an intermediate court in the first instance and higher court in the second instance. The Chinese Criminal Law provides that: "Except for judgments made by the Supreme People's Court according to law, all sentences of death shall be submitted to the Supreme People's Court for approval. Sentences of death with suspension of execution may be decided or approved by a high people's court." Such a review procedure can effectively prevent irreversible miscarriage of justice.

VII

Although the retention by China of the death penalty is allowed by international conventions and the Chinese law have provided for many restrictions on the application of the death penalty, there has been debates in Chinese academic and law circles on the question of whether to reduce the capital crimes in the Criminal Law. Before the revision of the Criminal Law in 1997, Professor Hu Yunteng and I submitted to the organ of state power a report on the death penalty on the basis of long period of research and preparation. This report, which has now been published, discusses the international trend of development toward the restriction and abolition of the death penalty, the relevant Chinese historical experiences, the criminal policies adopted by China in the past 20 years and their results, the change in crime rates in countries that have very few number of execution or stopped the execution of the death sentences, as well as those that have abolished the death penalty, and puts forward suggestions and recommendations on the reduction of the capital crimes in the Criminal Law. Regrettably, most of these suggestions and recommendations in the report have not been adopted by the state legislative organ.

We advocate reducing the use of the death penalty, but do not believe that the abolition of the death penalty is desirable under the currentcircumstances in China. In a sample investigation carried out by a Chinese legal research institution some years ago, 95% of the interviewees were against the abolition of the death penalty. Therefore, the current Chinese policy on the death penalty conforms to the will of the majority of the Chinese people. In my opinion, the main reasons why the majority of the Chinese people are against the abolition of the death penalty and a large number of capital crimes have been retained in the revision of the Criminal Law in 1997 are the followings:

1. In modern Chinese history, the invasion by western powers and Japanese militarists had resulted in over a century of wars and chaos. After the founding of the New China, China had enjoyed a short period of peaceful construction in the 1950s. However, under the guidance of erroneous ideological lines, Chinese leaders launched a series of political movements, such as the "Cultural Revolution", which again threw the country into chaos and seriously affected the economic development in China. During the more than 20 years of economic construction since 1978, the Chinese people have learnt that economic, scientific and cultural development depends on a peaceful and stable social environment and they demand harsh punishment of crimes, especially vicious crimes, that undermine such environment.

2. Currently China is in the process of transition from the planned economy to the market economy and of adjustment of social structure. In this process, some government officials abuse the power in their hand to seek personal gains and trade power for money. The Chinese people have a deep-seated hatred for these corrupt officials; with the widening gap in economic income, some people are consumed by greed and try to get rich by any means. Because of low cultural quality and weak consciousness of law, they commit all kinds of vicious crimes, such murder, arson, poisoning, setting off explosion, and kidnapping and trafficking in women and children. The death penalty must be imposed on these criminals.

3. Since the reform and opening up, citizens are enjoying more and more freedom of movement and the movement of population both within and

between national boarders is increasing. Since the southwest part of China boarders the drug-producing "Golden Triangle", activities of drug-trafficking and the population of drug users have been increasing rapidly in China in the past two or three decades. In history, the narcotic drug opium had cause great physical and mental harms to the Chinese nation: poisoned by opium, the Chinese people were once known as "the sick man of Asia" and after losing the Opium War, the China was forced to cede territory and pay indemnities to western invaders. Because of this humiliating history, the Chinese people strongly demand severe punishment for drug-related crimes. This, in addition to the international obligation undertaken by the Chinese government to fight against drug-related crime, has made it necessary for China to apply the death penalty to those who have committed the most serious forms of drug-related crimes.

4. Since such traditional Chinese ideas as "those who kill others shall be punished by death and those who wound others shall be given corresponding criminal punishments" and "those who take the life of others shall pay back with their own life, just as those who take money from others shall pay back with their own money" contain simple philosophy of equality, they have been passed down from generation to generation for thousands of years and still have major influence on society even today. Not imposing the death penalty on criminals who cruelly murder others is contrary to these traditional Chinese ideas about equality and fairness. Moreover, Chinese people are still deeply influenced by such traditional ideas as "a filial son must avenge the killing of his parents and would never live under the same sky with the killer of his parents" and in rural areas many people are still living in extended families. Under this circumstance, not imposing severe punishment on murders and paying attention to the protection of the human rights of only criminals but not the victims of crimes will easily lead to vendetta, social chaos and loss of more innocent lives.

5. Criminal punishments become what they are because they have deterrence against crimes. We should neither exaggerate nor underestimate the deterrence of the death penalty. More than 2000 years ago, an ancient Chinese thinker, Xun Qing, said that "The purpose of rewards and criminal punishments are giving people what they deserve". If those who have committed the most serious crimes are not given the death penalty that they deserve, the criminal law will lose its deterrence against the criminals, who will be encouraged to commit murder and

other serious crimes, resulting in the loss of more innocent lives.

VIII

As a Chinese idiom goes, "more haste, less speed". I think it is desirable to abolish the application of the death penalty to economic crimes and possible to reduce the application of the death penalty to some other non-violence crimes, but not appropriate to abolish the death penalty itself in China under the current situation. If, as suggested by some European friends, China abolishes the death penalty against the will of the people and in disregard of its national conditions, then the Chinese society will have to pay high price for it and more innocent lives will be harmed. A comprehensive approach should be adopted towards the safeguarding of human rights, namely attention should be paid to the protection of the human rights of criminals, victims of crimes, as well as the broad masses of people. Actually the question of how to strike a balance between the rights of criminals and the rights of victims of crimes is also bothering some European countries. An example in this respect is that in some countries that have already abolished the death penalty but are faced with rising crime rate, the public is demanding the reintroduction of the death penalty. In light to the actual situation in China, currently the correct policy for China to adopt is to limit and reduce the application of the death penalty. And when the necessary conditions have been created and the abolition of the death penalty can be achieve without high social cost, I will give my wholehearted support to the abolition. For the present time, we should make down-to-earth efforts towards the abolition of the death penalty, rather mouthing cheap high-sounding words.

Part III

Foreign Exchange in the Field of Human Rights

My Participation in Human Rights Dialogues and Exchanges Between China and Foreign Countries

Retrospect and Prospect[①]

Human rights dialogue is an important means by which the Chinese government engages in struggles and exchanges with western countries in the field of human rights. Such dialogue began in the 1990s and is still going on today. Reviewing my participation in this process during the past dozen or so years and summarizing the relevant experience will help China improve its human rights protection system and better carry out struggle, exchange and cooperation with foreign countries in the field of human rights.

I. The Initiation and the Course of Development Human Rights Dialogue with Foreign Countries

1. My Participation in Human Rights Dialogues and Exchanges

In 1991, the then Chinese president Jiang Zemin pointed out that China should not avoid, but should carry out research on, the issue of human rights. After receiving the task of carrying out human rights research from CPC Central Committee, Professor Hu Sheng, the then President of Chinese Academy of Social Sciences (CASS), entrusted this task to the two directors of CASS Law Institute at that time—Professor Wang Jiafu and myself. In order to fulfill this task and further improve human rights

---

① Originally published in Department of Retirement Affairs of Chinese Academy of Social Sciences (ed.), *The People's Republic: the Source of All Victories*, Beijing: World Affairs Press, 2009.

protection system in China, I decided to expand my research work from the field of ancient Chinese legal history to the fields of the rule of law and human rights. Professor Wang Jiafu and I were both nervous and excited to accept this task because not long before that, some mainstream media in China had published articles claiming that " 'human rights' is a bourgeois slogan" . We were nervous because we were afraid of making mistakes; and we were excited because the theoretical forbidden zone of human rights was ultimately broken through. On the basis of initial theoretical research, the CASS Law Institute held a nationwide seminar on human rights, which produced strong repercussions in the academic circle. In order to provide the CPC Central Committee with relevant information and policy proposals, we decided to carry out investigation tours to different types of countries to learn about their human rights ideas and institutions and collect relevant materials. In September 1991, the first CASS human rights delegation, led by myself, carried out investigation in North America. After the first delegation returned from North America, another delegation, led by Professor Wang Jiafu, made two investigation trips to Europe. Afterwards, another delegation, again led by myself, carried out investigations in three South Asian countries. At the end of each investigation, detailed report was submitted to the CPC Central Committee. From that time on, the scholars of CASS Law Institute, entrusted by the CPC Central Committee and relevant state organs, have been continuously engaging in domestic and international human rights exchanges in conjunction with the construction of the rule of law in the country. At the invitation of the Chinese Foreign Ministry, I, together with several of my colleagues, have participated in the human rights dialogues between China and many foreign countries and international organizations, including the EU, the U. S. , and Canada. I myself have, in accordance with the instructions of state leaders, participated in or presided over the EU-China Dialogue on Administration of Justice and Human Rights, dialogues held under EU-China Human Rights Network, and Sino-German and Sino-U. S. dialogues on administration of justice and human rights. Moreover, I have also visited the UN Headquarters in New York and Geneva five times to hold talks with officials of the Human Rights Commission, the Office of the UN High Commissioner for Human Rights, and the ICRC, invited as a Chinese expert to participate in the feasibility demonstration of a cooperation project between the Office of High Commissioner for Human Rights and China. In February 2008, to build good atmosphere for the

Beijing Olympic Games, I, together with the leaders of the Chinese Society for human rights Studies, held talks with senior leaders of Amnesty International and Human Rights Watch in London and New York, gave a lecture at London School of Economics and Political Science and participated in an academic colloquium at Colombia University. In April of the same year, I visited Hungary, Czech Republic and Poland and held talks with relevant parties in these three countries on the issue of NGOs. And in May 2009, I presided over the Sino-EU Seminar on Human Rights in Prague.

2. Human Rights and the Attitude of Western Countries on Human Rights Issues

Before discussing human rights dialogues and exchanges, we must first understand what human rights are and what the attitude of western countries towards human rights is.

The so-called human rights are, in brief, the rights of human beings, namely the rights enjoyed or ought to be enjoyed by human beings. The subjects of human rights are all human beings. The objects of human rights are all rights. The term "fundamental rights", often used in constitutions and international human rights conventions, refers to the most important, most basic rights. The realization of rights is conditioned by the level of social, economic, political and cultural development. Rights are closely related to obligations. In order to realize human rights, necessary conditions must be created.

The concept of human rights was put forward during the bourgeois revolution in the 17th and 18th centuries to oppose feudal theocracy and feudal monarchy. At that time, the bourgeoisie mainly publicized the universality of human rights in order to mobilize the working class and the masses of working people to join the revolution. After the victory of the bourgeois revolution, they abandoned the working class and the working people, even deprived some of the rights of women of their own class. It was only because of the persistent struggle by the working class and working people that the scope of subjects of human rights has gradually expanded and the content of human rights has been continuously enriched and developed. Historical facts show that, although the human rights conditions in capitalist countries have been improved over the years, the bourgeois human rights policy is to a large degree hypocritical in nature.

This hypocrisy manifests itself not only in the long-term domestic policy of inequality between and discrimination against different classes, gender and races, but also in the external human rights policy of capitalist countries. Take the U. S. for example. In order to maximize its own interests and dominate the world, the U. S. has introduced ideology and politics into international human rights intercourse and openly adopted a double standard on human rights, namely one standard for itself and its allies, another standard for its former colonies, semi-colonies and other developing countries, so as to suppress countries with social system or opinions different from its own, never considering how great harms such policy may cause to the human rights in these countries. Human rights have become an instrument of political struggle with foreign countries. The situation is further complicated when some European countries play the jackal to the tiger under the influence of and manipulation by the U. S.

3. International and Domestic Situation in Late 1980s and Early 1990s

Major changes in international and domestic situations took place in late 1980s and early 1990s. The Soviet Union, in the name of exposing and rectifying the mistakes made by Stalin, negated the leadership of the Communist Party and the socialist system. Lenin and Stalin had made great contribution to their country by leading the October Socialist Revolution, establishing a socialist state, realizing the industrialization and agricultural modernization of the country, and defeating Nazi Germany in World War II. Although in this process he had made some mistakes, such as carrying out the Great Purge, which resulted in many irreversible unjust, false and erroneous cases, such mistakes should not be used to blot out the great contributions made by Stalin and the Russian Communist Party. However, when I visited Moscow and Leningrad in 1989, I found out that Lenin and Stalin were demonized in the Soviet Union: the TV was full of denunciations of Stalin's mistakes. The contributions of Stalin and other Communist leaders were totally negated. This resulted in great ideological confusion among the Russian people, the weakening of the state political power and economic slump. At that time, even the senior researchers of the Law Institute of Soviet Academy of Sciences were unable to explain this situation. Because of the mistakes made by Mikhail Gorbachev, the Soviet Union gradually descended into chaos. Because the leaders of the Communist Party of the Soviet Union at that time divorced themselves from the people, and failed to treat history with a realistic attitude, the Soviet Union quickly disintegrated under the influence of western countries. In the process of disintegration of the Soviet Union, great changes had also taken place in the socialist countries in Eastern Europe. Although the communist parties in these countries had also led their own people in the fight against Nazi Germany during the World War II, these countries were mainly liberated by the Red Army from the German occupation and therefore were under the strong influence of the Soviet Union after the war. During the collapse of the Soviet Union, western countries took the advantage of the weakening of the Soviet influence and began to infiltrate into eastern European countries. During our visit to three eastern European countries, we learnt that some NGOs in these countries were financed first by the U. S. , then by the EU. Among their sponsors were George Soros and Madeleine Albright. These organizations became the backbone of the so-called " Color Revolution" that changed the political system in these countries. The disintegration of the Soviet Union and the collapse of the communist governments in eastern European countries were caused by both internal factors in these countries and the influence and infiltration from the U. S. and western countries.

After the disintegration of the Soviet Union and the collapse of the communist governments in eastern European countries, China had become the primary target of attack by the U. S. and other western countries. In late 1980s, some problems had also emerged in China with the intensification of social conflicts. The U. S. and other western countries thought that the time had come to destroy the socialist system in China and launched unbridled attacks against the measures taken by the Chinese government to stabilize the domestic situation and imposed or threatened to impose such sanctions as cutting off high-level contact, cancellation of loans, and arms embargo against the Chinese government. It was against this background that dozens of foreign scientists wrote a joint letter to Mr. Zhou Guangzhao, the then President of the Chinese Academy of Sciences, raising the issue of human rights situation in China and it was on his letter Comrade Jiang Zemin wrote the above-mentioned instruction to carry out research on human rights. Upon receiving the instruction, the Chinese theoretical circle went into action without delay and a new situation was created in the field of human rights research.

4. The Initiation of Human Rights Dialogue with Foreign Countries

In early 1990s, the economic reform in China expanded from rural areas to urban areas. In 1992, Deng Xiaoping, in a speech made during an inspection tour in southern provinces, reiterated his opinion on the development of socialist market economy: "I can't see why the market economy could not be implemented in a socialist country";① "A planned economy is not equivalent to socialism, because there is planning under capitalism too; a market economy is not capitalism, because there are markets under socialism too."②

The Communist Manifesto points out that, the development of the market economy, from the acquisition of raw materials and sale of products, has become globalized and cannot be limited to only one country. This means the development of socialist market economy in China depends on a good international environment. At that time, the imposition by the U. S. and other western countries of unitary or collective sanctions on China and the demonisation of China by mass media manipulated by western countries had a very negative impact on the reform and opening up as well as the development of the market economy in China. Human rights are in essence a domestic affair which should be dealt with by each state without interference from other states. The acts of the U. S. and other western countries at that time was taken with an ulterior motive, namely to overthrow the socialist system in China. However, they failed to recognize that China was not as vulnerable as eastern European countries because socialism was deeply rooted in Chinese society. As Deng Xiaoping pointed out: "The People's Republic of China was established as a result of 22 years of revolutionary war and has grown up while being constantly blockaded, sanctioned and isolated by western countries. Therefore, China will not collapse and the sanctions imposed by some western countries on China is destined to fail."③ The CPC and the socialist system are strongly supported by the Chinese people. Imposing sanctions on or

---

① Deng Xiaoping, *Selected Works of Deng Xiaoping*, vol. 2, Beijing: People's Publishing House, 1994, p. 236.

② Deng Xiaoping, *Selected Works of Deng Xiaoping*, vol. 3, Beijing: People's Publishing House, 2001, p. 373.

③ Literature Research Office of the Central Committee of the CPC (ed.), *Chronology of Deng Xiaoping: 1990*, Beijing Central Literature Press, 2004, p. 1312.

demonizing China will only enable Chinese people to see more clearly the hegemonic nature of U. S. and western countries, and adhere more steadily to the socialist road. In this process, some far-sighted persons in the political and academic circles in western countries had also realized that accusing, imposing sanctions on or isolating China does not work. A U. S. scholar said, you can not go to a neighbor's house to beat up his child. Even if your neighbor's child has done something wrong, it's up to your neighbor discipline him. Although this metaphor is not necessarily appropriate, its shows that they do not want to continue the confrontation with China in the field of human rights. The U. S. President Bush had also indicated that in a letter to Chinese leaders in August 1990 that: "The U. S. will not downscale U. S. -China relationship, which is of great strategic importance. "① And he expressed the hope to improve the relationship between the two countries. The condition had been ripe for the China to initiate human rights dialogue with western countries. The dialogue was first carried out with the U. S. and later expanded to include EU and other western countries. The dialogue with the U. S. was intermittent and the dialogue with EU became institutionalized in the 1990s.

II. The Form, Content and Effect of Human Rights Dialogue

1. The Form of Human Rights Dialogue

Human rights dialogues are inter-governmental activities as opposite to human rights confrontation and human rights exchanges are exchanges carried out in accordance with inter-governmental agreements and participated by government officials and scholars. Human rights dialogues and exchanges take the following forms:

(1) Inter-governmental human rights dialogues, which are organized by the foreign ministries of both countries and participated by the officials of relevant legislative, judicial and administrative organs. Sometimes researchers at CASS are also invited to participate in such dialogues in light of actual need. I myself and several of my colleagues at the CASS

① Literature Research Office of the Central Committee of the CPC (ed.), *Chronology of Deng Xiaoping: 1990*, Beijing Central Literature Press, 2004, p. 1319.

Law Institute have been invited to participate in China's human rights dialogues with the EU, Australia, Canada and the U. S.

(2) Human Rights Dialogue seminars (also known as seminars on human rights and administration of justice), which are follow-ups of human rights dialogues and broader theoretical discussions on issues already discussed in human rights dialogues. The participants of such seminars, apart from government officials who have participated in human rights dialogues, also include scholars and representative of NGOs. At such seminars, the participants discuss previously agreed-upon issues in connection with relevant international human rights and the laws and practices in their own countries, but not individual cases. The human rights dialogue seminar between China and EU has been held on a biannual basis since 1998. Up to now, a total of 18 such seminars have been held. As one of the chairpersons on the Chinese side, I have participated and chaired 16 of them.

(3) EU-China Human Rights Network and seminars on human rights and administration of justice between China and U. S. and between China and other countries. The EU-China Human Rights Network was a cooperation project between Chinese Foreign Ministry and the European Council. It was participated by the representatives of universities and research institutions in 15 EU member states on the EU side and the CASS Law Institute and a dozen or so universities and research institutions on the Chinese side. With the approval of Mr. Li Lanqing, the then Minister of Education, Mr. Li Tieying, the then President of CASS, and Mr. Qian Qichen, the then Foreign Minister, CASS Law Institute was made the Chinese coordinator of the Network and I was appointed by Mr. Li Tieying to be the person responsible for this project. The Network lasted for three years. Apart from six seminars, it has also organized three advanced training courses participated by university teachers, lawyers, judges and prosecutors. The human rights seminars between China and the Germany and between China and the U. S. were participated by government officials, scholars, and NGO representatives. I participated and presided over Sino-German Human Rights Seminar and, together with Professor Luis Henkin of Colombia University, I also presided over the Sino-U. S. Human Rights Seminar held in Washington.

Among the above human rights dialogues and exchanges, the inter-governmental dialogues are official while China-EU, Sino-German, Sino-U. S. human rights seminars are semi-official, sponsored by governments, addressed by government officials at the opening and closing ceremonies, but chaired by scholars; EU-China Human Rights Network is another form of human rights exchange platform established according to intergovernmental agreement but sponsored by academic institutions and presided over by scholars.

2. Content of Human Rights Dialogues and Exchanges

The content of human rights dialogues and exchanges are broad, including the economic, social, cultural, civil and political rights provided for in the Universal Declaration of Human Rights and the two 1966 international human rights covenants. Each of the above-mentioned categories of rights contains many specific rights. All human rights are interdependent and indivisible. Moreover, in the field of international human rights, there are special conventions on the protection of the rights of vulnerable groups in society, such as women, children, people with disability, and minorities. The rights provided for in these conventions are comprehensive. For example, children's rights involve many issues, such as support, education, health and judicial procedures. So are the rights of other groups. As for the main topics of each dialogue or seminar, those of intergovernmental dialogues are determined through the negotiation between the foreign ministries of the states participating in the dialogue; those of human rights seminars are proposed by leading academic institutions responsible for organizing the seminar in both countries and then approved by the foreign ministries of both countries; those of the seminars of EU-China Human Rights Network were determined through the negotiation between the leading academic institutions on both sides. As far as the process of development is concerned, the topics of the seminars of human rights dialogues and of EU-China Human Rights Network have undergone a process of development from general concepts to specific rights, for example, the concept of human rights, the universality and particularity of human rights, the right to development, human rights and state sovereignty, the ratification and implementation of international human rights conventions, women and human rights, right to work, right to health, the prohibition of racial discrimination, the rights of people with disability, religious freedom, freedom of association, transparency and the regulation of mass media, human rights and education, adequate standard of living, criminal defense system, prohibition of torture, the death penalty, etc. At each seminar, some more concrete issues under the above-mentioned topics, such HIV/AIDS, transplantation of human organs, unlawful detention, and application of the death penalty, will be raised and discussed. At official intergovernmental dialogues, many concrete issues, even individual cases, are discussed whereas at the academic seminars accompanying human rights dialogues or under the EU-China Human Rights Network, no individual case is discussed, although sometimes certain specific human rights issues are raised, and as a rule, no human rights issue of a third state is discussed.

3. Results of Human Rights Dialogues and Exchanges

As mentioned above, human rights dialogue is the opposite of human rights confrontation. Based on their own national interests and ideology, western countries often provoke confrontation with China in the field of human rights, accuse China on the basis of fabricated or distort facts, even adopt official statements or resolutions, or take or threaten to take other measures that negatively affect relationship between states. Confrontation has a strong emotional color and therefore often deviates from facts whereas dialogue enables problems to be discussed within a certain scope, in a rational way, and on the basis of facts. It has been proved that human rights dialogue and other forms of exchange in the field of human rights enable states to discuss their differences in a thorough and rational way, thereby helping them to reach mutual understanding.

(1) The human rights dialogues and exchanges have to a certain extent eased the tension between China and western countries. During the early 1990s, the U. S. and other western countries tried to use human rights issues to attack and defame China. As a result, their relationship with China deteriorated. The dialogues, by putting the problems on the table, and discussing them by presenting the facts and reasoning things out, have increased the mutual understanding and eased the tension between China and western countries.

(2) The human rights dialogues and exchanges created difference of opinions on human rights in China between some western countries and the U. S. In the past, many European countries often play the role of little brothers to the U. S. , taking the "information" provided by the U. S. for granted and guided entirely by the U. S in many issues of international relationship. The dialogues and exchanges enable them to find out that what the U. S. and western media say about the human rights situation in China

is not always true. The U. S. had tried to adopt an anti-China resolution at each annual sessions of the UN Human Rights Commission in Geneva. At first, this effort was supported by some European countries. But later the situation had changed. China was able to defeat over a dozen anti-China motions put forward by the U. S. and other western countries mainly because it had the support from developing countries, but partly also because the human rights dialogues and exchanges had successfully created difference of opinions between the U. S. and other western countries on the issue of human rights in China.

(3) The dialogues and exchanges enabled many scholars, experts, U. S. officials and NGOs to learn the true situation of human rights protection in China. At first, they had heavy prejudice and doubts about human rights in China. But after genuine contact with China, they found out that the Chinese government is truly a government for the people and that the human rights situation in China was not as bad as they thought. Many problems faced by China, such as the regional imbalance in development, the income gap between different groups of society, defects in educational, medical and social security systems, the poor economic condition and unemployment, environmental pollution and food safety, the relationship between the protection of the cultures and languages of ethnic minorities and modernization, and the protection of judicial rights, are also faced by many other countries. To promote human rights, different states should exchange experiences and cooperate with each other, rather than accusing each other, let alone discriminating or imposing sanctions on each other. Some foreign participants of exchanges praised China for its policy on the education of ethnic minorities, saying that China has a very preferential policy towards ethnic minorities in university admission: In China, every ethnic minority in the country has its own college students whereas in Europe many ethnic minorities do not have even one college student. He suggested that government officials in Europe come to China to learn from its experience. The former UN High Commissioner for Human Rights (and former Irish President) M. Mary Robinson, after hearing the discussion of human rights issues by scholars of CASS Law Institute during her visit to China, put aside her pre-prepared lecture and gave an impassionate impromptu speech in front of the leaders of the Chinese Foreign Ministry, in which she made comments on each speech made at the discussion by Chinese participants and repeatedly praised China for the high level of human rights research and practice. This meeting was praised

by the Chinese Foreign Ministry for playing a positive role in dispelling the misunderstanding of the human rights conditions in China by UN officials and improving China's international image.

(4) The human rights dialogues and exchanges have provided human rights training for a large number of cadres in China. Human rights research has been a theoretical forbidden zone in China during the period from mid—1950s until some time after the Third Plenary Session of the Eleventh CPC Central Committee. As a result, China has a late start in human rights research and was not familiar with the relevant information and codes of conduct in this field. The continuous human rights dialogues and exchanges have greatly changed this situation. They enabled China to acquire the relevant information and experience, trained a large number of cadres, and promoted theoretical research on human rights and the improvement of legislative and judicial systems of human rights protection in China.

(5) The human rights dialogues and exchanges enabled the government officials and scholars in the U. S. and other western countries to further realize the importance of dialogue and exchange. Although the dialogues and exchanges were first proposed by China, they received positive response from many government officials and scholars in the U. S. and other western countries this form of communication because they deepened the mutual understanding between China and western countries. Through these dialogues and exchanges, more and more people in the West have realized that human rights are universal and that the Universal Declaration of Human Rights and international human rights conventions have provided for universal principles and standards of human rights protection. However, differences in historical background, level of development and social system in different countries have determined the particularity of the human rights protection system. The practice of some states of trying to change the world by imposing their values or systems on other countries is bound to get into trouble on all sides. Just as the former Canadian Foreign Minister once said, it is not fair to require China to complete in several, dozens or several dozens of years the process which had taken western countries 200 or 300 years to complete. Now more and more far-sighted states and people in the West are demanding the strengthening of dialogue, exchange and cooperation between China and western countries in the field of human rights.

III. What I Have Learnt from My Own Experience in Participation in Human Rights Dialogues and Exchanges

Participating in China's dialogues and exchanges with foreign countries in the field of human rights is an important practice that enables me to apply what I have learnt to serve the country and the people. Through this activity I feel deeply that dialogue and exchange with foreign countries is an important part of the human rights cause in China and that adhering to the correct principles is the key to the success of human rights dialogue. These principles include:

1. Equality

Equality is one of the basic principles of international human rights conventions. In the process of human rights dialogue and exchange, China must adhere to the principle of equality both in terms of the content and in terms of the form of dialogue. As far as the content is concerned, a dialogue should not focus only on the human rights problems China, but problems in both parties to the dialogue should be discussed. Actually, all countries have human rights problems, which differ only in scale and degree in different countries. It is not fair for one country to focus only on the problems in another country, or for "the pot to call the kettle black". There are numerous human rights problems in western countries, such as the protection of the rights of migrant workers and ethnic minorities in some EU countries, the rights of indigenous peoples in Canada and Australia, the boat people in the coast of Australia, the rights of native Indian people, the extensive racial discrimination, the homeless people, and the frequent school shootings in the U. S., and killing of innocent civilians in the Gulf war. The purpose of discussing these problems is not to touch each others'sore spots, but to show that different states should make joint efforts to find solutions to human rights problems through the summarization and exchange of experiences. As for some people who make unjustifiable accusations against China in the dialogue, we should not engage in tit for tat wrangle with them, but rather patiently explain the issues to them. For example, an American representative, when discussing the Tibetan issue in one dialogue, claimed that it should be solved by a way similar to that of the American War of Independence. I immediately pointed out that the various states in North America were colonies before the American War of

Independence whereas Tibet had become part of China as early as in the 13th century. If we must find a comparable example in American history, it should be the American Civil War, which ended the slavery system in southern states by means of war whereas China had originally tried to end the serf system and theocracy in Tibet through peaceful reform before 1959. As for which system was more compatible with human rights principles at that time in Tibet, anyone with an unbiased mind can make an objective judgment. My speech had won the support of many U. S. representatives. Equality in form means equality in terms of the location, participants, chairpersons, and opportunity to speech at the dialogue. For example, at the China-EU Human Rights Dialogue Seminar held in Berlin in 2007, the EU invited the representatives from two non-EU members, one of them a self-proclaimed "Chinese" NGO, to participate in the dialogue despite repeated opposition from the Chinese Foreign Ministry. By the time I, as the Chinese chairperson, and the EU chairperson had already took our seat at the podium, the foreign ministers of the two countries were still in a deadlock over the matter. The seminar was ultimately canceled as a result. This incident was related to the policy adopted by the German government after Angela Merkel came to power and reflected the pernicious habit of some decision-makers in western countries of being unable to treat China as their equal partner.

2. Mutual Respect

Mutual respect is also an important principle provided for by the Universal Declaration of Human Rights and international human rights conventions. The Universal Declaration of Human Rights provides in Article 1 that "All human beings are born free and equal in dignity and rights." Mutual respect in human rights dialogue and exchange means to respect the dignity of the state and the representatives of the other party to the dialogue or exchange. According to the research by a French scholar, the use of the term "dignity" in Article 1 of the UDHR was the result of the insistence by the Chinese representative to the drafting conference of the UDHR, Mr. Zhang Pengchun. Mr. Zhang was and educator who participated in the establishment of Nankai University and Tsinghua University. He had personal experience of the aggression against China and humiliation suffered the Chinese people at the hands of colonialists and imperialists during the past century and knew very well the importance of the dignity of the Chinese state and nation in its relationship with foreign states. It was not by accident that he insisted that the principle of the equality of all human beings in dignity and rights be provided for in Article 1 of the UDHR. Respecting the dignity of other states and the representatives of other states has been a principle always upheld by China whereas some people in western countries are used to talking to Chinese people in a commanding tone, often using such terms as "helping", "instructing" and "influencing" Chinese people in human rights dialogues with China. Some even openly accuse China for human rights violations. An example in this respect was the human rights dialogue seminar held in Lisbon, Portugal in 2000. The discussions in the two-day seminar had been conducted smoothly in a friendly atmosphere. However, an unexpected incident happened during the closing ceremony. After the concluding speeches by the representatives of the foreign ministries of China and the hosting country, an EU official read a statement (later we found out that it was the same statement made at the annual session of the Human Rights Commission in Geneva) which attacked China by name. The statement was met with immediate response from Mr. Wang Ming, the representative of Chinese Foreign Ministry. As the last speaker at the closing ceremony, I gave the following response to this statement after making an objective assessment of the two-day seminar: "We are all striving for the full enjoyment of human rights by the people in China and around the world. In the past century, Chinese people had undergone a tortuous road in the struggle for human rights. In the end of the 19th century and beginning of the 20th century, China had suffered great harms at the hands of western powers. The scars left by the aggressions by western powers can still be seen in Beijing even today and, as was witnessed by my own generation, the invasion of China by Japanese militarists in the 1930s and 1940s had resulted in the death of over 20 million Chinese people. The aggressions by colonialists and imperialists have left deep scars in the soul of the Chinese nations and enabled us to truly understand what human rights are really about. In 1949, China gained national independence. The Chinese people who have stood up in the world are more concerned about their own human rights than anyone else. China has attracted worldwide attention for the efforts and achievements it has made in the domestic and international protection of human rights. We need the support of our friends in solving the problems in the field of human rights. However, such support should be in the form of equal dialogue, rather than unjustifiable accusation, especially accusation in a condescending tone. The practice of some people of using international forum to advance the interests of their own countries, to introduce politics and ideology into dialogue and academic seminars on human rights, and to harm the feelings and dignity of other nations runs counter to the purpose of this seminar and to the basic principles of human rights." My speech had won not only the support of Chinese representatives, but also the sympathy and approval of many EU representatives: the conference room burst into applause after I finished the speech. Before the beginning of the dinner party that night, the EU official who had attacked China during the closing ceremony went to my table and apologized to me. It had been proved that by stepping forward at the critical moment to uphold national dignity in a reasonable and restraint manner, we will be able to win the respect of even our adversaries.

3. Taking National Interests as the Starting Point and Drawing on Useful Experience

China has long history and culture and Chinese people has a glorious revolutionary tradition. After the establishment of the PRC in 1949, the Chinese people have gained national independence, freedom and emancipation and a historical development of the cause of human rights protection was achieved. Since the "reform and opening up", respecting and safeguarding human rights has become an important principle adhered to by the CPC and the Chinese government in ruling the country and people's political, economic, cultural and social rights have been gradually safeguarded. We will be able to keep to the right direction in the international human rights exchange as long as we recognize this basic fact. The CPC and the Chinese implement the socialist system, adhere to the principle of putting people first, and take the full enjoyment of human rights by the people as the starting point as well as the ultimate goal of their work. In order to further improve human rights protection system, we must carry forward the best parts of the Chinese culture and draw on the ideas and experiences in our own cultural tradition that are beneficial to human rights protection, and take every opportunity to disseminate them in the international community, thereby occupying moral high ground and increasing the soft power of China. Meanwhile, we must also draw on the outstanding achievements of human civilization. China's human rights ideas and systems have developed under the influence of western civilization and we must continue to draw on the useful experiences of foreign countries, including those of western countries, in the further development and improvement of human rights ideas and systems. In accordance with the basic spirit of international human rights, China does not introduce politics and ideology into human rights dialogues and exchanges with foreign countries. However, because of the differences in historical and cultural background, in social system, and in people ideology, it is very difficult to adhere to this principle in human rights dialogues, especially in the official dialogues between governments, which involve national interests. The U. S. and other western countries often adopt double standards in international human rights protection, turning it into a political struggle. Therefore, we should not be too naïve in human rights exchange with these countries. When they use human rights as excuse to interfere in China's internal affairs and to realize hegemony, we should see clearly through their tricks and make forceful response. Otherwise our national interests will be harmed. And history has proved that when national interest is harmed, people's rights will inevitably be violated. Of course, paying attention to political and ideological struggle in human rights dialogues and exchanges does not mean we should not pay attention to acquiring information and gaining experience from these dialogues and exchanges. In human rights dialogues, especially those carried out in the form of seminars, the representatives of some countries can explain human rights theories and principles of International Bill of Human Rights, and introduce the experiences on human rights protection in their own countries. We should draw on these theories and experiences and use them to improve the human rights protection system in China.

IV. Prospects of Human Rights Dialogues and Exchanges

In recent years, with the multi-polarization of international relations and the development of multilateral diplomacy, human rights dialogues and exchanges has been generally recognized both in China and abroad for their effectiveness and therefore are expected to continue in the future. As for their trend of development, from a general point of view, with the increase of the comprehensive national strength and the continuous improvement of human rights protection system in China, the struggle in this field will gradually ease off, although it will continue to exist for a long period of time and sometimes will even become intensified on some issues.

1. The Protracted Nature of the Struggle

(1) After taking office, the Obama Administration realized that the policy of dominating the world through unilateralism pursued by its predecessor has gone into a dead end and began to adjust this foreign policy. While continuing to take national strength as the basis of its foreign policy, it began to implement the so-called "smart power diplomacy". However, the external human rights policy of the U. S. is a part of its foreign policy and subjected to the overall national interest. Although adjustments have been made to this policy under new situation, this does not change the U. S. hegemonism that has swelled up since the end of the World War II.

(2) The U. S. and European countries, under the long-term influence of Christian culture, attach more important to individual rights and freedoms. In contrast, China attaches equal importance to individual and collective rights in accordance with socialist human rights principles. This will inevitably lead to conflict on certain concrete issues.

(3) Human rights diplomacy is the bedrock of the foreign policy of the U. S. and some other western countries. In the implementation of such policy, these countries also adopt a double standard. China will never accept such discriminatory policy.

(4) The long-term negative publicity against China by western media and the attack against China on so-called human rights issues by western politicians during general elections have resulted in prejudice against China among the general public in these countries, which is hard to eliminate in a short period of time and forms a relationship of a circular influence with the ideas and behaviors of some politicians.

(5) The Democratic Party in the U. S. has always flaunted the importance it attaches to human rights issues. In the early 1990s, the speaker of the US House of Representatives, Nancy Pelosi, displayed an anti-China slogan in Tiananmen Square during her visit to China. I met Ms. Pelosi at U. S. Congress during a visit to the U. S. in 1991, and she gave me the impression of a hard-edged politician who would take every opportunity to put up a show by making use of the so-called human rights issues in China. The current U. S. Secretary of State Hillary Clinton, who had participated the Fourth World Conference on Women in Beijing in 1995 while she was still the First Lady, also has very radical attitude

towards human rights issues in China and may take certain actions under certain circumstances.

(6) The U. S. and other western countries, based on their own national interests, often interfere in the internal affairs of some developing countries (such as Sudan and Burma), either by themselves or through UN or other international organizations, and demand the cooperation by China in the name of "accountability" or "stakeholder", or else they will direct their action towards China.

2. The General Trend of Development towards Détente

(1) After many years of efforts, the human rights protection system in China has been greatly improved and the principle of "respecting and safeguarding human rights" enshrined in the Constitution of the CPC and the Chinese Constitution and become an important principle for ruling the country by the CPC and the Chinese government. The government is attaching increasing importance to human rights research, publicity and education, the human rights consciousness among the people has been gradually raised, their economic, political, cultural and social rights further safeguarded, the advantages of the socialism and human rights protection system with Chinese characteristics are becoming more and more apparent, and China's development experience has become the focus of attention of people around the world. Under such circumstances, if the U. S. and other western countries continue to make a big fuss about the so-called human rights issue in China, they will not only offend the Chinese people, but also isolate themselves in the international community.

(2) The rulers in the U. S. are utilitarians. The White House and the spokesperson of the U. S. State Department never hide the fact that their human rights diplomacy is always based on their national interest. I once said to an American friend: "The spokespersons of the White House and the U. S. State Department are adorably frank. They always shield themselves behind "U. S. national interest" whenever they are unable to advance any further arguments to justify themselves." The U. S. "national interest" often extends to the fields of interest of other countries. It has been trying to interfere in China's internal affairs on the pretext of human rights by introducing anti-China motion at the Human Rights Conference in Geneva every year during the past dozen or so years—except for the three years of the Gulf War, during which period it needed China's support in UN Security Council on the Iraqi War and other

issues.

(3) In 2009, the Obama administration took office and Hillary Clinton became the U. S. Secretary of State. Many foreign media believed that she would again make a big issue of human rights during her first visit to China after taking office. To their surprise, however, she did not do so. When asked why she kept such a low profile on the issue of human rights, she replied that: "The issues of human rights, Tibet, religious freedom and the freedom of speech are part of Sino-U. S. dialogue. But now the U. S. and China should focus their attention on more important issues affecting the peace, progress, and prosperity of both countries and of the world." These issues include fight against international terrorism, the control of weapons of mass destruction, the financial crisis and the world economic crisis, the global warming and environmental problems, the Afghan issue, the Iranian issue, and the denuclearization of the Korean Peninsula.

(4) Although European countries are more radical than the U. S. on some human rights issues, they generally follow the lead of the U. S. in human rights diplomacy. Meanwhile, they also need the economic support from China. After many years of dialogue and exchange, they now have a better understanding of the human rights conditions in China and no longer wholeheartedly follow the U. S. in human rights policy.

(5) The UN Human Rights Council has established a mechanism of "Universal Periodic Review" of human rights conditions in various countries around the world. Although this mechanism can also be bogged down in political struggle, it is formally equal to all states. Through the assessment of human rights conditions in all UN member states, this mechanism has to a certain extent resolved or alleviated the conflicts between states in the field of human rights.

Finally, it should be pointed out that the purpose of engaging in human rights dialogues and exchanges with foreign countries is not to make a show or to do it after a fashion, but to eliminate the political interference in development of the human rights cause in China and the construction of socialism with Chinese characteristics by the U. S. and other western countries in the name of human rights. And the purpose of reviewing and summarizing the successful experience of human rights dialogue is to better carry out human rights dialogues and exchanges with foreign countries. In this process, we should never ignore the existing problems because of the great achievements we have already made, let alone becoming conservative or cover up our mistakes in the field of human rights protection. In the future dialogues and exchanges, we will, as always, continue to improve the human rights safeguarding system, strengthen international human rights cooperation, promote the construction of a harmonious world, and make further efforts for the "establishment of a new social and international order". ①

---

① Article 28 of UDHR, in CASS Law Institute (ed.), *International Instruments of Human Rights and International Institutions of Human Rights*, Beijing: Social Sciences Documentation Publishing House, 1995, p. 8.

Constructing Human Civilization and Strengthening Judicial Protection of Human Rights[①]

Good morning, ladies and gentlemen:

First, on behalf of all the members of the delegation of the Institute of Law of Chinese Academy of Social Sciences, I would like to thank Mr. Morten Kjaerum, the Director of the Danish Center for Human Rights, and his colleagues for inviting us to Copenhagen and to congratulate the opening of the Sino-Danish Seminar on the Protection of Human Rights in Administration of Justice.

During our stay in Copenhagen, we have received warm welcome from the Danish Center for Human Rights, and through the arrangement by the Center, have met the Danish Minister of Development and expressed our gratitude to him for his support of the academic exchange between China and Denmark. We have also held meetings with the Parliamentary Ombudsman, the National Commission of Police, and the Chairman of the Parliamentary Legal Committee, visited the Supreme Court, the National Museum, and a prison, and held informal discussions with the officers of a district police bureau in Copenhagen. In all these places we have received warm and thoughtful receptions. As a Chinese saying goes, "seeing is believing". These visits have greatly increased our understanding of the political, legal, and human rights safeguarding systems, as well as the history and culture of Denmark, and given us a sense of reality about this beautiful land of fairy tales, which has fired our imagination in our childhood as the "hometown of the Little Mermaid".

---

① Originally a speech given by the author at the opening ceremony of the Sino-Danish Seminar on the Protection of Human Rights in Administration of Justice, held in Copenhagen in November 1988.

We will bring back to China all these wonderful impressions together with the successful Danish experiences in the fields of politics, law, and human rights protection.

The topic under discussion in this seminar is the safeguarding of human rights in administration of justice, which covers a wide range of areas. In a modern state, it is not only the final solution to the political, economic, social and cultural disputes, but also the last and most reliable line of defense against violations of human rights. Generally speaking, it involves the individual, society and the state; specifically speaking, it involves parties, judges, prosecutors, and lawyers. It deals with not only specific persons and acts, but also various abstract social relationships. In this sense, administration of justice occupies an important position in the entire human rights safeguarding system. Administration of justice can be roughly divided into administrations of administrative, civil and criminal justice and it is hard to say which one of them is more important in real life. In the preparation for the seminar, my friend Mr. Kjaerum suggested that we concentrate our discussion on the administration of criminal justice, and especially torture, at the seminar. I agreed. Actually, the topic of torture has already been discussed at the second EU-China Seminar on Administration of Justice, held in Beijing on October 12—20 this year and consensus have been reached between Chinese and EU scholars on many issues relating to this topic. However, in view of the facts that torture is still widely practiced in many countries, either openly or secretly, despite that it is abhorred by good and honest people all around the worlds, that the prohibition of torture is of vital importance to international protection of human rights and to the advancement of human civilization, and that both China and Denmark are state parties to the Convention against Torture and Other Cruel, Inhuman or Degrading Treatment or Punishment, we believe that carrying out further discussion is conducive to deepening our understanding of this problem. Currently many problems still exist in the system of judicial protection of human rights around the world. We believe that, in the discussion of the issue of torture, or any other issue relating to human rights protection, all of us, whether scholars or politicians, should refrain from attacking or ridiculing each other, but carry out exchange and cooperation on an equal basis with a sense of responsibility for the construction of human civilization. Only in this way can the exchange and cooperation achieve the expected objectives.

As you know, China signed the International Covenant on Economic, Social and cultural Rights in October 1997 and the International Covenant on Civil and Political Rights in October this year. This is necessary for realizing the objectives of strengthening the legal system, ruling the country by law, and constructing a socialist state under the rule of law, as well as for improving China's human rights system and enabling China to actively participate in international protection of human rights. China is now in the process of deliberation on the ratification of the International Covenant on Economic, Social and cultural Rights and will begin the deliberation on the ratification of the International Covenant on Civil and Political Rights in due time. I believe that, after careful deliberation, the Chinese legislature will ratify both covenants. I also hope that, when ratifying the two covenants, China will make as few reservations as possible. China is faithful to its promises and enjoys a good reputation in fulfilling its obligations under international conventions. The two covenants will be conscientiously implemented in China once they are ratified by the Chinese legislature. Like many other countries, China will encounter various problems in the implementation of the two covenants. For this reason, we would like to carry out continuous exchanges and discussions with experts and scholars in Denmark, EU and other countries, so as to contribute to the comprehensive implementation of the two covenants in China.

My friends, although China and Denmark are separated by long distance, have different historical and cultural backgrounds and levels of development, and are faced with different challenges, the people of both countries are kindhearted, desire for peace and development, pursue the full enjoyment of human rights, and live in the same global village. Faced with the coming new century, we have every reason to carry out further exchange and cooperation in all fields, including the human rights field, so as to create a better life for ourselves as well as for the further generations.

The Chinese People Are More Concerned about Their Own Human Rights than Any Other People[1]

First of all, I would like to take this opportunity to thank the organizers of the Fourth EU-China Dialogue Seminar on Human Rights and Administration of Justice for this opportunity to speak at the closing ceremony of the seminar.

I am in full agreement with the assessment of this seminar by Mr. Wang Min of the Chinese Foreign Ministry and his response to the speech by the representative of the European Commission. It should be said that this seminar has been hectic, compact and straightforward: It is hectic because the Chinese delegates entered into the conference only hours after a 24-hour-long long journey from Beijing to Lisbon; it is compact because during the two-day seminar, the participants have been exchanging opinions and information with each other by various means from the moment they enter into the conference room at 9 am till the end of dinner

---

① This article was originally a speech given at the closing ceremony of the Fourth EU-China Human Rights Dialogue Seminar, held in Lisbon on May 8—9, 2000. The two-day seminar had been conducted in a friendly atmosphere, although one of the topics discussed at this seminar, the death penalty, was very sensitive. At the closing ceremony, however, the representative of European Commission suddenly attacked China by name in his speech, in violation of the rules of procedure of the seminar and the previously reached agreement between China and EU. This attack was met with immediate response from the representative of Chinese Foreign Ministry, Mr. Wang Min. As the last speaker at the closing ceremony, I, after making a brief summarization of the seminar, also gave a reasonable, forceful and restrained response to the speech by the EU representative. My speech won enthusiastic applause from participants of the seminar, including many EU representatives. At the dinner time, the EU representative apologized to me for his inappropriate remarks at the closing ceremony.

party at evening; an it is straightforward because all participants have freely expressed their opinions during the discussions of various issues. Generally speaking, the seminar has been held in a good atmosphere and, thanks to the concerted efforts made by the Chinese and EU organizers and participants, achieved expected results. The participants of the seminar carried out exchange of views and in-depth explorations on various issues relating to " the ratification and implementation of the two UN human rights covenants" and the "the death penalty", thereby getting a better understanding of each other's views and laying a sound foundation for further discussions.

The two human rights covenants are legally binding international conventions adopted by the UN after the promulgation of the 1948 Universal Declaration of Human Rights. They are the products of long struggle by the people of the world as well as the crystallization of the achievements of human civilization. Because of various reasons, such as the late restoration of its lawful seat at the UN, China has not yet ratified the two covenants. However, as one of the founding states of the UN and permanent members of the UN Security Council, China recognizes and respects the basic principles of the Universal Declaration of Human Rights and the two UN human rights covenants and follows these principles in the construction the socialist democracy and rule of law. As far as I know, the Chinese government had extensively solicited opinions in the whole society on the issue of ratification of the two UN human rights covenant in early 1990s. In 1992, the Law Institute of the Chinese Academy of Social Sciences submitted a formal recommendation on the ratification of the two human rights covenants to the Chinese government. After careful consideration of opinions from different quarters of society, the Chinese government signed the International Covenant on Economic, Social and Cultural Rights and the International Covenant on Civil and Political Rights in 1997 and 1998, respectively. Now, the Standing Committee of the National People's Congress has begun the deliberation on the ratification of the International Covenant on Economic, Social and Cultural Rights and will deliberate on the ratification of the International Covenant on Civil and Political Rights at an appropriate time. It is expected that China will ratify both covenants after the completion of the deliberation. All EU member states have already ratified the two covenants. As far as I know, all of them had made careful preparations before the ratification of the two covenants. For example, in order to implement the European Convention on Human Rights and the two UN human rights covenants, the British Parliament adopted in 1998 the Human Rights Act, which came into for in October 2000. Therefore, it is common practice for a state to make the necessary preparations in legislative, judicial and administrative fields before ratifying a human rights convention, which in a certain sense can be said to be a manifestation of responsible attitude towards the convention. At the seminar, the participants have carried out discussions on such issues as the positive significance of the ratification of the two UN human rights covenants to the domestic construction of democracy and the rule of law and the effect of the two human rights covenants and their relationship with domestic laws. There are three different kinds of relationships between international conventions and domestic laws in terms of legal effect: first, the legal effect of international conventions is higher than that of the national constitution, as is the case in the Netherlands, Germany and Belgium; second, the legal effect of international conventions is the same as that of the national constitution, as is the case in Portugal; third, the effect of international conventions is lower than that of the national constitution, as is the case in Austria. The methods for the implementation of international conventions can also be divided into three types: first, monism, namely incorporation, as is the case in Belgium and the Netherlands; second, dualism, namely transformation, as is the case in Denmark and Sweden; and third, pluralism, namely a combination of incorporation and transformation, as is the case in Greece. As for the situation in China, Professor Huang Lie has already explained in detail in her paper and presentation and currently a debate is going on in the Chinese academic circle on this issue. In his speech, Professor van Hoof expressed a consensus of the participants by saying that, although the method of implementation deserves careful study, a conscientious attitude is the key to the implementation of the covenants. To ensure the implementation of the covenants, all sate parties must improve their domestic laws and domestic and international human rights safeguarding mechanisms. China is faithful to its promises. Although it has not yet ratified the two human rights covenants, it has already begun the active preparation for their implementation by improving its legislative, judicial and administrative systems and by carrying out human rights education among citizens. And it has received support from EU and other countries in this process. For example, Sweden has provided training for the Chinese police officers, Canada provides training for Chinese judges, and the Netherlands and UK provide training for Chinese lawyers. Such support has produced positive effects and I hope that it will continue in the future.

Another subject for discussion at this seminar is the death penalty. The International Covenant on Civil and Political Rights provides in Article 6 that: "In countries which have not abolished the death penalty, sentence of death may be imposed only for the most serious crimes in accordance with the law in force at the time of the commission of the crime and not contrary to the provisions of the present Covenant and to the Convention on the Prevention and Punishment of the Crime of Genocide. This penalty can only be carried out pursuant to a final judgement rendered by a competent court." There is no doubt that this provision, which is based on kind-hearted humanitarian desire, should be strictly observed. All the EU member states have already abolished the death penalty and the information provided and opinions expressed by some EU delegates at the seminar are of certain reference value to China. Although China has not yet abolished the death penalty, it is very cautious in the application of the death penalty. All death sentences must go through strict trial, defense and review procedures. The current legal provisions and judicial practice relating to the death penalty in China is compatible with the basic spirit of the Covenant. As for the call by some EU delegates at the seminar for China to abolish the death penalty as soon as possible, although it expressed a kind-hearted wish for humane treatment of criminals, it does not confirm to the current situation in China. The fact that China has not yet abolished the death penalty is determined by the concrete situation in China. China is currently at the primary stage of socialism and will remain so for a long period of time to come. The question of whether to abolish the death penalty should be considered from the perspective of the overall need of social development and stability. On the one hand, the state should give humane treatment to criminals and protect their right of existence; on the other hand, it should also protect the rights of victims of crimes and their family members. By committing crimes, the criminals harm not only certain individual persons, but also certain social relationships. Under the concrete circumstances in China, not applying the death penalty on the most serious crimes will endanger public security. Since Emperor Liu Bang, the founder of the Han Dynasty, made the rule that "Those who commit murder shall be given death penalty and those who intentionally cause injuries to or steal from others shall be punished accordingly" more than 2000 years ago, the traditional idea that "anyone who takes another person's life must repay with his own life, just as anyone who takes another person's money must repay with his own money" has been deeply rooted in the mind of the Chinese people. Not imposing the death penalty on those who have committed the crime of vicious murder will easily lead to revenges by the relatives of victims against the relatives of the murderers, resulting in the violation of the right to life and the right of existence of more people and greater social costs. Nevertheless, China is very cautious in the application of the death penalty because it is after all the severest form of criminal punishment and a person can never be resurrected once executed. It is for this reason that the Chinese Criminal Procedure Law provides for strict procedures for the review of the death penalty. China retains the death penalty not because it has a blind faith in or an addiction to the death penalty. Several years ago Professor Hu Yunteng and I submitted to the Chinese government a recommendation on reducing the capital crimes in the Chinese Criminal Law. In fact, currently a debate is going on in Chinese academic circle on whether the death penalty should be applied to economic crimes. Just as introduced at the seminar, a sample investigation carried out by the academic circle shows that 95% of the people in China are against the abolition of the death penalty. The Chinese government, as a people's government, cannot but take into consideration public opinions and popular feelings in making criminal policies relating to the death penalty. The Chinese scholars, while actively advocating the reduction of the application of the death penalty, have also taken the abolition of the death penalty as their ultimate goal, and are creating conditions for the realization of this goal.

Ladies and gentlemen, up to now, a total of four EU-China seminars on administration of justice and human rights have been held, with each one of them more extensive and in-depth in content than the previous one. Meanwhile, the CASS Law Institute has also carried out bilateral exchanges with scholars of the Netherlands, Denmark, Norway and Switzerland on similar subjects, and after each seminar, a collection of papers from the seminar is published in both Chinese and English. It has been proved that such academic exchange is of great significance to increasing mutual understanding, developing cooperative relationship and promoting domestic and international protection of human rights. Due to the differences in historical and cultural backgrounds, social system and level of development, difference in opinions on some issues is inevitable.

However, I believe that, with the continuation of discussion, China and EU will deepen their mutual understanding in broader fields.

Friends, the world is beautiful and the struggle for the full enjoyment of human rights is a worthy cause. We are all striving for the full enjoyment of human rights by the people of our own countries as well as by all the people in the world. Here I would like to point out that the Chinese people have gone through a tortuous and bumpy road in the struggle for human rights during the past century. At the end of the 19th century and beginning of the 20th century, China had suffered great harm and humiliation at the hands of western powers. Evidences of aggression by western powers can still be seen in Beijing even today. As people of my generation have all witnessed, the invasion by Japanese imperialists in the 1930s and the 1940s had resulted in the death and injury of tens of millions of Chinese people. The aggressions by colonialists and imperialists have left a deep wound on the soul of the Chinese nation, and enabled us to understand the importance of human rights. In 1949, China finally gained national independence. The Chinese people who have stood up are more concerned about their own human rights than anyone else. They have made great efforts and achieved remarkable results in the protection of domestic and international human rights. In the process of solving the problems faced by our country, we need the support from our friends in other countries. With respect to issues of common concern, we expect more equal dialogue, less unwarranted accusations, especially accusations in a condescending tone, from western countries. Just a moment ago, at the closing ceremony of the seminar, an EU delegate, out of he selfish interest of his own country and organization, used international forum to make unwarranted accusations against China, thereby bringing politics and ideology into an academic seminar on human rights and harming the national feelings and dignity of the Chinese people. Such a behavior is against the purpose of this seminar and the basic principles of human rights.

Here I would like to reiterate that the struggle for human rights is a noble cause and we the Chinese people will always be grateful to those foreign friends who genuinely support and contribute to the cause of human rights protection in China and in the whole world. Finally, I would like to thank the organizers and participants of this seminar for their hard work and contribution.

Carrying forward the Ancient Chinese and Roman Civilizations and Promoting the Construction of Modern Civilization[①]

My colleges and I have come to Venice in beautiful mood to attend the Seminar on Administration of Justice and Human Rights.

Italy is a country with an ancient civilization and Venice is a poetic and picturesque city of water with unique charms and fascinating ancient buildings.

Ancient Rome and ancient Greece were the cradles of European civilization. The Roman Law, which was called by Carl Marx "the first world law of a commodity-producing society", is not only the source of the continental law system, but also played an important role in the formation of the contemporary common law system. The civilizations of ancient Rome and ancient Greece, together with those of ancient China, Babylon, Egypt, and India, had profoundly influenced the development of human history. Florence, which is not far from Venice, is also the birthplace of the European Renaissance, which is milestone in the development of Europe from a medieval society to a modern civilization. The main topic of this seminar—administration of justice and protection of human rights—is an important content of contemporary civilization that affects the well-being of over 1. 5 billion people in China and EU countries. In this sense, our seminar will contribute to the promotion of the development of modern civilization.

Today, both China and EU are undergoing a process of reform and transformation. On the basis of over 20 years of reform and rapid

---

① This article was originally a speech delivered at the opening ceremony of the Tenth China-EU Seminar on the Administration of Justice and Protection of Human Rights, held on December 15, 2003.

development, China has recently put forward the goal of building a well-off society in all-round way, and constructing socialist material, political and spiritual civilizations, so as to further promote the respect for and safeguard of human rights, as well as the full development of mankind. The EU, while expanding its membership, is planning to deepen the union of various European countries through the adoption of the EU Constitution. This constitution, if adopted and implemented, will enable EU countries to make new progresses towards to goal of establishing a United States of Europe. The transformation of China and EU will certainly promote the progress of the human civilization.

Up to now, China and EU have jointly organized nine seminars on the administration of justice and protection of human rights. In addition, four seminars and two training courses have been organized under the China-EU Human Rights Network. The training courses were held in China and participated by over 100 judges, prosecutors, lawyers and university and college teachers and have achieved very good results. As the Chinese chairperson and participant of the EU-China Human Rights Network, I feel gratified about these achievements. This is the tenth China-EU seminar on administration of justice and protection of human rights, which will be focused on the issues of "NGO Capacity Building and Judicial Protection of Human Rights". As a link in the chain of the China-EU exchange in the field of administration of justice and protection of human rights, it will certainly contribute to the progress of the Chinese, European and the entire human civilizations. I wish the seminar every success.

The Right to Criminal Defense and Corporate Social Responsibilities[1]

The Eleventh EU-China Dialogue Seminar on Administration of Justice and Human Rights is coming to an end. The Seminar is very successful, thanks to the joint efforts made by the EU and Chinese organizers, scholars and experts.

One of the important reasons for the success of this seminar is that it is, as all the previous seminars were, participated by a number of experienced legislative, judicial and administrative officials, NGO representatives, as well as accomplished scholars. Moreover, the participation by representatives of new EU member states enabled us to make new friends and expand the scope of the exchange.

Another reason for the success of the seminar is that, the EU and Chinese organizers of the seminar have decided through negotiation on two topics for discussion at seminar that are of great theoretical and practical significance. And, on the basis of thorough preparation, the participants of the seminar have carried out heated, candid and serious discussions around the two topics during the two-day seminar. They have never concealed their opinions when clarifying theoretical issues or avoided the existing problems in their own countries when discussing practical issues, thus truthfully imparted information and exchanged opinions. The discussions have promoted their mutual understanding, contributed to the elimination of their misunderstandings and increased their friendship.

The right to defense is a countervailing power against prosecution authorities, which as a part of state political power, may violate the lawful rights of criminal defendants. The ultimate objective of this right is to realize judicial fairness and social justice. Although the right to defense is a

---

① Originally a speech given at the closing ceremony of the Eleventh EU-China Seminar on Human Rights and Administration of Justice.

concrete system of criminal procedure, it is an indicator of the level of the development of the rule of law and human rights protection and the summarization of the experience of the progress of human civilization. It is exactly for this reason that this right has been fully affirmed by international human rights conventions and the Basic Principles on the Role of Lawyers. Article 14 of the International Covenant on Civil and Political Rights provides that: "In the determination of any criminal charge against him, everyone shall be entitled to the following minimum guarantees, in full equality: To be tried in his presence, and to defend himself in person or through legal assistance of his own choosing; to be informed, if he does not have legal assistance, of this right; and to have legal assistance assigned to him, in any case where the interests of justice so require, and without payment by him in any such case if he does not have sufficient means to pay for it." The Chinese Constitution and laws have also provided for the criminal defense system. Article 125 of the Chinese Constitution provides that: "The accused has the right to defense." and Article 11 of the Chinese Criminal Procedure Law provides that: "A defendant shall have the right to defense, and a people's court shall have the duty to ensure that a defendant acquires defense." This Law contains a special chapter on "Defense and Representation". Moreover, the Chinese Law on Lawyers also contains corresponding provisions on criminal defense. From the speeches given at the seminar we can see that EU countries have also adopted relatively complete legal provisions on the right to defense. Under normal circumstances, there are certain gaps between international human rights conventions and state constitutions and even greater gaps between legislation and law enforcement and administration of justice. Just as one of the European participants of the seminar points out, France, China and other countries all have a long way to go in improving their respective criminal defense system. This is why the word "strengthening" is added to the "right to defense" as one of the topics for discussion at this seminar.

Just as the European scholars and experts have pointed out at the seminar, the development of the system of the right to defense in EU member states is unbalanced: some of them have already developed a relatively sound system while some others still have many problems in their systems. China also has many problems in its own system of the right to defense, such as the low degree of consensus among state organs and the general public on the idea of criminal defense, the poor observance of the relevant legal provisions, the lack of protection of lawyers' rights, the low rate of criminal defense or lack of effective criminal defense, the lack of transparency and the lawyer's right to consult case file at various stages of criminal proceedings, and the lack of financial guarantee for legal aid... the raising of these issues is conducive to promoting the improvement of the relevant laws and the safeguarding of the right to defense. However, it should be pointed out that, although there are many problems in the criminal defense system in China, the deprivation of the defense right of those facing the death penalty is not one of them. As my Chinese colleagues and I have explained at the group discussion, the story about a criminal defendant named Deng Xing being sentenced to death while deprived of his right to defense is an unfounded hearsay.

We always believe that violation of the rights of defense and other rights of criminal defendants not only infringes the rights of an individual or a group of individuals, but also undermine social relationships as well as state laws and institutions. And the stability of the legal system is the guarantee of social stability and development. This is true for EU as well as for China.

As for corporate social responsibilities, it is a new issue that has emerged and caught people's attention in the process of construction of the rule of law and protection of human rights. As we know, human rights protection first of all focuses on state organs and government officials because of their important positions and responsibilities. NGOs or the civil society come next. They are playing an increasingly important role in the safeguarding of human rights whether in EU, in Europe, in China or in other parts of the world. Corporate social responsibilities are important to the safeguarding of political, economic, as well as social rights and involve such issues as the recruitment of employees, raising of capital, wages, working conditions, working hours, social security, industrial injuries, democratic management of enterprises, laying-off employees, the environmental threats posed by industrial production, and the impact of industrial products to people's physical and mental health, the plunder of nature resources, the seizure of market, and even the control of countries and regions. It is clear that the corporate behavior must be put into the orbit of the rule of law and corporations must abide by the laws of their home countries and their host countries as well as international codes of conduct and the relevant provisions of international human rights conventions. Just as Professor Schabas has pointed out, states must exercise supervision over corporate operations, so as to ensure the protection of the human rights of corporate employees and of the general public.

I am pleased to tell you that one of my colleagues at CASS Law Institute, Dr. Liu Junhai, began to pay attention to and carry out research on the issue of corporate social responsibilities as early as in 1995. His research work in this field was a pioneering exploration, whether in China and in the whole world, and was later supported and guided by Professor Asbjørn Eide, a famous international human rights expert, and achieved good results. Propelled by people all over the world, now the United Nations is also paying attention to and carrying out discussions on this issue. I believe that the research on and attentions pay to corporate social responsibilities will certainly be able to promote the development of the entire human rights cause.

Friends, this seminar is the eleventh held under the project of EU-China Dialogue on Administration of Justice and Human Rights and the five held under the EU-China Human Rights Network. Professor Wang Jiafu, Professor Chen Zexian, Professor Schabas, myself and many of our Chinese and European colleagues and friends are witnesses to the successful development of this form of exchange, which has forcefully promoted the development of the rule of law and human rights protection both in China and in EU. Now Professor Wang Jiafu and I are both at an advanced age and therefore will no longer be able to take an active part in this process in the future. But this exchange will continue develop in a healthy way. I am confident that, by the time the 21st or the 31st EU-China human rights dialogue or seminar is held, the rule of law and the safeguarding of human rights in China and EU will reach a new level and we will be able to make new contributions not only to the protection of human rights in China and EU, but also to the protection of human rights and the progress of human civilization in the whole world.

Speech at the Meeting of Senior Cadres of the Central Government of the People's Republic of Laos[1]

Vice-Premier Somsavat, Ambassador Liu Yongxing, Leaders of the Central Government of Laos, Ladies and Gentlemen, Comrades,

Good Morning!

First I would like to thank the Foreign Ministry of Laos for inviting us to Vientiane to exchange experiences in the field of human rights construction. Vientiane is a beautiful city with a strong local ethnic flavor. People here are very hospitable. We have been given a warm reception that made us feel at home. Especially, accompanied by comrades from the Laotian Foreign Ministry, we have visited the Memorial Hall of President Kaysone Phomvihane, the leader of the Laotian people, which enabled us to have a better understanding of the revolutionary history of Laos.

The Laotian people are great people who carried out several decades of extremely hard and heroic struggles under the leadership of the People's Revolutionary Party against the aggressions by the French colonialists and U. S. imperialists and ultimately won national independence. We have

---

① On June 24—24, 2005, I, accompanied by Mr. Dong Zhihua, acounselor at the International Department of Chinese Ministry of Foreign Affairs, and Ms. Wang Linxia, a section chief of the State Council Information Office, visited Vientiane, Laos at the invitation of the Government of the Lao People's Democratic Republic to give a lecture on China's experience in the construction of human rights system at a meeting attended by senior cadres of the Central Government of Laos. On June 24, 2005, Vice-Premier Somsavat of the Lao Government held a special banquet for me. Mr. Liu Yongxing, the Chinese Ambassador to Laos, told me that Vice-Premier Somsavat took the time out of his busy schedule to hold the banquet to thank me for the successful lecture, which he said had deepened the traditional friendship between the Chinese and Lao peoples.

learnt that, between the 1950s and the 1970s, the U. S. imperialists had dropped over three million tons of bombs in Laos, which at that time had a population of only three million, resulting in the death of large number of innocent civilians, including women and children. However, such atrocity failed to frighten into submission the Laotian people, who fought with ever greater bravery, and ultimately defeated the seemingly powerful aggressors. This story aroused in us deep respect for the Laotian Revolutionary Party, army and people and we are very proud to have such a great neighbor and friends.

The visit to the Memorial Hall reminded me of the Monument to the People's Heroes in Tiananmen Square in Beijing. The inscription on the Monument, composed by Chairman Mao Zedong, a close friend of President Kaysone and Prince Souphanouvong, and written by Premier Zhou Enlai, Reads:

"Eternal glory to the heroes of the people who laid down their lives in the people's war of liberation and the people's revolution in the past three years!

Eternal glory to the heroes of the people who laid down their lives in the people's war of liberation and the people's revolution in the past thirty years!

Eternal glory to the heroes of the people who from 1840on laid down their lives in the many struggles against domestic and foreign enemies and for national independence and the freedom and well-being of the people!"①

This inscription is both a tribute to the revolutionary martyrs and a declaration for the future generations: the liberation of the country, the independence of the nation and the realization of the freedom and wellbeing of the people, namely human rights, have always been the objective of persistent struggle by Chinese people, whether in the past, present or future. The Chinese people have been able to made huge achievements during the past several decades exactly because they have fallowed the spirit embodied in this inscription, carried forward the cause pioneered by their predecessors, forged ahead into the future in unity, and continuously summarized its own experience in the development of human rights cause.

---

① Mao Zedong, *Selected Works of Mao Zedong*, Beijing: People's Publishing House, 1977, p. 11.

Then, what are human rights? According to our understanding, the so-called human rights are the rights enjoyed or ought to be enjoyed by all persons by virtue of their status as human beings. Here, the term "persons" refers to all human beings and "rights" refers to all rights. The term "fundamental rights" often used in international human rights conventions refers to important rights indispensable to every human being. We recognize both the universality and the particularity of human rights. Just as the Universal Declaration of Human Rights points out, the universality of human rights means that everyone is entitled to enjoy human rights, without distinction of any kind, such as race, colour, sex, language, religion, political or other opinion, national or social origin, property, birth or other status. However, because of the differences in historical and cultural backgrounds, social system, and level of development in different countries, the particularity of human rights protection is inevitable. Such particularity is closely related to the main problems to be solved in the struggle for human rights by different states or nations in different periods of time.

Beginning from 1840, the Chinese people have taken the right to existence as the primary human rights in the struggle for human rights and in the development of human rights cause. In order to survive, China must adhere to the road of development. Deng Xiaoping once stressed that "development is of overriding importance." In China, the right to development is also regarded as an important human right. The development of human rights cause in China can be roughly divided into the following three stages:

First, struggling for national independence and establishing the People's Republic of China;

Second, improving the Constitution and laws and transforming due rights into legal rights;

Third, wholeheartedly seeking development and providing material and cultural safeguards for the realization of human rights.

The above three stages are closely related to each other. In the process of struggling for national independence, efforts had also been made in improving laws and institutions and developing the economy and the culture. The starting point and the ultimate goal of improving laws and institutions is to promote development, strengthen political power, and creating economic, political and cultural conditions for the full enjoyment of human rights.

I. Struggling for National Independence and Establishing the People's Republic of China

According to Marxism, the fundamental question of revolution is the political power, without which there will be no law to talk about. The proletariat, in order to liberate itself, must struggle for democracy and gain control of political power. After the 1840 Opium War, western imperialists invaded China with superior military power and turned China into a semi-colonial and semi-feudal society. From then on, the Chinese people had engaged in a long struggle for national independence and liberation, namely the struggle for human rights. This phase of history is summarized by the white paper Human Rights in China, published by the Information Office of the State Council in 1991, as the followings: "Under long years of oppression by the "three big mountains" -imperialism, feudalism and bureaucrat-capitalism-people in old China did not have any human rights to speak of. Suffering bitterly from this, the Chinese people fought for more than a century, defying death and personal sacrifices and advancing wave upon wave, in an arduous struggle to overthrow the "three big mountains" and gain their human rights." The process of this great struggle can be roughly divided into the following stages:

The denunciation of feudal ethics, with loyalty to the monarch and filial piety as its core, by Kang Youwei, Liang Qichao and others based on "nature rights" theory in the last days of the Qing Dynasty. Kang Youwei pointed out that: "All human beings, regardless of their gender, are born equal and endowed with the right of autonomy."① Liang Qichao also wrote that: "Human rights are natural rights. All human beings are born equal and endowed with the right of autonomy."② The reformists represented by Kang Youwei and Liang Qichao opposed feudal absolute monarchy and advocated democratic reform and the protection of human rights. They pointed out that: "The monarch is like the cart and the people like the horse. You cannot put the monarch before the people just as

① Kang Youwei, *Kang Youwei's Two Books on the Great Harmony*, Beijing: SDX Joint Publishing Company, 1998, p. 188.

② Liang Qichao (ed.), *Selected Commentaries on Current Events*, Vol. 1, Part I, Beijing: SDX Joint Publishing Company, 1960, p. 30.

you cannot put cart before the horse"① and that "of all political systems, only democracy accords with universal truth."② Although the reform failed under the suppression by the conservative forces in the Qing Government, the ideas disseminated by the reformists had exerted a positive influence on the intellectuals and the general public.

The failure of the reform by Kang Youwei, Liang Qichao and others fueled the determination of bourgeois revolutionaries headed by Sun Yat-sen to overthrow the Qing Government and struggle for human rights with "national revolution". Sun pointed out that "Popular sovereignty is a universally accepted principle of the state"③ and that "The state belongs to the people, rather than one or two families". ④He established the Chinese Revolutionary League (Tung Meng Hui) and summarized its political program as the Three Principles of the People, namely nationalism (national independence), democracy (establishment of a republic), and people's livelihood (equalization of land ownership). Faced with the brutal suppression by the Qing Government, Zou Rong cried out aloud: "Why must we have revolution? It is because the evil regime has deprived us of our natural rights. In order to restore our rights, we must overthrow this regime."⑤ In October 1911, the system of feudal absolute monarch was overthrow by the Wuchang Uprising and the Republic of China was established. In January 1912, Sun Yat-sen became the President of the Republic of China. In March of the same year, he promulgated a Presidential Order, declaring that: "All citizens of the Republic of China are equal and have inherent human rights."⑥ Meanwhile, the Temporary Constitution of the Republic of China provided

---

① Tan Sitong, *Complete Works of Tang Sitong*, Part II, Beijing: Zhonghua Book Company, 1981, p. 339.

② Liang Qichao, "Jean Jacques Rousseau's Theory of Social Contract", in *Xin Min Chong Bao*, No. 12, June 15, 1902.

③ Sun Yet-sen, *Complete Works of Sun Yet-sen*, vol. 3, Beijing: Zhonghua Book Company, 1984, p. 319.

④ Sun Yet-sen, *Complete Works of Sun Yet-sen*, vol. 5, Beijing: Zhonghua Book Company, 1985, pp. 628—629.

⑤ Liang Qichao (ed.), *Selected Commentaries on Current Events*, Vol. 1, Part II, Beijing: SDX Joint Publishing Company, 1960, p. 665.

⑥ See *Collection of Materials of Modern Chinese History*, the 1911 Revolution, vol. 8, Shanghai: Shanghai People's Publishing House, 2000.

for democracy, freedom, equality and human rights as the objectives of struggle for Chinese people. Later the fruit of the revolution was usurped by Yuan Shih-kai. The failure of the Revolution enabled Sun Yat-sen to realize that: "the constitution on paper alone is by no means sufficient to guarantee civil rights... the constitution can become truly effective only after the overthrow of the rules of western powers and warlords." ①

the May 4th Movement in 1919 and the establishment of the CPC in 1921 marked new phases in Chinese people's struggle for human rights. The founders of the CPC, such as Li Dazhao and Chen Duxiu, had not only vigorously advocated human rights, but also pointed out the relationship between human rights and the constitution: "the so-called human rights are the individual rights and freedoms that are enshrined in the constitution, which cannot be deprived by laws" ② and that "the constitution is the soul of modern citizenship, the guarantee of citizens' freedoms, and the creed of all citizens of Republic of China." ③ Ever since its establishment, the CPC has been devoted to the struggle for human rights. According to the spirit of its Second National Congress, the CPC established alliances for human rights in Beijing, Guangzhou, Shanghai, Shandong and Jiangxi. In February 1923, the CPC organized a major strike by the workers of Beijing-Hankou Railway Company and, faced with bloody suppression by warlord Wu Peifu, it put forward the slogan of "Fight for freedom and human rights!" After the Mukden Incident in 1931, the Japanese imperialists launched a full-scale invasion of China. At this critical moment of national subjugation, the Central Committee of CPC issued the Appeal to All Fellow Countrymen to Resist Japanese Invasion and Save the Chinese Nation on August 1, 1935, which called upon all Chinese compatriots to "Fight for our homeland! Fight for the survival of the Chinese nation! Fight for national independence! Fight for territorial integrity! And fight for human rights and freedoms!" The struggle for human rights and freedoms had always been a banner held by the CPC in the struggle against feudal warlords and

---

① Sun Yat-sen, *Selected Works of Sun Yat-sen*, Beijing: People's Publishing House, 1956, p. 522.

② Chen Duxiu, *Selected Works of Chen Duxiu*, vol. 1, Beijing: People's Publishing House, 1984, p. 166.

③ Li Dazhao, *Collected Works of Li Dazhao*, Part I, Beijing: People's Publishing House, 1984, pp. 157 and 168.

Japanese aggressors.

After the breakout of the Anti-Japanese War in 1937, the CPC, supported by the Chinese people of the whole country, began cooperation with Kuomintang (KMT) and established an Anti-Japanese national united front. In KMT controlled areas, a number of patriotic democratic personages, including Cai Yuanpei, Soong Ching-ling, Lu Xun, Yang Xingfo, Hu Shi, Xu Zhimo, Pan Guangdan, and Luo Longji, carried forward the tradition of the New Cultural Movement and vigorously advocated human rights. Madam Soong Ching-ling and others established in Shanghai China League for the Protection of Civil Rights aimed at mobilizing the people to participate in the struggle for civil rights. Their activities exerted great influence on Chinese people and forcefully supported the anti-Japanese war. In the anti-Japanese bases under the leadership of the CPC, the anti-Japanese democratic governments promulgated a series of laws and regulations on the protection of human rights, such as the Administrative Program of the Government of Shaanxi-Gansu-Ningxia Border Region, the Regulations of Shaanxi-Gansu-Ningxia Border Region on the Protection of Human Rights and Property Rights, Regulations of Shandong Province on the Protection of Human Rights, Interim Regulations of Hebei-Shandong-Henan Border Region on the Protection of People's Rights, and Regulations of Northwest Shanxi Province on the Protection of Human Rights. These laws and regulations contained specific provisions on the protection of property rights, personal rights and democratic rights and freedoms of the people as well as concrete measures on the their implementation and had played a positive role in mobilizing the people to participate in the war of resistance against Japanese aggressors.

During the period of the War of Liberation, the KMT counterrevolutionaries headed by Chiang Kai-shek and supported by the U. S. imperialists tore up the truce agreement reached between the CPC and KMT in Chongqing Negotiation and tried to eliminate the CPC by force. Faced with the suppression by ferocious counterrevolutionaries, the People's Political Consultative Conference in the KMT controlled areas decided to establish the Committee for the Protection of People's Rights in February 1942 and, at the first meeting of the Committee, the CPC representative Dong Biwu called on people in these areas to organize themselves to defend their own human rights. Later, the CPC launched an anti-civil war, anti-hunger, pro-democracy and pro-freedom patriotic democratic movement in major cities controlled by KMT. At the same time, governments in the liberated areas, while continuing to implement the human rights laws and regulations promulgated during anti-Japanese war period, adopted new regulations in the field of human rights protection, including the Announcement of the Government of Special Municipality of Harbin on the Prohibition of Unlawful Detention, Arrest, and Interrogation and Other Violations of Human Rights, adopted in April 1948, the Order of the Administrative Office of Henan-Anhui-Jiangsu Border Region Instructing Governments at Various Levels to Truly Protect Human Rights and Strictly Prohibit Arbitrary Arrest, Corporal Punishment and Extorting a Confession by Torture, adopted in May 1948, and the Revised Regulations of Bohai District on the Protection of Human Rights, also adopted in May 1948. The patriotic democratic movement in KMT controlled areas and the implementation of the human rights laws and regulations in liberated areas had provided strong support to the CPC in the war of people's liberation.

The establishment of the People's Republic of China in October1949 marked the end of the rules of imperialism, feudalism and bureaucratic capitalism, the control of political power by the people, and the beginning of a new chapter in human rights construction in China.

II. Improving the Constitution and Laws and Transforming Due Rights into Legal Rights

The CPC and the Chinese people had learnt from their personal experience that the basic question of revolution is political power. This was true both before and after the seizure of political power by the CPC. After taking control of the political power, the CPC must establish and improve the relevant legal systems aimed at consolidating its political power and safeguarding people's hard-won rights. It was based on this understanding that, soon after the establishing of the People's Republic of China, the people's government had adopted the Common Program of the Chinese People's Political Consultative Conference, which served as a provisional constitution at that time, and laws and regulations on the organization of the political power. In 1954, the Constitution of the People's Republic of China was adopted after thorough discussion by Chinese people in the whole country. It should be said that China had made quite remarkable achievements in the making of laws and establishment of relevant institutions during the period between 1949 and mid 1950s, despite the numerous difficult tasks faced by it at that time, such as carrying out democratic reform, suppressing armed bandits, engaging in the War to Resist U. S. Aggression and Aid Korea, and providing supports to peoples of Indo-China in their fight against imperialism. However, just as later pointed out by Deng Xiaoping and the CPC Central Committee, "From old China we inherited a strong tradition of feudal autocracy and a weak tradition of democratic legality. "① As a result, "we were liable, owing to the historical circumstances in which our Party grew, to continue to regard issues unrelated to class struggle as its manifestations when observing and handling new contradictions and problems which cropped up in the political, economic, cultural and other spheres in the course of the development of socialist society. And when confronted with actual class struggle under the new conditions, we habitually fell back on the familiar methods and experiences of the large-scale, turbulent mass struggle of the past, which should no longer have been mechanically followed. As a result, we substantially broadened the scope of class struggle"② and took a wrong path in the adoption of laws and construction of institutions. On reflecting this period of history, especially the lesson of the "Cultural Revolution", Deng Xiaoping pointed out at the Third Plenary Session of the Eleventh CPC Central Committee in 1978 that: "in order to safeguard people's democracy, we must strengthen the legal system",③ "and to ensure that there are laws to go by, that the laws are observed and strictly enforced, and that violators are brought to book. "④ To this end, the CPC and the Chinese government, supported by the people in the whole country, began to revise the Constitution. Before the revision of the Constitution, Deng Xiaoping especially pointed out that: "Our Constitution should be made more complete and precise so as to really ensure the people's right to manage the state organs at all levels as well as

① Deng Xiaoping, *Selected Works of Deng Xiaoping*, vol. 2, Beijing: People's Publishing House, 1995, p. 332.

② "Resolution on Certain Questions in the History of the CPC since the Founding of the People's Republic of China", in Department of Educational Administration of Party School of CPC Central Committee (ed.), *Selection of Important Documents of CPC and the Government Since the Third Plenary Session of the Eleventh Central Committee*, Beijing: Party School of CPC Central Committee Press, 2008, pp. 95—56.

③ *Supra* note 13, p. 146.

④ Ibid. , p. 147.

the various enterprises and institutions, to guarantee to our people the full enjoyment of their rights as citizens"①

The 1982 Constitution preserves the advantages of the 1954 Constitution, contains further provisions on the fundament rights of citizens, and moves the "Fundamental Rights and Freedoms of Citizens" from Chapter three to Chapter Two to give them more prominence. After the promulgation of the 1982 Constitution, the National People's Congress, in light of the actual need of socialist construction and the deepening of reform and opening up, adopted four constitutional amendments in 1988, 1993, 1999 and 2004, respectively. The main contents of these amendments include: first, the confirmation that "China will be at the primary stage of socialism for a long period of time", at which the main task of the country is to adhere to the policy of "reform and opening up" and to build socialism with Chinese characteristics; second, developing socialist market economy, adhering to the distribution system in which distribution according to work is dominant and diverse modes of distribution coexist; third, "The state establishes and improves the social security system fitting in with the level of economic development"; fourth, the establishment of constitutional principles of "ruling the country in accordance with the law and building a socialist country of law" and "the long-term existence and development of the system of the multi-party cooperation and political consultation led by the Communist Party of China"; and fifth, the establishment of "the state respects and protects human rights" as an important constitutional principle. The establishment of the above principles further improves the legal safeguards for economic, political, social and cultural rights in China.

Political rights. Political rights are the rights of people to participate in the management of state affairs. The Chinese Constitution provides that: "All power in the People's Republic of China belongs to the people. The National People's Congress and the local people's congresses at various levels are the organs through which the people exercise state power." People exercise this right mainly by electing deputies to the people's congresses, which in turn elect and appoint state functionaries. Deputies to people's congresses at the county and township levels are elected directly by their constituencies; deputies to the people's congresses of provinces, municipalities directly under the Central Government and cities divided

① *Supra* note 13, p. 339.

into districts are elected by the people's congresses at the next lower level in competitive elections; competitive election is applied to the vice chairmen of the standing committees of local people's congresses at various levels; competitive election is also applied to the chairmen of the standing committees of people's congresses, heads of various organs of the people's governments, presidents of people's courts and presidents of people's procuratorates at various local levels. However, single-candidate election can also be applied if only one candidate is nominated for the above-mentioned posts. Besides, the system of autonomous democracy is implemented in rural and urban grassroots units; and deliberative democracy is implemented by civil society and political consultative conferences at various levels. Through the above-mentioned forms of democracy, people exercise their right to supervise grassroots organizations, state organs and state functionaries.

Personal rights. Personal rights are rights relating to the human person, personal freedoms and human dignity. The Chinese Constitution provides that freedom of the person of citizens of the People's Republic of China is inviolable. No citizen may be arrested except with the approval or by decision of a people's procuratorate or by decision of a people's court, and arrests must be made by a public security organ. Unlawful detention or deprivation or restriction of citizens' freedom of the person by other means is prohibited, and unlawful search of the person of citizens is prohibited. The personal dignity of citizens is inviolable. Insult, libel, false accusation or false incrimination directed against citizens by any means is prohibited. Citizens' residences are inviolable. Citizens' freedom and privacy of correspondence are protected by law. In accordance with the Constitution, the state has adopted the Criminal Law, the Criminal Procedure Law and other relevant laws to further regulate judicial activities and strengthen the protection of personal rights. Chinese law strictly prohibits the practice of extorting a confession by torture or using any other unlawful means against a witness or his or her close relatives. Anyone who commits any of the above acts "shall be subject to criminal liability in accordance with law if it constitutes a crime; or shall be subject to punishment in public security administration in accordance with law if it is not criminally punishable."① To adapt to new developments of situation, China revised the Criminal Procedure Law and the Criminal Law in 1996

① See Article 49 of the Criminal Procedure Law of the People's Republic of China.

and 1997, respectively. The revised Criminal Law provides for the principle of "legally prescribed punishment for a specified crime" and the revised Criminal Procedure Law provides for the principle of "presumption of innocence". To ensure judicial fairness, the Constitution provides that the people's courts exercise judicial power, and the people's procuratorates exercise procuratorial power, independently, in accordance with the provisions of the law, and are not subject to interference by any administrative organ, public organization or individual. In the process of continuous practice, the state has carried out judicial reform through the revision of relevant laws, gradually established and improved the open trial system, the people's assessors' system, the legal supervision system, the death sentence review system, and the legal aid system.

Economic, social and cultural rights. Satisfying people's increasing material and cultural needs and safeguarding people's economic, social and cultural rights is the substitutive characteristic of the socialist system in China. In accordance with the constitutional principle that "The state implements socialist market economy", China has adopted the General Principles of the Civil Law, the Property Law, the Contract Law, the Patent Law, the Copyright Law, and the Trade Mark Law to guarantee the property right and the intellectual property right, which are the bases of socialist market economy. It has adopted the Company Law, the Partnership Enterprise Law, the Law on Individual Proprietorship Enterprises, the Law on Farmers'Professional Cooperatives, the Anti-Monopoly Law, and the Anti-Unfair Competition Law to safeguard the lawful status of the subjects of market, ensure their equal participation in market competition, and promote the healthy development of the market economy; it has adopted the Labor Law, the Labor Contract Law, the Employment Promotion Law, the Production Safety Law, the Law on the Prevention and Treatment of Occupational Diseases, the Regulation on Work-Related Injury Insurance, the Regulations on Unemployment Insurance, and the Regulations on Guaranteeing Minimum Subsistence for City Residents to promote employment and gradually improve social security system; it has adopted the Product Quality Law, the Food Hygiene Law, the Pharmaceutical Administration Law, and the Law on the Protection of Consumer Rights and Interests, the Environmental Protection Law, the Law on the Prevention and Control of Air Pollution, and the Law on the Prevention and Control of Air Pollution to safeguard people's living environment and physical health; and it has adopted the

Education Law, Law on Higher Education, Vocation Education Law, and Teachers' Law to implement the system of nine-year compulsory education, develop secondary and higher education, and improve people's cultural quality and their level of social civilization.

The rights of ethnic minorities. China is a unitary multi-national state with 56 nationalities. The Han nationality makes up 92%, and the other 55 nationalities 8%, of the total population of the country. "The unification of our country, the unity of our people and the unity of our various nationalities-these are the basic guarantees for the sure triumph of our cause."① The Constitution contains detailed provisions on the protection of the rights of minority nationalities. It provides in the General Principles that "All nationalities in the People's Republic of China are equal. The state protects the lawful rights and interests of the minority nationalities and upholds and develops a relationship of equality, unity and mutual assistance among all of China's nationalities. Discrimination against and oppression of any nationality are prohibited; any act which undermines the unity of the nationalities or instigates division is prohibited" and that "Regional autonomy is practiced in areas where people of minority nationalities live in concentrated communities; in these areas organs of self-government are established to exercise the power of autonomy." Chapter Three (State Organs) of the Constitution contains a special section on "The Organs of Self-Government of National Autonomous Areas". In accordance with the Constitution, the state adopted the Law on Regional National Autonomy in 1984. The organs of self-government of national autonomous areas share common characteristics with ordinary state organs while at the same time have their own unique characteristics. In the selection and appointment of cadres in a minority area, preferential treatment shall be given to the minority nationality exercising regional autonomy in the administrative area and other minority nationalities inhabiting the area. Compared with ordinary state organs at the same level, organs of self-government have greater power in making local regulations and separate regulations and in economic management; the percentages of members of minority nationalities among deputies to the National People's Congress and local people's congresses at various levels are much higher than the percentages of minority nationalities in the

① Mao Zedong, *Selected Works of Mao Zedong*, vol. 5, Beijing: People's Publishing House, 1977, p. 363.

population. The implementation of the system of regional national autonomy in China has upheld the unification of the country and unity of nationalities, and promoted the common development of minority nationalities within the big family of Chinese nation.

Rights of women and children. Women make up half of the population in the country and are a major force in the socialist construction. Children are the future of the country and their healthy development is the hope of the whole society. The Chinese Constitution provides that: "Women in the People's Republic of China enjoy equal rights with men in all spheres of life, including political, economic, cultural, social and family life" and that "Marriage, the family and mother and child are protected by the state." In accordance with the Constitution, the state has promulgated the Marriage Law, the Law on the Protection of Women's Rights and Interests, the Law on Maternal and Infant Health Care, and the Law on the Protection of Minors. In order to better implement the above-mentioned laws, the State Council promulgated programs of for the development of women and programs for the development of children's rights. The implementation of the above laws and programs has effectively safeguarded the rights and interests of women and minors.

Rights of disabled persons. Currently the number of disabled persons in China has reached 83 million, which make up over 5% of the total population in the country. The protraction of their rights has a direct bearing on the wellbeing of tens of millions of families and the stability and development of the whole society. The Constitution provides that: "Citizens have the right to material assistance from the state and society when they are old, ill or disabled" and that "The state and society help make arrangements for the work, livelihood and education of the blind, deaf-mutes and other handicapped citizens." In accordance with the Constitution, the state has promulgated the Law on the Protection of Disabled Persons. And in accordance with the Constitution Law on the Protection of Disabled Persons, the State Council has promulgated the Regulation on the Employment of Disabled Persons, Several Opinions on the Development of Education of Disabled Persons, and Five-Year Development Plan for Disabled Persons and other relevant laws and regulations. Various provinces, autonomous regions and municipalities directly under the Central Government have adopted local regulations on the safeguarding of the rights and interests of disabled persons in light of their respective local situations. Chinese laws strictly prohibit the discrimination against, insult, abuse, infringement upon the rights, and maltreatment and abandonment of disabled persons; infringements upon the right of person or other lawful rights of disabled persons by taking advantage of their disabilities that constitutes a crime shall be given a heavier punishment in accordance with the relevant provisions of the Criminal Law; to better uphold the rights and interests of disabled persons, the state has established federations of disabled persons in all provisions (with the exception of Taiwan), autonomous regions, municipalities, and in all prefectures and counties.

The above provisions in the Constitution and laws show that, during the past 30 years of "reform and opening up", China has been learning from the lessons of the "Cultural Revolution" and the mistakes made before that and continuously improving the system of law with the Constitution at its core, including the human rights safeguarding system. By basing itself on the actual situations in China and drawing on all the achievements of human civilization, China has been able to continuously raise the quality of legislation. Meanwhile, China has also actively participated in the international human rights protection and ratified a total of 23 international human rights conventions, including the International Covenant on Economic, Social and Cultural Rights, the International Convention on the Elimination of All Forms of Racial Discrimination, the Convention on the Elimination of All Forms of Discrimination against Women, the Convention against Torture and Other Cruel, Inhuman or Degrading Treatment or Punishment, the Convention on the Rights of the Child, and the International Convention on the Status of Refugees. And currently China has already signed the International Convention on Civil and Political Rights, and is in the process of deliberation for the ratification of the Covenant. The international human rights conventions ratified by China is a component of the system of human rights law in China and play an important role in the safeguarding of human rights in the country.

III. Wholeheartedly Seeking Development and Providing Material and Cultural Safeguards for the Realization of Human Rights

Karl Marx pointed out that "Right can never be higher than the economic structure of society and its cultural development conditioned thereby."[①] Its has been proven that, in order for legal rights to become the rights actually enjoyed by the people, the state must reform the social and economic structure and develop social, economic and cultural undertakings. China started to carry out this historical task immediately after the establishment of the People's Republic in 1949, and redoubled its efforts and went on a fast track of development after the Third Plenary Session of the CPC Central Committee in 1978, and since then has made achievements that attracted worldwide attention.

China had been a large country with a huge population and an agricultural natural economy. Land had been the most basic means of production in China. However, before 1949, most land was in the hands of landlords and rich peasants. Poor peasants who made up the majority of the population in the country had either no or little land. To change this situation, the Chinese government promulgated the Land Reform Law in 1950 and, on the basis of the land reform in the old liberated areas, carried out land reforms in the newly liberated areas to distribute land among peasants who had no or little land. The implementation of the land reform and the marriage law and the democratic reform carried out in cities enabled the broad masses of people to free themselves from the oppression by feudal forces, and greatly enhanced their enthusiasm for participating in socialist construction. While engaging in the War to Resist U. S. Aggression and Aid Korea, China rapidly restored the national economy, which had suffered serious damages during the long period of war. By the end of 1952, the level of agricultural and industrial production in China had reached the historical high.

On the above-mentioned basis, China began large-scale socialist economic construction in 1953, and decided to gradually realize socialist industrialization, socialist transformation of agriculture, handicraft industry and capitalist industry and commerce, and adjustment of social and economic structure. Between 1953 and 1956, the gross value of industrial output had been increasing at an average annual rate of 19.6%; and the gross value of agricultural output had been increasing at an average annual rate of 4.8%. During this period, the market had been brisk, the commodity price stable, people's living standard rising continuously and

① Marx and Friedrich Engels, *Selected Works of Karl Marx and Friedrich Engels* (Chinese Edition), vol. 3, Beijing: People's Publishing House, 1995, p. 305.

social order good.

Between 1956 and 1976, China implemented strict planned economy. Because of the lack of experience and the eagerness to defeat the blockade and containment by external hostile forces and to success in economic development, the Chinese leaders had made many big mistakes, including the "Cultural Revolution", and suffered major setbacks in economic construction. Fortunately, the broad masses of Chinese people still had not lost their confidence in CPC's leadership and a large number of CPC cadres and ordinary CPC members still adhered to the correct direction. During the ten years before the "Cultural Revolution", the socialist economy continued to develop. "By 1966, the value of fixed industrial assets, calculated on the basis of their original prices, was four times greater than in 1956. The output of such major industrial products as cotton yarn, coal, electricity, crude oil, steel and mechanical equipment all recorded impressive increases. Capital construction in agriculture and its technical transformation began on a massive scale and yielded better and better results. Both the number of tractors for farming and the quantity of chemical fertilizers applied increased over six times."① During the ten-year "Cultural Revolution", some progress was made in the development of the national economy despite tremendous losses: "Grain output increased relatively steadily. Significant achievements were scored in industry, communications and capital construction and in science and technology."②

In 1978, CPC at the Third Plenary Session of its Eleventh Central Committee summarized the historical experiences both in China and abroad and decided to implement the policy of emancipating the mind, reform and opening up, and shift the emphasis of work from class struggle to economic construction. From then on, the reform and development in China has been unfolding on a magnificent scale. Between 1978 and 1992, China had been groping the way forward in economic reform, first in rural areas, then in urban areas. In 1992, China set the goal of developing socialist market economy, thereby further determining the direction and speeding up the pace of the reform. The Outline of the Ninth Five-Year

---

① See *Resolution on Certain Questions in the History of the CPC since the Founding of the People's Republic of China*, adopted at the Sixth Plenary Session of the Eleventh Central Committee of the Communist Party of China on June 27, 1981.

② Ibid.

Plan for National Economic and Social Development and the Long-Term Goals to the Year 2010, adopted at the Fourth Session of the Eighth National People's Congress in 1996, set the goals of quadrupling the GNP of 1980 by the year 2000, basically eradicating poverty, raising people's living standard to a relatively comfortable level, and quadrupling the GNP of 2000 by the year 2010. In 2002, after reaching the goal of raising people's living standard to a relatively comfortable level, the CPC and the Chinese government decided that, in the first two decades of the 21 century, namely before the year 2020, China would concentrate on building a well-off society of a higher standard in an all-round way, to the benefit of well over one billion people. Today, the Chinese people are forging ahead towards this goal.

To realize healthy development and build socialism with Chinese characteristics, the CPC and the Chinese Government put forward the scientific outlook on people-oriented, comprehensive, harmonious and sustainable development, which means to take the realization of people's interests as the starting point, the process, and the ultimate goal of socialist development; to realize the comprehensive development of social production force, relations of production, economic basis and superstructure; to coordinate between economic, political, cultural, and social development and between the development in various sectors of the economy, and to coordinate the relations between the natural environment, human resources, and economic and political systems, so as to lay a sound foundation for sustainable development and for the development of the future generations. The purpose of putting forward the scientific outlook on development is to rectify the tendency of some government departments and officials of attaching too much importance to the growth of GDP while ignoring such problems as environmental pollution, the waste of resources, and the violation of the rights and interests, even the right to life, of the people, in the process of rapid development. This outlook is in complete agreement with the principles that "The human person is the central subject of development" and that "The right to development is a universal and inalienable human right" provided for in the UN Declaration on the Right to Development. It was exactly because China has recognized the overriding importance of development and adhered to the scientific outlook on development that it has been able to make huge achievements in the development of economic, political, cultural and social undertakings and in the safeguarding of human rights. In

2004, the GDP in China had reached 13.65 trillion yuan, 9.5% higher that of the previous year; 9.8 million new jobs were created in urban areas; the per capita disposable income of urban residents reached 9, 422 yuan, the rural per capita net income reached 2, 936 yuan, and there was a big increase in the level of social security of urban and rural residents with respect to housing, medical care, education. Meanwhile, China has also made great progress in the protection of people's political, personal and cultural rights. Indisputable facts have proved the genuineness of the human rights protection in China.

Comrades, the universality of human rights discussed above is not only embodied in the UN Charter and the Universal Declaration of Human Rights, but also proved by historical facts. In today's world of rapid scientific and technological development and economic globalization, the distance between peoples around the world is become shorter and shorter. While sharing common rights, interests and opportunities, they are also faced with common crises and challenges: natural disasters triggered by the greenhouse effect, the restrictions on social and economic development by the shortage of resources, the effect of soil erosion and air pollution on food safety and the survival of mankind, the threat of terrorism and weapons of mass destruction, and armed conflicts and local wars triggered by racial, ethnic, and religious conflicts and unilateralism, etc. The prevention and solution of these problems is beyond the capability of any one country and can be achieved only through international cooperation. Under this circumstance and in order to achieve lasting peace and common prosperity, China has put forward the idea of building a harmonious world. In the so-called harmonious world, states should promote democracy, respect each other politically, cooperate with each other economically, learn from each other culturally, trust each other in the matter of security, settle international disputes by peaceful means, assist and cooperate with each other in dealing with environmental issues and in taking good care of the Earth, the only home of human beings. The idea of building a harmonious world is a new development of the idea of establishing "a social and international order in which the rights and freedoms set forth in the Universal Declaration of Human Rights can be fully realized." China and Laos are close neighbors. The people of the two countries have fought side by side and built ties of profound friendship with each other in the struggle against imperialism and colonialism and continued to support each other after achieving national independence. Today, they are both devoted to the construction and improvement of human rights protection system in light of their respective national conditions. I believe that, under the leadership of the CPC and Lao People's Revolutionary Party, the peoples of the two countries will continue to co-operate closely with each other and jointly promote the development of the socialist cause and enjoy fuller human rights in the future.

Strengthening the Protection of Labor Rights and the Right to Information[①]

The convening of the Fifteenth EU-China Seminar on Human Rights and Administration of Justice coincides with the 40th Anniversary of the adoption by the UN of the 1966 International Covenant on Economic, Social and Cultural Rights (ICESCR) and International Covenant on Civil and Political Rights (ICCPR), which gives this seminar special significance as compared to the pervious ones. The adoption of the two international human rights covenants is a milestone in the development of international human rights law in that it turns the basic principles proclaimed in the Universal Declaration of human Rights into binding international code of conduct. This is a fruit of as well as a motive force for the development of human civilization. This year, the UN established in the process of reform the Human Rights Council which is aimed at strengthening the supervision over international protection of human rights. This is a result of the long-term influence of the two international human rights covenants and indicates that the international community is attaching increasing importance to the protection of human rights. Both China and EU play a very important role in human development because of their large territories and the proportions of their populations in the world population. For this reason, the contents of this seminar and the pervious ones are not only conducive to the implementation of the two human rights covenants and improvement of the human rights protection systems in China and EU countries, but also have profound influence on the entire international community. It has been proven that such seminar is a very good channel of communication and means of mutual leaning for scholars of different countries.

---

① Originally a speech given by the author at the closing ceremony of the Fifteenth EU-China Seminar on Human Rights and Administration of Justice.

The main themes of this seminar, namely labor rights and the right to information, are provided for in articles 23 and 24 of the Universal Declaration of Human Rights, articles 6, 7 and 8 of the ICESCR, and article 19 of the ICCPR. The basic principles and spirits of these provisions are also embodied in the Chinese Constitution, the constitutions of EU member states and the European Convention on Human Rights. Here I will not repeat the contents of these provisions, which you are all very familiar with and have been repeatedly quoted by many participants during the discussions at the seminar, but only point out that, just as many speakers have said, labor rights and the right to information are both composite rights, namely, none of them is as simple as its name suggests, but contains many other relevant rights. This shows that the interrelations and indivisibility of human rights is embodied not only in human rights in general, but also in each specific human right. For example, the realization of labor rights requires the enhancement of relevant knowledge, the improvement of work conditions, and the safeguarding of the livelihood of laborers; the realization of the right to information requires the necessary facilities, resources and institutional guarantees. Therefore, we should understand that, in real world, labor rights involve not only ICESCR and the right to information involves not only the ICCPR, and that corresponding conditions and safeguards must be created in order to realize these rights. The fact that labor rights and the right to information have been enshrined in national constitutions and international conventions means that these rights are not ordinary rights, but fundamental human rights protected by international law and international conventions. This understanding is very important to the realization of these rights.

The understanding of labor rights and the right to information as fundamental human rights guaranteed by domestic constitutions and international human rights conventions is conducive to enhancing people's consciousness of the government's obligations under domestic constitution and international conventions to safeguard human rights. Rights and obligations are closely related. The affirmation of a certain right as constitutional right means the government is under the obligation to take measures for the realization of this right. This is because the government is formed by the representatives elected by the people for the purpose of realizing and safeguarding their rights. After the adoption of the two international human rights covenants, the academic circle divides the rights provided for in the ICESCR and ICCPR into two categories:

"positive rights" and "negative rights", the former require the government to take measures to create conditions for their realization whereas the latter do not. Such a division is at best of limited significance. Actually, the realization of any right requires the fulfillment of certain obligations and the creation of certain conditions by the government. It has been proven that the role played by the government in the realization of labor rights and the right to information can be divided into direct role and indirect role. The former means the government or its subsidiary organs have to take direct measures to create conditions for the realization of labor rights and the right to information while the latter means that the government has to supervise enterprises, public institutions and social organizations in the fulfillment of their social responsibilities and their legal obligations relating to labor rights and the right to information. When discussing labor rights and the right to information, people tend to discuss only the direct obligations of the government, which are of course very important because the government plays a major role in creating jobs, providing training and social security to workers, improving facilities for the dissemination of information, increasing the transparency of its own operation, and mastering information resources. However, in the process economic globalization and rapid development of science and technology, there have emerged a number of large enterprises both in China and in EU member states. Some transnational corporations even have more wealth than many states. Their fulfillment of social responsibilities is of great importance to the safeguarding of labor rights, the right to information and other human rights. In order to safeguard human rights, the government must strengthen the supervision over them. Of course, emphasizing the government's negative obligation with respect to labor rights and the right to information does not mean that these rights can be exercised without any restriction. Generally speaking, the realization of labor rights is conditioned by social system and the level of social development whereas the right to information is restricted by national security and privacy. Article 19 of the ICCPR, while affirming the right to information, provides for the various restrictions on the exercise of this right, including "respect of the rights or reputations of others" and "the protection of national security or of public order (ordre public), or of public health or morals". The state must safeguard citizens' right to information and freedom of speech while at the same time regulate the exercise of these rights and strike a balance between freedom and order, so as to maintain social stability and promote development. This is exactly what China, EU member states and all the others countries trying to do.

Just as many speakers at the seminar have pointed out, the discussions on labor rights and the right to information at this seminar are of great theoretical as well as practical significance to China and EU member states. In the process of economic globalization, China is now developing the market economy and undergoing the transition from the planned economy to the socialist market economy. Some new EU member states are undergoing the same transition while many others are also carrying reform to varying degrees, so as to adapt to the new situation. This means that both China and EU are faced with opportunities and challenges in realizing labor rights and the right to information. Although China has already made great achievements in this respect, many problems remain to be solved. With respect to labor rights, the most prominent problems faced by China include the arrangement for the surplus labor force in urban and rural areas, the "three rural problems", the problems relating to education, and the problem of the coverage of medical services and social security. With respect to the right to information, the main problems faced by China include the transparency of the operation of the government and the regulation of the mass media. EU member states are also faced with the problem of unemployment, and problems with migrant workers relating to wages, social security and visits by their family members. With respect to right to information, some EU countries are faced with the problem of the propaganda for new Fascism and misleading of the public on such major issue as war. With respect to the issue of corporate social responsibilities, both China and EU have the problem of weak supervision. In order to attract foreign capital, some local governments in China give foreign enterprises preferential treatments that exceed the extend allowed by state laws and policies and conduct strict supervise over the behaviors of foreign and private enterprises, resulting in many serious problems relating to wages, production safety, environmental pollution, and product quality, which seriously violate the rights and interests, even endanger the life and health, of employees and the general public. Some European-based transnational corporations have adopted discriminatory policies towards Chinese employees in terms of wages and other treatments. All these problems should be dealt with at their sources. Namely, the home countries of these transnational corporations should strengthen the supervision over these corporations, so as to embody the universality of human rights.

Many examples given by the speakers at the seminar have shown that governments should publicize labor rights, the right to information, and other fundamental human rights provided for by the two international human rights covenants in light of the actual situation of the country and embody these rights in its domestic laws, judicial practices and policies, so as to better understand and implement them. In the past few years, especially since the signing of the two international human rights covenants and the ratification of the ICESCR, the Chinese government and NGOs have carried out systematic campaigns of dissemination of the knowledge of laws and human rights by such means of seminars, lectures, training courses, newspapers, magazines, books and other media, thereby greatly enhancing Chinese people's human rights awareness. To better mobilize the people to struggle for human rights and based on traditional Chinese culture, the Chinese government has used vivid languages to describe the objectives of different stages of socialist construction and development of human rights protection system: namely to have "adequate food and clothing for the Chinese people" at the beginning of the reform and opening up, "to lead a relatively comfortable life" in the early 1990s, and "to build a well-off society in an all-round way" in 2001, when China's per capita GDP reached 1, 000 US dollars. The objectives of "having adequate food and clothing" and "realizing a relatively comfortable life" are mainly embodied in economic indexes and emphasize material civilization, whereas the objective of "building a well-off society in an all-round way", while continues to take economic development as its basis, also contains the objectives of political, cultural, scientific, technological and social developments. Not long ago, the highest decision-making organ of the ruling party in China put forward in a resolution the objective of constructing a socialist harmonious society, namely a dynamic and stable society that is democratic, law-based, fair, just, honest and friendly where man and nature live in harmony. This objective includes economic, political, legal, cultural ideological, moral, as well as social and natural environmental content. It covers and further develops the objective of "building a well-off society in an all-round way". To realize these objectives, the highest decision-making organ in China has put forward the scientific outlook on people-oriented, comprehensive, coordinated and sustainable development. Here, the concept of "people" in "people-oriented" is the same as the "human" in "human rights", which refers to all human beings in contrast to "god" and "things". Being "people-oriented" means taking the people as the starting point, the basis and the ultimate goal of development. "Comprehensive development" means the development of not only the social and economic bases, but also the superstructure; "coordinated development" means the coordination of relations between economic, political, cultural and social developments as well as between various parts of each of the above-mention fields of development; "sustainable development" requires not only the conservation of resources and the protection of the environment, but also the cultivation of talents. Harmonious society is not only an objective of socialist construction, but also a social order necessary for the safeguarding of human rights in China.

To build a harmonious society and uphold world peace, the Chinese government has put forward the objective of promoting the construction of a harmonious world. To the end, China will devote itself to promoting the mutual respect between different countries and respect for the right of people of each country to freely decide their own social system and development road, the co-operation, common development, mutual benefit, and co-prosperity between different countries, the strengthening of mutual trust, dialogue, and cooperation between states, the peaceful solution of international disputes, and maintenance of international and regional peace and stability, the exchange between different cultures, the diversity of the world and the progress of human civilization. The EU-China seminar on human rights and administration of justice is a channel of communication between different cultures, which is conducive to promoting the mutual understanding and the establishment of a harmonious relationship between China and EU countries. At the seminar, some European experts expressed the concern that the construction of harmonious society in China will conflict with the publicity and implementation of human rights. This concern is unnecessary. The content of harmonious society shows that its construction will create material, political, spiritual and social conditions for the realization of human rights. It can be expected that, with the construction of the harmonious society, the various factors affecting social harmony will be eliminated one by one, and the human rights protection in China will certainly reach a new level.

Fair Trial: An Objective Yet to Be Achieved[①]

I

The Chinese government and the EU, after negotiation, have decided to make "fair trial" one of the two topics to be discussed at the Seventeenth EU-China Seminar on Administration of Justice and Human Rights. A similar topic, namely "access to justice", has been discussed several years ago in a seminar organized under the framework of EU-China Human Rights Network. The two topics are similar because they contain basically the same elements, such as "fairness" and "trial"; yet they are not identical because they have different emphases: unlike "fair trial", "access to justice" takes the great masses of the people as its starting point. Nevertheless, "fair trial" is still a positive concept whether in terms of the construction of state system or in terms of the protection of the protection of the rights of the people. In Chinese language, the "fair" in "fair trial" has two levels of meaning: first, "impartiality", namely being disinterested and observing the law; second, "justice", namely being reasonable and embodying the interests of the people. Together, "fair trial" refers to the attitude that should be adopted by the judge in the trial of a case and the value objective that should be achieved by the trial. An ancient Chinese thinker, when discussing the development of the legal system, said that "Ancient laws need not to be followed if they can no long meet the need of the contemporary times. A ruler should make laws and establish institutions in light of the actual situation of his country."[②] In today's world of rapid development of science and technology and

① Originally a presentation given at the Seventeenth EU-China Seminar on Human Rights and Administration of Justice.

② Shang Jun Shu, Reform of the Law.

economic globalization, the laws and institutions in China and in EU member states are in a process of transition. Therefore, even if the topic of this seminar is identical to that of the seminar held under the EU-China Human Rights Network several years ago, there will always new issues to discuss under the same topic because of passage of time and change of situation, and therefore the seminar will still has practical significance.

It should also be pointed out that the title of my presentation, "Fair Trial: an Objective yet to Be Achieved", is not intended to depreciate the current level of fair trial in China or in EU member states, but to remind you that the realization of fair trial is a long-term objective, for the realization of which unremitting efforts have been made by our ancestors, are still being made by our own generation, and will continue to be made by the future generations.

II

As early as 2, 000 years ago, ancient sages in China had attached great importance to the fairness of trial and the impartial application of criminal punishments. They pointed out that "fair administration of punishments and penalties give people the feeling of safety and stability"① and that: "arbitrary application of criminal punishments makes the people at a loss as to what to do." To achieve the objective of fair trial, they had put forward a series of principles, such as the principle of equality before the law: "ministers and commoners shall be treated alike in punishment and reward"② and "punishment shall be imposed on any one who commits a crime, including those who are close to and loved by the king."③ Ancient Chinese law prohibited the practice of soliciting favor before a judge on behalf of a party to lawsuit: "whoever solicits favor on behalf of a party to a case shall be punished with a flogging of fifty strokes. A judge who accepts such solicitation shall also be punished with fifty strokes of flogging; and those who bend the law for personal gains shall be given severer punishment."④ Extorting a confession by torture was not

① See Liji, Dazhuan.

② See Hanfeizi, Youdu.

③ See the Analects, Zilu.

④ See Commentary of Criminal Law of Tang Dynasty: the System of Government Officials.

encouraged in the interrogation of criminal suspects: "the best way to try a case is to be able to prove the guiltiness or the innocence of a defendant without resorting to torture; the bad way is to resort to torture; and the worst way is to resort to not only torture, but also terror..."①; ancient Chinese laws provided for the accountability of judges for unjust handling of cases: "What is the crime of unjust handling of cases? It's giving light punishment where heavy punishment should be given, or giving heavy punishment where light punishment should be given, or not prosecute a person who has committed a crime and should be prosecuted according to law."② Since the Qin Dynasty, the laws of every dynasty had provided for the crime of unjust handling of cases. In west history, Solon, a famous statesman in ancient Greece, in order to alleviate the conflicts between aristocrats and commoners, had put forward the idea of equality before the law: "laws shall treat equally without discrimination all citizens, whether nobles or commoners and enable everyone to play his proper role in society." In the field of litigation, the equity law, which was developed in the 14th century, two century after the emergence of the common law in Britain in the 11th century, on the basis of the case law of equity courts. According to this law, a party to a case who thinks that the case has not been handled in a fair way by a common law court may request a specially appointed judge to try the case in accordance with the principles of equity. A large amount of historical materials show that advanced ideas and systems had been developed both in ancient China and in ancient Europe, which had played certain role in promoting the development of history. However, such ideas and systems could not have been truly realized or implemented in slave or feudal societies. It was only in the 17th and 18th centuries that the situation began to change.

With the bourgeois revolution that began in Britain in the 16th century and the American War of Independence and the French Revolution in the 18th century, human history had entered into a new stage of development. The principles established during the revolution, such as democracy, freedom, human rights, separation of powers, legally prescribed punishment for a specified crime, and presumption of

---

① See *Qin Dynasty Bamboo Slips Unearthed in Suidihu: Rules on Criminal Procedures*, Beijing: Cultural Relics Publishing House, 1978.

② See *Qin Dynasty Bamboo Slips Unearthed in Suidihu: Questions and Answers on Issues of Law*, Beijing: Cultural Relics Publishing House, 1978.

innocence, and the criminal defense system that has been gradually developed after the revolution have provided institutional safeguard to fair trial. For a long period of time, however, this system had benefited only the bourgeoisie and excluded the poor and the colonial people from its scope of protection and, therefore, was an incomplete system. It began the process of benign development only after long struggle by workers, peasants and other laboring people.

III

The First World War between 1914—1918 and the Second World War between 1941—1945, whiling bring untold sufferings to the people of the world, also weakened the imperialist and colonial rules. The people of the world, baptized by the fire of war, become more aware of their own strength and confident of their ability to master their own fate. At the end of the Second World War, they threw themselves into the new struggle for national independence, freedom and liberation. As a result, a series of human rights instruments have been adopted which are directly related to the topic under discussion in today's seminar, including the UN Charter, the 1948 Universal Declaration of Human Rights, the two international covenants on human rights, and other international human rights conventions.

The UN Charter, declares at its very beginning the purpose of the United Nations: "to save succeeding generations from the scourge of war, which twice in our lifetime has brought untold sorrow to mankind, and to reaffirm faith in fundamental human rights, in the dignity and worth of the human person, in the equal rights of men and women and of nations large and small, and to establish conditions under which justice and respect for the obligations arising from treaties and other sources of international law can be maintained, and to promote social progress and better standards of life in larger freedom" . In accordance with the above provision of the UN Charter, the Universal Declaration of Human Rights provides in Article 8 that:

> "Everyone has the right to an effective remedy by the competent national tribunals for acts violating the fundamental rights granted him by the constitution or by law" ;

in Article 9 that:

> "No one shall be subjected to arbitrary arrest, detention or exile", in Article 10 that "Everyone is entitled in full equality to a fair and public hearing by an independent and impartial tribunal, in the determination of his rights and obligations and of any criminal charge against him";

and in Article 11 that:

> "1. Everyone charged with a penal offence has the right to be presumed innocent until proved guilty according to law in a public trial at which he has had all the guarantees necessary for his defence.
>
> 2. No one shall be held guilty of any penal offence on account of any act or omission which did not constitute a penal offence, under national or international law, at the time when it was committed. Nor shall a heavier penalty be imposed than the one that was applicable at the time the penal offence was committed."

To give legally binding force to the above provisions, the UN General Assembly adopted in 1966 the International Covenant on Civil and Political Rights, which provides in Article 9 that:

> 1. Everyone has the right to liberty and security of person. No one shall be subjected to arbitrary arrest or detention. No one shall be deprived of his liberty except on such grounds and in accordance with such procedure as are established by law.
>
> 2. Anyone who is arrested shall be informed, at the time of arrest, of the reasons for his arrest and shall be promptly informed of any charges against him.
>
> 3. Anyone arrested or detained on a criminal charge shall be brought promptly before a judge or other officer authorized by law to exercise judicial power and shall be entitled to trial within a reasonable time or to release. It shall not be the general rule that persons awaiting trial shall be detained in custody, but release may be subject to guarantees to appear for trial, at any other stage of the judicial proceedings, and, should occasion arise, for execution of the judgement.

4. Anyone who is deprived of his liberty by arrest or detention shall be entitled to take proceedings before a court, in order that court may decide without delay on the lawfulness of his detention and order his release if the detention is not lawful.

5. Anyone who has been the victim of unlawful arrest or detention shall have an enforceable right to compensation;

in Article 14 that:

1. All persons shall be equal before the courts and tribunals. In the determination of any criminal charge against him, or of his rights and obligations in a suit at law, everyone shall be entitled to a fair and public hearing by a competent, independent and impartial tribunal established by law...

2. Everyone charged with a criminal offence shall have the right to be presumed innocent until proved guilty according to law.

and in Article 15 that:

1. No one shall be held guilty of any criminal offence on account of any act or omission which did not constitute a criminal offence, under national or international law, at the time when it was committed. Nor shall a heavier penalty be imposed than the one that was applicable at the time when the criminal offence was committed. If, subsequent to the commission of the offence, provision is made by law for the imposition of the lighter penalty, the offender shall benefit thereby.

Today the Universal Declaration of Human Rights has already gained universal acceptance and the International Covenant on Civil and Political Rights have been ratified by over 140 countries and signed by China. According to the spirit of "respect for the obligations arising from treaties and other sources of international law", states that have already ratified the Covenant have the obligation to implement the Covenant and those that have already signed the Covenant and all other UN member states also have the obligation not to engage in any act that contravenes the Covenant.

To ensure the observance of the Covenant, the UN has adopted a series of related instruments, including the Basic Principles on the Independence of the Judiciary, the Guidelines on the Role of Prosecutors, the Basic Principles on the Role of Lawyers, the Convention against Torture and Other Cruel, Inhuman or Degrading Treatment or Punishment, the Code of Conduct for Law Enforcement Officials, and the Principles of Medical Ethics relevant to the Role of Health Personnel, Particularly Physicians, in the Protection of Prisoners and Detainees against Torture, and Other Cruel, Inhuman or Degrading Treatment or Punishment. The principles established in the Covenant and the above-mentioned instruments have become international standards that should be followed by all countries in improving their legislative and judicial systems relating to fair trial.

The international standards are clear and comprehensive. However, due to various factors, such as political prejudice, racial discrimination, defective system, and giving priority to substantive law over procedural law or vice versa, the level of their observance differs greatly from country to country and is very unsatisfactory. Plenty examples of unfair trial can be found all around the world. Here I will only give you two: The first is the O. J. Simpson case in the U. S. , in which the famous American football player who had murdered his own wife was acquitted in criminal trial, but found guilty and ordered to pay a huge sum of compensation by a civil court; the second is that, although the fact that many men and women in China and other Asian countries occupied by Japan during the World War II were forced by the Japanese army to become "comfort women" (sexual slaves) and slave labor has long been confirmed by international tribunal, the Japanese leaders and judicial authorities openly deny this fact by claiming they "could not find any evidence" to support it and refused to apologize or pay compensation to the victims and their families. Although, under the press of world opinion, they were forced to make some insincere understatements about these crimes, they continue to treat the former "comfort women" and slave labors with extreme coldness and showed no willingness to take any action to compensate for their sufferings. These are obvious examples of blatant violation of domestic and international standards of fair trial.

V

Like many EU member states, China is creating conditions for the realization of judicial fairness in the fields of criminal policy, legislation, and judicial practice. By summarizing historical experience and current practice, the Chinese government put forward in 2005 "the scientific outlook on people-oriented, comprehensive, coordinated, and sustainable development" with a view to constructing a harmonious socialist society. The "people" in "people-oriented", as the subject of development, is the same as the "human" in the "human rights". Comprehensive, coordinated and sustainable development includes economic, cultural, political and legal development as well as the development of the system of fair trial. Harmonious society takes democracy and the rule of law as its main content, fairness, justice, stability and order as its value objectives, and fair trial as one of its emphases. This shows that China is creating good conditions in terms of guiding ideology and state policy for the realization of fair trial. But, of course, this does not mean that China is faced with no difficulty or obstacle in the realization of fair trial.

In the process of modernization of the legal system in the past century, China has been continuously drawing on the fruits of the progress of human civilization embodied in the western system of the rule of law, while at the same time carrying forward its own traditional culture. However, mainly because of the aggressions by western powers and Japanese militarists, it has encountered many obstacles and difficulties in this process. For a long period of time after the established of the New China in 1949, because of the blockade by western countries, the Chinese people had concentrated their efforts on upholding national independence and striving for their own survival. As a result of these external and internal factors, China had been closed to the outside world for a long period of time, during which period the operation of the state machinery mainly depended on the policies adopted by state leaders without sufficient democratic discussion. This had resulted in a series of serious mistakes in decision-making which are hard to comprehend.

This situation has been fundamentally changed after 1978, when China established the ideological line of "emancipating the mind and seeking truth from fact" and implemented the policies of reform and opening up, taking economic construction as the center of work, and strengthening the construction of democracy and the legal system. China has made rapid advancement in the construction of the legal system by taking its own national condition as the starting point and drawing on the fruits of the progress of human civilization. Currently, under the general objective of constructing a harmonious society, the Chinese government has adopted a series of measures around the objective of fair trial, including improving legislation, reforming the judicial system and speeding up the training of judicial personnel. Here it should be especially pointed out that the Chinese government adopted in 2006 the criminal policy of "tempering justice with mercy" and made corresponding adjustments to the existing legislative and judicial policies. The so-called "tempering justice with mercy" is to take facts and the law as the criteria in the trial of criminal cases and to impose severe punishments in cases where the circumstance of crime is severe and lenient punishment in cases where the circumstance of the crime is relatively minor. This policy also emphasizes the strict observance of the procedural law. The famous Italian jurist Cesare Bonesana Beccaria once said that the severity of the criminal law is embodied not only in the harshness, but also in the certainty, of the criminal punishments. This scientific assertion has received more attention in China.

On the basis of implementing the system of open trial, the Supreme People's Court decided to take back the power of review of death sentences that had been previously delegated to lower people's courts and implement the system whereby the all the death penalty cases are heard in public in the second instance, so as to unify the legal system and reduce the application of the death penalty. In recent years, the number of death sentences has been decreasing every year and almost none of those who have been sentenced to death with a two-year suspension of execution had been executed after the two-year suspension.

The people's procuratorates have strengthened their legal supervision functions by carrying out strict examination of the criminal cases transferred by public security organs for prosecution, exercising trial supervision over cases where an unjust ruling is made by people's court, and actively seeking external supervision over the investigation corruption cases by themselves, and establishing the system of "people's supervisors". In order to more effectively implement its legal supervision functions, the People's Procuratorate of Beijing Municipality has also adopted provisions on safeguarding the human rights of various participants in proceedings, including victims of crimes, witnesses, defenders, and criminal suspects. This practice has a demonstrative effect on the whole country. The above measures have been taken not only because of the nature of procuratorates as the state organs of legal supervision, but also because of the rise in human rights consciousness of Chinese judicial organs and the

Chinese people.

Evidence is the main basis of trial. To prevent the practice of obtaining evidence by unlawful means, recently China has strengthened the supervision over the process of interrogation of criminal suspects by implementing the system of taking video recording of the whole process of criminal investigation.

Moreover, on the basis of the rise in people's rights consciousness, the Chinese mass media has also strengthened the supervision over the fairness of trial and such supervision has been proven to be very effective.

The above facts have shown that China has adopted a series of policies and laws for and achieve remarkable results in the realization of judicial fairness and fair trial. Its task at the next stage is to further improve the laws relating to fair trial, including the Criminal Law, the Criminal Procedure Law and the Lawyers' Law. I am confident that, with the implementation of the above-mentioned measures, the level of the fairness of trial in China will certainly reach a new high.

The Justiciability of Economic, Social and Cultural Rights[①]

The two-day seminar is drawing to an end. I fully agree with the representative of the Office of UN High Commissioner for Human Rights that this seminar is successful because it is based on adequate preparation by Chinese and foreign experts and scholars, who have expressed their own views from various perspectives at the seminar. These views are of great significance to deepening the understanding of the justiciability of economic, social and cultural rights and promoting the solution of the relevant problems. Here, I will not repeat the views of other participants of the seminar, but only share with you my own opinions on some of the issues discussed at the seminar.

I. One Characteristic of Economic, Social and Cultural Rights

The theoretical circle of international human rights defines economic, social and cultural rights as "positive rights" and civil and political rights as "negative rights". The so-called "positive rights" refer to the rights that require the government to take positive measures to create conditions for their realization and the so-called "negative rights" refer to the rights that require no positive measures, but only non-interference, from the

---

① This article was originally a speech made by the author at the closing ceremony of the "International Seminar on the Justiciability of Economic, Social and Cultural Rights", jointly organized by the Law Institute of Chinese Academy of Social Sciences and the Office of the UN High Commissioner for Human Rights. It was first published in Liu Huawen (ed.), *Study on the Justiciability of Economic, Social and Cultural Rights*, Beijing: China Social Sciences Press, 2008.

government for their realization. Some scholars have reservations on this division of human rights. They believe that all human rights take certain level of economic, political, cultural and social development as the condition for their realization, which can be created only if corresponding measures have been taken by the government. I agree with this opinion. The civil and political rights provided for in the 1776 American Declaration of Independence, the 1789 French Declaration of the Rights of Man and of the Citizen, the 1918 Russian Declaration of Rights of the Working and Exploited People, and the 1949 Common Program of The Chinese People's Political Consultative Conference were all the results of active campaigns and all depend on the positive measures by the government for their realizations. Otherwise, the "human beings" and "citizens" in the American Declaration of Independence and the French Declaration of the Rights of Man and of the Citizen could not have included people of different race, different gender, even different classes. It is clear that, even today, the realization of civil and political rights in any country is dependent on the adoption of corresponding measures and creation of necessary conditions by the national government for their realization.

II. The Justiciability of Economic, Social and Cultural Rights

Since neither economic, social and cultural rights nor civil and political rights are "negative" rights that can be realized without adoption of positive measures by the government, it is not appropriate to say that only the latter have justiciability while the former do not have or have only very limited justiciability. I believe that rights—people's rights—can not be regarded as true rights if not justiciable. Rights can be divided into due rights, legal rights and actual rights and justiciability can be understood in broad sense and in narrow sense. Before becoming legal rights, due rights are moral rights, which, although do not have justiciability in the narrow sense, do have justiciablity in broad sense. Namely, holders of these rights have the right to request assistance from the state and society for their realization. As both Chinese and foreign legislative practices show, people can also demand the government to transform moral rights into legal rights through legislation and, once a right has been transformed from moral right into legal rights, its justiciability becomes self-evident. Administrative justiciability means that the relevant government organs have the obligation to supervise over the implementation of laws. If they fail to fulfill this obligation and such failure has resulted in harms to citizens, the latter have the right to bring legal action against them. If the problem is not resolved after all domestic remedies have been exhausted, citizens can also uphold their rights through the complaint mechanism of the UN Human Rights Council. Of course, the above is only a theoretical possibility. Actually, no country, including China, has reached that level of protection of economic, social and cultural rights. The purpose of this seminar is to improve the economic, social and cultural rights safeguarding system. But of course, in order to do so, conditions must be created through economic, social, cultural development and the development of democracy and the rule of law.

III. Opportunities and Challenges Faced by China in Realization the Justiciability of Economic, Social and Cultural Rights

Justiciability is only one form of remedies for economic, social and cultural rights. As Professor Liu Cuixiao pointed out in her paper, justiciability is important because it is by nature a safeguard for the safeguarding of human rights. China, like many other countries in the world, is currently faced with good opportunities to realize the justiciability of economic, social and cultural rights. Firstly, after 30 years of reform and opening up, China has made rapid progress in economic, cultural, scientific and technological development. In 2007, China's GDP had reached 24. 66 trillion yuan, making China the fourth largest economy in the world. In the same year, the national revenue had reached 5. 13 trillion yuan and foreign exchange reserve had reached 1. 52 trillion US dollars. Socialist democracy and rule of law have been further strengthened, and are people have basic rules to go by in safeguarding their rights and interests. Under this circumstance, the level of the protection of people's economic, social and cultural rights has been raised, providing better material and legal safeguards for the realization of new development objectives. Especially noteworthy is that the highest decision-making organ in China has put forward the scientific outlook on people-oriented, comprehensive, coordinated and sustainable development and the strategy of building a well-off society and socialism with Chinese characteristics in an all-round way, and given priority to solving the increasingly prominent problems relating to people's livelihood, including the imbalance in development between different regions and between urban and rural areas, problems relating to the treatment, especially wage arrears, of migrant peasant workers, problems in compulsory, occupational and higher educations, the problem of the coverage of medical and health services and social security, and problems relating to the development of resources and protection of the environment. The solution of these problems will further facilitate the realization of the economic, social and cultural rights of the Chinese people, increase their enthusiasm in participating in socialist construction, and realize the virtuous cycle of development and safeguarding of rights. On the other hand, however, China is also faced with major challenges in this field. Firstly, with the progress of economic globalization, people's demands for economic, social and cultural rights will gradually increase, and the undertaking of obligations under international conventions will increase the pressure on China for the improvement of the system of safeguarding economic, social and cultural rights; secondly, China still has a long way to go in solving the problems in the safeguarding of certain rights (such as the urban-rural dual structure); the safeguarding of some rights is still at the stage of protection by policies, which must be translated into laws in order to be more stably and operable; thirdly, at the opening ceremony of this seminar, I quoted Mencius as saying "Virtue alone is not sufficient for the exercise of government; laws alone can not carry themselves into practice." In order to truly implement the existing laws, it is necessary to train conscientious law enforcement personnel and establish corresponding institutions; fourthly, the key to safeguarding economic, social and cultural rights is administrative law enforcement, namely the supervision by administrative organs over the fulfillment of social responsibilities by enterprises. In case administrative law enforcement is not in place, other remedies, namely judicial remedies, must be available; fifthly, judicial remedy is said to be the last line of defense for rights. However, the current judicial system in China, under which people's courts have jurisdiction over only cases involving specific administrative acts, but not those involving abstract administrative act, has inevitably limited the judicial remedy for economic, social and cultural rights. China must take positive measures to meet the above challenges in order to truly safeguard economic, social and cultural rights.

IV. Further Emancipating the Mind and Improving the relevant Systems, so as to Realize the Justiciability of Economic, Social and Cultural Rights

At the seminar, the participants have reached consensus on the importance of safeguarding economic, social and cultural rights to social development and human rights protection and exchanged information and opinions on ways to realize the justiciability of economic, social and cultural rights. In light of the current situation in China, the most important thing for China to do is to continue to emancipate people's mind, expand their vision, draw on the wisdom of the masses, summarize its experience in practice, so as to find out solution to the problems. Many years ago, I read an article written by a judge from a grassroots court in Henan Province. It discussed a case in which the land contracted by a woman in a village was requisitioned by the state and the woman received 5,000 yuan compensation for the requisition of land. The villagers' committee brought a lawsuit against the woman demanding her to return the 5,000 yuan compensation on ground that she had married into another family after the contract of the land. There was no concrete law applicable to this case at that time. The Court made a ruling in favor of the woman by invoking the provision on gender equality in the Constitution. This case shows that many difficult problems can be solved as long as we set our wits to work. Currently the Chinese academic circle carrying out discussions on the justiciability of the Chinese Constitution. Although China is not country of the case law system, precedents had been followed along with statutes in the trial of cases in most dynasties in Chinese history. As is pointed out by some Chinese scholars at the seminar, the Chinese Supreme Court has begun the compilation of selected cases and is planning to establish a case-guidance system, which may play a positive role in promoting the justiciability of economic, social and cultural rights. Some scholars also discussed the possibility of drawing on the practice of some countries of invoking international conventions by domestic courts in the trial of cases. In China, the position of international law in domestic legal system is still unclear. Some Chinese laws provide that international treaties shall prevail over Chinese legal provisions in case of conflict between the two. As for the practice of directly invoking international human rights law by domestic court, currently it exists only in a very few countries, such as the Netherlands and Norway. China adopted the approach of transformation towards international law, which is more suitable to its national conditions.

Ladies and gentlemen, this seminar is very important and successful in that the participants have exchanged their experiences and raised many questions on the issue of the justiciability of economic, social and cultural rights. Continuous researches will be carried out in the future on these issues. In order for these researches to get actual results and draw the attention of more people to the relevant issues, we must also carry out publicity of these issues, both among the general public and among government officials and leaders: while the former is important because it can raise people consciousness of their status as subjects of rights and give full play to their initiatives in solving the problems, the latter maybe even more important because the reform and opening in China is a top-down process carried out under the leadership of the CPC and the government. China is now in the process of building a socialist state under the rule of law and, in order to promote the strategy of ruling the country by law, the Chinese President Hu Jingtao recently put forward the principle of the supremacy of the Constitution and the laws. I believe that, with the progress of the construction of the socialist rule of law, China will be able to appropriately solve the problem of the justiciability of economic, social and cultural rights and provide better safeguard for these rights.

Appendix

The Establishment of the UN Human Rights Council and Issues to Which Special Attention Should be Paid by China[①]

In March 2006, the United Nations established the Human Rights Council, which replaces the UN Commission on Human Rights—a subsidiary organ of the UN Economic and Social Council—to become a organ subsidiary to the UN General Assemble and parallel to the Economic and Social Council, thus making the Un organ responsible for promoting human rights protection, together with the UN organs responsible for promoting security and economic and social development, the "three pillars" of the UN. As a result, human rights related activities become the focus of attention of countries, people as well as news media throughout the world. After over one year of efforts by the representatives of the 47 members of the Human Rights Council, including China, the basic system of the Council has already been established and put into operation in accordance with a resolution of the UN General Assembly. In light to the establishment of the Council and the review by the newly established Council of human rights conditions in some countries, China should pay special attention to the following issues and adopt corresponding measures.

I. New Provisions and Several Issues to Which Special Attention Should Be Paid

The purpose of establishing the Human Rights Council is to strengthen the UN human rights mechanism on the basis of the existing mechanisms, further mainstream human rights issues, and more effectively safeguard human rights. In the review of and supervision over the human rights

① This article was originally published in *CASS News in Brief* (2007) No. 56.

situation in various countries, the Council adheres to the principle of universality, objectivity and non-selectivity, advocates constructive international dialogue and the elimination of double standard and politicization. To embody these principles, the Council has established the mechanisms of "universal periodical review", "motion for country-specific review", "Advisory Committee", "special procedures", and "complaint procedure". However, because the Council is made up of representatives of countries with different social systems, levels of development and cultural backgrounds, double standard and political considerations are very difficult to avoid. China should, in light of the experience of the Commission on Human Rights and the actual situation in China, pay special attention of the operation of the above-mentioned mechanisms and related issues.

1. Universal Periodic Review (UPR)

The so-called UPR is the review every four years of the human rights records of all UN Member States. All member States of the Council are be reviewed during their term of membership. The basis of the review, apart from the human rights conventions ratified by the countries accepting the review, also include the UN Charter, the Universal Declaration of Human Rights, and voluntary pledges and commitments made by States, including those undertaken when presenting their candidatures for election to the Human Rights Council, and "the applicable international humanitarian law". The review is based on three kinds of basic materials: the national report submitted by the state under review; a compilation prepared by the Office of the High Commissioner for Human Rights of the information contained in the reports of treaty bodies and other human rights mechanisms; and excerpts from and compilation of materials provided by NGOs. The review is conducted in one working group, chaired by the President of the Council and composed of the 47 member States of the Council. Observer states may participate in the review and the dialogue during the review. A report shall be prepared after the review of each state. The report shall include a summary of the review, conclusions, recommendations and commitment voluntarily made by the state being review. The outcome of UPR "should be implemented primarily by the State concerned and, as appropriate, also by other relevant stakeholders". And "after exhausting all efforts to encourage a State to cooperate with the universal periodic review mechanism, the Council will address, as appropriate, cases of persistent non-cooperation with the mechanism. "

With respect to UPR, China should pay special attention to the following issues: (1) For many years, China has been able to defeat the motions to carry out discriminatory review of the human rights situation in China put forward by the U. S. and other western countries at the UN Commission on Human Rights. However, under the UPR system, the review of China's human rights condition cannot be avoided. (2) Since China is a member of the current Human Rights Council and is at the front of the list in alphabetic order, the review of China's human rights condition will be held at the latest in 2009, namely soon after the Beijing Olympic Games, despite the efforts made by the Chinese diplomatic representatives to delay it. This leaves China very little time to prepare. (3) Since the basis of the review includes the Charter of the United Nations, the Universal Declaration of Human Rights and "human rights instruments to which a State is party" (including the Vienna Declaration and Programme of Action), the basis of review actually include the International Covenant on Civil and political Rights, which China has not yet ratified. (4) The basis of the review also includes materials provided by NGOs. Some anti-China organizations have been attacking China's human rights systems for many years and those that have consultative status with the Council can also participate in the review. This will inevitably increase the complexity of the review.

2. Country-specific Review

Country-specific review refers to the special review of the human rights situation in a specific country in accordance with the provision on "Human rights situations that require the Council's attention" in the General Assembly resolution that creates the Human Rights Council. The motion for country-specific review should be brought by a member of the Council and supported by at least one third of all the Council members. The review is held in special session. The states under such review include those that have serious violated human rights and yet refused to cooperate with the review mechanism, or those that are accused of violation of human rights in the complaint procedure. The rules of procedure of special sessions are the same as those of the regular sessions. During the one year since its establishment, the Council has already carried out country-specific review on human rights situations in over a dozen countries and regions, including Israel and Darfur, Sudan. Some of these situations, such as the recent situation in Myanmar, have been considered to pose serious threat to the peace and security in neighboring countries or in the entire region and, as such, have been submitted to the Security Council for discussion.

With regard to country-specific review, China should pay special attention to the following issues: (1) Although, before the establishment of the Human Rights Council, China has been able to defeat many anti-China motions tabled by the U. S. and other western countries at the UN Commission on Human Rights, human rights diplomacy and double standard are the long-term national policies of the U. S. and, therefore, it is very possible that in the future it will play the same old trick again and make new accusations against China in the field of human rights. (2) China should adopt measures to prevent the occurrence of serious human rights incidents, especially mass incidents of bloodshed, so as not to provide the U. S. and other western countries with ammunition for attacking China in the field of human rights. (3) Faced with complicated situation in the Human Rights Council, China, as a member of the Council, should make a correct assessment of the situation, adhere to the basic principles, and take an appropriate stand in the UPR procedure at regular sessions and in country-specific review procedure at special sessions, so as uphold international human rights and promote the construction of a harmonious world.

3. Special Procedures

The "special procedures" under the Human Rights Council are special mechanisms established through the integration and reorganization of the special rapporteur system and other relevant systems established by the former UN Commission on Human Rights since 1979. These special rapporteurs are independent human rights experts with mandates to report and advise on human rights from a thematic or country-specific perspective. Country-specific rapporteurs investigate the human rights situation in a specific country; thematic rapporteurs investigate a specific human rights issue in different countries. After carrying out on-site investigation, they will make assessment of and submit reports on the human rights situation in the countries or fields concerned, thereby fulfilling their supervisory functions. Special rapporteurs must meet the following requirements: (a) expertise; (b) experience in the field of the mandate; (c) independence; (d) impartiality; (e) personal integrity; and (f) objectivity. They are not United Nations staff members and do not receive financial remuneration for their work. However, in the performance of their functions, they enjoy the rights provided for in the Convention on the Privileges and Immunities of the United Nations. The Resolution of Human Rights Council on "Institution-building of the United Nations Human Rights Council" provides for the election and terms of office of special rapporteurs and the principles they should follow in the performance of their functions. It especially provides that: "In case of situations of violations of human rights or a lack of cooperation that require the Council's attention, the principles of objectivity, non-selectivity, and the elimination of double standards and politicization should apply."

With respect to special procedures, China should pay attention to the following issues: (1) compared to representatives of states, experts under special procedures are less influenced by political factors, and have greater independence, objectivity and fairness in the review of human rights situation in countries or fields concerned. (2) However, most of these experts are from western countries or have been under the long-term influence by western countries and their selection is in fact determined by organs controlled by western countries. Therefore, their observation and assessment of the relevant human rights issues are inevitably influenced by western values and ideas. (3) Since 1994, the Chinese government has invited the Special Rapporteur on Religious Freedom, the Working Group on Arbitrary Detention, the Special Rapporteur on Education and the Special Rapporteur on Torture to visit China. Currently another six special rapporteurs have made the request to visit China. The reports they prepare after the visit to China will have significant impact on the review of the human rights situation in China by the Human Rights Council. In light of the experience of other countries, China should adopt an open attitude toward their visits and afford them the necessary facilities and assistances during their visits.

4. Complaint Procedure

The complaint procedure is a mechanism for addressing communications from individuals and NGOs about violation of human rights by governments. The working modalities of the complaint procedure are basically the same as those under the former UN Commission on Human Rights. According to the relevant provisions, in order to be admissible, a complaint must be submitted by a person or a group of persons claiming to be the victims of violations of human rights and fundamental freedoms, or by any person or group of persons, including non-governmental organizations, claiming to have direct and reliable knowledge of the violations concerned; it must not be manifestly politically motivated and its object must be consistent with the Charter of the United Nations, the Universal Declaration of Human Rights and other applicable instruments in the field of human rights law; It must not be exclusively based on reports disseminated by mass media; It must give a factual description of the alleged violations, including the rights which are alleged to be violated; and "domestic remedies have been exhausted, unless it appears that such remedies would be ineffective or unreasonably prolonged."

Two working groups have been established under the complaint procedure: the Working Group on Communications and the Working Group on Situations. The former screens, assesses and decides on the admissibility of communications while the latter decides, on the basis of the materials prepared by the former, whether to discontinue the consideration on a situation or to present the Council with a report on consistent patterns of gross and reliably attested violations of human rights and fundamental freedoms and to make recommendations to the Council on the course of action to take. In this process, the state concerned shall cooperate with the complaint procedure. Once the Council decides to take up a complaint for consideration, the state concerned has the right to take part in the consideration. Both the author of a communication and the State concerned should be informed of the final outcome of the consideration.

With regard to "complaint procedure", China should pay special attention to the following issues: (1) As far as I know, the Human Rights Council receives a large number of complaints against China every year; (2) although a large percentage of the complaints against China are politically motivated, some of them do reflect problems which should be dealt with by administrative and judicial organs in China; (3) I've learnt that the replays given by the competent Chinese authorities to the inquiries by the Human Rights Council with regard to complaints are too simple to explain the relevant issues, which is in stark contrast to the careful replays by many other countries.

II. Countermeasures to Be Adopted by China

Although China has greatly improved its human rights protection system and made remarkable achievements in the development of human rights cause in recent years, there is still a gap between the current human rights situation in China and the requirements of the International Bill of Human Rights and the Chinese Constitution and laws and many prominent problems in the field of human rights still need to be solved, for examples, the excessive application of the death penalty, the actual existence of the practice of extorting a confession by torture, the urgent need for the reform of the re-education-through-labor system, the frequent occurrence of accidents in factories and mines, the occasional occurrence of mass incidents, serious pollution of the environment, problems of product quality and food safety, problems in the compulsory education in urban and rural areas and in social security system, etc. Domestic affairs are the basis of foreign relations and a good domestic policy is the basis of a successful foreign policy. By further improving its human rights conditions, China can enhance national cohesion, improve its international image and create a good international environment for the development of the country. I suggest that the Chinese government take the following measures with a view to promoting the construction of socialism with Chinese characteristics, enabling the Chinese people to full enjoy human rights, winning a better assessment of China human rights conditions at the Human Rights Council, and upholding China international reputation.

1. Further Reducing the Application of the Death Penalty

Since the adoption by the Chinese government of the criminal policy of "tempering justice with mercy", the application of the death penalty in China has been gradually reduced. Especially after the Supreme People's Court took back the power of review and approval of death sentences, the application of death penalty has been further reduced. However, from the cases published in news media we can see that the number of death sentence in China is still very large. Currently most countries in the world have either abolished or are no longer applying the death penalty. In those that still retain the death penalty, the numbers of death sentences each year are very small. For example, in both India and the U. S. the numbers of death sentences are less than 100 each year. According to the statistics of relevant international organizations, China executes more people each year than the rest of the world combined. Both domestic and foreign experiences have shown that reducing the application of the death penalty will not affect public security and social stability. China should take not only judicial but also legislative measures to further limit the application of the death penalty. The currently Chinese Criminal Law provides for 68 kinds of capital crimes, which should be drastically reduced.

2. Eradicating the Practice of Extorting a Confession by Torture

Despite its strict prohibition by Chinese law, the practice of extorting a confession by torture is still very common in China, resulting in many unjust, false and erroneous cases, even execution of innocent people, in judicial practice. Extorting a confession by torture is a chronic social malady that has caused serious damages to the authority of the Party and the state as well as to China's international image. In 2006, the UN Special Rapporteur on Torture, after a visit to China, reported by quoting the official statistics published by the Chinese government that extorting a confession by torture had resulted in 241 deaths in the whole country during the two years between 1993 and 1994. In recent years, although the relevant government organs have already adopted such measures as strictly prohibiting the use of torture or threat to extort a confession and videotaping interrogation of criminal suspects, incidents of extorting a confession by torture continue to occur in some grassroots political-legal organs, calling for more drastic measures to be taken by the Chinese government.

3. Abolishing as Soon as Possible the System of Re-education through Labor

The system of re-education through labor was established in 1957. Later, the Standing Committee of the National People's Congress approved the Decision of the State Council on Re-education through Labor, which contains very general provisions on the system. The system has very a weak legal basis as the time period of reeducation through labor, the administration of persons undergoing reeducation through labor, and the termination and extension of reeducation through labor are all provided for by administrative regulations or administrative rules. According to the relevant provisions, the length of reeducation through labor is 1-2 years, and can be extended by one year when necessary. This kind of punishment against freedom is severer than the criminal punishments of public surveillance and criminal detention, even short-term imprisonment. This system is contrary to the 2000 Legislation Law and to the relevant international human rights conventions. As such, it has been met with strong opposition from the Chinese law circle and from some government officials and caused widespread concern by the international society. China should adopt positive measures to abolish this system through legislation.

4. Guarding against the Occurrence of Mass Incidents, Especially Large-scale Mass Incidents

Currently China is in a period of social transition, in which the old institutions and codes of conduct are being transformed while new institutions and codes of conduct have not yet been full established and the conflicts of ideologies and interests occur frequently. Moreover, because of the weak understanding of laws and policies, even corruption, on the part of some government officials, many problems involving the interests of masses of people emerged in the process of housing demolition and relocation and expropriation of land are not dealt with appropriately, resulting in the intensification of conflicts and the breaking out of mass incidents. Faced with such a situation, the relevant state organs should carry out careful investigation and deal with these conflicts in a timely and appropriate manner. In this process, administrative organs should abide by the principles of administration by law and civilized law enforcement and judicial organs should uphold judicial fairness, so as to resolve conflicts in a timely manner and prevent the occurrence of large-scale mass incidents, especially incidents of bloodshed, which have very negative domestic and international impacts.

5. Strengthening the Government's Supervision over the Implementation of Laws and Social Responsibilities by Enterprises

Under the socialist market economic system, enterprises are playing an increasingly important role the safeguarding human rights, especially in the fields of employment, occupational safety, wages and welfare, quality of products, and environmental protection. The question of whether enterprises can operate in accordance with law and strictly implement their social responsibilities has a direct impact on the welfare of large number of enterprise employees (including hundreds of millions of migrant peasant workers) and the livelihood of hundreds of millions of urban and rural families. The products manufactured by Chinese enterprises are circulated throughout the country and the world. The quality of such products has great national and international impacts. The basic way of strengthening the supervision over enterprises is to further improve the relevant institutions and truly implement the system of level-by-level accountability. Government should strengthen the supervision over and education of officials who fail to perform their obligations and bring to justice those who trade power for money and collude with unscrupulous merchants to engaging in illegal activities.

6. Further Cultivating NGOs in the Field of Human Rights

NGOs in the field of human rights are the products of reform and opening up and economic, political, cultural and social developments in China and are playing an important role in the theoretical research, policy and legal consultation, domestic and international publicity, protection of vulnerable groups, and national and international exchanges in the field of human rights. It has been proved that the free expression by these organizations of their independent opinions within the scope of constitution and law on issues of human rights protection both in China and abroad is conducive to the improvement of domestic human rights protection system and the international exchange and struggle in the field of human rights and, therefore, should be encouraged. Currently many NGOs and especially their activities are financed by foreign foundations. In the future, the Chinese government should allocate special funds for the support of these organizations, so as to ensure their healthy development, to allow them to take more initiatives in human rights research, in the protection of the rights of vulnerable groups, and in the exchange with foreign countries, and to give them stronger voice and enable them to present the true human rights situations in China in the UPR procedure and the country-specific review procedure at the UN Human Rights Council and in the deliberation procedures of other human rights treaty bodies.

7. Conscientiously Organizing the Preparation of National Human Rights Report and Reports on the Implementation of Other Human Rights Treaties and Implementing the Recommendations in the Outcomes of the Review

The UPR system requires states to submit national human rights reports to the Human Rights Council and many important human rights conventions also require state parties to submit reports on the implementation of the conventions. Submitting state reports and accepting consideration of these reports by the relevant human rights bodies is an obligation China has undertaken under international law as well as a platform for China to display the progresses it has made in the field of human rights. National human rights report covers a wide range of economic, political, cultural and social issues. Preparation of Reports under specialized conventions also involves more than one field or government department. This means that the Chinese government should organize relevant state organs to jointly prepare the national human rights report and reports on the implementation of various human rights conventions and to solicit the opinions of NGOs in this process. The UPR and the consideration of state reports on the implementation of human rights conventions are carried out on a periodical basis. The government should attach special importance to the preparation of the initial reports, which are taken as reference in the consideration of subsequent reports. The outcome of the consideration by the Human Rights Council of national human rights report and the conclusions of consideration by human rights treaty bodies of state reports on the implementation of human rights conventions all contain recommendations on further improving the relevant human rights, which should be conscientious implemented by the government.

8. Making Serious Reposes to Communications in the Complaint Procedure

The task of the complaint procedure is to "to address consistent patterns of gross and reliably attested violations of all human rights and all fundamental freedoms". As mentioned above, the Human Rights Council receives a large number of complaints against China each year. Although the admissibility criteria for communications require that a communication should "not be manifestly politically motivated", a large percentage of complaints against China are politically motivated. The rest involve complicated administrative and judicial issues. Communications to China under the complaint procedure are mostly forwarded by the Working Group on Communications as part of the procedure of investigation and screening of complaints. The relevant organs of the Chinese government should carry out careful examination of these communications. They should help the Working Group to screen out those that are politically-motivated, and conduct carefully investigations on others. With regard to those that contain well-founded charges of violation of human rights, they should adopt measures to provide necessary remedies to the victims; with regard to those contain ill-founded and unreasonable accusations, they should also give detailed reply and provide relevant information and materials, so as to enable the complaints to be resolved while they are dealt with by Working Group on Communications. If the complaint is transmitted to the Working Group on Situations, the relevant government departments should assist Chinese diplomatic representatives to make further efforts to prevent the Working Group on Situations from referring the matter to the Human Rights Council for deliberation. If a complaint is referred to the Council and a resolution has been adopted by the Council on the matter, the Chinese government should also cooperate with the Council in resolving the issue in accordance with the relevant procedures, so as to prevent the further intensification of the conflict and further damage to China's international image.

9. Inviting with More Open Attitude Famous Human Rights Scholars and Experts of UN Human Rights Council to Come to China to Exchanges Opinions

China has a late start and is currently still in a passive position in foreign exchange in the field of human rights. Because of the influence of the U. S. and other western countries and the media under their control, many foreigners, including some UN officials, can not have an objective assessment of the actual situation of human rights protection in China. The original purpose of establishing the UN Human Rights Council is to avoid political wrestling in the field of human rights. However, since the Council is composed of state representatives, political factors will still play a role in the activities of the Council. Although famous international human rights scholars and experts are also influenced by western ideology, most of them are able to maintain a relatively high degree of independence. Their opinions carry great weight in the UPR at the Human Rights Council as well as in the deliberation of state party reports by human rights treaty bodies. Although the human rights situation in China still needs to be improved, it is by no means as bad as claimed by some western countries or western media. The relevant foreign affairs department of the government, academic institutions and NGOs in China should invite famous foreign human rights scholars and activists who have close relationship with the UN to visit China to exchange opinions with their Chinese counterparts. As long as we treat them with thoughtfulness and frankness, and sincerely accept their unbiased criticisms and constructive opinions, they will be able to make relatively objective assessment of the human rights situation in China.

10. Establishing a National Coordination Mechanism for the Construction of Human Rights Protection System

China, as a permanent member of the UN Security Council and a member of UN Human Rights Council, has already ratified over 20 international human rights conventions. China has already signed the International Covenant on Civil and Political Rights and it is only a matter of time before the Covenant is ratified by China. Respecting and safeguarding human rights and promoting the comprehensive development of human beings has become a basic Party policy and constitutional principle, as well as the ultimate objective of the people-oriented scientific outlook on development and socialism with Chinese characteristics. Human rights protection is a very important part of China's domestic and foreign policy. However, currently China has not yet established a national institution to coordinate theoretical research, policy-making, improvement of laws, dissemination and education, implementation of relevant systems, internal and external relations, and liaison with NGOs in the field of human rights. Such a situation is not conducive to the construction of human rights system in the country or to international exchange and struggle in the field of human rights. In order to adapt to the new situation, China should establish a national mechanism under the direct leadership of the CPC Central Committee and participated by the relevant government departments, including the Foreign Ministry, to be responsible for coordinating major affairs in the field of domestic and international protection of human rights.

Postscript

When the first electronic draft of this book came out, I was suffering from hyperostosis and lumbar disc herniation and had to stay in bed at doctor's order. As a result, I was unable to carry out further revision of the manuscript. Fortunately I was offered generous help by Professor Jiang Chengzhao of Shenzhen University, who, despite her old age, completed the careful proofreading of the whole manuscript during the hottest days of summer and provided me with many valuable suggestions on the revision of the manuscript. Here I would like to express my deepest gratitude to her for her kind help. Now, at the time when this book is ready to go to press, I would also like to thank the following colleagues and friends for their contributions to the book: Ms. Wang Yalan who took the time out of her busy schedule to proofread part of the manuscript; Ms. Gu Weidong who helped me with the first draft of the book; Mr. Zhao Lixin who had done a lot of work at the later stage of the editing work; Ms. Zhang Huiqiang, who helped me with the search for materials and with the verification of part of the citations and footnotes; and Dr. Xie Zengyi and Mr. Zhang Jinggui who have provided me with much assistance in contacting the publisher.

The author

This book is the result of a co-publication agreement between China Social Sciences Press (China) and Paths International Ltd (UK)

Title: Sixty Years of the Protection and Development of Human Rights in China
Author: Liu Hainian
Translated by Bi Xiaoqing
ISBN: 978-1-84464-266-3
Ebook ISBN: 978-1-84464-389-9

Paths International Ltd
PO Box 4083
Reading
United Kingdom
RG8 8ZN
www.pathsinternational.com

Published in United Kingdom

CPSIA information can be obtained at www.ICGtesting.com
Printed in the USA
BVOW09*1118300516

449556BV00005B/15/P

9 781844 642663